NEW PROCLAMATION

D1402413

NEW PROCLAMATION

Year C, 2007

Easter through Christ the King

David L. Tiede
Rebecca J. Kruger Gaudino
Gary E. Peluso-Verdend
David Schnasa Jacobsen

From the Library of
David C. Morgan

David B. Lott, editor

FORTRESS PRESS
Minneapolis

NEW PROCLAMATION
Year C, 2007
Easter through Christ the King

Copyright©2006 Fortress Press, an imprint of Augsburg Fortress. All rights reserved. Except for brief quotations in critical articles or reviews, no part of this book may be reproduced in any manner without prior written permission from the publisher. Visit http://www. augsburgfortress.org/copyrights/contact.asp or write to Permissions, Augsburg Fortress, Box 1209, Minneapolis, MN 55440.

Unless otherwise noted, scripture quotations are the author's own translation or from the New Revised Standard Version Bible, copyright © 1989 by the Division of Christian Education of the National Council of the Churches of Christ in the USA, and are used by permission.

Scripture quotations marked NIV are taken from the Holy Bible, New International Version,® copyright © 1973, 1978, 1984 International Bible Society. Used by permission of Zondervan. All rights reserved.

Scripture quotations marked NEB are taken from the New English Bible, copyright © Oxford University Press and Cambridge University Press 1961, 1970. All rights reserved.

The responsive readings listed from the Roman Catholic Lectionary follow the chapter and verse numbering of the New American Bible, as indicated in *The Lectionary for Mass* (1998/2002 U.S.A. edition).

Illustrations: Lucinda Naylor, *Icon II: Visual Images for Every Sunday*, copyright © 2004 Augsburg Fortress.

The Library of Congress has catalogued this series as follows.
New proclamation year A, 2001–2002: Advent through Holy Week / Francis J. Moloney . . . [et al.].
     p. cm.
Includes bibliographical references.
ISBN 0-8006-4245-7 (alk. paper)
     1. Church year. I. Moloney, Francis J.
BV30 .N48 2001
251'.6—dc21   2001023746

New Proclamation, Year C, 2007, Easter through Christ the King
ISBN-13: 978-0-8006-4256-3
ISBN-10: 0-8006-4256-2

The paper used in this publication meets the minimum requirements of American National Standard for Information Sciences—Permanence of Paper for Printed Library Materials, ANSI Z329.48-1984.

Manufactured in the U.S.A.
10   09   08   07   06   1   2   3   4   5   6   7   8   9   10

CONTENTS

THE SEASON AFTER PENTECOST: PROPERS 13–22
GARY E. PELUSO-VERDEND

THE SEASON AFTER PENTECOST:
PROPERS 23-29, REIGN OF CHRIST SUNDAY, AND THANKSGIVING
DAVID SCHNASA JACOBSEN

PREFACE

N*ew Proclamation* continues the time-honored Fortress Press practice of offering a lectionary preaching resource that provides first-rate biblical exegetical aids for a variety of lectionary traditions. This present volume covers the lections for the second half of the church year, from Easter Sunday through Christ the King Sunday.

Thoroughly ecumenical and built around the three-year lectionary cycle, *New Proclamation* focuses on the biblical texts, based on the conviction that acquiring a deeper understanding of the pericopes in both their historical and liturgical contexts is the best means to inform and inspire preachers to deliver engaging and effective sermons. For this reason, the most capable North American biblical scholars and homileticians are invited to contribute to *New Proclamation*.

Although we provide contributors with common instructions and a general "template" for their writing, each is given the freedom to alter and improve that pattern in ways they think will be most helpful to the user. What is most important is that the biblical texts themselves, set in their liturgical context, provide the basis on which each writer determines the format he or she chooses to follow. So, for example, you will note that while most authors have combined their exegesis and application into one section rather than separating them into two distinct segments, some have chosen to provide separate sections titled "Response" and "Putting the Texts Together."

In general, *New Proclamation* is planned and designed to be user-friendly in the following ways:

- *New Proclamation* is published in two volumes per year, with a large, workbook-style page, a lay-flat binding, and space for making notes.
- Each season of the church year is prefaced by an introduction that provides insights into the background and spiritual significance of the period, as well as ideas for planning one's preaching during the season.
- The application of biblical texts to contemporary situations is an important concern of each contributor. Exegetical work is concise, and thoughts on how

the texts address today's world, congregational issues, and personal situations have a prominent role.

- Although the assigned psalms ("Responsive Reading") are infrequently used as preaching texts, brief comments on each are included so that the preacher can incorporate reflections on these in the sermon. The psalms, for the most part, represent the congregation's response to the first reading and are not intended as preaching texts.

- Boxed quotations in the margins help signal important themes in the texts for the day.

- The material for Year C is here dated specifically for 2007 for easier coordination with other dated lectionary materials. However, we hope the text itself has a timeless quality so that preachers can keep these volumes on their shelves and refer to them in future years for preaching inspiration.

- These materials can be adapted for uses other than for corporate worship on the day indicated. They are well suited for adult discussion groups or for personal meditation and reflection.

The authors in this latest edition of *New Proclamation* not only represent a variety of Protestant faith traditions, but hail from diverse disciplines and professional backgrounds—and even nationalities!—as well. What they hold in common is a love for God's Word, clearly interpreted and well preached. It is a particular pleasure to welcome the eminent Luke-Acts scholar David L. Tiede, who last wrote on Holy Week for *Proclamation 4* in 1989, back to the series. Rebecca Kruger Gaudino, to whom Walter Brueggemann has referred as his "prize student," serves the United Church of Christ in Oregon as a writer. Also a teacher of world religions, she brings her considerable writing and editing skills to the opening weeks of Pentecost. I first met Gary Peluso-Verdend when I edited his book *Paying Attention: Focusing Your Congregation on What Matters* for the Alban Institute. It is a delight to work with Gary again on this volume, as he brings his eloquence in congregational studies and stewardship matters to open new insights on the texts for the middle weeks of Pentecost. David Schnasa Jacobsen, who has published several well-received books on Scripture and preaching, brings his deep knowledge of both disciplines—as well as a binational perspective—to the closing weeks of Ordinary Time. We are grateful to each of these contributors for their insights and their commitment to effective Christian preaching, and we are confident you will find in this volume ideas, stimulation, and encouragement for your ministry of proclamation.

David B. Lott

THE SEASON OF EASTER

DAVID L. TIEDE

The liturgical calendar emulates the cyclical change of seasons, inhabiting the natural rhythms of morning and evening, seedtime and harvest, birth and death with the mystery of God's love. In the northern hemisphere, the Easter season also coincides with the new life of springtime, filling Christian worship with rich vernal metaphors.

The incarnation of the down-to-earth God, Emmanuel, means God has come to dwell with us in the daily joys and sorrows, growing and aging our earthly lives. But Easter proclaims the resurrection, God's prophetic action, transforming the natural order. The resurrection of Christ Jesus is an *eschatological* event in ordinary time, a new creation from God's time and space, not to end human history but to renew mortal life.

By raising the crucified Jesus from the dead, God even renewed the Scriptures. The words in Israel's Scriptures were not altered, but in the light of Easter, God's Law and the Prophets were brought forward as testimony to reinterpret the world. Generation after generation, disputes continue as to whether Jesus is Israel's Messiah, but those who know him to be vindicated by God press on, confident all of God's promises are fulfilled in Jesus the Christ. Reading Israel's Scriptures and the testimonies to Jesus' resurrection in the twenty-first century, the church again announces, "God is making all things new." Proclaiming this transformation throughout God's earth is the joy of Easter preaching.

I

In the Easter story of the walk to Emmaus, the risen Messiah, still unrecognized by those with whom he was walking, chides them for being "slow of heart to believe all that the prophets have declared" (Luke 24:25). "Then beginning with Moses and all the prophets, he interpreted to them the things about himself in all the scriptures" (v. 27). Christians read the Hebrew Bible theologically as the "Old Testament" because in the light of Easter, the Scriptures bear witness to what God has accomplished in Christ Jesus.

It is historically accurate to describe the New Testament as one of the surviving commentaries on the Scriptures of Israel. The other major tradition of interpretation belongs, of course, to the synagogues across the street where the Messiah is still awaited. The commentaries (*midrashim*), instruction (*mishnah*), and learning (*Talmud* or *gemara*) of Judaism took their definitive forms in the same decades the letters, Gospels, and writings of the New Testament were compiled, then collected. Both were Jewish traditions of interpretation, populated in their origins by communities that sought to be faithful to the God of Abraham and Sarah, Isaac and Rebekah, David and Wisdom, Isaiah and Deuteronomy. In his remarkable account of the origins of Judaism and Christianity in the Roman world, Alan Segal compares these traditions to the fraternal twins Esau and Jacob, once contending in Rebecca's womb, now with "competing claims to divine favor" with "different, even opposing ways to preserve their family's heritage."[1]

> THE EASTER SEASON DISCLOSES THE NEW TESTAMENT AS THE RESURRECTION INTERPRETATION OF ISRAEL'S SCRIPTURES.

It is, therefore, historically possible and religiously necessary to remember that the Scriptures of Israel are both the common ground and the contested ground for Judaism and Christianity. Jesus is credited with raising two questions that still unite and divide Christianity and Judaism: "What is written in the Torah? How do you read?" (Luke 10:26, my translation). Even when the assigned New Testament readings for a particular Sunday are only weakly linked with passages that have been selected as Old Testament lessons, the interpretation of Israel's Scriptures stirs deeply in the New Testament stories themselves. The Hebrew Bible did not disappear into the Christian canon as if the church superseded Israel. Both Judaism and Christianity continue to lay claim to Israel's election. Thus, the New Testament is filled with challenging theological convictions, and the Christian claims are profound, especially in the Easter season. The Easter season discloses the New Testament as the resurrection interpretation of Israel's Scriptures.

Both the risks and the power of Christian interpretation are felt deeply when paying careful attention to the ways New Testament letters, Gospels, and writings use Israel's Scriptures. The risks are inescapable when it becomes clear to the twenty-first-century interpreter that the Christian writers are regularly drawing upon Israel's Scriptures to make sense of what God has done in Jesus. Of course, they were also drawing upon memories of what happened and coloring the stories with scriptural allusions, confident that even before they saw the connections, Jesus was enacting God's script. The apostolic witnesses testified not merely to brute facts but to the fulfillment of God's will and purposes. All the New Testament writers know well that Jesus' identity as Messiah and Lord is contested, with many in Israel rejecting Jesus as a false messiah. The resistance to Jesus as the enacted presence of Israel's God and the rejection of apostolic testimony within a divided Israel drive the interpreter deep into Israel's Scriptures. Christian interpreters, therefore, continue to enter a Jewish conversation in which the stakes are very high about who is truly faithful to God, who is true Israel. Preaching these stories in later Gentile communities outside of that intra-Jewish struggle constantly risked what Marilyn Salmon calls "unintended anti-Judaism."[2] On the other hand, the Easter witness promises to reveal God's heart and will in the interpretation of Israel's Scriptures.

Pontius Pilate, Jerusalem, Galilee, and Jesus' followers did not go away, but the witness of Easter is that God was doing a new thing among them, in their places. The Easter lectionary fills ample chapters and verses with the testimony for this truth.

Jesus is the Messiah, crucified and raised. How then shall we live? Week after week in the Easter season, the readings bear witness to how both heaven and earth are transformed by this new thing God has done. Most of the first readings are drawn from the Acts of the Apostles, taking the faithful beyond Pentecost into the Holy Spirit's mission through the apostolic witnesses. Many of the second readings are taken from the Revelation to John, with glimpses of Jesus' reign in heaven about to come to earth. The Gospel lessons are predominately from the Gospel according to John, testifying to the unity of the

> WEEK AFTER WEEK IN THE EASTER SEASON, THE READINGS BEAR WITNESS TO HOW BOTH HEAVEN AND EARTH ARE TRANSFORMED BY THIS NEW THING GOD HAS DONE.

Son, suffering and exalted, with the Father's love. The calling of the people of God, the divine drama in heaven, and the very being of the triune God are all affected by the death and resurrection of Jesus. God's mission of moving into the world in love is not finished, but it is both culminated and inaugurated anew in the resurrection of Christ.

Easter proclamation, therefore, deals with the "what?" of God incarnate in first-century Jewish history, the "so what?" of the transformation of the people of God into an apostolic movement in the Greco-Roman world, and the "now what?" of the church's calling in the world. The resurrection of Jesus Christ crucified demonstrates the miracle of divine mercy, shown in his dying even for the ungodly; bestows the irrepressible hope of life in Christ for believers; and sends the church into the world to testify to God's ultimate love.

Notes

1. Alan F. Segal, *Rebecca's Children: Judaism and Christianity in the Roman World* (Cambridge: Harvard University Press, 1986), 179.

2. Marilyn J. Salmon, *Preaching without Contempt: Overcoming Unintended Anti-Judaism*, Fortress Resources for Preaching (Minneapolis: Fortress Press, 2006).

RESURRECTION OF THE LORD / EASTER DAY

APRIL 8, 2007

REVISED COMMON	EPISCOPAL (BCP)	ROMAN CATHOLIC
Acts 10:34-43 or	Acts 10:34-43 or	Acts 10:34a, 37-43
Isa. 65:17-25	Isa. 51:9-11	
Ps. 118:1-2, 14-24	Ps. 118:14-29 or	Ps. 118:1-2, 16-17,
	118:14-17, 22-24	22-23
1 Cor. 15:19-26 or	Col. 3:1-4 or	Col. 3:1-4 or
Acts 10:34-43	Acts 10:34-43	1 Cor. 5:6b-8
John 20:1-18 or	Luke 24:1-10	John 20:1-9
Luke 24:1-12		

FIRST READING

ACTS 10:34-43 (RCL, BCP)
ACTS 10:34a, 37-43 (RC)
ISAIAH 65:17-25 (RCL ALT.)
ISAIAH 51:9-11 (BCP ALT.)

Peter's proclamation in Acts 10 is an elegant and concentrated summary of the Easter gospel. As the story is told in Acts, this sermon is a direct response to the request from the Roman centurion Cornelius and the first non-Jewish or Gentile household gathered "in the presence of God to listen to all that the Lord has commanded you to say" (10:33). The apostle himself is learning the Easter meaning of the long-standing conviction that "God shows no partiality."

Much earlier, Deuteronomy affirmed that "God, mighty and awesome, is not partial and takes no bribe" and even that God "loves the strangers, providing them food and clothing" (Deut. 10:17-18; see also Sir. 35:14-26). Although the history of Jewish reception of "God fearers" and "righteous Gentiles" is difficult to reconstruct precisely, the synagogues of the Greco-Roman era apparently also understood God's "acceptance" (Gk.: *dektos*) of "God fearers" from every nation (Gk.: *ethnos*—Gentile) who "perform righteousness" (Gk.: *ergazomenos dikaoisynēn*;

NRSV: "does what is right," Acts 10:34-35). In Luke's story, another Roman centurion who asked that his slave be healed by Jesus was commended by the Jewish elders on just such terms: "He is worthy [Gk.: *axios*] of having you do this for him, for he loves our people, and it is he who built our synagogue for us" (Luke 7:4-5). Cornelius was also introduced with high Jewish commendations as "a devout man who feared God with all his household; he gave alms generously to the people and prayed constantly to God" (Acts 10:2). Thus far in the story, even Peter's entry into the Gentile's house was probably not beyond the boundary of Hellenistic Jewish practice. In Luke's telling, however, neither Peter nor "the circumcised believers who had come with Peter" (v. 45) were prepared for the profound acceptance that God was about to extend to Cornelius and his household.

Verses 36-42 are precisely what the Lord *commanded* his apostles to say (vv. 33, 42). God first sent the message "to the people of Israel, preaching peace by Jesus Christ" (v. 36). It is God who identifies Jesus within Israel as Lord and Messiah (Christ). Then "after the baptism that John announced . . . God anointed Jesus of Nazareth with the Holy Spirit and with power." Luke is emphatic in his Gospel (chaps. 3–4) that Jesus' baptism was his divine royal anointing, even telling the story of John's arrest before Jesus' baptism and mentioning only the agency of the Holy Spirit in the event, identifying Jesus in the words of royal enthronement as God's Son (Ps. 2:7). What human beings who were set against God did by putting Jesus "to death by hanging him on a tree" (v. 39), God transformed by raising him "on the third day" and allowing him to appear to the chosen witnesses (vv. 40-41). Then God's righteousness will be finally demonstrated by the agency of the resurrected Jesus in the last judgment "of the living and the dead" (v. 42).

> THE POURING OUT OF THE HOLY SPIRIT "EVEN ON THE GENTILES" IS AN EASTER MIRACLE, UNEXPECTED BY PETER AND THE CIRCUMCISED BELIEVERS.

Without citing specific passages, Peter's testimony concludes with an appeal to "all the prophets" that "everyone who believes in him receives forgiveness of sins through his name" (v. 43). This is the ultimate "acceptance," even in the last judgment, not resting on "performing righteousness" (NRSV: "doing what is right") in honoring Jewish traditions or observing food laws and circumcision, but brought about by faith in Jesus Christ.

Verses 44-48, therefore, indicate the consequence of the evident faith of these "righteous," that is, "believing," Gentiles. The pouring out of the Holy Spirit "even on the Gentiles" is an Easter miracle, unexpected by Peter and the circumcised believers. They had received the commissioning of the Holy Spirit, the renewal of Israel's vocation to be a light to the nations (Isa. 49:6; Acts 1:6-8). Now by faith in the Messiah and Lord whom God raised from the dead, these non-Israelites also received God's ultimate acceptance.

As is common in Luke's narrative, the hearer is confronted with a theodicy, a demonstration of the righteousness of God perfected in the resurrection, calling forth faith in God as the new righteousness that is "acceptable" to God. Easter preaching does not conclude with a description of this redefinition of righteousness, as if one way of being worthy before God was displaced by another. Easter preaching is the announcement to all who are gathered "in the presence of God" (v. 33), inviting faith in Jesus the crucified Messiah, vindicated by God, and praying for the Holy Spirit to confirm this faith and the callings to which it leads.

The alternative readings from Isaiah 51:9-11 (BCP) and 65:17-25 (RCL) resound with the magnificent promises in which Israel has hoped. Modern non-Jewish Christians may feel consternation with the specific focus of these promises. Isaiah 51:9-11 promises not only the end of human tears, but the fulfillment of the hope of the return of "the ransomed of the LORD" to Zion. And Isaiah 65:17-25 envisions the creation of "a new heaven and a new earth" specifically in terms of the recreation of Jerusalem as a "joy." It is not difficult to see why Jesus' disciples immediately connected his resurrection with the hope of the restoration of the kingdom to Israel (Acts 1:6), and a modern literalism has led some Christians to interpret the Zionism of the state of Israel as a fulfillment of these promises. Several of the Easter readings from the Revelation to John will confirm that Jesus' resurrection does indeed foreshadow the re-creation of heaven and earth with the heavenly Jerusalem "coming down out of heaven from God" (Rev. 21:10).

> WITHOUT CONTROLLING THE FUTURE, THESE DECLA-
> RATIONS OF ESCHATOLOGICAL HOPE ARE HYMNS IN
> PRAISE OF GOD'S GLORY.

The grandeur of these visions challenges both those who try to tie down God's ultimate actions to the chaotic conflicts of the politics of the Middle East and those who think God has abandoned the promises to Israel. Without controlling the future, these declarations of eschatological hope are hymns in praise of God's glory. The resurrection of Jesus is a glimpse of God in action with great surprises still to come. As the apostle Paul declared, "For in him [Jesus], every one of God's promises is a 'Yes!' For this reason, it is through him that we say the 'Amen,' to the glory of God" (2 Cor. 1:20).

RESPONSIVE READING
PSALM 118:1-2, 14-24 (RCL)
PSALM 118:14-29 OR 118:14-17, 22-24 (BCP)
PSALM 118:1-2, 16-17, 22-23 (RC)

The verses that are excerpted from Psalm 118 in each of the lectionaries clearly reflect editing to give voice to the personal praise of Christian believers. The preacher who seeks to grasp the force of the assurances will do well also to attend to the deep struggles in the omitted verses 3-13. The longer and more continuous readings at least indirectly maintain the critical question implied in verses 19-20 concerning "the gates of righteousness" through which "the righteous shall enter." If the hearer presumed to know what "righteousness" would provide access to "the gate of the LORD," it would be well to rehearse the lesson God taught the apostle Peter in Acts 10 about the Easter righteousness of faith in the God who raised Jesus.

On the other hand, the briefer selections of verses from Psalm 118 provide personal and corporate praise for what God has done. The festival praise of ancient Israel now sings with Christian hope. The God who promised a new creation (see also Isa. 65:17-25, the RCL alternative for the first reading) has now "made" this Easter day, and faith in the stone the builders rejected has become "my salvation."

SECOND READING
1 CORINTHIANS 15:19-26 (RCL)
COLOSSIANS 3:1-4 (BCP, RC)

The brief reading from 1 Corinthians 15:19-26 raises wonderful hopes and complex questions about the consequences of the resurrection of Christ. The larger context is the discussion of whether there is such a thing as a resurrection at all, no matter how people experienced Jesus to be alive after his death. As will be noted in the comments on John 20 in the Second Sunday of Easter, Paul's witness is rich in confidence of the bodily resurrection, while deeply reserved about attempts to reduce what happened to a mere "explanation." In 1 Corinthians 15, he moves from the question of the general resurrection to the particular resurrection of Christ, then back to the hope Jesus' resurrection offers to all.

> THE RESURRECTION OF CHRIST JESUS TRANSFORMED THE FUTURE INTO THE REALM OF HIS TRIUMPH, AND ALL WHO ARE IDENTIFIED WITH HIM SHARE IN ITS PROMISE.

The first human being (Adam) and second human being (Christ) are linked with death and the resurrection of the dead, not merely as a typology, but as an identity of all who belong to the mortal race, subject to the slings and arrows of powers and systems, and all who are also called to belong to Christ. Christ's dominion until the end, therefore, is a sign of a new order, a reign no longer trapped by the vicissitudes of mortal existence. The resurrection of Christ Jesus transformed the future into the realm of his triumph, and all who are identified with him share in its promise.

Verse 24 has prompted rich wonder and speculation among Christian interpreters through the ages. This vision relies on the great promises of Romans 8:38; Ephesians 1:21; and Colossians 2:10, 15. It also provides a flitting glimpse of the unity and ultimate obedience of Christ's role in God's cosmic, prophetic drama (see also 1 Cor. 3:23).

Preachers and interpreters must not flee too quickly from these complex questions into a realm of divine mystery. But as Paul himself allows later in this same chapter, the consequences of Christ's resurrection are a mystery (1 Cor 15:51; Gk.: *mystērion*), both in the sense of an experience beyond mere mortal knowledge (see vv. 35-36) and in the sense of a prophetic revelation. God's time has come into human time, disclosing a reality that is not yet manifest (vv. 23-26). Speculative musings about the history of the Trinity are inescapable. The apostle's witness, however, moves the focus toward the hope and confidence the resurrection of Jesus gives for mere mortals, beginning in the present.

Colossians 3:1-4 is pure promise, with a surprising affirmation of the resurrection as a present reality for believers (see also Col. 2:12). In 1 Corinthians 15:22-23; Romans 6:3-5; and Philippians 3:10-11, by contrast, believers participate in the sufferings and death of Christ in baptism, but await participation in his resurrection. Paul's usual emphasis on the future or eschatological reality of the resurrection is essential to his testimony to its embodied character. In Colossians, however, the focus is on living in the confidence of what has already happened in the heavenly realms.

> CHRISTIANS ARE NOT INVITED TO PRETEND THAT HEAVEN HAS ALREADY COME ON EARTH. BUT THEY KNOW THAT CHRIST HAS BEEN RAISED.

When read in the light of the subsequent affirmations, these verses offer a Christian understanding of why followers of Christ are called to live by high moral standards. The lists of virtues and vices in Colossians 3 are not dramatically Christian but reflect the spirit and strength by which Christians are encouraged, "Whatever you do, in word or deed, do everything in the name of the Lord Jesus" (v. 17).

Christians are not invited to pretend that heaven has already come on earth. But they know that Christ has been raised. In the confidence of this reality, they already see the world in a new light, and they are invited to live now in newness (see also Rom. 6:4), even in perils. Verse 3 also could be dangerous to literal readers if they assumed that no dangers could harm them because their lives are "hidden with Christ in God." In the light of Christ's death and resurrection, this ultimate truth brings authentic comfort exactly to those who know it is still a promise when sufferings and trouble are real. Verse 4, therefore, is essential to keeping the promise of future glory in the future.

1 CORINTHIANS 5:6b-8 (RC ALT.)

See the second reading for the Resurrection of the Lord/Easter Evening, below.

ACTS 10:34-43 (RCL ALT., BCP ALT.)

See the first reading for the Resurrection of the Lord/Easter Day, above.

THE GOSPEL
JOHN 20:1-18 (RCL)
JOHN 20:1-9 (RC)
LUKE 24:1-12 (RCL ALT.)
LUKE 24:1-10 (BCP)

The magnificent stories of Easter morning welcome those who have never heard into the wonder of faith and draw believers into ever-greater depths of thanksgiving. Preachers who have poured their energies into the disciplines of Lent and Holy Week may be as weary as the women at the tomb and may be caught up in the joyful confusion as if no one has told them before what God has done. These are narratives of faith, not proof.

John 20:1-18 (RCL) includes both the story of the disciples at the empty tomb (vv. 1-9; RC) and the story of Jesus' appearance to Mary Magdalene (vv. 10-18). In the numbering of the Fourth Gospel, these stories will be followed by three appearances of Jesus to his disciples (see 21:14). These first Easter stories, therefore, do not need to carry the full weight of the meaning of the resurrection. The evangelist appears content providing as many questions as answers, leading to faith (20:30-31).

IN JOHN'S GOSPEL, THE CONFUSION OF THE DISCIPLES IS NOT DISBELIEF, BUT LACK OF UNDERSTANDING, PREPARING THE WAY FOR MARY MAGDALENE'S TESTIMONY.

In John's narrative Mary Magdalene is the first to the tomb, which would heighten the risk if she were thought to have traveled in the dark of the night without the companions mentioned in the Synoptic accounts. Her repeated testimony is already more than a worry about a missing body: "They have taken away the [my] Lord, . . . and we [I] do not know where they have laid him" (vv. 2, 13).

The depiction of Peter and "the other disciple, the one whom Jesus loved" (v. 2; see 19:26-27) running to the tomb is so awkward as almost to be humorous. Modern scholars have posited the weaving in of other source materials. At least one ancient commentator thought that "the other disciple outran Peter" because he wasn't married. Then the disciple peered in and waited outside the tomb until Peter entered to inspect the details, then "he also went in, and he saw and believed"

(v. 8). This theme of seeing and believing will appear again in the story of Thomas (20:24-29), but then it will be seeing the risen Lord. In this scene, it is not clear what the disciple or Peter "believed," because verse 9 indicates they did not yet "understand the scripture, that he must rise from the dead." As in Luke 24:44-47, the conviction is strongly stated that Jesus' death and resurrection were necessary ("he must rise") for a scriptural reason, that is, to be in accord with God's will. But no specific scriptures are cited in either of these Easter contexts. In Luke, at least, the risen Messiah will point the reader to the fulfillment of "everything written about me in the law of Moses, the prophets, and the psalms" (24:44). In John's Gospel, the confusion of the disciples is not disbelief, but lack of understanding, preparing the way for Mary Magdalene's testimony.

The rich and strong depiction of Mary Magdalene is worth noting, especially in the light of the historical nonsense of *The Da Vinci Code*, and she is mentioned explicitly in the Easter stories of all four Gospels (Matt. 28:1; Mark 16:1; Luke 24:10; John 20:1). She is also mentioned among a group of remarkable women in Luke 8:1-3, where the twelve disciples were accompanied by "some women who had been cured of evil spirits and infirmities; Mary, called Magdalene, from whom seven demons had gone out, and Joanna, the wife of Herod's steward Chuza, and Susanna, and many others, who provided for them out of their resources." Whatever modern minds make of the delivery from evil spirits, even this strange passage accredits Mary Magdalene and the other women social prominence, economic capacity, and standing among the disciples (all who also had their histories). Later centuries would develop fantastic and adverse speculations about these important women, including associating Mary Magdalene with an adulterous past (that is, presuming she was the unnamed woman of Luke 7:36-50) to the prurient delight of people who sell fiction or the comfort of those who are anxious about powerful women. But in all the Gospels, Mary Magdalene is a significant and authoritative disciple. Whether with or without the other women, whether encountered by angels or the risen Lord himself, Mary Magdalene is a first witness to the resurrection.

> WHETHER WITH OR WITHOUT THE OTHER WOMEN, WHETHER ENCOUNTERED BY ANGELS OR THE RISEN LORD HIMSELF, MARY MAGDALENE IS A FIRST WITNESS TO THE RESURRECTION.

The focus of the story shifts from describing her confusion to relating the testimony of the risen Lord. We read that she was still looking for the body of the "Lord," and her inability to recognize Jesus is consistent with Luke's account of the travelers to Emmaus (see the Gospel for Easter Evening, below). The exchange between Mary as "Woman" and Jesus as "Sir," the apparent gardener, changes suddenly when he addresses her by name. "Mary" evokes "Rabbouni." Scholars disagree on whether this term is more personal that "Rabbi," another Semitic word for "teacher" used often in the Fourth Gospel. In any case, the recognition leads beyond a personal conversation to a further revelation from the risen Lord. She will announce her vision and bear the good news of what he said to the disciples (v. 18).

The good news is not only that Jesus has been raised, and Jesus' resurrection is not merely his physical return to the community, nor is his exaltation about his absence. Beginning on the cross, Jesus is being lifted up to the Father (see John 12:32-33; 14:12, 28; 16:5, 10, 28). The theological testimony of the resurrection stories, therefore, is centered in Jesus' exaltation for the giving of the Spirit. Jesus' message through Mary Magdalene to "my brothers" is therefore his promise, "I am ascending to my Father and your Father, to my God and your God" (20:17). He is not distancing himself from them by not being "held" (v. 17), but his ascent to the Father is necessary to the unity of the Father, Son, Spirit with the community in God's love for the world (see also the promise of the sending of the Holy Spirit in John 14:23-29, the Gospel reading for the Sixth Sunday of Easter, below).

This profound theological conviction of God's mission of love in Jesus will draw the interpreter deep into John's narrative. It cannot be explained in an eight-minute message on a busy Easter Sunday. On the other hand, even reading the story slowly and thoughtfully can communicate the vision it provides of the unity of the Son with the Father's mission of love, including care for Mary and the disciples. This love extends to the mere mortals in Easter worship. Jesus is on his way to the Father, in his ministry, in his being raised up on a tree in crucifixion, in his resurrection and exaltation to God, not to abandon his disciples and friends but to send the Spirit to dwell with them.

In the alternative reading from Luke 24:1-12 (RCL) or 24:1-10 (BCP), the empty tomb causes as much wonderment as that described in John's account. Compared to Mark 16:1-8, which only includes the shocking story of a heavenly messenger in the empty tomb, Luke's version anticipates the appearances of Jesus in 24:13-49. The verdicts of disbelief of the women's words as an "idle tale" and Peter's amazement (vv. 11-12) open the Easter season to an exploration of such questions as "Is it true?" and "What does it mean?"

Luke's account also includes many details linking this story to the narrative whole of Luke-Acts. The story of Jesus' burial in 23:50-56 concluded with the women preparing spices and ointments for the body, awaiting the end of the Sabbath rest. The early dawn is again featured along with the deep perplexity at the missing body, now followed by an encounter with two angelic figures in "dazzling clothes"

READING THE STORY SLOWLY AND THOUGHTFULLY CAN COMMUNICATE THE VISION IT PROVIDES OF THE UNITY OF THE SON WITH THE FATHER'S MISSION OF LOVE, INCLUDING CARE FOR MARY AND THE DISCIPLES.

(see also Luke 9:29-31; Acts 1:10). The angels' words echo Mark and Matthew, but with important nuances. Their command to "remember how he told you" (v. 6) closely follows the passion predictions for the suffering of the Son of Man, especially in Luke 9:22 (see also 9:44; 18:31-33). The note of necessity (*"must be handed over,"* v. 7) is grounded in the fulfillment of the Scriptures (see 18:31: "Everything that is written about the Son of Man by the prophets will be accomplished").

In verse 10, the women are partially identified (only Mary Magdalene, Joanna, and Mary the mother of James are mentioned along with "the other women") as the messengers to the apostles (earlier identified as the eleven because Judas is gone; see Acts 1, along with "all the rest"). Was their report dismissed as an "idle tale" (Gk: *lēros hrēmata,* "foolish talk") because of cultural biases against the testimony of women or simply because the story was incredible? Peter's amazement, even after corroborating the empty tomb, leaves the question unresolved.

Luke is a master storyteller, drawing the hearer into the narrative. As will be even more evident in the Emmaus story of 24:13-35 (see the Gospel reading for Easter Evening, below), the reader or hearer of the story knows more than those in it. Their perplexity invites faith from those who know how the story turns out, still sharing amazement and wonder about the question, what does it all mean?

RESURRECTION OF THE LORD / EASTER EVENING

APRIL 8, 2007

REVISED COMMON	EPISCOPAL (BCP)	ROMAN CATHOLIC
Isa. 25:6–9	Acts 5:29a, 30–32 or Dan. 12:1–3	Acts 10:34a, 37–43
Psalm 114	Psalm 114 or Psalm 136 or Ps. 118:14–17, 22–24	Ps. 118:1-2, 16–17, 22–23
1 Cor. 5:6b–8	1 Cor. 5:6b–8 or Acts 5:29a, 30–32	Col. 3:1–4 or 1 Cor. 5:6b–8
Luke 24:13–49	Luke 24:13–35	Luke 24:13–35

FIRST READING

ISAIAH 25:6-9 (RCL)
ACTS 5:29a, 30-32 (BCP)
DANIEL 12:1-3 (BCP ALT.)

In the alternative readings from both Isaiah and the Acts of the Apostles, small excerpts are brought forward to sing the song of Christian hope. The Isaiah passage describes a festival for the accession to rule of a new king. Most remarkable is the connection between this enthronement and the swallowing up of death forever (Isa. 25:8). This hymn of praise to God is an eschatological protest against the Canaanite myths in which death is the one whose giant mouth swallows all (see Isa. 5:14). Paul picks up this theme again in 1 Corinthians 15:24–26, where the ultimate reign of God means the destruction of all the rulers and powers and "the last enemy to be destroyed is death" (see the RCL second reading for Easter Morning, above).

The context for the sermon of Acts 5 is the trial of the apostles before the high priest's council. The apostles' sharp word of obedience to God rather than human authorities has been omitted, yet Peter's testimony still includes a prophetic reproof of those who were complicit in Jesus' death. Peter's statement emphasizes the fulfillment of God's enduring will to redeem Israel since "the God of our ancestors raised up Jesus" (v. 30). The resurrection of Jesus, therefore, is the

vindication of God's purposes, not to condemn, but to "give repentance to Israel and forgiveness of sins" (v. 31). This "repentance" (Gk.: *metanoia*) is not mere penance but the "change of mind" or "turn" or "return to God" in confidence of mercy and forgiveness. In the following story, the Pharisee Gamaliel prevails in the council on behalf of restraint lest the Temple authorities "be found fighting against God" (v. 39). Peter's brief sermon, therefore, is properly read as an appeal to all hearers to accept God's gift of return and forgiveness offered in the death and resurrection of Christ Jesus.

The alternative reading from Daniel 12:1-3 (BCP) declares the remarkable vision of the awakening of "many of those who sleep in the dust" to "everlasting life" or "everlasting contempt" (v. 2). This is one of the few pre-Christian testimonies to the resurrection of the dead. Groups such as the Sadducees who "say that there is no resurrection" (Acts 23:8) also excluded Daniel from their canons. As the apostle Paul testified before King Agrippa in Acts 26:22-23, the resurrection of Jesus is a confirmation of Daniel's vision as being in accord with all of Israel's Scriptures: "To

> PETER'S SERMON IS PROPERLY READ AS AN APPEAL TO ALL HEARERS TO ACCEPT GOD'S GIFT OF RETURN AND FORGIVENESS OFFERED IN THE DEATH AND RESURRECTION OF CHRIST JESUS.

this day I have had help from God, and so I stand here, testifying to both small and great, saying nothing but what the prophets and Moses said would take place: that the Messiah must suffer, and that, by being the first to rise from the dead, he would proclaim light both to our people and to the Gentiles."

ACTS 10:34a, 37-43 (RC)

See the first reading for the Resurrection of the Lord/Easter Day, above.

RESPONSIVE READING
PSALM 114 (RCL, BCP)
PSALM 136 (BCP ALT.)

Psalms 114 and 136 resound with the praise of God who created the world and redeemed Israel. In the context of Easter, these hymns fill in the picture of Jesus' resurrection. This is consistent with what God had been doing since the creation of the earth (see also John 1:1), and the magnificence of God's reign is now made manifest for all the world to see. As the apostle Paul testified to Agrippa, "This was not done in a corner!" (Acts 26:26).

PSALM 118:14-17, 22-24 (BCP ALT.)
PSALM 118:1-2, 16-17, 22-23 (RC)

See the responsive reading for the Resurrection of the Lord/Easter Day, above.

SECOND READING
1 CORINTHIANS 5:6b-8 (RCL, BCP, RC ALT.)

Preaching on 1 Corinthians 5:6b-8 on leavened and unleavened requires attention to the moral context of Paul's words. Here the apostle invokes deep Jewish memories of purification for Passover, whereby a household was to be thoroughly cleansed of all yeast as a ritual of eliminating contamination. The ancient testimony to eating unleavened bread before the exodus had become a call to renewed obedience, now in preparation for God's redemption. Before rushing with liturgical delight into the Lord's Supper as a paschal feast, Christian preachers must remember that Paul's moral argument against the contamination of "malice and evil" is not a warrant for excluding those who are not morally worthy from the Lord's table. Yes, the "malice and evil" of those who boast of flagrant sins is a danger to the sanctity of the Lord's table, but this warning against flagrant sins are not directed at sensitive souls who are aware of their need of mercy. Only sinners come to Jesus' feast, and in his sacrifice as the Paschal Lamb, they become saints.

ACTS 5:29a, 30-32 (BCP ALT.)

See the first reading for the Resurrection of the Lord/Easter Evening, above.

COLOSSIANS 3:1-4 (RC)

See the second reading for the Resurrection of the Lord/Easter Day, above.

THE GOSPEL

LUKE 24:13-49 (RCL)
LUKE 24:13-35 (BCP, RC)

The Gospel reading for Easter Evening is a Lukan literary masterpiece. If Luke 2:1-20 is known and read throughout the world as the "Christmas Gospel," the walk to Emmaus deserves the same oral rendition every Easter. The Revised Common Lectionary extends the story until almost the last verses of Luke's account, much like the long readings from Passion (Palm) Sunday and Good Friday. Although the text is rich in details, preachers (and commentators) need to take care not to intrude on the narrative flow with too many particular observations. Three brief notes will suffice in this context: one literary, one scriptural, and one theological.

The literary note is an encouragement to dramatize the story or at least read it slowly and with expression for its tensions and resolutions. The inability of the travelers to recognize Jesus is consistent with many of the resurrection appearances in the Gospels, but more sustained, more confounding in this narrative. As in a theater where the audience can see what the players on the stage cannot, Luke's telling draws the audience (that is, the hearers) into a prophetic perplexity of why people "see and do not see" or "hear and do not understand" (see Isa. 6:9-10; Luke 8:10; Acts 13:40-41; 28:26-27). The opening of their eyes in the breaking of the bread (vv. 30-31) is filled with eucharistic faith, and their burning hearts in Jesus' opening of the Scriptures draw the hearer with them into the holy realm of faith. As this story reveals, the prophets and evangelists knew the contrary wisdom that believing is seeing.

The scriptural note is an encouragement to the preacher to observe how central scriptural interpretation is to the meaning of the resurrection, that is, what the resurrection means to God, its theological significance. Luke reports that on the road, "beginning with Moses and all the prophets, he interpreted to them the things about himself in all the scriptures" (v. 27). If one is going to be literal, it must have been a very long journey. More important, this summary verse discloses that to understand Jesus, one does not need to dwell in Israel's Law, Prophets, and Writings. In the context of the story, Jesus was illuminating their understanding of the redemption of Israel (v. 21), not rejecting it, but preparing to turn Israel's restoration into its vocation to be a light to the nations (Isa. 49:6; Acts 1:6-8; 13:47). The repeated themes of "necessity" undergird this story with the scriptural narratives Jesus is fulfilling, and his apostles will enact the same script.

> AS THIS STORY REVEALS, THE PROPHETS AND EVANGELISTS KNEW THE CONTRARY WISDOM THAT BELIEVING IS SEEING.

The theological note is an invitation to wonder faithfully about where Jesus' resurrection fits within God's purposes and vocation for the people of God. This lovely story follows many chapters of growing conflict, betrayal, and brutal execution. Jesus is acclaimed by the Roman centurion as the "righteous" or "innocent" (Gk.: *dikaios*) one. He is identified as a prophet (Luke 4:24; 7:16; 13:33; 24:19) and the Messiah of God, Son of God, Son of Man, King of the Jews, and God's Chosen One (see especially Jesus' trial and execution in Luke 23–24). Killing a righteous person earns reprisal. Killing a prophet puts a nation at risk. What about the Messiah and Son of God? What will God do when Jesus is killed? This question is pursued directly in Peter's first sermon in Acts 2:36-38 and indirectly in Luke 20:1-19. Luke 24 is a revelation of what God actually did, what the resurrection meant to God, disclosing the ultimate meaning of the vindication of God and God's Messiah. This vindication is fulfilled not in vindictiveness, but in the proclamation of "repentance and forgiveness of sins . . . in his name to all nations, beginning from Jerusalem" (v. 47; see also Acts 1:6-8).

> LUKE 24 IS A REVELATION OF WHAT GOD ACTUALLY DID, WHAT THE RESURRECTION MEANT TO GOD, DISCLOSING THE ULTIMATE MEANING OF THE VINDICATION OF GOD AND GOD'S MESSIAH.

Easter Evening already begins to lean toward Pentecost!

SECOND SUNDAY OF EASTER

APRIL 15, 2007

Revised Common	Episcopal (BCP)	Roman Catholic
Acts 5:27-32	Acts 5:12a, 17-22, 25-29 or Job 42:1-6	Acts 5:12-16
Ps. 118:14-29 or Psalm 150	Psalm 111 or Ps. 118:19-24	Ps. 118:2-4, 13-15, 22-24
Rev. 1:4-8	Rev. 1:(1-8) 9-19 or Acts 5:12a, 17-22, 25-29	Rev. 1:9-11a, 12-13, 17-19
John 20:19-31	John 20:19-31	John 20:19-31

The weeks between Easter and Pentecost invite Christians to see the world in the new light of the resurrection of Jesus. This is a brief season for wonder at the mystery of God's presence and power, while still embedded in human and earthly realities. Although it looks to be the same, the world will never return to normal, if measured by pre-Easter criteria. On the other hand, how has life itself been transformed and the creation with it? First steps into uncharted regions totter from tentative, to misguided, to purposeful.

FIRST READING
ACTS 5:27-32 (RCL)
ACTS 5:12a, 17-22, 25-29 (BCP)
ACTS 5:12-16 (RC)
JOB 42:1-6 (BCP ALT.)

The varied readings from Acts 5 provide a composite picture of divine power and authority stirring the community of Jesus' followers and disturbing the peace of the Roman order as enforced by the Temple authorities. None of the lectionaries includes all of the verses from Acts 5:12 to Acts 5:32, but interpreting any smaller selection of verses without reading at least this much context may be a risky practice.

The healing stories in Acts 5:12-16 (from the Roman Catholic lectionary) have often been abused by religious hucksters as precedents for their own claims to divine powers. This story about the healing power of Peter's shadow is imbued with the popular piety of religious amulets and the saints. Such stories are not only disturbing to modern rationalists. As is evident in the similar account about Paul's handkerchiefs and aprons in Acts 19:11-20, the early Christians understood that the line between these displays of divine power and mere magic is easily blurred. Taken by itself, the story of Peter's shadow doesn't even convey normal Christian clarity that healing occurs in the name of the risen Jesus. It does, however, express an enduring conviction that the apostolate of healing is an authentic Easter ministry, contending with spiritual and physical forces.

> THIS EPISODE IS A DISPLAY OF DIVINE AGENCY, EVIDENT ONLY TO THOSE WHO CAN SEE GOD AT WORK IN THE LIGHT OF THE RESURRECTION.

The snippets of Acts 5:12a, 17-22, 25-29 in the Episcopal lectionary interpret the "signs and wonders" of 5:12a in terms of God's evident siding with the apostles in their conflicts with the Temple authorities. This excision of verses compounds the risk of focusing on the Temple leadership's "jealousy" (v. 17), "perplexity" (or "utter confusion," v. 24), and ignoble fear of the people (v. 26), as if the apostles were heroes and their opponents merely political. But this story is not a simple ordeal of virtue, proving the apostles more noble than the Temple authorities. This episode is a display of divine agency, evident only to those who can see God at work in the light of the resurrection. In the prophetic diagnosis of the Acts of the Apostles, the officials' jealousy and dismay manifest their spiritual ignorance about "what might be going on" (v. 24), as if the apostles' filling "Jerusalem with your teaching" were mere civil disobedience or insurrection. The apostolic conclusion "We must obey God rather than any human authority" (v. 29) is thus a positive version of Gamaliel's later warning: "You may even be found fighting against God!" (v. 39).

The Revised Common Lectionary selection of verses 27-29 from this narrative context omits both the popular reaction to apostolic displays of power and the disclosures of the spiritual blindness of the authorities. The risk of this excerpt is that the hearer can no longer tell why the apostles are in such trouble in the story, other than that they disobeyed an order. The larger context reveals that the God who raised Jesus from the dead is continuing to confront the leadership of Israel with displays of both power and authority. Now on trial before the Temple leadership, the apostles bear witness, but not in their own self-defense. Back in the court where the Lord Jesus had also been tried, the apostles put the accusers on trial, bearing witness against Jesus' wrongful death, testifying that in raising him from the dead, God turned Jesus' hideous crucifixion into a gift of restoration for Israel.

The concluding words of the apostle's testimony, therefore, announce the mercy God intends for all who have opposed Jesus: "that he might give repentance to Israel and forgiveness of sins" (v. 31). Repentance is more than "penance" that God could rightly demand. God *gives* the "turning," the "change of mind" and of spirit to return. (Here the BCP alternative selection of Job 42:1-6 may be helpful if the point is not the groveling "in dust and ashes," but the discovery of "things too wonderful for me, which I did not know.") The forgiveness of sins will be the restored mission of Israel, as promised by the prophets, "to the ends of the earth" (Acts 1:8), wrought of the blood of the witnesses (Acts 8:1; 10:43).

Job 42:1-6 (BCP alternative) is a classic story of a mortal's encounter with God. Job's long narrative rejects all the easy answers about human suffering. Any Israelite who knew the story of Abraham's argument with God over the fate of Sodom in Genesis 18 would not be surprised or offended by Job's demand for his day in court. Even as he submits to a wisdom beyond his understanding, Job agrees with God's charge that he has "darken[ed] counsel by words without knowledge" (Job 38:2), but he has also girded "up [his] loins like a man" (38:3) so that the engagement with God does not end in Job's shame but in his enlightenment. Job is chastened but not humiliated. God who could have ignored this mere mortal, instead took his questions seriously and then blessed him with understanding. How much more will the God who could have justifiably destroyed those who killed Jesus now be glorified by "giving repentance," that is, the return and restoration of vocation to Israel.

> THE LARGER CONTEXT REVEALS THAT THE GOD WHO RAISED JESUS FROM THE DEAD IS CONTINUING TO CONFRONT THE LEADERSHIP OF ISRAEL WITH DISPLAYS OF BOTH POWER AND AUTHORITY.

RESPONSIVE READING

PSALM 118:14-29 (RCL)
PSALM 118:19-24 (BCP ALT.)
PSALM 118:2-4, 13-15, 22-24 (RC)
PSALM 150 (RCL ALT.)
PSALM 111 (BCP)

As on Easter Day, various excerpts from Psalm 118 appear in all of the lectionaries for the Second Sunday of Easter. The psalm sounds a profound note affirming God's steadfast love, emphatically to Israel (v. 2, Roman Catholic lectionary). The recitation of Psalm 118:22-24 is common to all the readings, now heard as a compelling Easter metaphor that Jesus Christ, "the stone that the builders rejected," has become God's cornerstone. Christian interpreters will do well to appreciate how this ancient affirmation of "the LORD's doing," which is "marvelous in our eyes," is again a call to turn to God as the source of life, hope, and joy. Read in the light of the resurrection of the crucified Messiah, Easter is "the day the LORD has made." The Psalms reveal that long before Jesus, Israel was practiced in joyful repentance, confident of returning to God's steadfast love.

Psalm 150 resounds with God's praise, inviting instrument after instrument and calling the whole creation to join the song. The specific reason for this exuberance is only hinted at in verse 2: "for his mighty deeds . . . according to his surpassing greatness." Whatever ancient Israel had in mind, the praise of Easter is for God's "mighty deeds" and "surpassing greatness" in raising Jesus from the dead and exalting his reign of mercy to the blessing of all nations and the joy of heaven.

Psalm 111 has been similarly appropriated for Christian praise. Here verses 5-6 hint at God's mighty acts in the exodus from Egypt, and verse 9 alludes to the giving of the law. The integrity of this praise was well established before Jesus, but now in the worship of Christian communities, the praise of God is filled with the substance of God's having raised the Messiah from the dead to the blessing of Israel and the nations.

SECOND READING
REVELATION 1:4-8 (RCL)
REVELATION 1:(1-8) 9-19 (BCP)
REVELATION 1:9-11a, 12-13, 17-19 (RC)

This is the first of a series of Easter season readings from the Revelation to John. The sequence of Sunday readings provides a rich opportunity for reciting and teaching this material, which is often misread as a kind of magical codebook by which to predict the future. Written in the semblance of a letter that includes other letters and many visions, the Revelation to John is thoroughly doxological, with angelic hosts and earthly figures contending with forces and powers while singing the praise and announcing the triumph of the Lamb who was slain (5:12; 13:8).

While the Acts of the Apostles announces that God "has exalted him [the crucified Jesus] as Leader and Savior" (5:31), the Revelation to John is a heavenly dramatization of scenes of the reign of the exalted Jesus, "the faithful witness, the firstborn of the dead, and the ruler of the kings of the earth" (1:5; see Ps. 89:27). Jesus' followers are priests in his reign (1:6; see Exod. 19:6), and the liturgical phrases ring with a heavenly, political glory that surpasses the hierarchies of the empires, within and beyond Israel. The "grace and peace" of his reign (1:4) come from the Lord God, who set the stars in the heavens (Gen. 1:14–19). Now the seven stars are the seven churches, not spinning in astrological necessity, but surrounding the Messiah's reign as heavenly lights corresponding to the seven earthly lampstands (see also Rev. 1:13).

The vindication and exaltation of Jesus Christ are scripted in the prophecies and revelations of Israel's holy writings. The narrative and the hymnic poems of the Revelation to John are filled with refrains from Daniel, especially in allusions to the one like a Son of Man "coming with the clouds" who has been "pierced" (Rev. 1:7, 13; Dan. 7:13; Zech. 12:10–12). This is not a mechanistic codification of prophecy, but the enactment of a divine drama in accord with the Scriptures.

An hour invested tracing the scriptural allusions with the help of a study Bible will reward the interpreter with an awareness of the wealth of scriptural images in Revelation. Where this leads, however, is not merely into an arcane history of sources behind the text, but toward a confident understanding of the world in front of the text. Writing an account of what he "saw" (1:10–12) equips John both to report this vision of the heavenly court and to see the world lying before it. John's vision pro-

> ALL WHO HAVE STARED INTO THE OPEN GRAVE OF SOMEONE THEY LOVED UNDERSTAND THAT JESUS' COUNSEL AGAINST FEAR DOES NOT MEAN A SPIRITUAL ESCAPE FROM THE WORLD.

vides a revelation of the present as the time in which the risen Jesus is already enthroned. What now is happening in heaven anticipates the manifestation of Jesus' reign on earth.

Revelation is filled with visions, scriptural allusions, poetry, and hymns. Looking to "see whose voice it was," the seer's eyes are directed to the seven golden lampstands, in the midst of which stood "one like the Son of Man." This is more than mere physical sight (see also Isa. 6:1–13). Small wonder that artists and musicians probably have the best chance among all interpreters of doing justice to the testimony of this book! Another hour invested with the church musician investigating the hymnic resources the church has developed from Revelation will help the people of God draw from the wells of this book to sing their Easter faith, surpassing prosaic interpretation with the faith of the heart and soul as well as the head.

Verses 17-19 (included in both the Episcopal and Roman Catholic lectionaries), therefore, also invite dramatization, or at least disciplined public reading, drawing the hearer and observer into the awesome presence of the one who is "the first and the last, and the living one." This heavenly figure is not a disembodied spirit, some otherworldly ideal or Gnostic avatar. This is Jesus who "was dead, and see, I am alive forever and ever." His gaze is now turned to the seven churches on earth for whom the seven golden lamps burn in heaven. All who have stared into the open grave of someone they loved understand that Jesus' counsel against fear does not mean a spiritual escape from the world. Rather, the one who was slain has invested human embodiment with divine dignity forever.

ACTS 5:12a, 17–22, 25–29 (BCP ALT.)

See the first reading for the Second Sunday of Easter, above.

THE GOSPEL

JOHN 20:19–31 (RCL, BCP, RC)

These appearances of the resurrected Jesus to his disciples and Thomas are deeply treasured in Christian history. They defy empirical explanation by either those who intend to disprove the historicity of the resurrection or those who hope to prove it on some grounds other than the testimony of the evangelist to the gospel truth.

A pious rationalist was heard to assert that people who don't believe Jesus came out of the tomb, "hair, bones, and teeth," don't believe in the resurrection. Of course, he was right in a way, and he seemed to have Thomas on his side of the argument, and perhaps even the risen Lord who showed his hands and sides to his astonished disciples and told Thomas to put his finger in the wounds of his crucified body. At the same time, how does modern or ancient rationalism deal with Jesus' appearance among his disciples when "the doors of the house where the disciples had met were locked" (20:19; or "shut," 20:26)? The disciples in the story and the evangelist who told it don't themselves supply evidence that can be empirically reproduced, nor could they about the resurrection itself. This is not the revivification of Lazarus complete with bandages and the fear of stench. The bodily resurrection does not eliminate the spiritual reality of the resurrection, as the ancient Ebionites may have thought. The New Testament testifies that Jesus' bodily resurrection was one of a kind, so far, the "first fruits of those who have died" (1 Cor. 15:20). All of us who have confidence in our rationality may still be tempted to ask, "How are the dead raised? With what kind of body do they come?" To which Paul answers, "Fool! . . . God gives it a body as he has chosen. . . . So it is with the resurrection of the dead. . . . Just as we have borne the image of the man of dust, we will also bear the image of the man of heaven" (1 Cor. 15:35–49). The resurrected body is still a body, but it is transformed in a manner mere mortals have yet to experience.

> THE RESURRECTED BODY IS STILL A BODY, BUT IT IS TRANSFORMED IN A MANNER MERE MORTALS HAVE YET TO EXPERIENCE.

The Fourth Evangelist attests both that Jesus appeared among them when the doors were locked and that his body was visible and apparently palpable. To say it was "apparently palpable" does not mean that it only seemed to be so, as the Docetics and Gnostics argued. John's Gospel is confident of the incarnation: "The Word became flesh" (1:14). Still, the evangelist stops short of reporting that Thomas or the others actually touched the resurrected Jesus when invited to do so, and Jesus' caution to Mary Magdalene that she not "hold on to" him (John 20:17) is again filled with the New Testament's restraint about "explaining" the resurrection by mere human experience.

The segments of this story, therefore, move through the wondrous and unknown toward that which can be received in faith. Verses 19-21 open with the awesome appearance of the resurrected Jesus, who like countless heavenly and earthly visitors greets the disciples with "Peace be with you!" The story is not preoccupied with the wonder of the resurrected body, but drives toward bringing the disciples into God's sending (the Latin word for this sending is *missio*, and in this context it is God's sending or the *missio Dei*). That is, as God has "sent" Jesus (said over twenty times in John; Gk.: *apostellein*; Lat.: *missio*), so Jesus sends (*pempein*) his disciples. It is intriguing to note the Fourth Evangelist doesn't use the noun *apostle* or even the verb *apostellein* to describe the sending of the disciples.[1] Nevertheless, Jesus' giving of the Holy Spirit results in the authorization of Jesus' followers to forgive or retain sins (20:22-23). Thus, as in the promise of Acts 1:6-8, the gift of the Holy Spirit moves beyond the spiritual enrichment of the disciples to the agency they are empowered to exercise.

The story of Thomas similarly builds beyond his problem of doubt or disbelief. It never was a condition of unbelief, but his "seeing" prompts his confession, "My Lord and my God!" In contrast to the prophetic denunciations of those who "see and do not see" or "hear and do not perceive" (Isa. 6:10), Thomas is blessed to believe not simply because he understands, but because he sees Jesus for who he is (see also Peter's confession in Mark 8:29, following the allusions to Isaiah 6 in Mark 8:18 and 4:10-12). In a classic Jewish rhetorical turn ("so much the more"), Jesus announces the greater blessing of those who "have not seen and yet have come to believe" (20:29).

> THE STORY IS NOT PREOCCUPIED WITH THE WONDER OF THE RESURRECTED BODY, BUT DRIVES TOWARD BRINGING THE DISCIPLES INTO GOD'S SENDING.

Verses 30-31, therefore, are the proper conclusion to this story and also to the whole narrative of the first twenty chapters. The sense of an ending is so strong that John 21 has regularly been called an "epilogue." Perhaps it was even written separately. In any case, the testimony of John 20:30-31 is important for its candor about all the "signs" "that are not written in this book." Was that "book" even a separate "book of signs" that was later assembled into the larger narrative of the

Fourth Gospel? At a minimum, the remarkable differences from the Synoptic Gospels (Matthew, Mark, and Luke) in content, sequence, and literary mode reinforce the recognition that the Fourth Gospel was not written simply to record all the "facts." Rather, it was composed with an evangelical purpose of leading people to "come to believe that Jesus is the Messiah, the Son of God, and that through believing you may have life in his name" (v. 31).

Was this a public evangelistic purpose, calling all people to faith? Or was this Gospel written with a more specific goal of getting faith in Jesus the Messiah straight among his followers?[2] Study of how John speaks of Jesus as the Son of God reveals the evangelist's careful work to communicate that the King of the Jews (see John 18:33-38; 19:19-22) who was raised up in crucifixion is truly the Son of God sent into the world on God's mission of love (see also John 3:16-17) and now raised up as the ensign of life (see also John 3:14).

Notes

1. See Raymond E. Brown, *The Community of the Beloved Disciple* (New York: Paulist Press, 1979), 81.

2. See D. Moody Smith, *John*, Proclamation Commentaries (Philadelphia: Fortress Press, 1986), 83–86.

THIRD SUNDAY OF EASTER

APRIL 22, 2007

REVISED COMMON	EPISCOPAL (BCP)	ROMAN CATHOLIC
Acts 9:1-6 (7-20)	Acts 9:1-19a or Jer. 32:36-41	Acts 5:27-32, 40b-41
Psalm 30	Psalm 33 or 33:1-11	Ps. 30:2, 4, 5-6, 11-12, 13
Rev. 5:11-14	Rev. 5:6-14 or Acts 9:1-19a	Rev. 5:11-14
John 21:1-19	John 21:1-14	John 21:1-19 or 21:1-14

The Third Sunday of Easter is manifestly the day for the story told in the Fourth Gospel of "the third time that Jesus appeared to the disciples after he was raised from the dead" (John 21:14). As Christians of every age dwell in these narratives, God's calling resounds with both a profound sense of apostolic purpose and a growing awareness that discipleship means vulnerability, even suffering and death.

FIRST READING

ACTS 9:1-6 (7-20) (RCL)
ACTS 9:1-19a (BCP)
ACTS 5:27-32, 40b-41 (RC)
JEREMIAH 32:36-41 (BCP ALT.)

The passage from Jeremiah (the BCP alternative) stands apart from the stories in Acts, recalling God's undying love for Israel. The mystery of God's bond with "my people," against all odds, remains challenging for all the other nations and families gathered in the light of Easter and Pentecost as heirs to God's promises. Still, the nations or "Gentiles" can never boast of having displaced empirical Israel in God's heart. These verses stand in the lectionary as a reminder of the faithfulness of God's love, not only giving assurance to Israel, but also offering enduring consolation to all the nations who are now claimed in the name of the Messiah of this same God (see also Romans 9–11, especially 11:17-24: no gloating is allowed). In the end, there is no comfort in the thought that Israel, God's first love, would be abandoned. All the nations that are now included in this bond are also made worthy only through God's forgiveness and ardor for them and the world.

Some of the verses from Acts 5 in the Roman Catholic lectionary for this Sunday were already cited in the readings for last Sunday, and the danger of excerpting small portions of Acts 5 was noted in my comments there. The verses that have been lifted into the first reading in the Roman Catholic lectionary convey the particular danger of Christians thinking that the apostles were indeed "determined to bring this man's [Jesus'] blood on us" (meaning the high priests; Acts 5:27-28).

The response from Peter and the apostles does hold the high priests accountable for having Jesus killed by Roman crucifixion, but the apostles are not announcing a final judgment even on the high priests, and certainly not on all of Israel. Instead, this is an occasion for testimony to God's mercy, as in the classic biblical conviction that what sinful people meant for evil, God means for good to accomplish the salvation of Israel (Gen. 50:20). The ending of the first portion of this reading, therefore, is not condemnation, but God's *gift* of "repentance to Israel and forgiveness of sins" with the apostles as testamentary witnesses along with the Holy Spirit. Even in the face of persecution (vv. 40b-41), the apostles continue to announce the news of Jesus the Messiah. In the preaching of the apostles, this is good news of God's mercy for Israel and for the whole world.

> ACTS 9 IS NOT A CONVERSION STORY IN THE MODERN SENSE OF THAT WORD OF "CHANGING RELIGIONS."

The story of Saul's call in Acts 9 should be read through verse 20, as is the alternative suggestion in the Revised Common Lectionary. This is often called Paul's "conversion," which is apt in the biblical sense of the "change of mind" (*metanoia*) of "turning" or "returning" to God. This is not a conversion story in the modern sense of that word of "changing religions." Through the vision and words of the resurrected Jesus, Saul's zeal was redirected from doing evil, when he was trying to do good by his own lights, to doing what was good in God's eyes.

The first nine verses tell of this encounter but only as far as Saul's blindness. It is a call story with a light from heaven (v. 3), the divine voice repeating Saul's name (see also Moses in Exod. 3:4 and Samuel in 1 Sam. 3:4, 6, 10). If the reading stops here, it is merely a dramatic account of how an enemy of the followers of Jesus, who were called "the Way" (v. 2), was struck down. Jewish readers would likely have seen the similarities with the 2 Maccabees story of how, in the midst of an epiphany of divine power, the Greek general Heliodorus was struck down into "deep darkness" when he attempted to plunder the Temple treasury. When healed by God through the high priest's prayer, Heliodorus also "made very great vows to the Savior of his life" and "bore testimony to all concerning the deeds of the supreme God, which he had seen with his own eyes" (2 Macc. 3:35, 36). Saul's story is recounted twice more in the Acts of the Apostles in his own testimony (22:6-16; 26:12-18), but Saul/Paul's witness will be about more than his own experience.

Verses 10-19 change the scene to Damascus, where Saul is about to be taken, no longer under his own power. Obscure Ananias has his own vision and call, and he responds in authentic Jewish fashion: "Here I am, Lord" (v. 10; see 1 Sam. 3:4, 6, 10; Acts 22:12). His protests against Saul's "evil" doings are coupled with fear of the high priests' powers. Once again, God is about to do a good thing out of people's evil intents, making this enemy into "a chosen instrument" or vessel (see 2 Cor. 4:7) for bringing God's mission before "Gentiles and kings and before the people of Israel" (v. 15). Even Paul's apostolate to the nations (Gentiles) includes continued witness in Israel. When the risen Lord promises to show him "how much he must suffer for the sake of my name" (v. 16), he is sounding the note of the divine necessity of God's mission prompting the inevitable struggle with humans (see also Luke 9:22; 17:25; 22:37; 24:7, 26, 44; Acts 4:27-28).

The restoration of Saul's sight (vv. 17-19) is a sign of the fulfillment of God's promises (Luke 7:22; Isa. 29:18; 35:5-6). Even if he didn't change religions, Saul's story is a classic "conversion" in the deepest sense of the change of heart and mind of the new believer. The refrain of the hymn "Amazing Grace" sounds this same confidence that new sight is a miracle of faith: "I once was blind, but now I see." Quick to submit to baptism, he also begins "immediately . . . to proclaim Jesus in the synagogues, saying, 'He is the Son of God.'" As Acts 9:22 demonstrates, Saul's declaration of Jesus as God's Son is not an abstract speculation about Jesus' divine nature, but an affirmation that Jesus is God's Anointed, the Messiah, the one who rules with divine authority, as did King David (Psalm 2).

EVERY CHRISTIAN COMMUNITY THAT BASKS IN THE JOYFUL LIGHT OF EASTER IS SOON CALLED BEYOND ITS COMFORT ZONE INTO PUBLIC WITNESS AND MISSION.

Once again, the Easter season stories explore the ways in which the world is changed by Jesus' resurrection. Saul/Paul has still not taken the news beyond Israel, but the risen Jesus has already announced that his mission will also reach the Gentiles and kings (9:15). Every Christian community that basks in the joyful light of Easter is soon called beyond its comfort zone into public witness and mission. The reign of the Lord Jesus quickly extends beyond every ethnic enclave into the world God so loves.

RESPONSIVE READING

PSALM 30 (RCL)
PSALM 30:2, 4, 5-6, 11-12, 13 (RC)
PSALM 33 OR 33:1-11 (BCP)

Psalm 30 (RCL, RC) is a song of thanksgiving, probably used by those who experienced healing (v. 2) when death was apparently close (v. 3). In verses 4-5, others are invited to join the song, aware of God's wrath but confident in the joy of God's favor. The psalm gives voice to all who have been brought low from their self-confidence, then renewed in their callings of praise to God. Both Saul in Acts and Peter in John's Gospel fit this profile, and all who are exploring the world in the light of Easter may also know the joy of being drawn into the chorus of the praise of God.

Psalm 33 (BCP) is a song of praise, full of Israel's confidence in God as the creator (vv. 6-9) and ruler of the nations and all humankind (vv. 10-15). Preaching in the Easter season is marked by this grand confidence in God. The picture of God watching all "from where he sits enthroned" (v. 14) brings alive the wonderfully earthy images of "the waters of the sea" gathered "as in a bottle," "the deeps in storehouses," the warrior, and the warhorse. Still, this is not a picture of a detached god watching "from a distance." Rather, Israel's God is caring for "those who hope in his steadfast love, to deliver their soul from death, and to keep them alive in famine" (vv. 18-19). Verses 20-21 thus sound the conclusion of thanksgiving, with trust and hope focused on God.

SECOND READING

REVELATION 5:11-14 (RCL, RC)
REVELATION 5:6-14 (BCP)

The fifth chapter of the Revelation to John continues the glimpse into the court of heaven that began in Revelation 4. The splendid and strange living creatures (see also Isa. 6:1-7), along with the twenty-four elders, are seen singing the praise of God, who is seated on the throne. A remarkable epiphany is about to occur with the unrolling of the scroll. The seals on a scroll were used to keep successive levels of confidentiality, as each waxen seal was broken by the authorized person until the most secret message was disclosed only to the eyes of the one authorized to unroll the last section.

The liturgy and hymns ought somehow to be reenacted for modern hearers so they can grasp the drama of this scene. Verse 5 identifies the "Lion of the tribe of

Judah, the Root of David" as the conqueror who is able to unroll the scroll and all of its seven seals. Verse 6 identifies this Lion with the "Lamb standing as if it had been slaughtered." The Lion of Judah is the Davidic king, and the Lamb who was slaughtered is Jesus.

Deep within this concatenation of images lies the faith that the crucified Jesus is truly the King of Israel, to whom the reign of heaven and of earth has been entrusted. Jesus is the one around whom the heavenly creatures and elders are gathered as the script of what will be is disclosed, but this story is no simple imposition of an imperial plan, not even a rigid script from heaven. And what does it mean when God's people still experience privation and rejection? The Lion of Judah appears to be an image of triumph, which is not complicated to understand, but what happens in heaven and on earth when the Lion of Judah is the Lamb once slain?

The few biblical writers who provided glimpses of what was occurring in the courts of heaven (for example, Daniel; Isaiah 6, 24–27) understood such events to be engaged with or affecting things that occur on the plane of human history. The unrolling of the scroll in the heavenly court is, therefore, an event of consequence to

> WHAT HAPPENS IN HEAVEN AND ON EARTH WHEN THE LION OF JUDAH IS THE LAMB ONCE SLAIN?

both earth and heaven, but it is prophetic, not fatalistic, alive to God's purposes and relationships, not driven by a necessity whose power lies beyond the gracious will of God.

These distinctions are crucial to the interpretation of the Revelation to John. God and the Lamb are the ultimate mysteries, the ones to whom all honor and glory are due. The great hymns of Revelation 5 accord honor and praise to God and to Jesus the Lamb. The interpreters who reduce these visions to mechanistic codes to be cracked make idols of the images as if they no longer pointed to God's presence and care for the saints. No promises are given that the disciples of the Lamb once slain will be exempt from suffering, but the praises of the Lamb and God are filled with confidence in the dignity and worth of those who will now "be a kingdom and priests serving our God, and they will reign on earth" (v. 10). To which the chorus of heavenly creatures and angels sings *Amen*.

ACTS 9:1-19a (BCP ALT.)

See the first reading for the Third Sunday of Easter, above.

THE GOSPEL

JOHN 21:1-19 (RCL, RC)
JOHN 21:1-14 (BCP, RC ALT.)

These wonderful stories convey the human realities, the symbolic power, and the transcendent experiences of the Easter season. Readers and proclaimers do well to enjoy the specific details, to explore the world of meaning, and to wonder at the many things they do not and will not fully understand in the stories.

Both the Episcopal lectionary and the alternative reading of the Roman Catholic lectionary conclude the reading at verse 14, where the story specifi-cally identifies this as "the third time that Jesus appeared to the disciples after he was raised from the dead." The story holds together in three scenes: a fruitless night fishing (vv. 1-3) is followed by the risen Jesus' appearance on the shore, pointing them to a good catch (vv. 4-8), then hosting a meal (vv. 9-14). This excerpt has the narrative virtues of a clear beginning, middle, and end; an intriguing tension about how their work changes when they see Jesus; and a satisfying focus on his hospitality. The story almost preaches itself.

THE HEARER AND INTERPRETER MUST DEAL NOT ONLY WITH *WHAT* HAPPENED WHEN JESUS APPEARED BUT ALSO WITH THE CONSEQUENCES OF HIS APPEAR-ANCE—THAT IS, *SO WHAT?*

When the lectionary reading continues through verse 19, the interpreter's task is more complex, and perhaps more interesting. Now the hearer and interpreter must deal not only with *what* happened when Jesus appeared, but also with the consequences of his appearance—that is, *so what?* The literary coherence of the whole episode now begins with the disciples' night fishing, followed by Jesus' appearance on the shore and his hosting them for a meal, and concludes with his new commission to Peter (vv. 15-19).

As was noted in last week's comments, John 21 as a whole appears to be an epilogue or even an addition to the narrative. Although no ancient manuscripts omit this chapter, scholars are intrigued with identifying possible literary sources. But theological interpreters of the narrative itself probably do better to credit the evangelist's evident attention to introducing new material (see 20:30-31, "signs . . . which are not written in this book. But these are written . . ."; 21:1, "After these things Jesus showed himself again . . ."). Whatever the sources behind the narrative might have been, the evangelist presents these stories as sequels to chapters 1–20, pressing toward another literary conclusion in 21:25 with comments about how much more could have been written.

Verses 1-3 alert the reader that a resurrection appearance is about to be recounted, but the focus is on the disciples who follow Simon Peter. "I am going fishing!" he declares. Interpreters who hear echoes of Peter's call in Luke 5:1-11 know that Jesus called Simon and the sons of Zebedee away from their nets to become fishers of people. But apart from mentioning the sons of Zebedee and a dramatic catch after a night of failure, no specific connections to that Lukan call story are made in John's account. If interpretation is closely textual, therefore, bringing story elements in from Luke may be questionable. On the other hand, memory and oral tradition were lively in the first century and remain so. Jesus doesn't scold Simon Peter for taking out the nets of his former professional life. He intercepts him and shows him a more excellent way.

Verses 4-8 present an epiphany fish story. The details about nets and where to cast them and men toiling in their skivvies have fascinated imaginations for centuries. "Just after daybreak, Jesus stood on the beach; but the disciples did not know it was Jesus" (v. 4). This lack of recognition recalls the disciples walking to Emmaus (Luke 24:16, "Their eyes were kept from recognizing him"). Without overdrawing the parallels, it is noteworthy that again while surrounded by a stupendous catch of fish, Peter recognized Jesus as "the Lord" (see Luke 5:8, "Go away from me, Lord, for I am a sinful man"). This time it is "the disciple whom Jesus loved" (see also John 21:20 and 25 for links with the author) who alerts Peter, "It is the Lord!" (21:7). The graphic details of epiphany call stories in the Bible alert the hearer to divine presence in the ordinary (see Exodus 3, Moses herding sheep; Judges 6, Gideon threshing; Isaiah 6, Isaiah in the Temple).

Verses 9-14 continue to explore the details with such attention that each begins to attain symbolic status: charcoal fire, fish, and bread already set out by Jesus (v. 9). As the story progresses, the evangelist clearly invites wonder, perhaps even speculation. What difference does it make that Peter went back on the boat, that the fish were "large," that there were 153 of them, and that "the net was not torn" (v. 11)? The allegorical interpreters in the early church had a field day with these details, confident that the 153 was much more than a literal count. But the evangelist's restraint in not answering the questions these details raise cautions interpreters to let them work in the hearers' imagination without "explanations."

The disciples themselves don't dare to ask Jesus the central question of the Gospel: "Who are you?" It is not merely that they don't ask "because they knew it was the Lord," but that none of them "dared to ask him" (v. 12). First they didn't literally recognize who was standing on the beach (v. 4); now they know him by sight, but

AS THE STORY PROGRESSES, THE EVANGELIST CLEARLY INVITES WONDER, PERHAPS EVEN SPECULATION.

they are clearly depicted as yearning to know something more they don't dare to ask. Those who have stood by the bedside of their own sleeping child have sensed some of this wonder: "Who are you?" But with Jesus, the mystery is still deeper.

At least the whole gospel story is needed to answer this question, and these are Jesus' disciples who have been with him. Then he gave them the answer in another way, again as servant and host as he had been in sharing bread and fish with the crowd (John 6:11) and in giving bread to his betrayer in his farewell supper with the disciples (John 13:1—17:26; see 13:26). The question, "Who is Jesus?" requires more than a pat answer. His living presence as Lord and host transforms the community of his disciples.

Verses 15-19 begin to demonstrate the consequences of Jesus' appearance. It is impossible to sense the depth of the agony in Jesus' threefold question to Peter, "Do you love me?" without remembering Peter's threefold denials during Jesus' arrest (John 18:15-27). The entire Gospel of John sounds the theme of God's costly love for the world (3:16) and Jesus' love for his followers (see 15:9; 16:27; 17:25-26; and so forth). Peter's commission, therefore, is focused pastorally on the care and feeding of the community of believers: "Feed my lambs! Tend my sheep! Feed my sheep!"

THE LOVE, THE CARE OF THE FLOCK, THE DISCIPLESHIP TO WHICH THE RESURRECTED JESUS CALLS PETER IS CONSISTENT WITH JESUS' OWN MISSION.

Verses 18-19 sound the note of the costly love of discipleship. Jesus makes no assurances of personal ease or adulation. In a metaphor that causes all geriatrics to shudder, Jesus promises only the loss of control of being led around by his belt coupled with an allusion to his glorifying God by stretching out his hands in crucifixion (see John 19; 12:23). The love, the care of the flock, and the discipleship to which the resurrected Jesus calls Peter are consistent with Jesus' own mission. It is the crucified and resurrected Jesus who renews his call to discipleship: "After this he said to him, 'Follow me'"!

FOURTH SUNDAY OF EASTER

APRIL 29, 2007

REVISED COMMON	EPISCOPAL (BCP)	ROMAN CATHOLIC
Acts 9:36-43	Acts 13:15-16, 26-33 (34-39) or Num. 27:12-23	Acts 13:14, 43-52
Psalm 23	Psalm 100	Ps. 100:1-2, 3, 5
Rev. 7:9-17	Rev. 7:9-17 or Acts 13:15-16, 26-33 (34-39)	Rev. 7:9, 14b-17
John 10:22-30	John 10:22-30	John 10:27-30

FIRST READING

ACTS 9:36-43 (RCL)
ACTS 13:15-16, 26-33 (34-39) (BCP)
ACTS 13:14, 43-52 (RC)
NUMBERS 27:12-23 (BCP ALT.)

The story of Tabitha or Dorcas in Acts 9 (RCL) is a remarkable account of revivification, filled with narrative details that provide glimpses into a community of Jewish Christians in a cosmopolitan city. Her name, which seems to be of bicultural interest itself in Aramaic and in Greek, can be translated as "gazelle" in English. Her reputation for "good works and acts of charity" (v. 36) identifies her as a person of good standing in the Jewish community (see Luke 11:41; 12:33; Acts 3:2; and especially Acts 10:2). Careful attention is paid in Jewish practice to preparation of a body for burial (Luke 23:50—24:1; on "the saints and widows," see also Luke 2:37; Acts 6:1). Peter's residence with Simon the tanner is reported as a matter of fact, although strictly observant communities may well have regarded this work with dead skins to be ritually unclean.

The significance of the story may well be embedded in its context, following the healing of a paralyzed man in Lydda (9:32-35) and preceding the remarkable story of the conversion of the Roman centurion Cornelius (10:1-48). Peter is enacting the script as Jesus' apostle, healing a paralyzed man as Jesus did (Luke 5:17-26) and reviving a dead woman, complete with echoes of Jesus' command to the little girl (Luke 8:54, "Child, get up!"; Mark 5:41, "Talitha cum!"; Acts 9:40, "Tabitha, get up!").

It is important to note that in the New Testament, such stories of revivification are not confused with the resurrection. Lazarus (John 11), the widow's son at Nain (Luke 7), and Jairus's daughter (Luke 8) join Dorcas as those who were miraculously revived. These stories are also filled with scriptural precedents from the Law and the Prophets, Moses, Elijah, and Elisha. Thus, the story of Dorcas concludes with the spreading of the news throughout Joppa, "and many believed in the Lord," but no one worshiped Dorcas. As an apostle, Peter bears the authority of One who was not merely revived; the resurrection of Jesus confirms that God has made him Lord and Messiah (Acts 2:36; 10:37-41).

Major sections of the second half of Acts 13 are included in both the Episcopal and Roman Catholic lectionaries, but neither tradition overlaps the other. In verses 14-16, readers are introduced to a depiction of the hospitality extended to visiting interpreters in the synagogues of Asia Minor. In Nazareth, Jesus "stood up to read" and "sat down" to comment on the Scriptures in Nazareth (Luke 4:16, 20). Here Paul "sat down" for the reading of the "law and the prophets," then "stood up . . . to speak" when invited to offer a word of exhortation. The lectionaries offer differing portions of his extended comments in the synagogue.

Verses 26-33 (34-39) are cited as alternatives for the first and second readings in the BCP lectionary. This is an excerpt from one of the classic "speeches in Acts," all of which are scriptural expositions. The "message of this salvation" (v. 26) proclaims Jesus as the promised Savior who along with his adversaries fulfills "everything that was written about him" (v. 29). The apostle's testimony is a first-century Jewish Christian interpretation of Psalms 2 and 16:10 and Isaiah 55:3. These royal psalms were no longer just about ancient King David, but about David's son who is now exalted as God's Son and the Lord. Such "messianic" exposition of the Scriptures was also consistent with the declaration of the risen Jesus that "everything written about me in the law of Moses, the prophets, and the psalms must be fulfilled" (Luke 24:44). The ways in which Israel's Scriptures are cited seem strange to modern interpreters, but these verses demonstrate how the early followers of Jesus read Israel's Scriptures in a new light following Jesus' resurrection.

AS AN APOSTLE, PETER BEARS THE AUTHORITY OF ONE WHO WAS NOT MERELY REVIVED; THE RESURRECTION OF JESUS CONFIRMS THAT GOD HAS MADE HIM LORD AND MESSIAH.

Verses 43-52 (RC) skip over the scriptural exposition to focus on the responses to Paul's message to the synagogue. In order to prevent a misguided judgment by modern interpreters against all of Israel, it is essential to notice the report in Acts that "many Jews and devout converts to Judaism followed Paul and Barnabas" (v. 43). Nevertheless, this story will become dangerously anti-Jewish when the Christian movement becomes predominately composed of non-Jews. The theme of "jealousy" (v. 45; see also Acts 5:17; 7:9) is a prophetic indictment, although it sounds merely petty and self-justifying. So also, Paul and Barnabas's denunciation of those who have rejected them is no harsher than many historic words against Israel by her own prophets (see Isa. 6:9-13), which is not to say these are easy words. Fiercest of all is the citation of Isaiah 49:6 as a prophetic reproof so that the success of the Gentile mission is a judgment against Israel (see also Romans 9–11). This is the same prophetic passage to

> PAUL AND BARNABAS'S DENUNCIATION OF THOSE WHO HAVE REJECTED THEM IS NO HARSHER THAN MANY HISTORIC WORDS AGAINST ISRAEL BY HER OWN PROPHETS, WHICH IS NOT TO SAY THESE ARE EASY WORDS.

which the risen Lord alluded in Acts 1:6-8, announcing the witness of his followers to the end of the earth as a fulfillment of God's promise to true Israel. The Acts of the Apostles, therefore, declares that in raising Jesus and exalting him as Lord, God was keeping the promises to Israel, for the restoration of their vocation as a light to the Gentiles, if they could receive it. The "joy" and "Holy Spirit" that filled the disciples (v. 52), therefore, were not in the rejection they were receiving from some Jews, even if they were a majority, but in the believers' bold confidence that God was fulfilling Israel's vocation as they bore the light of Christ Jesus to the Gentiles.

Numbers 27:12-23 is a story of Joshua's commission by God as Moses' successor. It anticipates the Gospel lesson in its strong affirmation of the trustworthy agency of God's "spirit" caring for the welfare of the community when Moses or Jesus is gone (see also John 14:15-30). The Gospel's affirmation of care that God's people not be left as a flock without a shepherd echoes with the assurances of Numbers 27:17. Whereas Moses was Israel's shepherd and Eleazar the priest, Jesus is both the Good Shepherd who lays down his life for the sheep (John 10) and the High Priest interceding on behalf of the people (John 17:9-13).

RESPONSIVE READING
PSALM 23 (RCL)
PSALM 100 (BCP)
PSALM 100:1-2, 3, 5 (RC)

Psalm 23 (RCL) echoes the promise in the Gospel lesson, "My sheep hear my voice. I know them, and they follow me. I give them eternal life, and they will never perish" (John 10:26-27). Although many Christian interpreters find it difficult to follow the way the psalms were being read in the passages from Acts 13, their own experience of the pastoral assurance of Psalm 23 causes them to hear Jesus all through it. Since this psalm is used regularly in the context of funerals, the traditional refrain "even though I walk through the valley of death" still rings in Christian ears, even when the NRSV reads "even though I walk through the darkest valley," with no overt reference to death. Although the snippets of text are brief in the lectionary and the memory of the people shorter, the Scriptures, especially when they are memorized or oral, continue to interpret the Scriptures. Psalm 23 is a telling example.

Psalm 100 is a brief hymn of thanksgiving, still shorter if verse 4 is omitted, as in the Roman Catholic lectionary. Again the reference to us as God's "people, and the sheep of his pasture," links the psalm to the Gospel lesson. This psalm stands along John 10 as an explication of the Lord's "steadfast love" that "endures forever." The promise of "eternal life," therefore, is filled with God's enduring love and "faithfulness to all generations." This is a promise not only for life beyond death but for God's continuing care for the generations alive and to come.

SECOND READING
REVELATION 7:9-17 (RCL, BCP)
REVELATION 7:9, 14b-17 (RC)

The pastor who has chosen to preach on the Easter readings from the Revelation to John will have a feast on the Fourth Sunday of Easter! Handel's "Hallelujah Chorus" will ring in people's ears, and the vision of the "great multitude that no one could count" will overwhelm all fussy and mechanistic explanations of the numbers of Revelation. This is not a passage to be droned through by a weak reader. To do it justice, the congregation may need trumpets or timpani or at least a vigorous recitation.

The great multitude appears to be a vision of the nations who have come to faith, the Gentiles in contrast to the tribes of Israel who were just numbered in verses 4-8. There is no hint that the Gentiles have superseded Israel, but their astonishing numbers manifest the fulfillment of Israel's vocation to be a light to the nations. Now they are also in the light, white-robed in the purity given to them by the blood of the Lamb (v. 14).

The Bible does not often reveal much about heaven, its architecture, or its life. Those who dream of escaping this "late great planet earth" may miss the joy of their callings to be the hands of Christ to their neighbors. Even when the Revelation to John pulls back the curtain of the firmament for glimpses of the heavenly realm, what is disclosed is the splendor of the God and the Lamb whom the faithful have trusted and worshiped on earth. And these glimpses are given to encourage all who have already received eternal life by belonging to the Lamb. There is more to come!

Thus, "they who have come out of the great ordeal" may be martyrs whose confession of faith cost them their mortal lives, but the image is larger, at least including all who endured times of suffering prior to the revelation of the ultimate reign of the Messiah. Even now in the times of their death, these holy ones are safe with God. "The Lamb ... will be their shepherd, and he will guide them to springs of the water of life, and God will wipe away every tear from their eyes" (v. 17). But the end of the story is not getting to heaven. It is, rather, a holy city, a new Jerusalem, "coming down out of heaven from God," and "the home of God is among mortals" (Rev. 21:2-3). This is when death itself will be no more.

THERE IS NO HINT THAT THE GENTILES HAVE SUPER-SEDED ISRAEL, BUT THEIR ASTONISHING NUMBERS MANIFEST THE FULFILLMENT OF ISRAEL'S VOCATION TO BE A LIGHT TO THE NATIONS.

Easter proclamation, therefore, includes assurance concerning those who have died. The resurrection of Jesus is his exaltation to heavenly dominion, for now. Revelation is a glimpse of the gathering of all the faithful dead, all those for whom the Lamb was slain. And it is a vision of a new creation, come to earth, for the living and the dead.

ACTS 13:15-16, 26-33 (34-39) (BCP ALT.)

See the first reading for the Fourth Sunday of Easter, above.

THE GOSPEL
JOHN 10:22-30 (RCL, BCP)
JOHN 10:27-30 (RC)

This brief reading is filled with peril and promise. The peril lies in the temptation for Christian self-justification at the expense of the Jews. The promise is given in the profound revelation of the unity of Jesus in the will, heart, and purposes of God.

The peril must be faced directly. It does not help to berate the Gospel of John for the fact that it has so long been read as an anti-Jewish polemic. Once the New Testament Gospels fell into almost exclusively non-Jewish (Gentile) hands, the fierce intra-Jewish struggles of the first century ceased to lie within the family.

One partial explanation is to remember that Jesus was from Nazareth in Galilee, not from Judea. The Gospel of John is keenly aware of the harsh question of whether anything good could come from Nazareth (1:45) and of the fact that the Judeans expected neither the Messiah nor a true prophet to come from Galilee (7:41, 52). Another partial explanation is that when Jesus is dealing with the "Jews" (*hoi Ioudaioi*) in John 10, he is being confronted by the Judean Temple authorities. Historically, these were the leaders who were most threatened by challenges to their authority. Not only did they have huge personal and professional investments in defending their Temple leadership; they also were held accountable by the Roman occupation forces to keep the peace. It must still be granted, however, that scholars who have tried to sort out all of the fierce words in John's Gospel about "the Jews" have concluded that some struggle must have been continuing during the time the Gospel was being written, perhaps concerning followers of Jesus who were expelled from the synagogue (9:22).

THE PROMISE OF THIS READING LIES IN THE DEEP ASSURANCE OF THE UNITY OF JESUS WITH THE WILL, HEART, AND PURPOSES OF GOD.

The evangelist seems to use the word *Ioudaioi* with at least an indirect reference to ongoing adversaries of the unity of the community.

The promise of this reading, however, lies in the deep assurance of the unity of Jesus with the will, heart, and purposes of God. It has been said that Jesus is God's way of being in the world or even that Jesus the Messiah is God's way of ruling the world. These comprehensive convictions find sound foundations in John 10, notably in the declaration "The Father and I are one" (see also John 17:11).

John's Gospel begins to fill out this declaration in the prologue (1:1), where the evangelist declares, "In the beginning was the Word, and the Word was with God, and the Word was God." The metaphysical philosophers of later Christian centuries explored these depths with the great joys and glories of trinitarian theology. Part of the truth to be proclaimed from John 10, therefore, is the testimony that Jesus' story is God's story. The apostle Paul announced that "in Christ God was reconciling the world to himself, not counting their trespasses against them" (2 Cor. 5:19). In the Fourth Sunday of Easter, therefore, John 10 at least anticipates the doxological splendor of Trinity Sunday.

But this story is more pastoral than philosophical. In the face of hostile critics, Jesus speaks a word of comfort to his own flock, his sheep that hear his voice, and his assurance to them that "no one will snatch them out of my hand" (v. 28) rests on his unity with the Father. The discussion will continue about how "I am in the Father and the Father is in me" (14:10), but for now, the confidence that "no one can snatch it out of the Father's hand" (v. 29) provides the deepest assurance of the eternal well-being of Jesus' sheep.

THE PREACHER WILL DO WELL TO GIVE JESUS' PROMISE FLESH BY LISTENING CAREFULLY TO THE LOSSES AND FEARS OF DISHONOR OF THOSE MEMBERS OF THE FLOCK TO WHOM SHE OR HE IS PREACHING.

The promise Jesus delivers to his flock in John 14 is compactly stated, and it is stated under duress. To grasp its joy, the preacher will do well to give this promise flesh by listening carefully to the losses and fears of dishonor of those members of the flock to whom she or he is preaching. Then let the resounding hymns of Revelation break loose in their splendor and joy. "For the Lamb at the center of the throne will be their shepherd, and he will guide them to springs of the water of life, and God will wipe away every tear from their eyes!" (Rev. 7:17).

FIFTH SUNDAY OF EASTER

MAY 6, 2007

REVISED COMMON	EPISCOPAL (BCP)	ROMAN CATHOLIC
Acts 11:1-18	Acts 13:44-52 or	Acts 14:21-27
	Lev. 19:1-2, 9-18	
Psalm 148	Psalm 145 or 145:1-9	Ps. 145:8-9, 10-11,
		12-13
Rev. 21:1-6	Rev. 19:1, 4-9 or	Rev. 21:1-5a
	Acts 13:44-52	
John 13:31-35	John 13:31-35	John 13:31-33a,
		34-35

FIRST READING

ACTS 11:1-18 (RCL)
ACTS 13:44-52 (BCP)
ACTS 14:21-27 (RC)
LEVITICUS 19:1-2, 9-18 (BCP ALT.)

Acts 11:1-18 (RCL) is Peter's rehearsal of the conversion of Cornelius that was just described in Acts 10, now repeated in response to criticism for eating with Gentiles. Although this text appears in the Easter season, it rightly follows the story of Pentecost. The Cornelius story is profoundly significant as a chapter in the history of the mission of the church, because this is how the Christian movement broke out of the enclave of Israel.

The criticism against Peter comes from "circumcised believers" (v. 2), which reflects the reality that many Jewish Christians could not accept the Gentile mission if it meant the violation of Torah observance, or the keeping of the law, as was commonly practiced. Believers like these show up again in Acts 15, insisting, "Unless you are circumcised according to the custom of Moses, you cannot be saved" (v. 1), and are joined by "some believers who belonged to the sect of the Pharisees" who insisted, "It is necessary for them to be circumcised and ordered to keep the law of Moses" (v. 5; see also Paul's arguments with the "Judaizers" in Galatians). Non-Jewish cultures often have difficulty understanding why this was so important to Jews that people would die martyrs' deaths rather than abandon circumcision. But even modern Gentile Christians can understand the problem of justifying full membership by those who refuse to observe a clear biblical command. How can Christians claim to be faithful Israel when circumcision is neglected?

Peter's vision is understood as God's answer to such a question. The kosher food laws were also clear and prescriptive. Eating with noncircumcised people threatened to dishonor God's presence in table fellowship. The voice from heaven was called the *bat qol* among Jews, and the threefold repetition of the message was understood to be required to confirm its

> EVEN AFTER INDICTING THEM FOR COMPLICITY IN JESUS' DEATH, THE APOSTLE ANNOUNCED GOD'S GIFTS OF REPENTANCE AND THE HOLY SPIRIT.

validity. But even voices from heaven were subject to debate. As Paul observed in protecting the freedom of the gospel from the requirement of circumcision, "Even if we or an angel from heaven should proclaim to you a gospel contrary to what we proclaimed to you, let that one be accursed!" (Gal. 1:8).

Verse 18 states the conclusion that moved the church into its vocation to be a light to the nations: "God has given even to the Gentiles the repentance that leads to life." What matters here is that this "repentance" is not just another obligation, but God's gift and gracious invitation to "turn" to God, the source of life. This is a testimony of divine election because God is the one who chooses who will be God's people. In Acts 2, Peter announced the renewal of God's election of Israel. Even after indicting them for complicity in Jesus' death, the apostle announced God's gifts of repentance and the Holy Spirit (2:37-39; see also 3:19-26; 5:31[!]). So also in Acts 10-11, the gift of the Holy Spirit (10:44; 11:15-16) is a confirmation of God's blessing on the inclusion of Gentiles.

Acts 14:21-27 (RC) is a "summary section" in the Acts narrative. It does not report a new episode but provides a lovely and loving overview of how the community was being shaped (see also Acts 2:43-47; 8:2-3). And in the midst of all this affirmation, the apostles declare, "It is through many persecutions [or tribulations] that we must enter the kingdom of God" (v. 22). The reader is thereby alerted that the struggle to liberate the Christian mission for its broader reach among the nations or Gentiles is far from over. Paul and Barnabas would soon be summoned to Jerusalem to account for their missionary activities among the Gentiles. But meanwhile, they returned to communities that had been evangelized, where they "strengthened the souls of the disciples and encouraged them to continue in the faith" and "with prayer and fasting they entrusted them to the Lord" (vv. 22-23). Verses 24-28 continue beyond this reading with an account of the warm reception Paul and Barnabas received on their return to Antioch.

The BCP alternative reading from Leviticus 19 is an important reminder that Jesus' call to his disciples to love one another was already deeply embedded in Israel's Scriptures, notably in the book of Leviticus that is often taken lightly by Gentile Christians. These verses identify the holiness to which Israel is called (v. 2) in terms of observance of such socially significant practices as leaving harvest gleanings for the poor (vv. 9-10) and several of the core commands of the Deca- logue (vv. 11-16). The command of love of neighbor already serves as a levitical summation of the whole law, offering an enduring definition of the holiness of the Lord (v. 18; see also the two commands cited by Jesus in Mark 12:31; Matt. 22:34-40; and Luke 10:26-27; see also Gal. 5:14).

ACTS 13:44–52 (BCP ALT.)

See the first reading (RC) for the Fourth Sunday of Easter, above.

RESPONSIVE READING

PSALM 148 (RCL)
PSALM 145 OR 145:1–9 (BCP)
PSALM 145:8–9, 10–11, 12–13 (RC)

Psalm 148 exults in the all-inclusive praise of God. This is a marvelous hymn for Easter faith, gathering voices from far beyond all narrow enclaves of the faithful. All of God's creatures have a voice in this choir, animate and inanimate: sea monsters and all deeps, fire and hail, mountains and all hills, fruit trees and all cedars, kings of the earth and all peoples. In the final verse, the expansive confi- dence of this psalm opens the community of the faithful to the conviction that all of these voices join the praise of God's elect.

Psalm 145 sounds a softer voice than Psalm 148, but with an equal confidence in God. All the alternative excerpts include verses 8-9, and these affirmations express the remarkable purposes and divine freedom to which the Cornelius story in Acts 10–11 also bears witness. The Psalms were Israel's prayerbook long before they were recited in the church. But the radical mission to the Gentiles to which Israel is called by the Holy Spirit in Acts gives new meaning to Israel's confidence in God's grace, mercy, steadfast love, goodness to all, and compassion for all God has made.

SECOND READING

REVELATION 21:1-6 (RCL)
REVELATION 19:1, 4-9 (BCP)
REVELATION 21:1-5A (RC)

The opening verses of Revelation 19 (BCP) are more forceful if verses 2-3 are not excluded as they are in the Episcopal lectionary. To be sure, the reference to "the great whore" and the delight over the smoke going up from her destruction "forever and ever" sound like the words of a wild-eyed fundamentalist cleric, whether Christian or Muslim. But without outrage against the corruption of the earth and the persecution of the faithful (see 18:24), what is the content of the "salvation and glory and power" of God (v. 1)?

This passage is a shout of triumph from "the loud voice of a great multitude in heaven" (v. 1). This triumph in heaven must not be confused with triumphs of the kingdoms of the world, although the liturgies may be similar. The Revelation to John is well aware of the political theater of the Roman Empire. Triumphal processions, choruses of praise, and acclamations of victory were not joyful occasions for subjugated people. Their conclusions were but the beginning of harsher times.

TRIUMPHAL PROCESSIONS, CHORUSES OF PRAISE, AND ACCLAMATIONS OF VICTORY WERE NOT JOYFUL OCCASIONS FOR SUBJUGATED PEOPLE.

But this heavenly liturgy of triumph concludes with the impending "marriage of the Lamb," a vision of a purified and restored Jerusalem. The invitations to the marriage feast must go out first, then the marriage, then the reign. However literally or metaphorically Christians interpret this revelation, it is indisputably a vision of Jesus' lordship being ultimately established on earth. No political movement, Christian or otherwise, will bring in this kingdom, but the consummation of history is not the destruction of the earth but its restoration. The blessing on those who are invited to the marriage supper of the Lamb is their election. The bride's "fine linen, bright and pure" is "the righteous deeds of the saints," probably living and dead. But even these garments are not badges of human achievement because the garments have been made white in the blood of the Lamb (7:14; 19:13).

THE REVELATION TO JOHN IS A GLIMPSE INTO THE COURT OF HEAVEN WHERE GOD'S WILL IS ALREADY BEING DONE WITHOUT THE NEED OF PRAYER.

The vision is of a fulfillment of the prayer Jesus taught his disciples: "Your kingdom come. Your will be done on earth as it is in heaven" (Matt. 6:10). The Revelation to John is a glimpse into the court of heaven where God's will is already being done without the need of prayer. Heaven's preparations for the marriage of the Lamb, however, envisions the engagement of the powers of heaven to accomplish the prayer for the coming of the reign of Jesus and the doing of God's will on earth as in heaven.

Only the Revised Common Lectionary includes verse 6 in the Revelation 21 reading. The first word from the one on the throne echoes the ultimate declaration of the seventh angel in Revelation 16:17: "It is done!" God has begun the reign among mortals (v. 3). The new creation (v. 5) is no mere future escape into fantasy. For those who are privileged to be given this glimpse into the heavenly courts through John's vision, the promised future is already manifestly breaking into the mundane present.

ACTS 13:44–52 (BCP ALT.)

See the first reading (RC) for the Fourth Sunday of Easter, above.

THE GOSPEL

JOHN 13:31–35 (RCL, BCP)
JOHN 13:31–33a, 34–35 (RC)

This brief reading is complex in at least three ways. First, in its literary context, the glorification of the Son of Man is apparently linked with Judas's betrayal. Second, the liturgical context of the Easter season draws the meaning of being glorified "at once" into the resurrection. Third, the commandment to love may be heard simply as obligation, not promise.

The literary link with Judas is only hinted at in the first words of verse 31, "When he had gone out." Casual hearers will probably assume it is Jesus who has "gone out" somewhere. Preachers who are fearful of the confusions created by the recent publication of *The Gospel of Judas* may choose simply to ignore this link and move on to more "spiritual" questions. But this may cause the proclaimer to miss a teaching opportunity.

In fact, the tendency to "spiritualize" the Gospel narratives is a major cause of ancient and modern fascination with Judas. The Gospel of John is particularly susceptible to this misuse because of its rich spirituality. By the second century when Gnostic and Docetic interpretations of Christ flourished in the Hellenistic world, Jesus' crucifixion seemed unreal or an embarrassment from a more earthy

THE TENDENCY TO "SPIRITUALIZE" THE GOSPEL NARRATIVES IS A MAJOR CAUSE OF ANCIENT AND MODERN FASCINATION WITH JUDAS. THE GOSPEL OF JOHN IS PARTICULARLY SUSCEPTIBLE TO THIS

Jewish time. But if Jesus only seemed (*dokein*) to have suffered and died as a flesh-and-blood mortal, then Judas appears to have been the mortal scapegoat, set up by God or Jesus to play the hard role of betrayer to get the drama to move. Modern attraction to the antihero has also increased Judas's popularity in dramatic productions such as *Jesus Christ Superstar* or novels such as Frank Yerby's *Judas My Brother.* "Poor old Judas," sings the chorus in *Jesus Christ Superstar*, as if it were he who died for our sins.

John's Gospel, however, is anti-Docetic and anti-Gnostic in its strong affirmation that Jesus is glorified exactly in his suffering and death. John's account of the crucifixion comes the closest in style to the literary historiography of the Synoptic Gospels, with no spiritualized escapes from his death. The famous Johannine allusion to the lifting up of the serpent in the wilderness (Num. 21:9) points directly to the exaltation of Jesus in his being lifted up as the Son of Man on the stake of execution (John 3:14; 8:28; 12:32-34). Thus, the glorification of the Son of Man (v. 31) has begun with his betrayal, but will be completed "at once" on the cross. The glory of the Son of Man is in Jesus' death for the sake of all who look on him for eternal life (see 12:32-34). To imply with modern Gnostics that Judas was used by Jesus or the church misses the scandal of the cross. Judas's betrayal was an evil act (see 13:27), but Jesus blessed the world.

The glorification of the Son of Man had a long history, at least since Daniel 7:13-15, where "one like a human being" (or "Son of Man"—Aramaic) comes "with the clouds of heaven . . . to the Ancient One. . . . To him was given dominion and glory and kingship, that all peoples, nations, and languages should serve him." In John's narrative, the one who is vindicated in his resurrection is exactly the one who was glorified "at once" (v. 32) in his crucifixion as "Jesus of Nazareth, the King of the Jews" (John 19:19).

Jesus' command to his disciples who will be "left behind" is thus more a promise than an obligation. Perhaps the preacher is helped by recognizing that this story is located far earlier than the Easter appearances. Some commentators have even suggested that this is one of the post-Easter stories written back into an earlier narrative. But whatever the literary history, this story is about Jesus. His mission of God's love for the world offers a basis for Christian love for the world and merciful care for the community. Jesus is not merely cajoling the Christian community like a weary parent: "You really *ought to* love each other." No, this is a promise to the community and the world grounded in the self-giving love of Christ Jesus.

JESUS' MISSION OF GOD'S LOVE FOR THE WORLD OFFERS A BASIS FOR CHRISTIAN LOVE FOR THE WORLD AND MERCIFUL CARE FOR THE COMMUNITY.

SIXTH SUNDAY OF EASTER

REVISED COMMON	EPISCOPAL (BCP)	ROMAN CATHOLIC
Acts 16:9-15	Acts 14:8-18 or Joel 2:21-27	Acts 15:1-2, 22-29
Psalm 67	Psalm 67	Ps. 67:2-3, 5, 6, 8
Rev. 21:10, 22—22:5	Rev. 21:22—22:5 or Acts 14:8-18	Rev. 21:10-14, 22-23
John 14:23-29 or John 5:1-9	John 14:23-29	John 14:23-29

FIRST READING

ACTS 16:9-15 (RCL)
ACTS 14:8-18 (BCP)
ACTS 15:1-2, 22-29 (RC)
JOEL 2:21-27 (BCP ALT.)

All three lectionaries cite passages from the middle chapters of Acts of the Apostles as the first reading appointed for the Sixth Sunday of Easter, but each selection is different. Since Acts is a large book by biblical standards (Luke and Acts together comprise about one-third of the length of the New Testament), it is difficult to sustain a sense for the literary whole when only excerpts can be read in successive weeks. The preacher, however, can read all of chapters 14–16 in a matter of minutes to begin to grasp the story of the struggles the apostolic mission faced as it moved within and beyond the synagogues of Asia Minor. This is a realistic narrative of the risk and resistance that accompany change in a religious tradition in which continuity is treasured. For the sake of honoring the flow of the story, my comments

> PAUL AND BARNABAS OBJECT THAT THEY ARE "MORTALS JUST LIKE YOU," CONNECTING WITH THE COMMON GREEK VIEW THAT THE GODS WERE FREE FROM HUMAN PASSIONS AND SUFFERING.

will follow the sequence of the chapters from which the appointed readings are excerpted.

In Acts 14:8-18 (BCP), the story of Paul's healing of the man from Lystra who was "crippled from birth" immediately recalls Jesus' healing of the paralyzed man (Luke 5:17-26) and Peter's healing of the man "lame from birth" (Acts 3:1-10). The detail that the man from Lystra "sprang up" echoes Peter's healing, where "jumping up," the man "entered the temple with them, walking and leaping and praising God" (3:7-8). The story in Acts 3 is an enactment of the promise in Isaiah 35:1-10 of Israel's restoration like a leaping lame man. Now Paul, "looking at him intently" (v. 9; see 3:4), performs the same sign among the Gentiles. The healing in Acts 3 prompted "wonder and amazement" (3:10) and led to Peter's proclamation in the Temple (3:11-26), followed by the arrest of Peter and John. In Lystra, the crowds' acclaim provoked a different theological problem.

When the Lycaonians declare that Barnabas and Paul are "the gods come down to us in human form" (v. 11), they are not assuming a full Jewish or biblical sense of incarnation. Their verb (Gk.: *homoiōthentes*) implies the gods "have been made something like human," since stories of visitations from the realm of the gods were well known. Zeus was at the top of the assembly (pantheon) of the Greek gods, and Hermes was the mes-

THE WORDS FOR "CONVERSION" AND "REPENTANCE" ARE ABRASIVE IN EVERY LANGUAGE ONCE IT BECOMES CLEAR THAT BELIEVING IN ISRAEL'S GOD CAN'T BE A SPIRITUAL SUPPLEMENT.

senger with winged feet. Even myths of their appearances would be magnified and marketed to the benefit of the local temple and its economy (see also the slave girl of Philippi, Acts 16:16-24). But Paul and Barnabas object in verse 15 that they are "mortals just like you" (Gk.: *homoiopatheis*, "of the same feelings or human passions"), connecting with the common Greek view that the gods were free from human passions and suffering. Well trained by Israel's prophets, the apostles are also opposed to idols, calling the people to "turn from these worthless things to the living God, who made the heaven and the earth" (v. 15; see also Paul's speech on the Aeropagus in Acts 17).

Greek religion practiced "adhesion," that is, adding gods to its pantheon, but Peter's call to "turn [Gk.: *epistrephein*] from these worthless things to the living God" (v. 15) invited a "change of mind" or "conversion." The words for "conversion" and "repentance" are abrasive in every language once it becomes clear that believing in Israel's God can't be a spiritual supplement. Prophetic religions of the Abrahamic tradition (Judaism, Christianity, Islam) call for change in people's lives and practices, identifying things that are "worthless" or idolatrous in the light of the actions, will, and purposes of "the living God." This story ends without clarity about whether the crowds grasped the deeper promise.

The Roman Catholic lectionary selection, Acts 15:1-2, 22-29, reports portions of how the church dealt with the crisis in faith and practice that was prompted by the flourishing of the apostolic mission among the non-Jews (Gentiles). Pastors who have seen congregations split over the powerful symbolic question of whether a national flag can be placed in the chancel (or even where to place it) have a small clue as to how deeply divisive was the question of the observance of God's command for circumcision of all males among the people of the promise. Twenty-first-century churches that are in agonizing debates about the clergy status of homosexual persons have only a short list of scriptural passages with which to contend, compared with the number of places in the Torah, Prophets, and Writings where circumcision is mandated.

Acts 15 is the story of the "Jerusalem Council" at which the circumcision issue was deliberated, a spiritual discernment was made, and the inclusion of non-Jews (Gentiles) was decisively endorsed, setting the course for the Christian movement in the pluralism of the Greco-Roman world. Verses 3-21 tell the story of the Council, with rich and respectful details about the various parties, including the "believers who belonged to the sect of the Pharisees" (v. 5), that is, Pharisees who accepted Jesus as the Messiah! Although the connection between these "believers" and the "false believers" Paul mentioned in Galatians (2:4) is debated, the result of the consultation by all accounts was the full reception of the Gentile believers. In Acts 15, the resolution turns on Peter's testimony that "God, who knows the human heart, testified to them [the Gentiles] by giving them the Holy Spirit, just as he did to us." Thus, instead of "putting God to the test," "we believe that we will be saved through the grace of the Lord Jesus, just as they will" (vv. 7-11). James then rehearsed the argument for why this was a sign of God's restoration of Israel (vv. 16-17), announced the decision, and identified the compromises necessary for Jews and Gentiles to live together.

The lectionary resumes (vv. 22-29) with the sending of a letter with Judas called Barsabbas and Silas in the company of Paul and Barnabas, communicating the decision throughout the churches. The most telling line is the phrase "It has seemed good to the Holy Spirit and to us" (v. 28). This is the formal language of declarations, but the conditions to be observed are modest and the tone is that of discernment of the will and Spirit of God. The letter reinforces the conviction that the scriptural basis of the decision was not a strict legal construction of the Torah, but a claiming of the promise given

IN JEWISH-CHRISTIAN MISSION PRACTICE, HOSPITALITY WAS NOT MERELY A PERSONAL VIRTUE BUT A SIGN OF COMMUNITY WITH GOD.

by the prophet Amos of God's consistent intentions that Israel's restoration will be a blessing to the Gentiles (vv. 16-17; see Amos 9:11-12; Isa. 49:6; Gen. 12:3). The concessions required of the Gentiles (v. 29) show respect for Jewish sensitivities: that is, food sacrificed to idols was a continuing issue of religious significance for both Jews and Gentiles (see Paul in 1 Cor. 8:7-13; 10:23-30); "blood" could mean murder, but probably again connects with Jewish aversion to eating the "life" that belonged to God; "what is strangled" clearly means nonkosher butchering; and "fornication" probably refers to all sexual immorality, which the Jews linked with idolatry (see Wisd. of Sol. 14:12).

In Acts 16:9-15, the RCL selection, the apostolic mission is prompted onward by a heavenly vision. The ascending Lord's commission to "be my witnesses to the ends of the earth" (Acts 1:8) is being enacted with divine engagement, first through the church being scattered in persecution beyond Jerusalem to Judea and Samaria (8:1), and now through a dramatic calling to cross the geographic boundary between Asia Minor and Europe (Macedonia). Whether Lydia, "a worshiper of God," was Jewish or Gentile, she was a woman of means (see also Luke 8:1-3), traditionally identified as the first "convert" in Europe because "the Lord opened her heart" to hear Paul's apostolic testimony (v. 14). Her hospitality is a sign of her having received the message and being accepted by the apostles (see Luke 10:5-6; 19:5; 24:29). As when Peter accepted lodging in the home of the Roman centurion Cornelius (Acts 10), Paul's entry into Lydia's home included the baptism of her household (10:47-48; 16:15). In Jewish-Christian mission practice, hospitality was not merely a personal virtue but a sign of community with God.

The BCP alternative reading from Joel 2:21-27 sounds the hope for the earth itself in God's triumph, a testimony also heard in Psalm 67 and Revelation. The Joel text had specific connections with Israel's military perils from the north. In the context of the Easter faith of the church, Joel's prophetic oracle awaits the redemption of the earth as a sign of the sustained dwelling of God for protection from harm and prevention of shame.

RESPONSIVE READING

PSALM 67 (RCL, BCP)
PSALM 67:2-3, 5, 6, 8 (RC)

When Psalm 67 is recited in the Easter season, this song of community thanksgiving resounds with renewed confidence that God's "way" and "saving power" are intended for all the earth and all its peoples (vv. 2-3). Of course, this psalm was sung in Israel's thanksgivings long before Jesus, demonstrating to the Christian believers that the mission of God (*missio Dei*) is exactly the calling into which the risen Lord summons the faithful. This is what God intended as Israel's calling all along. Now the gladness and joy of the nations (v. 4) are filled with the content of the reign of the exalted Messiah and Lord. The reverence of "all the ends of the earth" (v. 7) is the intended result of the witness of Jesus' disciples "to the ends of the earth" (Acts 1:8).

SECOND READING

REVELATION 21:10, 22—22:5 (RCL)
REVELATION 21:22—22:5 (BCP)
REVELATION 21:10-14, 22-23 (RC)

The excerpts appointed from this portion of the Revelation to John vary slightly, but all of the lectionaries bring the community into the vision of "the holy city Jerusalem coming down out of heaven from God" (21:10). Earlier generations of interpreters were often absorbed with the details of the jewels, measurements, precious materials, and architecture of the city (21:10-21). Those whose attention moved beyond the glorious details were often interested in correlating this vision with that of Ezekiel (Ezekiel 40). Many readers have offered complex allegorical interpretations of these details, and some have sought to reduce these rich symbols to codes by which the future could be cracked.

WOODEN LITERALISM AND CRYPTOGRAPHIC INTER-
PRETATIONS BOTH FAIL TO DO JUSTICE TO THE FLOUR-
ISHING OF IMAGES OF THE REVELATION.

The Roman Catholic lectionary sustains the reader's attention on the city. The twelve angels, twelve tribes of the Israelites, and twelve foundations of the city wall, inscribed with the names of the twelve apostles of the Lamb (vv. 10-14; see also Luke 22:30, where the twelve are identified as those who will judge the twelve tribes of Israel), gather the history of Israel into the future God is creating. All the lectionaries move toward the vision of this heavenly city come to earth, without a temple (v. 22). The declaration is emphatic that no temple is needed because the Lord God is the temple, dwelling among the faithful, which contrasts on a literal level with Revelation 3:12, where the church in Philadelphia is assured, "If you conquer, I will make you a pillar in the temple of my God." But wooden literalism and cryptographic interpretations both fail to do justice to the flourishing of images of the Revelation. Modern readers who seldom experience deep darkness in most days, weeks, and months might also be less dazzled by God's being the "light" or sun while the Lamb is the "lamp" or moon. But all efforts merely to "explain" the images miss the inspiring expanse of the vision of a new creation.

The echoes of the creation accounts in Genesis, Psalms, and Job reverberate powerfully in the opening verses of Revelation 22. Just as Paul envisioned Christ Jesus raised from the dead in terms of the new Adam (Romans 5; 1 Corinthians 15), the Revelation to John visualizes a new urban Eden, a paradise where the water of life flows in the city with the tree of life restored for the healing of the nations (22:1-2). One could speculate how the tree of life apparently stands on both sides of the river (22:2), but then the vision is reduced to mechanistic details. Who knows how that tree grows?

The joy of this vision, the gospel to be preached, lies in its profound affirmation of the goodness God has in store for the creation, anchored in the promises to Israel, now renewed because the Lamb who was slain has already been exalted. The faithful are invited to live in the promise of this renewal that has already begun.

ACTS 14:8-18 (BCP ALT.)

See the first reading for the Sixth Sunday of Easter, above.

THE GOSPEL

JOHN 14:23-29 (RCL, BCP, RC)
JOHN 5:1-9 (RCL ALT.)

A brief note on the RCL alternative reading from John 5:1-9 must suffice. John's account of this healing does not stand by itself, not even in the manner such stories are often presented in the Synoptic Gospels. This is one of the "signs" in John's Gospel, and one only begins to grasp its larger significance when at least all of John 5 is reviewed.

All of the lectionaries, however, identify John 14:23-29 as the primary Gospel lesson for the Sixth Sunday of Easter. The liturgical context of this Sunday is affected by the fact that Ascension Day will occur within the week and Pentecost is two weeks away. Biblical scholars regularly object when the liturgical context overwhelms the literary or historical context in the interpretation of any passage. This is a risk of the entire venture of lectionary commentaries such as *New Proclamation*. At the same time, John 14 can appropriately be read for its testimony concerning the apparent absence of Jesus in the present time.

> THE NARRATIVE OR LITERARY CONTEXT OF THIS LESSON IS INTIMATE COMMUNICATION AMONG BELIEVERS, ASSURING THEM JESUS' DEPARTURE WILL NOT LEAVE THEM "ORPHANED."

John's Gospel is deeply sensitive to the charges that Jesus is a false Messiah, even a blasphemer who claimed to be the Son of God (see 5:16-18; 6:52; 7:25-36; 8:39-59; 9:24-34; 10:22-29; 11:45-53; 12:36-43). In 13:1—17:26, Jesus delivers his "testament" or parting words to his disciples (compare Genesis 48–49; Acts 20:18-38) during his last meal with them. The narrative or literary context of this lesson, therefore, is intimate communication among believers, assuring them his departure will not leave them "orphaned" (14:18). This is not a narrative to prepare for Jesus' absence, but for those who love him, Jesus promises (1) his abiding loving presence along with that of the Father (vv. 23-24); (2) the sending of the Advocate, the Holy Spirit (vv. 25-26); and (3) the gift of his peace (vv. 27-29).

Verses 23-24 are best understood as an answer to the question asked by Judas (not Iscariot) in verse 22 that precedes the lectionary reading. The question is how Jesus' presence will be revealed to Christians and not to the world. Abiding in Jesus' word brings the believer inside the indwelling of the Father where love is alive. The prophet Zechariah (2:10) declared God's promise, "Lo, I will come and dwell in your midst." The Son was sent into the world because of God's love (John 3:16), and the resurrection of Jesus will mean not the loss of that love, but its presence now as God and Jesus "make [their] home" (v. 23) with the believers as they keep Jesus' word. This is not mere required obedience, but receiving Jesus' word as the word of life of the loving Father (v. 24; contrast 12:48-49). One of the profound mysteries of the Christian life that experienced saints report is their sense of the abiding presence of God throughout their years. As Augustine said, "Love separates the saints from the world."

Verses 25-26 takes the inquiry about divine presence deeper into the fellowship of the Trinity, from which the Holy Spirit is sent as God's Advocate. Jesus is described as speaking "while I am still with you" (v. 25), but also promising to remain as the Holy Spirit reminds them of and teaches them the full meaning of Jesus' words. The spiritual power of this learning is reminiscent of Colossians 3:16, where the saints are advised, "Let the word of Christ dwell in you richly; teach and admonish one another in all wisdom, and with gratitude in your hearts sing psalms, hymns, and spiritual songs to God."

PREACHERS WHO RETURN TO JESUS' WORDS YEAR AFTER YEAR IN THE LECTIONARY MAY DISCOVER THE ABIDING PRESENCE OF THE ADVOCATE, REMINDING AND TEACHING THEM AND THE COMMUNITY OF THE LIVING LORD.

Preachers who return to Jesus' words year after year in the lectionary may discover the abiding presence of the Advocate, reminding and teaching them and the community of the living Lord.

Verses 27-29 then state the promise of Jesus' abiding presence in terms of his "peace." Once again, Colossians 3:15 understands the active agency of this peace: "Let the peace of Christ rule in your hearts, to which indeed you were called in the one body." When Christians greet each other with "the peace of Christ," they are not simply wishing one another well. They are practicing their Easter faith in the enduring strength of the peace of Christ's presence, surpassing whatever fears or troubles may come (v. 27).

ASCENSION OF THE LORD

May 17/20, 2007

REVISED COMMON	EPISCOPAL (BCP)	ROMAN CATHOLIC
Acts 1:1-11	Acts 1:1-11 or 2 Kgs. 2:1-15	Acts 1:1-11
Psalm 47 or Psalm 93	Psalm 47 or 110:1-5	Ps. 47:2-3, 6-7, 8-9
Eph. 1:15-23	Eph. 1:15-23 or Acts 1:1-11	Eph. 1:17-23 or Heb. 9:24-28; 10:19-23
Luke 24:44-53	Luke 24:49-53 or Mark 16:9-15, 19-20	Luke 24:46-53

FIRST READING

ACTS 1:1-11 (RCL, BCP, RC)
2 KINGS 2:1-15 (BCP ALT.)

It is not difficult to see why the story of the assumption of Elijah in 2 Kings 2 has been linked with the exaltation of Jesus in Acts 1, but the apparent similarity with regard to bodily assumptions may raise as many problems as it solves. Fascination with the physics of physical assumptions also prompts comparisons with Mohammed ascending to heaven on his horse. Enoch is the only other biblical figure who was "taken by God" apparently directly into heaven without dying (Gen. 5:24). Like the story in Acts, however, the "assumption" of Elijah is primarily about succession. The recognition by "the company of prophets" that "the spirit Elijah rests on Elisha" (v. 15) further confirms what Elisha had already tested when he struck the water on his return to the river. The "mantle of Elijah" is an image of prophetic power, and the parting of the waters recalls Israel's safe passage through the Red Sea. The important question is not "Where did Elijah go?" as a matter of speculation, but "Where is the LORD, the God of Elijah?" (v. 14).

The answer is that the power of this God continues to be present among God's people in the person and ministry of Elisha.

The story in Acts 1 is also little concerned with Jesus' place in the space-time continuum. In fact, Jesus' response to the disciples' very earthbound question about God's timetable for the restoration of the kingdom redirects their attention to their vocation, and the angels divert their gaze from the clouds. The story of the "ascension" is thus about how the risen and exalted Jesus prepared his followers to receive "the promise of the Father" in the living presence of the Holy Spirit (vv. 4-5).

The opening verses mark the resumption of the narrative that began in Luke 1:1-4 by means of a brief historical prologue and touch upon the closing verses of Luke 24 concerning the "instructions" Jesus gave "through the Holy Spirit to the apostles whom he had chosen." This allusion in verse 2 appears to imply that the Holy Spirit's agency was already at work in the discourses the resurrected Jesus had with his apostles, and was not merely the promise of the power that was to come in Pentecost (Luke 24:49; Acts 1:4).

The heart of the passage is the apostles' question in verse 6 and Jesus' answer in verses 7-8. Their question about "the restoration of the kingdom" is historically natural, since the prophets of the Babylonian exile had taught Israel God's saving purpose in the midst of her trials. Jesus appears to reject the timing portion of the question: "It is not for you to know the times or periods," but his commission of them as witnesses constitutes a positive and prophetic answer to the hope for restoration. The logic of "not this, but this" originated in the word of the Lord of the Isaiah prophet of the exile. God did not abandon God's promises for Israel's restoration, but Israel's glory lay in the restoration of her vocation. "It is too light a thing that you should be my servant to raise up the tribes of Jacob and to restore the survivors of Israel; I will give you as a light to the nations that my salvation may reach to the end of the earth" (Isa. 49:6).

> GOD DID NOT ABANDON GOD'S PROMISES FOR ISRAEL'S RESTORATION, BUT ISRAEL'S GLORY LAY IN THE RESTORATION OF HER VOCATION.

The commissioning of the witnesses "in Jerusalem, in all Judea and Samaria, and to the ends of the earth" not only echoes Isaiah; it constitutes the literary outline of the Acts of the Apostles. In Acts 8:1, after conflict and persecution, the narrative indicates that the mission now moves to its next stages, and when Paul and Barnabas carry the message into the pluralism of the Roman world, they again conclude that "it is through many persecutions that we must enter the kingdom of God" (14:22). Restoring God's reign to Israel begins with Jesus' departure to send the Holy Spirit to confirm the calling of the people of God in God's dominion. Jesus will return in God's good time. The restoration of God's reign among God's people has already commenced in their callings.

RESPONSIVE READING
PSALM 47 (RCL, BCP)
PSALM 47:2-3, 6-7, 8-9 (RC)

See the responsive readings for the Seventh Sunday of Easter, below.

PSALM 93 (RCL ALT.)
PSALM 110:1-5 (BCP ALT.)

Psalm 93 is one of a series of psalms (see also Psalms 95–99) celebrating God's enthronement as king. In the context of his ascension, this psalm gives voice to faith that Jesus' assumption into heaven is his exaltation to dominion. The themes from creation ("he has established the world," v. 2) and the ordering of chaos ("The floods lift up their roaring," v. 3) identify the measures at which God's reign excel. In Psalm 93, God's everlasting holiness is linked with the law ("Your decrees are very sure," v. 5). The exaltation of Jesus establishes him as the measure and sign of God's reign.

Psalm 110 was probably used as an enthronement psalm when a new king was anointed in Judea. The speaker in the psalm is the Lord, who also identifies the king as "a priest forever according to the order of Melchizedek" (v. 4; the royal priest who came out to welcome Abram from his victory in Genesis 14:18). Early Christian interpreters understood this as God's acclamation of Jesus and linked it with his being anointed as the Davidic Son of God in the language of Psalm 2 (see Acts 2:34; Luke 20:42-44; see also Luke 3:22; Acts 10:37). In the context of the worship of the early Christian community, therefore, Psalm 110 defined Jesus' ascension as his receipt of heavenly authority and declared his reign.

SECOND READING
EPHESIANS 1:15-23 (RCL, BCP)
EPHESIANS 1:17-23 (RC)
HEBREWS 9:24-28; 10:19-23 (RC ALT.)

The reading from Ephesians develops the promise of the power of the Holy Spirit into a remarkable understanding of the church as Christ's body in the world. Whether the affirmation of Christ's lordship "over all things for the church" (v. 22) can be properly called an "ecclesiology," this great thanksgiving in Ephesians is focused primarily on the dominion of the exalted Lord Jesus Christ. In the context of the festival of Ascension, this witness from Ephesians makes it clear that the exaltation of the risen Jesus to dominion is also the beginning of the church's identity and mission for the sake of the world.

The alternative readings in the Roman Catholic lectionary from Hebrews 9 and 10 lead the community into a remarkable vision of a symbolic universe where earthly beings ascend to heaven through the high priesthood of Jesus. The Platonic or middle-Platonic sense of the earthly Temple's being "a mere copy of the true one" (Heb. 9:24) stands in striking contrast to the visions of the Revelation to John in which God descends to earth and there is no longer need for a temple because God's presence has come (see Rev. 21:22, the second reading for the Sixth Sunday of Easter). But Hebrews breaks through the spatial speculation of Platonism, insisting that Jesus' entry into the heavenly realm was "once for all at the end of the age to remove sin by the sacrifice of himself" (Heb. 9:26). Furthermore, while Hebrews uses Platonism's rich spiritual metaphors, the "new and living way" that Jesus has provided into the heavenly sanctuary passes through the curtain of "his flesh" (Heb. 10:20). Denying the flesh-and-blood incarnation is thereby excluded, and the link with the believer is not through some higher understanding or "gnosis," but through holding "fast to the confession of our hope without wavering, for he who has promised is faithful" (Heb. 10:23).

> WHILE HEBREWS USES PLATONISM'S RICH SPIRITUAL METAPHORS, THE "NEW AND LIVING WAY" THAT JESUS HAS PROVIDED INTO THE HEAVENLY SANCTUARY PASSES THROUGH THE CURTAIN OF "HIS FLESH."

ACTS 1:1–11 (BCP ALT.)

See the first reading for the Ascension of the Lord, above.

THE GOSPEL
LUKE 24:44–53 (RCL)
LUKE 24:49–53 (BCP)
LUKE 24:46–53 (RC)
MARK 16:9–15, 19–20 (BCP ALT.)

The concluding verses of Luke's narrative might better be read prior to the lesson from Acts (that is, prior to what the lectionary calls "the first reading"). Not only does this honor the narrative sequence of Luke and Acts; it allows the briefer version of the story to point forward to the more complete account.

It will also be generally easier to preach on the story in Acts where the crucial point of Israel's vocation within God's reign is made with strong prophetic warrants. The major themes are present *in nuce* in Luke 24: fulfillment of the Scriptures, the divine purpose of responding to the Messiah's execution by renewed gifts and grace, and the renewed calling of the "witnesses" to "all nations, beginning from Jerusalem."

The concluding verses (vv. 50-53) present Jesus' assumption into heaven with almost no dramatic details. The blessing is reminiscent of Moses' "departure" in Deuteronomy 33, and careful readers of Luke's narrative will remember that in Luke 9:31 Moses and Elijah appeared in glory on the mountain with Jesus, and they "were speaking of his departure [Gk.: *exodon*], which he was about to accomplish at Jerusalem." Like the Gospel of John, Luke interprets Jesus' "ascension" within the larger framework of his death, resurrection, exaltation, and dominion through the sending of the Holy Spirit. Jesus is "accomplishing an exodus" that far exceeds Moses' rescue of Israel from Egypt.

Mark 16:9-15, 19-20 (the Roman Catholic alternative reading) includes most of the verses commonly called "the longer ending of Mark." As the notes in study Bibles will confirm, these verses have little claim to being original to Mark's Gospel, although the medieval Greek manuscript tradition (the *textus receptus*) from which the pre-twentieth-century modern translations were made included them. The longer ending disrupts the elegant consternation Mark's narrative provokes when it

> LUKE INTERPRETS JESUS' "ASCENSION" WITHIN THE LARGER FRAMEWORK OF HIS DEATH, RESURRECTION, EXALTATION, AND DOMINION THROUGH THE SENDING OF THE HOLY SPIRIT.

ends at 16:8. Verses 16-18, which are not included in the lectionary, have been famous in cults in which handling poisonous snakes is an ordeal to prove true discipleship. If the appointed verses are going to be read in the community's worship, they are probably best understood as an early Christian expansion of Mark's narrative, drawing freely from the stories of resurrection appearances in the other Gospels and offering another version of the Great Commission.

SEVENTH SUNDAY OF EASTER

MAY 20, 2007

Revised Common	Episcopal (BCP)	Roman Catholic
Acts 16:16-34	Acts 16:16-34 or	Acts 7:55-60
	1 Sam. 12:19-24	
Psalm 97	Ps. 68:1-20 or	Ps. 97:1-2, 6-7, 9
	Psalm 47	
Rev. 22:12-14,	Rev. 22:12-14,	Rev. 22:12-14,
16-17, 20-21	16-17, 20 or Acts	16-17, 20
	16:16-34	
John 17:20-26	John 17:20-26	John 17:20-26

FIRST READING

ACTS 16:16-34 (RCL, BCP)
ACTS 7:55-60 (RC)
1 SAMUEL 12:19-24 (BCP ALT.)

The reading from Acts 16:16-34 (RCL, BCP) follows directly on the first reading in the Revised Common Lectionary for the Sixth Sunday of Easter, providing two more episodes of the first missionary encounters in Europe with the slave girl and her masters and the jailer and his family. These stories are rich in novelistic details, also providing numerous glimpses into these cross-cultural encounters. Read within the liturgical context of the Easter season, these stories manifest the power and presence of the reign of the Lord Jesus.

The "power of divination" (Gk.: *pneuma pythona*) of the slave girl could be translated more directly as "a Pythian spirit." At the shrine in Delphi, women prophets identified their powers of divination with the mythical python slain by Apollo, and this slave girl was apparently thought to share these or to be under their control. Her "fortune-telling" (Gk.: *manteuomenē*) was probably mantic or ecstatic, perhaps by shouting or trances. As in the stories of encounters with demonic spirits that shout out Jesus' identity (Luke 4:34; 8:28), the spirits possessing the person recognize powers greater than their own. "The Most High God" (v. 17) is a biblical title that Luke uses frequently, especially in contexts of praise or doxology (Luke 1:32, 35, 76; 2:14; 6:35; 8:28; 19:38; Acts 7:48). For the "Pythian spirit," however, the term is a recognition of the perilous presence of a more powerful spirit. Thus, when annoyed with the slave girl's shouting, Paul did not hassle her but confronted the spirit possessing her "in the name of Jesus Christ" (v. 18). Jesus' name has the power of the exalted Lord of heaven and earth (see also Acts 3:6, 16; 4:10, 30).

The fierce response of the owners of the slave girl is focused solely on their loss of her mercenary worth to them. Both Jewish and Hellenistic authors often discredited hucksters who were only interested in profits (see Acts 8:14-24; 19:23-40). In Luke's narrative, Paul is not attacking the religious culture of Philippi so much as exposing hustlers. They, however, rally the magistrates around a standard anti-Jewish charge of "advocating customs that are not lawful for us as Romans." Circumcision was one of those customs that had been outlawed for Romans, but there is no evidence in the text that Paul or the Jews were advocating such practices with the Philippians.

The encounter demonstrates, however, how the many cultures and religions in Philippi were hardly a "melting pot." The Roman colony is depicted as being more protective of its ethos than the Jewish enclave that welcomed Paul to "the place of prayer" (16:13, 16).

This story is a remarkable example of the irrepressible hope with which the apostolic movement was sustained in its encounters in the disparate and contentious urban contexts of the Roman order. By its very convictions, prophetic, biblical faith is seen by spiritually diffuse cultures to be intolerant. The "Most High God" simply does not fit into the pantheon of many gods. Christian, biblical faith thus provokes resistance, especially from those who have vested or economic interests in traditional gods. Stories of beatings and imprisonments (vv. 23-24) have always accompanied Christian mission.

The jail releases in Acts display the confidence of the believers in God's greater power and authority (see also Acts 5:19-20; 12:6-10), and even when Paul remains in chains, he bears witness to his "hope in God" that sustains his spirit in the midst of dishonor and confinement (Acts 24:10-16). The picture of Paul and Silas "praying and singing hymns to God" at midnight (v. 25) recalls the doxology and prayer throughout the whole story (see Acts 1:14; 2:42, 47; 4:23-31; 6:4; 9:11; 10:2, 9; 12:12; 13:2-3). Paul's assurance to the jailer is also consistent with this confidence, and he and Barnabas will refuse to be released quietly in verses 35-40, claiming their rights as Roman citizens.

> THIS STORY IS A REMARKABLE EXAMPLE OF THE IRREPRESSIBLE HOPE WITH WHICH THE APOSTOLIC MOVEMENT WAS SUSTAINED IN ITS ENCOUNTERS IN THE DISPARATE AND CONTENTIOUS URBAN CONTEXTS OF THE ROMAN ORDER.

The Roman magistrates are not merely dealing with two Jews, even two Jews who are Roman citizens. This is an encounter of powers, first spiritual with the Pythian spirits, then political. The Roman jailer is not required to undergo circumcision to be "saved," nor is his household subject to food laws. Isaiah 49:6 is being enacted (cited directly in Acts 13:47; harshly in 18:6; 28:26-28; and indirectly in Acts 1:8) as the "salvation" of being drawn close to God is also extended to the Gentiles. Paul's invitation to him to "believe on the Lord Jesus" becomes the means by which he and his household become believers in God (16:31, 34; compare Luke 8:26-39, where the demoniac confronts Jesus as "Son of the Most High God"; Jesus tells him to "declare how much God has done for you," and thus he proclaims "how much Jesus had done for him"). Believing in Jesus, crucified, raised, and exalted, is faith in the Most High God.

> BELIEVING IN JESUS, CRUCIFIED, RAISED, AND EXALTED, IS FAITH IN THE MOST HIGH GOD.

The Roman Catholic lectionary reading from Acts 7:55-60 steps back in the story to before Saul/Paul's call or conversion (see notes on the first readings for the Third and Fourth Sundays of Easter). In the liturgical context of the Easter season, the focus is less on Stephen's death and Saul's complicity and more on Stephen's vision into heaven. The heavens (plural in this context) also "opened" at Jesus' baptism (Luke 3:21) and in Peter's vision (Acts 10:11), revealing divine engagement in human affairs. Stephen's vision not only confirms divine sanction of his death and witness (martyrdom), but provides a fleeting glimpse or disclosure of the heavenly court itself.

Daniel 7:13 and Psalm 110:1, with their visions of God's ruler and heavenly agent of judgment, are embedded in this vision. The prophecy in Luke 9:26 of the Son of Man coming "in his glory and the glory of the Father and of the holy angels" has an even more complete correlation. The explicit references to the Son of Man "standing at the right hand of God" (vv. 55-56) may imply Jesus rising from his enthroned judgment seat (Ps. 110:1) to welcome Stephen. The executioners "covered their ears" as a sign that Stephen was speaking blasphemy (see Lev. 24:14 on stoning blasphemers outside the camp). Stephen's prayer for his executioners echoes Jesus' intercession for his (see Luke 23:34 and 23:46—"I commend my spirit"). The irrepressible hope of Easter faith rests on Jesus' resurrection as his vindication and exaltation as Lord, Messiah, and Son of Man.

> THE END OF DAVID'S FASTING IS A SIGNAL NOT ONLY OF HIS ACCEPTANCE THAT HE COULD NOT CHANGE GOD'S JUDGMENT, BUT IT IS THE BEGINNING OF THE RESTORATION OF HIS LIFE AND REIGN.

2 Samuel 12:19-24 (BCP alternative) is part of a longer and frightening story of human pathos, political intrigue, and faith. The pathos is as real as the death of an unnamed child, complicated by the fact that this child was conceived by David

with Uriah's wife, Bathsheba, while she was still married to Uriah. After confronting David with his sins of adultery and murder, the prophet Nathan announced that the child would die (v. 14). Verse 15 reports that "the LORD struck the child," and in spite of the king's pleading and fasting, it happened.

David and Bathsheba's second son was conceived in wedlock and was named Solomon (v. 24). "Solomon" means "his replacement." This story of the death of the first illegitimate son and the birth of "his replacement," therefore, discloses divine judgment on David's sin while still showing how the Davidic line was preserved. The end of David's fasting is not only a signal of his acceptance that he could not change God's judgment, but the beginning of the restoration of his life and reign, which Nathan also promised (see vv. 13, 25). As cool and detached as David's response appears, both the king and the Lord had now closed the chapter of David's sin.

RESPONSIVE READING
PSALM 97 (RCL)
PSALM 68:1-20 OR PSALM 47 (BCP)
PSALM 97:1-2, 6-7, 9 (RC)

Old Testament scholars regularly object that the first readings in the Easter season are almost always from the New Testament and the psalms are chosen to give voice to specifically Christian convictions about the lordship of Jesus Christ in God's reign. These objections are rightly founded historically, and the psalm selections for this Sunday are clear examples of drawing from pre-Christian Israel's hymnbook to sing Jesus' praise. With all the rich allusions to Psalm 110 and Daniel 7 in the first reading from Acts 7, New Testament scholars might also complain theologically at the choice of Psalms 47, 68, and 97, since the rich interpretations of Israel's Scriptures by the earliest Christians have largely been bypassed for the grand images of divine kingship that captured the attention of Christians moving beyond their Jewish roots to deal with Imperial Rome. Moderns with little patience for ancient views of authority, governance, and kingship may simply ignore or merely tolerate these doxologies as liturgical trappings.

In preaching from the Easter season lectionary, however, each of these psalms has a powerful capacity to evoke profound connections between the testimonies of the other readings and the lives of believers. A few examples must suffice to welcome the poetic or doxological force of these psalms in the interpretive context of the Easter season.

Psalm 47, for example, gives the slave girl's acclamation of the "Most High God" social and political definition (see Acts 16:17; Ps. 47:2). God's reign contends with "principalities and powers" that are spiritual and systemic on the one hand and human and historical on the other. In an era when the three Abrahamic religions (Judaism, Christianity, and Islam) contend with each other, God's reign "over the nations" places them all in subservience. God's dominion is now invested in the lordship of Jesus, who prays for the unity of all in the love of God (John 17). Thus, when "the princes of the peoples gather as the people of the God of Abraham" (v. 9), none is entitled to wreak havoc on the other. The triumph and exaltation belong to God, not to a warring people, "for the shields of the earth belong to God" (v. 9).

Psalm 68:1-20 is a portion of a processional song of thanksgiving, again focused on God's triumph, but this is not an Oriental Baal captive to nationalistic pride. This is the God whose righteousness is fulfilled in fatherly care for orphans and widows. Read as a lesson of the Easter season, the promised presence of God is signaled in the quaking earth (Ps. 68:8; see Acts 16:26), and God's salvation, even escape from death (Ps. 68:20), extends to the salvation of the Gentiles (Acts 16:31) and the welcome of the martyrs into the courts of heaven (Acts 7:59).

> IN AN ERA WHEN THE THREE ABRAHAMIC RELIGIONS CONTEND WITH EACH OTHER, GOD'S REIGN "OVER THE NATIONS" PLACES THEM ALL IN SUBSERVIENCE.

Psalm 97 fills the New Testament images of God's reign in Jesus with sturdy convictions of divine righteousness and justice (v. 1). The supremacy of the "Most High God" in Acts 16 is more adversarial in Psalm 97 to the "images, worthless idols, and gods" (vv. 7-9). The overwhelming confidence of this enthronement psalm, however, is a cause for rejoicing in the Lord and thanksgiving for "his holy name." In the New Testament, therefore, the name of Jesus bears the authority of the divine name (Acts 16:18).

SECOND READING
REVELATION 22:12-14, 16-17, 20-21 (RCL)
REVELATION 22:12-14, 16-17, 20 (BCP, RC)

All three lectionaries include the same verses from the ending of the Revelation to John, and all three exclude the judgments and warnings of verses 15 and 18-19. These exclusions are consistent with the tendency to exclude harsh and imprecatory psalms from the worship of the churches of Christendom. When sectarian Christians move apocalyptic words of judgment to the center of the proclamation, the churches of European origin that were (and still are legally) established remember why the Revelation to John had such difficulty even gaining canonical recognition. On the other hand, reciting all the promises and blessings of the closing verses of the Revelation without listening to the warnings risks offering the faithful mild medicine for dire conditions. The preacher, at least, must see the visions of promise against the dark clouds of warning.

The washing of the robes (v. 14) is truly a blessing, because the right to enter the holy city is granted by the blood of the Lamb, not by garments of human righteousness. The vision of the city as the ultimate place of promise does not contradict the biblical image of the garden of paradise (Genesis 2), but it fits with the conviction of Revelation that "the home of God is among mortals" (21:3). The divine goal of history is not the destruction of human community, but its redemption in communion with God.

The "root and the descendant of David" (v. 16) are images of the royal or messianic identity of Jesus (see Isaiah 11; Num 24:17), and the poetry of verse 17 echoes Isaiah 55, the prophecy of the restoration. The assurance, "I am coming soon!" (v. 20) has prompted many who tried to use the Revelation to John as God's code to be cracked to disobey the Lord's direct instructions against second-guessing the Father's timetables (Mark 13:32; Acts 1:6-8). This promise has also comforted generations of believers to trust the promises.

RECITING ALL THE PROMISES AND BLESSINGS OF THE CLOSING VERSES OF THE REVELATION WITHOUT LISTENING TO THE WARNINGS RISKS OFFERING THE FAITHFUL MILD MEDICINE FOR DIRE CONDITIONS.

ACTS 16:16-34 (BCP ALT.)

See the first reading for the Seventh Sunday of Easter, above.

THE GOSPEL
JOHN 17:20-26 (RCL, BCP, RC)

The five chapters of John 13:1—17:26 hold together as a literary unit beginning with the meal and continuing through Jesus' lengthy last discourse, often called "The Testament of Jesus." This pericope from John 17 has the quality of a summation, with rich associations with the rest of the story. It is followed by John's version of the passion narrative in chapters 18–19. As a Gospel lesson for the Easter season, it first seems like a flashback to the time before Jesus' death and resurrection. On the other hand, Jesus' final words in this lengthy discourse point beyond his mission (17:1-19) toward the mission of believers who will follow after him. Jesus is depicted as praying for the continuation of the mission God entrusted to him beyond the time of Jesus' glorification (17:1-5).

Verse 20 focuses Jesus' prayer for the benefit of those who come to believe in Jesus through the word of his disciples. The closely parallel clauses in verses 21 and 22-23 conclude with the purpose that "the world may believe that you have sent me" (v. 21) and that "the world may know that you have sent me and have loved them even as you loved me" (v. 23). This is a prayer, not a prediction, because while Jesus' purpose is clear, the desired result is not established. The unity of Jesus with the Father is already established, but the unity among Jesus' followers is a divine sign to be prayed for, not a human achievement.

The unity of the followers of Jesus is desired both for the well-being of the Christian community and for its witness to those who are still nonbelievers in Jesus. This is more than an absence of community conflict that would scandalize nonbelievers. The prayer that they will be "completely one" (v. 23) can be measured only by the standard of the Son's unity with the Father. This unity, therefore, means full alignment with the mission or purpose for which the Father sent the Son. This "glory" of Jesus is made manifest in his being raised up on the cross and in his exaltation. Peter will discover this includes "the kind of death by which he would glorify God" (21:19). The prayer is that when the nonbelievers see this deep bond of unity, they too will believe in God and be called into God's mission in the world.

> THE UNITY OF THE FOLLOWERS OF JESUS IS DESIRED BOTH FOR THE WELL-BEING OF THE CHRISTIAN COMMUNITY AND FOR ITS WITNESS TO THOSE WHO ARE STILL NONBELIEVERS IN JESUS.

God's love for the world lies at the heart of the Father's mission (John 3:16). This is the love in which the Father has held the Son "before the foundation of the world" (v. 24; see also the Word in John 1:1-18—"It is God the only Son, who is close to the Father's heart, who has made him known," v. 18). The evangelist draws the reader/hearer into the divine mystery of God's love, touching again on its revelation in the incarnation. As in 1 John 4:2-3, the belief that the glory and love of God have come in the flesh in Jesus Christ separates those who are one with God from those who oppose God. The love of God is not an abstract notion, but a dynamic force in the heart of Jesus and his followers. The love of God is the same love, continuing at work in Jesus' followers in a world that "does not know" the Father (v. 25).

> THE GOSPEL IS ABOUT GOD'S LOVE, FULFILLED IN THE GLORIFICATION OF THE SON AND HIS FOLLOWERS IN THEIR SELF-GIVING FOR THE WORLD, TO THE POINT OF DEATH.

The old gospel tune "They Will Know We Are Christians by Our Love" tells only a small part of the story. The deeper truth is that the world will learn to know and glorify God when the Father's profound love is seen to be at work in the Son and his disciples. The gospel is about God's love, fulfilled in the glorification of the Son and his followers in their self-giving for the world, to the point of death. This is their glorification, not in the sense of their heroic achievement, but in the reflection of God's love at work in them.

VIGIL OF PENTECOST

Revised Common	Episcopal (BCP)	Roman Catholic
Exod. 19:1-9 or Acts 2:1-11	Gen. 11:1-9 or Exod. 19:1-9a, 16-20a; 20:18-20 or Ezek. 37:1-14 or Joel 2:28-32	Gen. 11:1-9 or Exod. 19:3-8a, 16-20b or Ezek. 37:1-14 or Joel 3:1-5
Ps. 33:12-22 or Psalm 130	Ps. 33:12-22 or Canticle 2 or 13 or Psalm 130 or Canticle 9 or Ps. 104:25-32	Ps. 104:1-2, 24, 25, 27-28, 29, 30
Rom. 8:14-17, 22-27	Acts 2:1-11 or Rom. 8:14-17, 22-27	Rom. 8:22-27
John 7:37-39	John 7:37-39a	John 7:37-39

The lessons and psalms for this infrequently observed festival are so varied as to defy brief comments. Perhaps the best strategy in this context is simply to applaud the oral recitation of this wealth of texts, several of which testify to divine epiphanies. The liturgy may allow time for many readings and hymns, as often occurs in Easter vigils. Like the apostles in Jerusalem, the community is gathered together awaiting the promise of the Father. In Acts 1:14 (which does not appear in any of the lectionaries), we read, "All these were constantly devoting themselves to prayer." The litanies, prayers, and hymns provide the unhurried context for the readings of this vigil of waiting.

> PENTECOST IS A MOMENT, A *KAIROS*, WHERE GOD'S TIME MET ORDINARY TIME.

In this setting, the Gospel reading, brief as it is, unfolds the flower of the revelation of the Holy Spirit. As the Johannine witness has repeatedly affirmed in the

Easter season, Jesus' exaltation begins with his being lifted up on the cross, flows into his being raised up from death, is renewed in his resurrection appearances, and is fulfilled in his unity with the Father. Even in the Vigil of Pentecost, the focus remains on Jesus as he fulfills God's mission of love. The statement in John 7:39 that "as yet there was no Spirit, because Jesus was not yet glorified" is remarkably abrupt, but it expresses the conviction of both John and Luke that Jesus' exaltation was crucial to the Holy Spirit's coming in power.

Pentecost is a moment, a *kairos*, where God's time met ordinary time. Without fully understanding why Jesus' glorification was essential to the Holy Spirit's coming, the Vigil of Pentecost enters into God's holy time with the prayer, "Come, Holy Spirit."

Then the promises flow. Echoing the water from the rock in Numbers 20 and the water for thirsty lands in Isaiah 44 and Zechariah 14, the gift of God's Spirit is a wellspring of new life in parched souls. The refreshment of living waters is also the promise to the woman at the well in John 4. "The water that I will give," declares Jesus, "will become in them a spring of water gushing up to eternal life" (4:14).

With the woman at the well, the people say, "Sir, give me this water!" And with the saints of every generation, they praise God and declare, "Thank you for sending Jesus into our world and our lives. Send now the Holy Spirit that we may be fountains of living water for a thirsty world."

PENTECOST AND THE SEASON AFTER PENTECOST

REBECCA J. KRUGER GAUDINO

The Day of Pentecost, or "fiftieth" day, has its roots in the Jewish celebration of the Feast of Weeks, so called because this feast was celebrated seven weeks from the second day of Passover, or fifty days from the first day of Passover, although some Jewish sects advocated other beginning dates. In Hebrew Scripture, this pilgrim festival came at the end of the grain harvest and was also called the Day of First Fruits, a day of offerings in gratitude for God's generosity and care. Over time, however, and particularly after the Temple's destruction in 70 C.E., this feast was linked to God's covenant with Israel and the giving of the Torah.

For Christians, Easter Sunday became the first day from which Pentecost was counted. In some ways, the Jewish and Christian festivals are similar. It's possible to say that Christians also celebrate a harvest festival, not of life-giving grains, of course, but of the life-giving Spirit. And it is also a time to remember God's covenant with the new humankind, to use Paul's metaphor, for with the giving of the Spirit, the early church was empowered to proceed into the era of the new covenant inaugurated by Jesus Christ, the new lawgiver. No wonder Tertullian found Pentecost second only to Easter as that time of the church year most suited to baptism, the rite welcoming the catechumenate as people of the new covenant.

But here the two celebrations diverge because of the Christian Day One that begins the count to the fiftieth day: Easter Sunday, the day when the followers of Jesus learned that Jesus had triumphed over sin and death. What this triumph meant for them became clearer as they pondered and lived with this mystery: forgiveness, new beginnings, a place in the new family of God, and future hope. Easter Sunday, with all its newness and hope, shines brightly in the immediate background of Pentecost. But this one-day festival also has its own luminous quality, for because of Jesus' triumph, the presence and power of God became available to all Jesus' followers, for the first time, Luke tells us, on Pentecost. You might say that Pentecost completes the Extraordinary Time of Lent—Easter with a bang—loosing the Spirit among Jesus' followers and for the world. And this "bang" calls for great celebration!

Following this bang, however, is a season often called Ordinary Time. It seems to me that this season is poorly named. Now, I know that in this case "ordinary" derives from the term *ordinal*, referring to the fact that these Sundays are numbered rather than named, but doesn't this numbering suggest that these Sundays aren't significant enough to warrant a name, that they're just too "ordinary," somewhat like prisoners who receive numbers in place of names? Fortunately, Ordinary Time does not have all the bells and whistles of Advent–Christmas and Lent–Easter. Preachers and worship planners can wipe their brows and sit back for a bit. But an urgent question echoes in this long "ordinary" season: what in us and in our lives now reflects the Extraordinary?

> PENTECOST COMPLETES THE EXTRAORDINARY TIME OF LENT—EASTER WITH A BANG—LOOSING THE SPIRIT AMONG JESUS' FOLLOWERS AND FOR THE WORLD.

The calendar of the church year—with its cycle of reflection upon the great stories of God who transforms all of life, and then upon the call to live out the amazing truth of these stories in our own lives—reminds me of the movement of waves, rolling in to shore and then out, in and then out again, tumbling all the stones in its surf until they are beautiful in their smoothness and deep color. Well, the waves have just tumbled over us once again with the "God news" of Easter and Pentecost, and now they rush out. What new beauty in the stones—in us—lies upon the sand?

Or if talk of beauty makes us uncomfortable, let me shift metaphors: now is the time to take up our staffs. We have drunk down the stunning miracles, staggered on the hill outside Jerusalem, stared into the empty tomb, beheld flames burning above the holy. Now what do we do with all this treasure?

The lectionary texts of this next season of the church call on us to answer these questions creatively and faithfully. These texts do not permit us to forget who we now are as the followers of Jesus, the new people of God, freed from binding, deathly ways to spacious, new life. Always they call us to live out of the power of our new identity and life, even as they remind us of those who have walked God's paths long before us and have bequeathed to us the stories and lessons of their journey.

At this time of the church year, I think of a poem by Rainer Maria Rilke in which the poet imagines God as the One who creates us and then sends us into the territory of life, urging us to follow our yearning in large ways, to:

> Flare up like flame
> and make big shadows I can move in.

Indeed, the One who has re-created us as people of the Pentecost sends us out into the world to live out our love for God boldly and fully and to embody the Divine in our lives. Now is our time to flare up with the flame of the Spirit that makes room for the mysterious workings of God in our midst. This territory into which we journey is serious, Rilke imagines God informing us. From time to time, we may forget the God who has made and commissioned us. But we do not travel alone, for, as Rilke closes the poem, God holds out a hand to us.[1]

> NOW IS OUR TIME TO FLARE UP WITH THE FLAME OF THE SPIRIT THAT MAKES ROOM FOR THE MYSTERIOUS WORKINGS OF GOD IN OUR MIDST.

So let us put our hand in God's. And may this Ordinary Time be extraordinary in the power of the triune God flowing through our lives to the glory of our divine Creator and Companion and the full coming of the Realm.

Note

1. Rainer Maria Rilke, "*Gott spricht zu jedem nur, eh er ihn macht,*" in *Rilke's Book of Hours: Love Poems to God*, trans. Anita Barrows and Joanna Macy (New York: Riverhead Books, 1996), 88.

THE DAY OF PENTECOST

MAY 27, 2007

REVISED COMMON	EPISCOPAL (BCP)	ROMAN CATHOLIC
Acts 2:1-21 or Gen. 11:1-9	Acts 2:1-11 or Joel 2:28-32	Acts 2:1-11
Ps. 104:24-34, 35b	Ps. 104:25-37 or 104:25-32 or Ps. 33:12-15, 18-22	Ps. 104:1, 24, 29-30, 31, 34
Rom. 8:14-17 or Acts 2:1-21	1 Cor. 12:4-13 or Acts 2:1-11	1 Cor. 12:3b-7, 12-13 or Rom. 8:8-17
John 14:8-17 (25-27)	John 20:19-23 or John 14:8-17	John 20:19-23 or John 14:15-16, 23b-26

FIRST READING

ACTS 2:1-21 (RCL)
ACTS 2:1-11 (BCP, RC)

As Acts describes it, the first Pentecost was a time of fullness, in fact, overflowing-ness. Three Greek verbs pertaining to filling appear in the first four verses of this passage. Pentecost day "had come," the NRSV says in Acts 2:1, but the Greek says that this day is *fulfilled*: time is finally filled (*sympléroö*) with all the necessary ingredients for what may now happen. In 2:2, "a sound like the rush of a violent wind" fills (*pléroö*) the house. And in 2:4, all who sit in this house are filled (*pimplēmi*) with the Spirit. Notice the other words that also drive home the idea of saturation: "the *entire* house" (v. 2), "a tongue rested on *each* of them" (v. 3), and "*all* of them were filled" (v. 4). There is an all-embracing sweep in this story. Looking at the literary antecedents of the list of nations in 2:9-11, biblical scholar Gary Gilbert points to Roman propaganda that used these lists to emphasize the universality of Rome's rule. But Luke begs to differ: from east to west, from north to south—as these nations, past and present, roughly line up on a map—the realm of God is all-encompassing, and its citizens are those who have just experienced the realm of God.[1]

The reference to filling continues in 2:13 when some spectators give their read of the situation: "They are filled with new wine." In answer, Peter repeats Joel's words in which God promises to "pour out my Spirit upon all flesh" (vv. 16-17). "The Spirit fills these new followers, *not* new wine," Peter corrects the scoffers. But here Peter seems to have forgotten what Jesus once said about new wine that bursts old wineskins (Luke 5:37-38). These new followers of Jesus are not filled with new wine. They *are* the new wine! Watch them burst the seams of convention.

With this bursting, we learn of God's initiative in new twists on old stories. We hear hints of the creation story—the Spirit-wind of God that orders chaos into new life, in Acts, a new community. We hear echoes of the story of Babel, but now geographical and linguistic differences are no longer barriers. We hear of Joel's Day of the Lord, finally arrived with joyful and disruptive power. God's Spirit-vitality has been poured into the community. Watch it bubble and flow far and wide with God's love and power.

> GOD'S SPIRIT-VITALITY HAS BEEN POURED INTO THE COMMUNITY. WATCH IT BUBBLE AND FLOW FAR AND WIDE WITH GOD'S LOVE AND POWER.

GENESIS 11:1-9 (RCL ALT.)

Our reading tells the story of how the one family of Genesis 10 comes to inhabit different places and speak different languages. One time, the story begins, all humans lived together and spoke the same language. These humans seem to have been very enterprising, committing themselves to particular aims, which they then ably enacted. Three times we hear these humans say, "Let us": "Let us make bricks," "Let us build," and "Let us make a name" (11:3-4). Interestingly, the "us" never refers to God. Indeed, YHWH speaks of the plans of these people as what "*they* propose to do" (v. 6). There is no "we" here—God and people. God understands that this insular focus yoked to the vastness of human potential can be devastating: "This is only the beginning of what they will do; nothing that they propose to do will now be impossible for them" (v. 6). And so God scatters the people, making it impossible for them to understand one another and to work together again in the same way.

JOEL 2:28-32 (BCP ALT.)

Joel responds to a catastrophe that assails the entire postexilic community. Swarms of locusts have devoured crops. Fires have broken out in the dried fields.

And people and livestock thirst and starve. Joel calls the community to repentance and then speaks of the plenteous rains and harvests that will return because of God's mercy. Joel adds another oracle that promises the presence of God—"my spirit." The Hebrew verb for "pour out" is used of liquids, and in the context of a chapter segment that speaks of rain and overflowing vats (2:23-24), we have the sense of God's abundant presence gushing forth. Who will receive this bounty? "All flesh" (2:28): in particular, sons and daughters, old men, young men, male and female slaves. Raymond Bryan Dillard refers to this oracle as "a sociological overhaul" and asserts that it holds out for an era of "the prophethood of all believers."[2] In this time of Spirit-drenching, Joel imagines a day when God intervenes definitively to determine the outcome of history. Called to special roles in this day are God's prophet-people.

RESPONSIVE READING
PSALM 104:24-34, 35b (RCL)
PSALM 104:25-37 OR 104:25-32 (BCP)
PSALM 104:1, 24, 29-30, 31, 34 (RC)

Verse 24 is key to this reading, for it sets the stage for the remainder of this psalm about creation. Verses 27-30 powerfully state that God not only creates but also preserves and renews all life, a fitting Pentecost statement. And these acts of "newing" and renewing are continual, indeed, daily, for without God's gifts of food and breath, we would surely die. The psalmist closes this song with praise to a God so delighted in creation (104:26, 31b), so steadfast and generous in its tending, that we—and all creatures "filled with good things" (v. 28b)—can only cry out, "Bless the LORD, O my soul. Praise the LORD!"

PSALM 33:12-15, 18-22 (BCP ALT.)

This response is excerpted from a creation psalm; however, the response itself has to do with the God of history. While God watches over all peoples and nations, the psalmist refers to a different kind of watching over for those specially accompanied by God: "Truly the eye of the LORD is on those who fear him, on those who hope in his steadfast love" (33:18). The psalmist says of those who rely on this God, "Our soul waits for the LORD" (v. 20). The Hebrew word translated "soul" is much more expansive: "Our life [*nefesh*] waits for the LORD." The whole of who we are as God's people waits upon God. This is the God upon whom the Jesus community waits in Jerusalem.

SECOND READING

ROMANS 8:14–17 (RCL)
ROMANS 8:8–17 (RC ALT.)

In this passage, Paul lays out the struggle within Christians between life in the flesh and life in the Spirit. He is not advancing a Platonic argument here, valuing the spiritual life over the physical. Rather, he uses the language of flesh and Spirit to contrast, respectively, a life closed to, with a life open to, God's presence and purposes. Paul uses two images to highlight what he sees as a stark choice. The first describes life lived without God's presence as death (8:10, 13) and life filled with the Spirit as true life (v. 10). With his second image, Paul describes life lived out of our own power alone as slavery to the powers of sin and death with all the trappings of slavery, especially fear, while life lived out of God's power is adoption into the very family of God. It helps to hear this metaphor from the perspective of the ancient world in which kinship alone determined most people's possibilities in life. From slaves to "heirs of God and joint heirs with Christ" (v. 17)!

Paul also uses the mysterious language of mutual indwelling to describe the Christian's newly defining vitality and adoption: "You are in the Spirit, since the Spirit of God dwells in you" (v. 9). For Paul, this new relationship makes all the difference for both the joyous and the solemn responsibilities we as children of God must now accept (v. 17).

1 CORINTHIANS 12:4–13 (BCP)
1 CORINTHIANS 12:3b–7, 12–13 (RC)

In reading this lesson, it helps to remember that Paul is writing to a church dealing with divisive issues, a number of them about status. Paul's primary point in this lesson is that the Spirit of God is the leveling presence and energy in the community. But perhaps "leveling" is not quite the right word here, for *uplift for all* is what Paul is trying to communicate. The Spirit gives significance to everyone in the congregation. All are of great value because of the Spirit who gives each a gift to enact, through the power of God (1 Cor. 12:6), on behalf of the whole community.

EACH AND EVERY MEMBER IS ESSENTIAL, EACH AND EVERY MEMBER OF EQUAL VALUE IN THE EYES OF GOD.

Paul then employs the analogy of the body to communicate the sense of unity and interdependence that the new community has through the Spirit. This analogy was used in Roman political rhetoric to reinforce the empire's hierarchy. In one oration by Livy, for example, a Roman senator, Menenius Agrippa, called on the plebeians of Rome, what he termed the limbs of the imperial body, to end a strike and get back to work feeding the all-important stomach—those who governed—for without the stomach the body itself would die.[3] But Paul reads against the grain with his use of this analogy. Each and every member is essential, each and every member of equal value in the eyes of God. Paul's vision of the community prizes all, no matter their stations in life—"Jews or Greeks, slaves or free" (v. 13). There is only one credential in this community, and that is baptism, as Paul sees it, the gift of the Spirit *for all*. Here Paul describes baptism as the Spirit-water in which we are immersed and the Spirit-water that we drink—a total experience, inner and outer, that locates us in the Spirit and the Spirit in us.

ACTS 2:1-21 (RCL ALT.)
ACTS 2:1-11 (BCP ALT.)

See the first reading for the Day of Pentecost, above.

THE GOSPEL
JOHN 14:8-17 (25-27) (RCL)
JOHN 14:8-17 (BCP ALT.)
JOHN 14:15-16, 23b-26 (RC ALT.)

The RCL Gospel lesson is a lesson in the mystical logic of divine presence. Jesus gives his struggling disciple, citizen of the Show-Me state, a lesson in God's real presence. This lesson is essential, for Jesus will soon depart his disciples, and they need to understand how they will still experience his presence. Jesus first establishes that he, Jesus, is in the Father and the Father in him. "Just look at the miraculous works I have done, and you can see and know God in me and me in God—right before your eyes." Jesus goes on to explain that Philip and his friends will do even greater works because *they* will invoke Jesus' name and power. In other words, God's presence will be with them, too. They will experience the mystical indwelling that Jesus claims, for God will send to his faithful disciples another Advocate like Jesus, and this Advocate will abide with the disciples, and "he will be in you" (John 14:17). The Roman Catholic alternative reading makes this point even fuller: "[My Father and I] will come to them and make our home with them" (v. 23b). Talk about a full house! Now the disciples themselves are to become the dwelling of God's mysterious and rich presence, and they will be mobilized for dynamic, Jesus-like lives in this world.

> THE DISCIPLES THEMSELVES ARE TO BECOME THE DWELLING OF GOD'S MYSTERIOUS AND RICH PRESENCE, AND THEY WILL BE MOBILIZED FOR DYNAMIC, JESUS-LIKE LIVES IN THIS WORLD.

JOHN 20:19-23 (BCP, RC)

Set on the eve of the day of resurrection, this reading finds the fearful disciples locked in a house. They tremble, no doubt, because someone might recognize them as the executed Jesus' followers, as Peter was recognized, and decide they deserve a fate like that of Jesus. How appropriate then that Jesus appears in their midst with the words, "Peace be with you," not just once but twice (20:19, 21). But what is this peace about? Jesus immediately explains: "As the Father has sent me, so I send you" (v. 21). This peace is not about staying locked up in safe places but about heading back into the world with all its dangers and opportunities. But the disciples do not go out alone. Jesus gives them the gift of the Holy Spirit. That Jesus breathes this Spirit on them recalls the creation story, God's breath of life into Adam. Here we have the new humankind in-spired by Jesus, but this breath will be more than the breath of life for humanity. It will be what Jesus promised earlier: the Holy Spirit, the Spirit of truth, the Advocate sent by God in Jesus' name (14:15-17, 26). This divine breath and presence will take up residence in the new community of God, offering power to grant forgiveness and new beginnings to the despairing and defeated as well as power to unmask and counteract evil (v. 23).

RESPONDING TO THE TEXT

All of the texts for this special day are rich in preaching possibilities. One theme that recurs is the overflowing life of God's new people, filled with the Spirit's presence that spills forth from its human containers. Given the lively imagery of the Spirit that pours out from God to fill God's people, it would be appropriate on this joyous day to

HISTORY IS FILLED WITH EXAMPLES OF BABEL-LIVING THAT HAS LED TO DESTRUCTION OF SELF AND OTHER.

act out this theme with pitchers of water and various containers (a baptismal font?), all prepared for overflow. As liturgists read from Joel, Acts, and 1 Corinthians, other participants could splash water into the containers. These biblical texts are getting at the excitement of what it means to live out of resources far more than our own and for more than ourselves. What does Spirit-effervescence mean for us today?

A related theme deals with the remarkable statement of God in Genesis 11— that we humans when unified might be able to accomplish whatever we propose! This is an incredible recognition of the gifts given humankind in our creation. And yet how do we choose to use these gifts? The Genesis text describes the Babel life, lived with a self-absorbed concentration that does not recognize God's presence. We are living these days with so many factions building their own towers, walling their cities, considering only their own reputation, security, and future. History is filled with examples of Babel-living that has led to destruction of self and other. With the readings from Acts and 1 Corinthians, however, we encounter the new and lively Spirit-life that flows with divine power, presence, and purpose for all. This power set free for all of God's people outstrips even that implied in Genesis 11 and is a power for the salvation of all. In Acts 2, God's plans have entered the picture in a way that answers the judgment of Genesis 11. God dissolves the ancient barrier of language and soon will dissolve the barrier of distance. God's new· community will span the earth, and the Spirit will be the mortar that holds the new community of Jesus together. How much truer will God's comment of Babel be for the new church—"This is only the beginning of what [we] will do; nothing that [we] propose to do will now be impossible for [us]"—if this "us" truly includes God.

Yet a third theme is the intimate and mysterious relationship between human and divine that John describes as dwelling together and Paul (in Romans 8) as kinship. And yet even these seemingly peaceful household images speak of how God's power is incarnated and mobilized in the world through the church. What is remarkable about the ethic of these images is that those writing them, imbued with the empire's understanding of status and hierarchy, nonetheless saw a wholly new community being formed, free of longstanding bias and prejudice. The Spirit flowed into history to change the world and its earthly forms, and this change began with backwater Galileans, slaves, women, and old men and women, among others. Cyril of Jerusalem gets at the beauty of this new, en-Spirited diversity in reflections on this biblical text that are timely for the season in which Pentecost often falls:"One and the same rain comes down on all the world, yet it becomes white in the lily, red in the rose, purple in the violets and hyacinths, different and many-colored in manifold species. Thus it is one in the palm tree and another in the vine, and all in all things, though it is uniform and does not vary in itself. For the rain does not change, coming down now as one thing and now as another, but it adapts itself to the thing receiving it and becomes what is suitable to each."[4]

THE SPIRIT FLOWED INTO HISTORY TO CHANGE THE WORLD AND ITS EARTHLY FORMS, AND THIS CHANGE BEGAN WITH BACKWATER GALILEANS, SLAVES, WOMEN, AND OLD MEN AND WOMEN, AMONG OTHERS.

Notes

1. Gary Gilbert, "Roman Propaganda and Christian Identity in the Worldview of Luke-Acts," in *Contextualizing Acts: Lukan Narrative and Greco-Roman Discourse,* ed. Todd Penner and Caroline Vander Stichele (Atlanta: Society of Biblical Literature, 2003), 249–56.

2. Raymond Bryan Dillard, commentary on Joel, in *The Minor Prophets: An Exegetical and Expository Commentary; Hosea, Joel, and Amos*, vol. 1 (Grand Rapids, Mich.: Baker, 1992), 295.

3. Anthony C. Thiselton, *The First Epistle to the Corinthians: A Commentary on the Greek Text*, The New International Greek Testament Commentary (Grand Rapids, Mich.: Eerdmans, 2000), 993.

4. Cyril of Jerusalem, Catechesis 14.12, in *Fathers of the Church: A New Translation*, vol. 64 (Washington, D.C.: Catholic University of America Press, 1947–), 83, quoted in *Ancient Christian Commentary on Scripture, New Testament*, vol. 7, ed. Gerald Bray (Downers Grove, Ill.: InterVarsity Press, 1999), 123.

HOLY TRINITY SUNDAY / FIRST SUNDAY AFTER PENTECOST

JUNE 3, 2007

REVISED COMMON	EPISCOPAL (BCP)	ROMAN CATHOLIC
Prov. 8:1–4, 22–31	Isa. 6:1–8	Prov. 8:22–31
Psalm 8	Psalm 29 or Canticle 2 or 13	Ps. 8:4–5, 6–7, 8–9
Rom. 5:1–5	Rev. 4:1–11	Rom. 5:1–5
John 16:12–15	John 16:(5–11) 12–15	John 16:12–15

This Sunday is dedicated to the celebration of God as Holy Trinity. It may be tempting to some of us preachers to use this Sunday to explain the trinitarian doctrine to our congregations. Certainly this doctrine is a mystery to many sitting in the pews, and a pedagogical sermon may be just the thing. But it seems to me that what this Sunday and its biblical texts are really about is not the mystery of a doctrine but the mystery of God. Each of the texts for Trinity Sunday dovetails with the trinitarian doctrine in fascinating ways that suggest that this doctrine is—no matter how significant to our faith—just one door that we open in our efforts to gaze upon and understand the Divine. Some of the texts get at the immense and elusive otherness of the Divine that we often associate with the God language of Creator and Father/Mother. Others speak of the intimate, comforting familiarity of the Divine—Jesus and the Spirit—but in strange and elusive terms. Yet another text, a Proverbs text about Woman Wisdom, suggests territories of God's life and being that we humans have yet to fathom. Like the trinitarian doctrine itself, all these texts give us a toehold on this craggy mountain we call God—but just a toehold, for we have yet to ascend this mountain. Its summit remains without flag, and its flanks are often cloud swathed. There are those days when the clouds part, and we see meadows, sheer cliffs, cataracts, and even a path. But then the clouds close before we have traveled very far. Perhaps

> IT SEEMS TO ME THAT WHAT THIS SUNDAY AND ITS BIBLICAL TEXTS ARE REALLY ABOUT IS NOT THE MYSTERY OF A DOCTRINE BUT THE MYSTERY OF GOD.

this Sunday is the day to celebrate this Mystery: to stand in awe before the One, to cast down our crowns, to sing our praises as best we know, in the name of the Father/Mother, the Son/Child, and the Holy Spirit. Amen.

FIRST READING

PROVERBS 8:1-4, 22-31 (RCL)
PROVERBS 8:22-31 (RC)

This reading is much debated among scholars and yet largely neglected by preachers. First of all, let me say that verses 1-4 are essential to verses 22-31, for they identify the speaker in the latter verses. But including these verses will also most likely raise the difficult question, just who or what is Wisdom? Scholars have identified Woman Wisdom as a figure of poetry, as the principle of order in creation, as a divine attribute personified, even as God's very own self. This last possibility seems to claim too much for Proverbs 8 itself, although later deuterocanonical passages depict Woman Wisdom in divine terms (for instance, Wisdom of Solomon 10–11). Ancient understandings of this figure seem to have grown richer and more complex over time. It may be easy to dismiss Woman Wisdom as just a poetic device, but the sustained attention to this figure in the Old Testament invites us to reflect on what Israel's sages were saying through this figure. Kathleen M. O'Connor puts it this way: Woman Wisdom "articulates an intuition about reality. . . . She brings with her an aura, a haunting series of hints, allusions and revelations about the world and about God. In the riddle she poses for us to unravel, she is a metaphor leading us into deepest mystery."[1] Roland E. Murphy terms Woman Wisdom "God's communication, extension of self, to human beings."[2] Katharine Dell defines this figure as "the essence of what human beings need for a meaningful life, and as the form in which Yahweh makes himself present and in which he wishes to be sought by humankind."[3]

> IT MAY BE EASY TO DISMISS WOMAN WISDOM AS JUST A POETIC DEVICE, BUT THE SUSTAINED ATTENTION TO THIS FIGURE IN THE OLD TESTAMENT INVITES US TO REFLECT ON WHAT ISRAEL'S SAGES WERE SAYING THROUGH THIS FIGURE.

Translating some of the significant words of this passage shows why it has been difficult to know how much to claim for Woman Wisdom in Proverbs. The key verb in "The LORD *created* me" can be translated "fathered" or "acquired" (*kana*, v. 22). The verb in "Ages ago I was *set up*" (*nasak*, v. 23) can also be translated with the birth imagery of "poured out." The key verb of 8:24, "I was *brought forth*" (*ḥul*), is a mothering birth image. About these verses, Leo G. Perdue comments that God is described as both father and mother of Woman Wisdom.[4] All the verbs play with images that tie Yahweh intimately to Woman Wisdom, although there is no Nicene sense of begetting/birthing that identifies Woman Wisdom as God. Another troublesome word, *'amon*, translated "master worker" (v. 30), can also be translated, among yet other possibilities, "little child," in keeping with the parenting imagery as well as the play imagery of 8:30. But as "master worker," Woman Wisdom is an architect-builder, partnering with the Creator (compare Prov. 3:19).

What about preaching on this text? It allows preachers to introduce congregations to a new version of the creation story that celebrates creation as a wise and delightful process of both play and business and to a spirituality that sounds amazingly contemporary. Proverbs 8 reminds me of a story of a parent trying to get some serious work done while a child prances about him or her, pleased to be a part of things, giving a hand here and there, instilling joy and laughter in the whole process. Or if we focus on this figure as architect, we have the story of God relying on the great gifts of W/wisdom to lay out the world. That this female figure is placed at the very beginning as God's first creation is one of the few biblical affirmations of the joy and value that God finds in the company of women.

Without getting into the profound arguments about this figure, one can say that she is at the very least the good and joyful order at the heart of everything. Delighting in humankind, seeking us with the joy that God has in her, she is a mediator between the Creator and the created, taking upon herself the solemn aim of teaching humankind about God's order and purposes. From her, we learn to pay attention to creation. Nothing is too small for us to notice and consider, for everything can teach us more about God's ways in the world. Answering Wisdom's call is to practice a spirituality in our everyday lives that invites us to see the mystery and presence of the Divine in the details of our life and world so that all of our life becomes a mindful meditation on the Divine.

ISAIAH 6:1–8 (BCP)

"The King has died. Long live the King!" So the Isaiah text seems to read, like the traditional British proclamation intended to indicate both change and stability. King Uzziah has died—and who does Isaiah see but "the King, the LORD of hosts!" (6:5). The setting is most likely the Jerusalem Temple, which morphs into the throne room of God. The temple roof seems to telescope out into the heavens so that all that fills the temple is the hem of God's royal robe, while God sits "high and lofty" (v. 1) on the throne, engaged in decisions about the world. As Walter Brueggemann comments, "The throne room of God is the policy room of world government."[5]

Standing in the folds of the royal hem in this temple/throne room/policy room is Isaiah, aware that he has stepped into the presence of the Holy One, aware that he is "lost" and "unclean" before the one who is thrice holy. But his confession is met with divine absolution and followed by boldness as Isaiah overhears the discussion in the policy room and volunteers for duty: "Here am I; send me!" (v. 8). This text focuses on God as wholly Other, nonetheless engaged in the business of this world, indeed, in the very lives of individuals and nations.

RESPONSIVE READING
PSALM 8 (RCL)
PSALM 8:4-5, 6-7, 8-9 (RC)

This psalm is the first praise psalm in the psalter. Its opening and closing verses state the theme: the majesty of the Creator who has established the wonders of the heavens and yet has found time to attend to lowly human beings, finite and limited—"mortals" (v. 4), as the NRSV translates "son of Adam," the being created out of earth itself. God has given humans special standing and responsibility in the earth's created order. The closing verse, however, reminds us that while we humans might be tempted to blow our standing out of proportion, Yahweh, the Creator, is "our Sovereign" (v. 9).

PSALM 29 (BCP)

This psalm is a fitting response to the Isaiah text and a good prelude to the Revelation text. In what seems to be a heavenly council of gods, it celebrates the sovereignty of Yahweh, God of Israel, over all heavenly beings. Eighteen times, the poet states the name of Yahweh, as if to hammer home the point that Yahweh alone deserves worship. Indeed, Yahweh alone has tamed the power of chaos and "sits enthroned over the flood . . . as king forever" (vv. 10-11). And because of this certainty, the poet may pray for strength and peace, the blessings of God's enthronement.

CANTICLE 2 OR 13 (BCP ALT.)

This canticle is an excerpt from the "Song of Three Jews." Standing unharmed in Nebuchadnezzar's fiery furnace, the three friends of Daniel glorify God, calling praises from all of creation. All must sing out the majesty of a God who has created such an earth—mountain, seas, plants, and whales—and yet has seen the plight of these three men and rescued them. God is God of all, large and small, individual and community.

SECOND READING

ROMANS 5:1–5 (RCL, RC)

This lyrical text reminds me of the ancient stone steps found at the Acropolis, for it is a staircase of words and ideas that invites us Christians to mature, or climb step by step, in our faith.[6] The firm ground at the bottom of this stairway is the starting point of this prose poem: "peace with God," what Paul also terms "this grace in which we stand" (v. 2). We may boast of this foundation, certainly, for it points to the glory we will one day share with God.

But do we have anything to boast of now, in the midst of sufferings? Paul asserts that suffering is a first step on the journey to sharing God's glory. Paul knows that we humans often interpret suffering as a dead end. Here I think of Robert Louis Stevenson's *Kidnapped*, in which an evil uncle sends his unwanted nephew, true heir of the family wealth, up a ruined staircase and, so the uncle hopes, to his death.

> GOD HAS ALREADY GIVEN US THE GIFT OF PEACE AND EVEN NOW POURS INTO OUR HEARTS THE GIFT OF DIVINE LOVE SO THAT WE MAY JOURNEY ON IN THE KNOWLEDGE OF GOD'S HERENESS AND NOWNESS.

Paul writes, however, that from this first step of suffering we may mount to the second: "Suffering produces endurance" (v. 3). And then we may rise from endurance to character, which permits us to reach the step of hope. Luke Timothy Johnson writes that, for Paul, hope is not just some expectation of the future but our understanding of the present as God-filled that allows us to move into the future.[7] God has already given us the gift of peace, Paul writes, and even now pours into our hearts the gift of divine love so that we may journey on in the knowledge of God's hereness and nowness.

We can all think of people like Nelson Mandela or Rosa Parks who mounted Paul's staircase, climbing through suffering to hope that could not be extinguished, given their knowledge and experience of God's power and presence. But perhaps we need to remember the steadfast climbing of people like our parents, our grandparents, our teachers, our children, who also mount this staircase and testify in one way or another to the presence of the triune God—Jesus who won our peace with God for us (v. 1); God who grants us the gift of love (v. 5); and the Spirit who conveys God's love to us here and now (v. 5)—a Presence that draws us all to true hope.

REVELATION 4:1–11 (BCP)

As in Isaiah 6:1–8, we read the story of a human who enters the throne room of God to see yet again the mysterious and thrice holy one "seated on the throne" (4:2). While in Isaiah, this throne room is both earthly and heavenly, here it is entirely heavenly, as if John would show us a reality yet more fully Other than that in Isaiah. Scholars have identified the symbols of this passage: the twenty-four elders as the twelve tribes of Israel and Jesus' twelve disciples; the four living creatures, according to rabbinic traditions, as representatives of various classes of beasts (for instance, wild and domestic) in God's eyes, thus representing all creation; the sea of glass as the waters of chaos fully stilled and soon to be obliterated (see Psalm 93; Rev. 21:1). Scholars also note the political commentary of this passage. According to tradition, Domitian commanded those who approached him to address him as "Lord and God" and surrounded himself with twenty-four functionaries. And vassal kings of Nero supposedly set their crowns before the image of the emperor in deference.[8] John gathers all of history and creation into this heavenly scene and declares the mysterious one upon the throne "the God-center of reality," to use Eugene Peterson's phrase.[9] All falls under the holy sway of the Creator, who has much in mind for creation, entitling the true Lord and God "to receive glory and honor and power" (v. 11).

The Gospel

JOHN 16:12-15 (RCL, RC)
JOHN 16:(5-11) 12-15 (BCP)

We return once again to Holy Week, not in church time, but certainly in this lesson. Jesus has yet to endure the great rejection of all that he has done and claimed. From this context of sorrow that will deepen before it is answered with joy, Jesus seeks to prepare his disciples for the end of their close human companionship. The setting is intimate: a table around

> JESUS HOLDS THAT TRUTH COMES FROM GOD ALONE AND WILL BE DECLARED TO THE DISCIPLES THROUGH THE SPIRIT OF TRUTH.

which the disciples sit, Jesus with a bowl of water and a towel, a meal that takes them into the night, and finally the presence of dear friends only, after Judas's departure. And as twilight lengthens, Jesus begins to speak his love and hopes for those he will soon leave behind. He begins to speak about his departure.

The longer BCP reading is helpful because it lays out the epistemological challenge that the disciples face in following an absent Jesus. In verses 8-11, Jesus states that the coming Advocate and Spirit of truth will "prove the world wrong about sin and righteousness and judgment" (v. 8). The world has rejected Jesus as the one sent by God to save the world. And because of this rejection, the "ruler of this world has been condemned" (v. 11). Whether this ruler is Satan or evil personified, Caesar or Pontius Pilate, makes no difference, for this ruler represents the world's knowledge and power.

What, then, is truth? Jesus holds that truth comes from God alone and will be declared to the disciples through the Spirit of truth. Truth is and will be in line with what Jesus has already taught and yet must be further revealed over time. As Jesus puts it, the Spirit "will take what is mine and declare it to you" (v. 15). He adds that what is his belongs to the Father as well. But is this new Advocate a flesh-and-blood Advocate, as Jesus was? No. The Advocate is, as John writes, Spirit! But how can a Spirit that cannot be seen be presence?

This Johannine text teaches us humans about what we call absence. For early Christians, scholars say, Jesus' absence—whether after his death or his ascension—posed a major problem of faith. For us Christians today, living in an era in which what you can see, measure, and duplicate is defined as truth, the problem of absence continues. But Jesus teaches that absence does not mean nothingness and aloneness.

> JESUS' ABSENCE IS HIS PRESENCE IN A WAY THAT IS EVEN MORE POWERFUL AND ENDURING, SO MUCH SO THAT HE TELLS THE DISCIPLES THAT "IT IS TO YOUR ADVANTAGE THAT I GO AWAY."

In Mahayana Buddhism, there is a mysterious doctrine about Ultimate Reality called the Void or *s(h)unyata*. The interesting thing about this doctrine is that it does not mean nothingness. Rather, it means everything. It means totality so vast that any attempts to describe Ultimate Reality fail.

In some ways, Jesus' teaching is like that of the Void. Jesus' absence is his presence in a way that is even more powerful and enduring, so much so that he tells the disciples that "it is to your advantage that I go away" (v. 7). There is something about the Advocate—despite its seeming nothingness—that is the continuing presence of Jesus as well as the presence of the Father, all three available, present to the disciples. Absence becomes an experience of incredible fullness of presence. I think of Celtic prayers when I imagine this kind of presence:

> God be with thee in every pass,
> Jesus be with thee on every hill,
> Spirit be with thee on every stream,
> Headland and ridge and lawn;
>
> Each sea and land, each moor and meadow,
> Each lying down, each rising up,
> In the trough of the waves, on the crest of the billows,
> Each step of the journey thou goest.[10]

Absence is not so cut and dried as our world would have us believe. Through Jesus Christ, in the company of the Spirit, and in the power of our Mother/Father, we are invited into an experience of deep and direct knowing of the Divine among us, with us, in us. And it is this deep knowing that permits us to walk through all our holy weeks to the experiences of resurrection in our lives. The truth of this world—that the Void *is* nothingness and absence is *not* presence—is threadbare. Look through this flimsy cloth and see the light of the Divine shimmering on this side of that great divide called death or absence.

Notes

1. Kathleen M. O'Connor, *The Wisdom Literature*, Message of Biblical Spirituality, vol. 5 (Collegeville, Minn.: The Liturgical Press, 1988), 64.

2. Roland E. Murphy, *The Tree of Life: An Exploration of Biblical Wisdom Literature*, 2nd ed. (Grand Rapids, Mich.: Eerdmans, 1990), 147.

3. Katharine Dell, *"Get Wisdom, Get Insight": An Introduction to Israel's Wisdom Literature* (Macon, Ga.: Smyth & Helwys, 2000), 169.

4. Leo G. Perdue, *Proverbs*, Interpretation: A Bible Commentary for Teaching and Preaching (Louisville: John Knox Press, 2000), 143.

5. Walter Brueggemann, *Isaiah 1–39*, Westminster Bible Companion (Louisville: Westminster John Knox Press, 1998), 59–60.

6. In seminary, I heard a fellow classmate, Timothy Slemmons, preach on this text and use the image of the staircase to explain the rhetorical device used by Paul in verses 3-4. I have remembered that wonderful image all these years, even though I have forgotten how Tim developed his sermon. I thank Tim for the gift of that image and hope I have done it justice in my own exegesis.

7. Luke Timothy Johnson, *Reading Romans: A Literary and Theological Commentary*, Reading the New Testament series (New York: Crossroad, 1997), 80.

8. For further historical information, see M. Eugene Boring, *Revelation*, Interpretation: A Bible Commentary for Teaching and Preaching (Louisville: John Knox Press, 1989).

9. Eugene Peterson, *Reversed Thunder: The Revelation of John and the Praying Imagination* (San Francisco: HarperSanFrancisco, 1988), 61.

10. *Carmina Gadelica: Hymns and Incantations Orally Collected in the Highlands and Islands of Scotland and Translated into English*, ed. Alexander Carmichael (Scottish Academic Press, 1900–1928), 3:195, quoted in Esther de Waal, *The Celtic Way of Prayer* (New York: Doubleday, 1997), 11.

SECOND SUNDAY AFTER PENTECOST

The Solemnity of the Most Holy Body
and Blood of Christ (Corpus Christi) /
Tenth Sunday in Ordinary Time / Proper 5
June 10, 2007

Revised Common	Episcopal (BCP)	Roman Catholic
1 Kgs. 17:17–24 or 17:8–16 (17–24)	1 Kgs. 17:17–24	Gen. 14:18–20
Psalm 30 or Psalm 146	Psalm 30 or 30:1–6, 12–13	Ps. 110:1, 2, 3, 4
Gal. 1:11–24	Gal. 1:11–24	1 Cor. 11:23–26
Luke 7:11–17	Luke 7:11–17	Luke 9:11b–17

First Reading
1 KINGS 17:17–24 (RCL, BCP)

In today's text, we find the prophet Elijah in Sidon, outside Israel, living in the home of a widow and her only child, a son. Our pericope opens with news that an illness strikes this child until "there was no breath left in him" (v. 17). The widow turns her pain and anger upon Elijah, who has previously spoken to her of "the Lord the God of Israel" (v. 14). "Have you come to convict me of my sins and cause my son to die?" she cries out. She believes that she has been judged for past wrongdoing.

Elijah accepts neither her logic nor this outcome but takes the child from her arms and commands God's attention in the upper room of this home. He finds it hard to believe that God would strike down the son of the very woman in whose house he has found refuge from King Ahab. "Have you killed the son of the woman who has been caring for me?" he calls out in dismay. And then three times he calls on God to return the child to life. And "the Lord listened to the voice of Elijah" (v. 22).

> ELIJAH CARRIES INTO GOD'S PRESENCE NOT ONLY THE BODY OF THE CHILD BUT ALSO THE IMMENSE GRIEF OF THE CHILD'S MOTHER.

This story is about bringing pain and questions about our lives to God. The bereft widow expresses her honest pain, even if it isn't pretty. Elijah, who never pulls any punches himself, does not remonstrate her for what she has said. He does not argue with her theology. Rather, he carries into God's presence not only the body of the child but also the immense grief of the child's mother. His actions are the response of one who *suffers with* in the raw honesty of the moment. What we learn, and what the widow learns, is that the prayers and responses of men and women of God make a huge difference in this world. As the widow says, "Now I know that you are a man of God, and that the word of the LORD in your mouth is truth" (v. 24).

1 KINGS 17:8-16 (17-24) (RCL ALT.)

When the prophet Elijah goes into hiding from Ahab, he travels to Sidon, near the worship center where Baal is proclaimed the true god, ruler of the rains and the earth's fertility. But the drought that Elijah proclaimed for Israel in 17:1 also prevails in Sidon, despite Baal. Yahweh, God of Israel, is indeed supreme. One powerful motif about good kings in ancient Near

> THIS NARRATIVE ASSERTS THAT GOD HAS LOCKED DOWN POWER IN THE USUAL PLACES AND IDENTIFIES GOD'S POWER IN OUT-OF-THE-WAY PLACES.

Eastern belief was that they were abundant water-providers for their people, given their alliance with their nations' gods. According to Ras Shamra stories, good kings also helped widows with children.[1] But in our text, everything is awry in both worship and governance. And so Elijah meets a widow gathering the last sticks for a last fire over which she will make a last meal.

When Elijah hears of her situation, he announces, "Do not be afraid" (v. 13). Walter Brueggemann writes that these words are the typical Old Testament formula introducing an oracle of salvation. They announce that Yahweh is on the scene.[2] This story promises God's power for life on behalf of the powerless and the vulnerable. It also locates men and women of God with the powerless and the vulnerable. As Brueggemann suggests, it matters that Elijah dines at the widow's table and not at the table of King Ahab and Queen Jezebel, where the Baal-worshiping prophets dine (18:19).[3] Where we receive our nourishment shapes our loyalties, decisions, and actions.

Henri Nouwen speaks of the freedom or "critical distance" Christians need to call the world to conversion. He writes: "The Christian witness is a critical witness because the Christian professes that the Lord will come again and make all things new. The Christian life calls for radical changes because the Christian assumes a critical distance from the world and, in spite of all contradictions, keeps saying that a new way of being human and a new peace are possible. This critical distance is an essential aspect of true prayer."[4] He goes on to say that prayer is "breaking through the veil of existence and allowing yourself to be led by the vision which has become real to you."[5]

How do we Christians attain this critical distance? How do we push ourselves away from the tables of the powerful? This narrative asserts that God has locked down power in the usual places—palaces, marketplaces, capital cities—and identifies God's power in out-of-the-way places.

GENESIS 14:18–20 (RC)

This text follows the story of a battle in which Abram defeats invading kings and returns with the goods they stole and the people they captured. Coming to congratulate Abram is King Melchizedek (meaning "the king is just") of Salem. Scholars speculate that the narrator, in mentioning Salem, refers to the city that will someday be Jerusalem (see Ps. 76:2) and points to future Israel and King David in this Canaanite ruler. Melchizedek is both king and priest, a common pairing of roles in the ancient Near East. With bread and wine, he as king feeds the weary warriors and celebrates their victory. When he blesses Abram by God Most High (*El Elyon*), Creator of all, and then blesses this God as the source of the power behind Abram's victory, he as priest offers Abram bread and wine, the fruits of creation that take on sacramental meaning. Scholars debate what to make of *El Elyon*, although *el* is the Canaanite word for "god." Abram accepts the blessings of Melchizedek as blessings of one who worships the God of Abram (14:22). And then the enigmatic Melchizedek disappears. In some of the traditions of Judaism and early Christianity, however, he lives on, a "numinous figure" for Jews at Qumran, sign of the coming messianic liberator, and for Christians, sign of Jesus Christ.[6]

RESPONSIVE READING

PSALM 30 (RCL, BCP)
PSALM 30:1–6, 12–13 (BCP ALT.)

This psalm, a thanksgiving for deliverance, is a fitting response to the 1 Kings and Luke 7 texts. Its praise is founded in anguished prayers for help that precede this psalm's composition (vv. 2, 8–10). We hear the "before" and the "after" of these prayers for help: for example, the experience of the Pit (v. 3) and then the relief of being drawn up (v. 1). To the God to whom we cry in deep distress and whose restoration we experience time and again, the psalmist gives thanksgiving and praise.

PSALM 146 (RCL ALT.)

The last five psalms of the psalter open and close with *Hallelujah*: "Praise the LORD!" Psalm 146 is the first of these five. Why are we called to praise Yahweh in this psalm? Because Yahweh, thank goodness, is unlike any human ruler. Because princes are mere mortals, they will fail in their promises, the psalmist tells us. Yahweh alone offers help, especially to those who are vulnerable. This psalm is the song of all whom Elijah and then Jesus save from hunger.

PSALM 110:1, 2, 3, 4 (RC)

This psalm is a coronation psalm, celebrating the rule of the Davidic king, upheld by Yahweh's own power and commitment. The king will be ruler and priest, as was the ancient Canaanite priest-king of Jeru/Salem, Melchizedek. Christians have read this psalm as an anticipation of the enthronement of Jesus, the Davidic messiah "for whom and through whom God is working out his purpose in the world."[7]

SECOND READING
GALATIANS 1:11-24 (RCL, BCP)

In this text, Paul writes more about himself than he usually does in his epistles but not enough to answer the many questions that this text raises. Scholars have long debated why Paul spends so much time on his credentials. Is he defending himself against attacks that he is a renegade or that he just parrots other early apostles' teachings because he has no personal experience of Jesus? We do know from Paul's letter that the churches of Galatia were struggling over the issue of whether Gentile Christians were to follow Jewish law. Paul's credentials seem to serve an important purpose in this argument, for they identify Paul's authority as beyond all human factions.

Imagine one of the instruments many of us used in our high school geometry classes, the compass. In this text, Paul's primary purpose seems to be to establish the fixed arm of his life's compass: God as the origin of Paul's gospel as well as his understanding of that gospel. As Frank J. Matera says, Paul is not saying that he has learned nothing from his fellow Christians (see, for instance, 1 Cor. 15:3-5), but that the heart of the gospel that he teaches was revealed by God directly to him.[8] Scholars do not agree that Paul refers to the revelation recorded in Acts 9:3-6. Nor do they agree what to call this revelation—*conversion, call,* and/or *commissioning*—since Paul does not understand his gospel as a new religion. Whatever the experience, this revelation and the one who gave it comprise the fixed arm of Paul's life: only God "set me apart before I was born and called me through his grace, [and] was pleased to reveal his Son to me, so that I might proclaim him among the Gentiles" (1:15-16).

Now for the drawing arm of the compass that runs far from the fixed arm, but never too far: Paul's own apostleship. Paul's experience of the gospel sent him traveling far and wide on behalf of all Gentiles, including travel to Arabia that some scholars speculate may have included time in Petra of the Nabatean kingdom (1:17, 21). But this is just the beginning of his travel, both geographically and theologically. Would that this distance had been greater for Paul with regard to the issue of women in the church! Nonetheless, Paul's life is an example of the incredible power loosed and freedom given by the grounding experience of God's revelation. This text invites us to question what grounds our lives and what gives us freedom and energy to live for God. How would we speak of the compass of our lives?

PAUL'S LIFE IS AN EXAMPLE OF THE INCREDIBLE POWER LOOSED AND FREEDOM GIVEN BY THE GROUNDING EXPERIENCE OF GOD'S REVELATION.

1 CORINTHIANS 11:23-26 (RC)

Ben Witherington III writes that in the ancient world the wealthy sometimes set aside money in their wills for the purpose of their own annual memorial feasts. But, Witherington comments, Jesus is not calling for this kind of feast that dwells on the past. Jesus speaks of a rite that is a sign and seal of a new, living relationship—which Jesus terms a new covenant (Jer. 31:31)—and of a vital expectation for the future.[9] This rite is about the real presence of Jesus in our lives that invites us to more than recollection of our Savior. When Jesus says, "This is my body that is for you" (11:24), he identifies *us* as his disciples and covenant partners. We stand in that growing, living circle of disciples that includes Juliana of Liège, specially called in 1246 to advocate for a feast day first called Corpus Christi.

THE GOSPEL
LUKE 7:11-17 (RCL, BCP)

This text is another story of a life-giving encounter outside a city gate (see 1 Kgs. 17:10), threshold between safety and danger, life and death. As Jesus approaches this gate, he encounters a funeral procession. Luke fills in a few details about one of those who grieves, a widow whose only son is now being borne to his burial. In his study of gender and class in early Christianity, James Malcolm Arlandson categorizes the widow in this story as one of the "expendables" in society.[10] Without a husband and now without a son, she has lost her status in society and most likely her sole source of support.

The following verse is key to what happens next. We read that Jesus, whom Luke calls *kyrios* for the first time, sees this woman. Despite the large crowd accompanying her, he notices *her* and "had compassion for *her*" (v. 13). He is moved by her presence; note the many references to her in these few verses.

He steps forward and touches the bier on which lies the corpse—an unheard-of act among people who know the purity codes. Luke writes, ". . . and the bearers stood still" (v. 14). Certainly they are shocked at Jesus' actions, but there is more to this stillness. Jesus has just ended their funeral procession. Jesus has other intentions: "Young man, I say to you, rise!" Jesus speaks to this dead body as a living being.

> WE ALL EXPERIENCE LIFE OUTSIDE THE CITY GATE, OUTSIDE OUR SEEMINGLY SECURE AND PROTECTED AREAS WHERE WE FIND WE MUST GIVE UP SOMETHING WE CHERISH AS NO LONGER POSSIBLE.

Luke quotes the Greek translation of 1 Kings 17:23, drawing the parallel between Jesus and Elijah, this widow and the widow of Zarephath: "Jesus *gave him* [the dead man] *to his mother*" (v. 15).

The response is fear—and then praise, for "a great prophet has risen among us!" The rising of the dead man (*egeirō*, v. 14) is the sign of the rising (*egeirō*, v. 16) of a new and great prophet. The second claim of the onlookers—that "God has looked favorably on his people!" (v. 16)—could just as well be translated, "God has visited [*episkeptomai*] his people." A procession of death is now turned to a procession of life.

This miracle story still speaks to us today, for we all experience life outside the city gate, outside our seemingly secure and protected areas where we find we must give up something we cherish as no longer possible. God is at work in all of our territories, even in what seem to be our most dangerous and deathly places.

As a sign of Jesus' special attention to one of the "expendables," this story tells of God's special love for the forgotten and the vulnerable. And the compassion that Jesus feels for the widow is the very compassion to which he calls his followers throughout Luke (see 6:36; 10:33). We are all called to become signs of God's visitation.

In a pastoral note, the remarkable way in which Jesus addresses the dead man is an incredible testimony to a God who does not forget the dead but recognizes and continues to uphold their personhood. This story foreshadows the death and resurrection of Jesus and points to our fullness of being even in death because of a God of life who intends freedom from death.

LUKE 9:11b-17 (RC)

Jesus is nowhere near a Super 8 motel or a Kentucky Fried Chicken. The travelers following him have not been thinking about these amenities either. They have come for hope and healing. And Jesus "welcomed them" (v. 11). Even in this deserted place they will experience his hospitality. When evening arrives, along with the crowd's hunger pangs, the disciples ask Jesus to disperse the crowd.

> THE DISCIPLES DO NOT RECOGNIZE THAT THE RESOURCE OF PLENTY AND WELCOME—JESUS HIM-SELF—IS ALREADY PRESENT.

Jesus' response is interesting: "You give them something to eat" (v. 13). There is no boy in Luke to step forward with his basket of food. We have just these twelve disciples whom Jesus has recently welcomed back from an internship of traveling, proclaiming, and healing. He had instructed them to travel without food or money (9:1-6). And now Jesus seems to be challenging these twelve to remember their "enoughness" in these travels. He suggests that they already have the resources they need to feed this crowd.

While the disciples consider buying food for everyone, no doubt shaking their heads at the thought of trying to purchase this much food with such slim funds, Jesus moves ahead, aware that they are captive to the usual economics of goods and services, supply and demand, all of which convince us that we never have enough. "We'll just have to scatter and do the best we can to take care of old number one." The disciples do not recognize that the resource of plenty and welcome—Jesus himself—is already present. And so Jesus teaches them again in a meal that foreshadows the eucharistic meal with its distinctive actions: taking, blessing, breaking, and giving. This story is about the abundant giving of Jesus, a giving that will be for all humankind. And it is about the giving of Jesus' disciples, called to recognize the dynamic power already in their common life.

Notes

1. John Gray, *1 and 2 Kings: A Commentary*, 2nd ed., The Old Testament Library (Philadelphia: Westminster, 1970), 380–81.

2. Walter Brueggemann, *1 and 2 Kings*, Smyth & Helwys Bible Commentary (Macon, Ga.: Smyth & Helwys, 2000), 211.

3. Ibid., 214.

4. Henri J. M. Nouwen, *With Open Hands* (Notre Dame, Ind.: Ave Maria Press, 1995), 105.

5. Ibid., 118.

6. Victor P. Hamilton, *The Book of Genesis, Chapters 1–17*, The New International Commentary on the Old Testament (Grand Rapids, Mich.: Eerdmans, 1990), 414.

7. James L. Mays, *Psalms*, Interpretation, A Bible Commentary for Teaching and Preaching (Louisville: John Knox Press, 1994), 354.

8. Frank J. Matera, *Galatians*, Sacra Pagina series, vol. 9 (Collegeville, Minn.: The Liturgical Press, 1992), 56, 64.

9. Ben Witherington III, *Conflict and Community in Corinth: A Socio-Rhetorical Commentary on 1 and 2 Corinthians* (Grand Rapids, Mich.: Eerdmans, 1995), 250.

10. James Malcolm Arlandson, *Women, Class, and Society in Early Christianity: Models from Luke-Acts* (Peabody, Mass.: Hendrickson, 1997), 125.

THIRD SUNDAY AFTER PENTECOST

REVISED COMMON	EPISCOPAL (BCP)	ROMAN CATHOLIC
2 Sam. 11:26—12:10, 13-15 or 1 Kgs. 21:1-10 (11-14) 15-21a	2 Sam. 11:26— 12:10, 13-15	2 Sam. 12:7-10, 13
Psalm 32 or Ps. 5:1-8	Psalm 32 or Ps. 32:1-8	Ps. 32:1-2, 5, 7, 11
Gal. 2:15-21	Gal. 2:11-21	Gal. 2:16, 19-21
Luke 7:36—8:3	Luke 7:36-50	Luke 7:36—8:3 or 7:36-50

FIRST READING

2 SAMUEL 11:26—12:10, 13-15 (RCL, BCP)
2 SAMUEL 12:7-10, 13 (RC)

For this text to make sense, the congregation will need to hear a summary of the story behind the story: David's adultery with Bathsheba and the murder of Uriah the Hittite. The text for this Sunday begins with news of Uriah's death in battle and the period of mourning that precedes David's marriage to "the wife of Uriah" (11:26), as the text calls Bathsheba. Life seems to return to normal for the king and his new queen in verses 26-27, until the ominous second sentence of 11:27 announces otherwise: "But the thing that David had done displeased the LORD. . . ." The human players are ready to move on, put the whole sordid affair behind them, but God has yet to weigh in on the matter.

The prophet Nathan soon stands before David, telling a parable that likens David to a rich man, Uriah to a poor man, and Bathsheba to "one little ewe lamb" (12:3). Telling of a rich man who takes the poor man's lamb in order to kill and serve it at a feast for a guest, Nathan uses the metaphor of eating stolen food to speak of David's sexual misdeed. According to the text, David bears responsibility for what has happened, despite the long history of readers who have condemned Bathsheba (Why was she bathing where she could be seen? Why didn't she just say no?). The text, however, gives us little help sorting out Bathsheba's intentions and accountability. But the image of the lamb suggests that in God's eyes, she is the vulnerable party. The rich man, the king, is the one with the commanding power in this scenario. While his soldiers are capturing the city of Rabbah, his messengers are sent to *get* or *take* Bathsheba (*laqaḥ*, 11:4; also "*took* the poor man's lamb," 12:4; and "[David] *took* the crown of Milcom [king of Rabbah] from his head," 12:30). While we may worry about Bathsheba's role, the narrator is concerned with David's role and God's response.

God then reminds David of the king's long dependence on God's powerful commitment: *I* anointed you king, *I* rescued you from Saul, and *I* gave you the house of Saul. God reminds David that the king of Israel was the least likely son, the hunted fugitive, the hated upstart. God reminds David of his vulnerability, answered by God's loyal protection (a great contrast to the rich man's care for the lamb). And how has David responded to this steadfastness? He has broken the covenant with adultery and murder. With the power given to him by God, he has defied the boundaries that God has put in place for Israel as community. As God says, I gave you all you have, "and if that had been too little, I would have added as much more" (12:8). You have been greedy, David. Greed backed by heedless power is exactly what the prophet Samuel warned the twelve tribes about when telling them that kings would only take and take (1 Sam. 8:10-18; *laqaḥ* is used throughout)—sons, daughters, grain, fields, livestock, vineyards.

> THIS STORY DEMONSTRATES WHAT HAPPENS TO POWER WHEN HUMANS FORGET GOD, SOURCE OF ALL POWER, AND THE GOD-GIVEN BOUNDARIES THAT PROTECT LIFE AND COMMUNITY.

This story demonstrates what happens to power when humans forget God, Source of all power, and the God-given boundaries that protect life and community. Out of control, power becomes a devouring force that harms all around. When David repents of his sins, Nathan tells him that God puts away, or forgives, his sin. At the same time, consequences have already been loosed within David's own family, for it will continue to be divided by trouble and violence. Upcoming chapters tell the story of the rape of David's daughter Tamar by David's eldest son Amnon, and then the vengeance killing of Amnon by Absalom. We have a picture of a family experiencing the chaos of human power that recognizes no Maker. Today we might speak of family systems in which abusive and violent patterns of behavior are passed down through a family.

It is a story almost too sober to consider, especially when we learn of the innocent baby's death. But we also know the brutal truth of innocent children who bear the brunt of their parents' choices and sins. It is a hard but real story about decisions that destroy relationships and set down patterns seductive to those who exercise power and control—an important story for congregations to hear and ponder.

REBECCA J.
KRUGER GAUDINO

1 KINGS 21:1-10 (11-14) 15-21a (RCL ALT.)

The story of Naboth versus King Ahab and Queen Jezebel is a tremendous challenge to systems of human governance. Naboth lives according to the old tribal ways of Israel that understand the true owner of the land to be God and God alone (Lev. 25:23-25), who has granted the descendants of the freed slaves an inheritance of land in Canaan (see Joshua 13–14). Those who own land are simply stewards of the land, which is to remain within the family. Laws protect it from being stolen (Deut. 19:14; 27:17; Lev. 25:10, 13-14). Old tribal understandings of rulership also seem to prevail for Naboth, who boldly says "no" to the king of Israel. The king is king, certainly, but he must obey the same covenant laws to which Naboth is bound (Deut. 17:14-20).

> ELIJAH THE PROPHET MAY BE AHAB'S ENEMY, BUT HE IS A FIERCE FRIEND TO GOD AND TO ALL WHO SUFFER UNDER TYRANNY.

But Naboth comes up against another model of rulership, that of the despot who cannot be slighted or disobeyed, the model that Jezebel waves before Ahab's face: "Do you now govern Israel?" (21:7). Rulers take what they want! And both Jezebel and Ahab understand land to be something that represents only monetary value and thus can traded, bought, and sold—or taken—at will.

This story is about old covenantal ways colliding with human power and initiative unfounded in covenantal concerns about justice, compassion, and *shalom*. The judicial, political, and religious systems fail to protect an innocent man. Who then can stand against this kind of might, this kind of disdain for humanity?

Elijah and the God of Elijah, Yahweh. The prophet may be Ahab's enemy, but he is a fierce friend to God and to all who suffer under tyranny. While Ahab strolls through his new piece of property, envisioning rows of cucumbers and mounds of melons, thinking that he has gotten away with murder, God has set in motion a new initiative that will give hope and courage to all other Naboths who wonder if they must give up their backbone and land and whatever else tyrants might want. How would the Mosaic covenant allow us to reenvision just and godly rule and the proper relationship of ruler and ruled before God?

PSALM 32 (RCL, BCP)
PSALM 32:1-2, 5, 7, 11 (RC)
PSALM 32:1-8 (BCP ALT.)

This psalm of thanksgiving tells the story of healing that comes from forgiveness, a story that has some parallels to that of David in 2 Samuel 12. This psalm/story has four movements: deceit before God about one's sins, a deceit that drains away life and energy; speech that finally acknowledges sin to God; forgiveness of sin and healing by God; and praise to God, who helps the desperate and continues to guide and teach the faithful so that they may remain in "the way you should go" (32:8). This psalm speaks the good news that the unnamed woman of Luke 7:36-50 learns.

PSALM 5:1-8 (RCL ALT.)

This psalm is sung by the Naboths of the world, calling for God to enter situations of injustice in order to protect the innocent and to right wrong. It seems a shame to delete the final three verses. Including verse 10 seems an honest admission that we humans hope God will deal with workers of injustice in some powerful way that resolves injustice.

SECOND READING
GALATIANS 2:15-21 (RCL)
GALATIANS 2:11-21 (BCP)
GALATIANS 2:16, 19-21 (RC)

While Martin Luther and many readers since him have interpreted this passage as a contrast between faith and works, scholars today often invite us to read this text in light of its immediate literary context. Paul's contrast between faith and works occurs in a letter and chapter dealing with Jewish laws regarding Jewish identity, such as laws about circumcision, food, and table fellowship. So when Paul speaks of "works of the law" (v. 16), he most likely refers specifically to laws that divide Jews from Gentiles. Following these laws will not save us, Paul holds. Only "faith in Jesus Christ" (v. 16), as the NRSV trans-

> JESUS' FULL COMMITMENT TO THE DESIRES OF GOD FOR HUMANITY'S SALVATION IS WHAT HAS RESTORED OUR RELATIONSHIP WITH GOD AND ONE ANOTHER.

lates it, makes us just and whole. Scholars point to the possibility that this phrase may very well be "faith *of* Jesus Christ." In other words, Jesus' full commitment to the desires of God for humanity's salvation is what has restored our relationship with God and one another. What Christ has accomplished is blasphemous ("sin," v. 17) to some, but a wholly new way of life to Paul and many other Jesus followers who accept the faithful work of Jesus Christ as "the grace of God" (v. 21) and an act of freedom and love—the tearing down of walls that divide us (v. 18).

THE GOSPEL
LUKE 7:36—8:3 (RCL, RC)
LUKE 7:36-50 (BCP, RC ALT.)

Our Gospel lesson tells a story of two contrasting characters—Simon the Pharisee and an unnamed woman. Simon has invited Jesus to his home for dinner, a home well enough known in the community for the woman to find. Most likely, a large dining table graces the room, surrounded by couches for reclining guests, Jesus one of them. Standing behind Jesus in Simon's home is the second character in this story: an uninvited woman. Weeping, she bends down to bathe Jesus' feet with her tears, to dry them with her hair, and to anoint them. We never hear her speak, but her tears as well as her actions speak. They reveal a woman filled with grief who chooses a path of utmost humility born of deep yearning.

PREACHING ABOUT THIS TEXT PERMITS US TO LOOK AT PRIDE AND HUMILITY IN AN AGE THAT TEACHES THE SIGNIFICANCE OF SELF-ESTEEM.

Simon speaks little as well, but the narrator permits us to hear his inner thoughts as he watches the woman and Jesus, and these thoughts reveal a man closed to people who do not meet his standards. He sits in secret judgment of both the woman and Jesus, confident of his own analysis of the situation: Jesus cannot be a prophet of God, for how could he be so and allow this sinful woman to touch him?

Both Simon and the woman are present in our story because of one figure, Jesus, who has drawn their notice for different reasons and now becomes the center of attention. He has been observing these two characters carefully, reading Simon's mind and the woman's life, and what he has noticed in them is rather astonishing. In his parable of the two debtors, he says in essence that Simon and the woman are really very much the same. They are both debtors, sinners! Perhaps one owes more than the other, but both owe. And then Jesus forgives the one who seems to owe more, the woman.

The story of Simon and the uninvited woman brings to mind a saying of one of the desert mothers of Egypt, Amma Syncletica, whose *Life and Regimen* was written by Pseudo-Athanasius in the fifth century: "Just as it is impossible to be at the same moment both a plant and a seed, so it is impossible for us to be surrounded by worldly honor and at the same time to bear heavenly fruit."[1] Amma Syncletica's life was a testimony to this wisdom. Born into a wealthy Christian family in Alexandria, she sold all her family owned and gave this money to the poor after her parents and brothers died. She then took her remaining sister, who was blind, to a makeshift sanctuary outside the city—a tomb—where they lived for many years. Other women began to gather around her, and she served as their spiritual mother, or *amma*, always reminding them to relinquish the things that might stand in their way to God.

Preaching about this text permits us to look at pride and humility in an age that teaches the significance of self-esteem. Simon has social standing and status, education and learning, enough wealth for dinner parties and guests, and he has, or so he believes, what some in his particular social circle prize perhaps most of all: moral rectitude. In his eyes, he is a righteous man. In contrast to Simon, the unnamed woman puts aside all worries about honor and shame, appearance and reputation, in order to find Jesus. She comes uninvited into the company of men—she a woman known in the community as a sinner (we are not told her sins)—and tenderly cares for Jesus, whose forgiveness permits us to understand her grief as repentance. One might liken her to a prodigal daughter who returns home in longing, too sorrowful to worry about shame. But Simon, so caught up in his analysis of righteousness and purity, is entirely untouched by this homecoming enacted under his own roof. She is just a sinner. His pride in his own righteousness, in his reputation as the upstanding Simon, is his undoing. It leaves him blind to his own debts and the one before him who could and would cancel them. In the end, the uninvited woman is invited by Jesus to new life and possibility. Her humility has touched the heart of Jesus.

One of the early church monastic leaders who thought deeply about humility and its significance in our lives was St. Benedict. Benedictine sister and author Joan D. Chittister writes that the Rule of Benedict teaches that humility is the realization that "human limitation is the gift that relates us to God, to the world, to the self, and to others. Pride drives a wedge between us and reality; humility is its glue." The first of St. Benedict's twelve principles of humility is the most important, for it creates the foundation of one's entire way of life in community: "the *memoria dei*, 'the awareness of God,' at all times, in all places, at the center of all things." This awareness permits us to learn, Chittister writes, that God "is not a goal to be reached; God is a presence to be recognized."[2] From this foundational principle that reorients our lives from self to divine Presence, all the other principles flow: how we bear ourselves, how we speak, how we live in community, and to what degree we may reveal ourselves to others. In all things, we live out of the humility that comes in recognizing God's presence among us.

In Luke's story, the unnamed woman is the only one who seems to recognize the God-with-us of Jesus, the one who has authority in her life and over her losses, who forgives and renews. Even though we have no words from her confessing Jesus as Lord, she alone, of all the guests in Simon's dining room, knows to whom she may reveal herself and find new life. She is our model in her humility and honesty.

The final verses in the longer RCL and RC reading are an interesting addition to the story of the unnamed woman, for they name three women and refer to "many others" who join Jesus in his ministry. For centuries, the church taught that Mary Magdalene, mentioned in 8:2, was the unnamed woman of 7:36-50 and that Mary/the unnamed woman was a prostitute. Biblical criticism has finally caught up with these assumptions and demonstrated their problematic nature. What we have in the first four verses of chapter 8 is a rare look at the women in Jesus' life. We see that they share his company and even provide for his needs. As a whole, this entire lesson is a fascinating look into the lives of some of the first followers of Jesus—women who recognized their need and chose the path of humility: God-awareness. Perhaps the unnamed woman was one of the women who traveled with Jesus.

> IN LUKE'S STORY, THE UNNAMED WOMAN IS THE ONLY ONE WHO SEEMS TO RECOGNIZE THE GOD-WITH-US OF JESUS, THE ONE WHO HAS AUTHORITY IN HER LIFE AND OVER HER LOSSES, WHO FORGIVES AND RENEWS.

Notes

1. Amma Syncletica, *The Life of Blessed Syncletica by Pseudo-Athanasius*, trans. Elizabeth Bryson Bongie (Toronto: Peregrina Publishing, 1995), quoted by Laura Swan, *The Forgotten Desert Mothers: Sayings, Lives, and Stores of Early Christian Women* (New York: Paulist Press, 2001), 60. The information about the life of Amma Syncletica also comes from this source (p. 42).

2. Joan D. Chittister, *Heart of Flesh: A Feminist Spirituality for Women and Men* (Grand Rapids, Mich.: Eerdmans, 1998), 98.

FOURTH SUNDAY AFTER PENTECOST

FOURTH SUNDAY AFTER PENTECOST

TWELFTH SUNDAY IN ORDINARY TIME / PROPER 7
JUNE 24, 2007

REVISED COMMON	EPISCOPAL (BCP)	ROMAN CATHOLIC
Isa. 65:1-9 or 1 Kgs. 19:1-4 (5-7) 8-15a	Zech. 12:8-10; 13:1	Zech. 12:10-11; 13:1
Ps. 22:19-28 or Psalms 42 and 43	Ps. 63:1-8	Ps. 63:2, 3-4, 5-6, 8-9
Gal. 3:23-29	Gal. 3:23-29	Gal. 3:26-29
Luke 8:26-39	Luke 9:18-24	Luke 9:18-24

FIRST READING
ISAIAH 65:1-9 (RCL)

The image of God that opens this passage is poignant. Walter Brueggemann points out that the God who calls out, "Here I am!" (v. 1) is the same God of comfort we find in the Isaiah 40 "'gospel' pronouncement: 'Here is your God!'"[1] But in our text, God receives no joyful response. The people to whom God calls are now "following their own devices" (v. 2): worshiping other gods, seeking the dead for oracles (although the *living* God calls to them). The prophet uses a verb that often describes what God's people have promised: to *keep* God's covenant and precepts (*naṣar*; Deut. 33:9; Ps. 119:33-34). But now the people "sit among the graves and spend their nights *keeping secret vigil*" (NIV; *naṣar*, v. 4). Those who have violated their promises to God will be punished, but for the grapes that still yield juice for wine—God's people who remain a blessing—a way forward opens once again. In our Gospel lesson, we meet one who unwillingly dwells in the tombs. Here we meet those who choose deathly ways and places even though the God of life awaits with open arms.

1 KINGS 19:1-4 (5-7) 8-15a (RCL ALT.)

Fresh from winning a contest against the prophets of Baal, Elijah hightails it out of Queen Jezebel's reach as soon as he hears that the queen, patron of the defeated prophets (18:19), has put out a contract on his life. His courage evaporates. He collapses in the wilderness, exhausted, ready to give up on life. To God, Elijah twice tells the story of his flight and then his sense of aloneness: "I alone am left" (19:10, 14). But his report misses some key points: that the people who observed Elijah's victory confessed their faith in the God of Israel (18:39) and that Elijah is not alone, for the palace steward has told him that a hundred prophets of God are hidden from Jezebel (18:3-16). Perhaps this story gets at our temptation to think that we are alone, especially when we feel discouraged, or that we alone count in the crucial work. Perhaps it's about fear that clouds our faith and sense of reality. Perhaps it gets at God's patience with our discouragement, seen in the ministrations of angels (19:5-7). Or maybe it's about the incredible power of God who splits rocks and quakes the earth but finally reveals God's self to a discouraged faithful prophet in silence. Indeed, God is generous to Elijah throughout his flight. But in the end, God lets Elijah know that this wilderness experience is a temporary retreat. God has a new, even more dangerous plan for Elijah!

> THIS STORY GETS AT OUR TEMPTATION TO THINK THAT WE ARE ALONE, ESPECIALLY WHEN WE FEEL DISCOURAGED, OR THAT WE ALONE COUNT IN THE CRUCIAL WORK.

ZECHARIAH 12:8-10; 13:1 (BCP)
ZECHARIAH 12:10-11; 13:1 (RC)

Zechariah wrote in a time of hope. The Persian Empire was in a state of chaos, facing Babylonian rebellion. It seemed that the Jewish people were just about to experience liberation with the fall of their old master. As Zechariah writes, it had been a "day of small things" (4:10) for the returned exiles. But in this oracle the prophet speaks of a day of the immense: renewal of the nation, return of Davidic rule, and destruction of the nation's enemies. But there is more: renewal of the people's hearts with compassion and cleansing from all sin. The prophet looks longingly for a day when God will do what no human can.

RESPONSIVE READING
PSALM 22:19-28 (RCL)

This response moves from the anguished desperation of someone at the edge of life to praise that ripples out from the individual to encompass the entire community—the congregation, the poor, the ends of the earth, the families of the nations, posterity. Set against the backdrop of Isaiah 65:1-9, this text perhaps is the response of one who has turned to God at the sound of God's "Here I am!"

PSALMS 42 AND 43 (RCL ALT.)

These psalms could be the laments of Elijah or the possessed man of Luke 8, discouraged by tribulation, in search of God and yet unsure of God's fidelity. They are the honest expression of desolation and so belong, doubts and all, in synagogue and church. Where else are we to bring the realities of our lives?

PSALM 63:1-8 (BCP)
PSALM 63:2, 3-4, 5-6, 8-9 (RC)

This psalm comes from one who has lived too long in the presence of constraint and threat (vv. 9-10), experienced as withering barrenness. The only remedy for this kind of shriveling up is the abundance of God, who waters our thirsty lives, feeds our hungry souls, demonstrates power in our feebleness, and upholds us when we fall.

SECOND READING
GALATIANS 3:23-29 (RCL, BCP)
GALATIANS 3:26-29 (RC)

Reading this part of Galatians is somewhat like sitting down in an oak-lined study with the family lawyer Paul. An ancient will lies upon the desk, made out to Abraham by (the still-living) God (3:15-18), and a host of possible offspring crowd into the study to hear what this document means for their futures. Before our portion of this discussion opens, Paul explains that Jesus Christ alone has inherited one of the promises made to Abraham: in and through Jesus the blessing given to Abraham by God is now available to all peoples. This inheritance is finally to be portioned out!

We can see hands in the air. Someone asks, "Yes, but I'm related to Abraham by blood. Does this mean nothing?" The explanations that follow take some exceptional turns that continue this legal family discussion: (a) all those related to Abraham by blood have been under the supervision of the law, like minors under the protective eye of the "disciplinarian" (v. 24), the *paidagōgos* or family slave charged with watching over the children, keeping them from harm, essentially given the right to command them[2] (the NRSV "imprisoned and guarded" of v. 23 is too negative); (b) now that the inheritor Christ Jesus has come, all these children are coming into their majority; (c) since the blessing has been activated for all peoples, all who claim Jesus as Savior are adopted into the family through baptism and come into their majority as well; (d) the ancient models of Hellenistic and Jewish hierarchy that separate people into groups of more or less power and significance are abolished.[3] This is a new family in which all are full members and kin. And what does this coming into our majority mean for us? Clothing ourselves with Christ, living as our Savior and Brother did, utterly faithful to God.

Julia A. J. Foote was born in 1823 in New York to parents who had been slaves. Sent into service early in her life and cruelly treated by her mistress, she found deep comfort in the Bible. When she was older, she had a vision in which God called her to preach—something she resisted because she, like her church, opposed the idea of women preachers. When she finally began preaching, she was excommunicated from her church. She found strength and comfort in Galatians 3:28 as well as other New Testament texts. Of Ephesians 6:21, she writes, "When Paul said, 'Help those women who labor with me in the Gospel,' he certainly meant that they did more than to pour out tea."[4] She also faced considerable racism and writes of being forced to sit on the deck of a boat because white passengers would not permit her in the cabin. Near the close of her autobiography, she writes, "Sisters, shall not you and I unite with the heavenly host in the grand chorus? If so, you will not let what man may say or do, keep you from doing the will of the Lord or using the gifts you have for the good of others."[5] How can we today more fully live out the truth of our family? How can we more fully live out our great freedom to be like our Brother, the embodiment of faithfulness to God?

> WHAT DOES THIS COMING INTO OUR MAJORITY MEAN FOR US? CLOTHING OURSELVES WITH CHRIST, LIVING AS OUR SAVIOR AND BROTHER DID, UTTERLY FAITHFUL TO GOD.

THE GOSPEL
LUKE 8:26–39 (RCL)

Today's miracle story appears right after the story about Jesus' calming the stormy waves of the lake. Jesus steps from the boat of now-serene waters onto firm ground and immediately meets another storm, this time in human form: a man possessed by demons. That Luke describes the possessed as "a man of the city" (v. 27)—in other words, a man used to living among others and following the usual conventions most of us city dwellers follow—suggests how far this man has fallen. He wears no clothes. His home is the tombs. He greets Jesus shouting "at the top of his voice" (v. 28). But these signs of his desolation are just the symptoms of an even deeper loss: the loss of himself. When he begins to speak, we do not hear the man speak. Instead, the unclean spirit that manifests itself as multiple demons speaks. Bound by humans who fear him, bound by demons who possess him, this man has lost almost everything as he is driven far from his home. The tomb dwelling of the man suggests his death-in-life. And the defeat of this death-in-life is the drowning of the possessed swine, for the demons do not escape the abyss but return to the lake, symbol of the primordial watery chaos defeated by the Creator, here by Jesus, "Son of the Most High God" (v. 28).

This story is about what it means to fall to the bottom of life where all is lost, and life itself becomes a way of death. The man of the city has lost his community, his very own self. Those who once knew him as friend, colleague, or brother now know him as community menace and failure. Have we not known people who have battled these powers beyond their control? Perhaps we have known what it is to be at the mercy of powers that have no mercy.

> JESUS UNDERSTANDS OUR WILDERNESS ENCOUNTERS AND CAN RESTORE US WITH THE GIFT OF THE CALMED WATERS OF INNER BEING AND PURPOSE.

They drive us away from all we know and love to the very brink of life—the tombs. Luke writes that they drive this man "into the wilds" (*erēmos*, v. 29), an interesting word choice, for Jesus too has journeyed into the wilderness (*erēmos*, 4:1) where he has battled forces that sought to undercut his unique calling and personhood. Jesus understands our wilderness encounters and can restore us with the gift of the calmed waters of inner being and purpose.

Perhaps we can also identify with the people from nearby towns and farms who arrive to see what has happened to the man. Interestingly, they respond with fear. They hurry Jesus back into his boat and gratefully see him gone. We humans get so used to the patterns of our lives—the dysfunctions, the failures, the unresolved problems—that we sometimes resign ourselves to defeat or sometimes try the shackles again and again and again. Striking out in radically new directions is frightening indeed, opening everything up once again to our sense of futility and pain. Better to drive the hope away and live with familiar defeat. This story is a story of hope for both the possessed man and the community, if they will claim it.

LUKE 9:18-24 (BCP, RC)

Jesus asks the disciples to report who the crowds say he is and then asks the disciples who they think he is. Peter answers that Jesus is "the Messiah of God" (v. 20). Jesus then explains what lies before him—in other words, what his experience as God's Messiah will be: suffering, rejection, death, and raising. But Jesus quickly

> JESUS CALLS US TO LIVE WITH SUCH FAITHFULNESS TO THE REALM OF GOD THAT WE ARE WILLING TO ENDURE REJECTION SO THAT ALL MAY KNOW THAT THEY ARE SONS AND DAUGHTERS OF GOD.

turns to what his life means for his disciples: they are to follow his example. The questions that Jesus asks the disciples about his own identity become, in essence, the questions that we Christians are invited to ask about our identity: Who am I? Am I a follower of Jesus? Jesus speaks of the signs of those who follow him: denying the self, taking up the cross daily, following Jesus, and having new priorities. The call to self-denial and different priorities is a call to step beyond the narrow interests and concerns in our own lives only. Jesus' life, death, and resurrection point to a more encompassing goal—the salvation of all humanity—that invites and needs our participation. Jesus calls us to live with such faithfulness to the realm of God that we are willing to endure rejection so that all may know that they are sons and daughters of God. Jesus' call to pick up the cross is rooted in the realization that suffering is not a closed door or a locked room. It is part of the path of new life that also includes joy. We walk this path of both joy and sorrow with Jesus—forerunner and companion. As Dietrich Bonhoeffer writes, using the image of the yoke as well, "Under his yoke we are certain of his nearness and communion." When we lift up our cross, we discover Jesus with us.[6] And that is the joy!

Notes

1. Walter Brueggemann, *Isaiah 40–66*, Westminster Bible Companion (Louisville: Westminster John Knox Press, 1998), 239.

2. Frank J. Matera, *Galatians*, Sacra Pagina series, vol. 9 (Collegeville, Minn.: The Liturgical Press, 1992), 139.

3. Paul responds to two models of hierarchy that inform the lives of those in the churches of Galatia: the rule of the Hellenistic household by the *paterfamilias*, the foundation of a successful state, according to Aristotle's political thought; and the ordering of the ancient Jewish community that places males above females and Gentiles entirely outside the Jewish community. See Judith Plaskow, *Standing Again at Sinai: Judaism from a Feminist Perspective* (San Francisco: HarperSanFrancisco, 1990), who writes of "the Otherness of women" at the center of the Sinai covenant (p. 25).

4. Julia A. J. Foote, *A Brand Plucked from the Fire: An Autobiographical Sketch* (Cleveland: W. F. Schneider, 1879), reprinted in *Sisters of the Spirit: Three Black Women's Autobiographies of the Nineteenth Century*, ed. William L. Andrews (Bloomington, Ind.: Indiana University Press, 1986), 209.

5. Ibid., 227.

6. Dietrich Bonhoeffer, *The Cost of Discipleship*, rev. ed. (New York: Collier, 1959), 103.

FIFTH SUNDAY AFTER PENTECOST

Thirteenth Sunday in Ordinary Time / Proper 8
July 1, 2007

Revised Common	Episcopal (BCP)	Roman Catholic
1 Kgs. 19:15-16, 19-21 or 2 Kgs. 2:1-2, 6-14	1 Kgs. 19:15-16, 19-21	1 Kgs. 19:16b, 19-21
Psalm 16 or Ps. 77:1-2, 11-20	Psalm 16 or 16:5-11	Ps. 16:1-2, 5, 7-8, 9-10, 11
Gal. 5:1, 13-25	Gal. 5:1, 13-25	Gal. 5:1, 13-18
Luke 9:51-62	Luke 9:51-62	Luke 9:51-62

First Reading
1 KINGS 19:15-16, 19-21 (RCL, BCP)
1 KINGS 19:16b, 19-21 (RC)

For background information, please see the comments on the RCL alternative reading for the Fourth Sunday after Pentecost. Our text begins with Elijah's new marching orders from God: to anoint two new kings and one new prophet. To this point in the story, Elijah has been discouraged, feeling alone in his work and burdened by its danger. Having fled to the wilderness and Mt. Horeb/Sinai, he is sent back to Israel and to assignments yet more dangerous: initiating revolution in two kingdoms. God's response to Elijah is not warm and fuzzy, but it is a response that demonstrates God's continuing power and presence in the world.

ELISHA IS CALLED FROM A LIFE THAT FOLLOWS THE CYCLE OF THE SEASONS TO A LIFE OF UNPREDICTABILITY AND SURPRISE.

Elijah's first stop is to find his apprentice and successor, Elisha. While Elijah does not anoint Elisha, he throws his mantle over him, an act that signifies God's call. Elisha will wear the clothes of—take on the life of—his teacher. Elijah permits him to kiss his parents good-bye and to prepare a farewell feast for all whom he leaves.

Elijah has called Elisha to a life of loyalty to God and thus of grave danger. Good-byes are fitting. The slaughter of the oxen marks Elisha's break with his previous life.

Our text tells the story of disruptions in our lives that come from God's initiatives. Elijah is mobilized from despair to new service to God. Elisha is called from a life that follows the cycle of the seasons to a life of unpredictability and surprise. Behind this new call and energy is a God for whom human governance is so important that rulers and nations bear continual divine scrutiny and justice, as do poor widows and children—those who most clearly bear the brunt of human misrule. And the role of the spokesperson of God who stands up to power, despite threat, is crucial. God prepares for the time when Elijah will no longer be God's prophet—and when Ahab and Jezebel will no longer rule Israel. The disruptions in our lives are sometimes God's preparations for the future.

2 KINGS 2:1-2, 6-14 (RCL ALT.)

This text tells the story of Elijah's chariot ride and Elisha's new power. It's a story full of bold images that elude easy understanding. The long journey of master and student (vv. 2-5) builds the story's suspense while suggesting the close relationship between these two men, for Elisha refuses to leave his master's side.

The parting of the Jordan keeps in sight the dangerous work of these two. Like Moses, Elijah has been working to liberate those who live under the unjust rule of Pharaoh Ahab and consort Jezebel. Crossing into the wilderness and freedom, Elijah experiences his own exodus from a life of hard duty and threat to the promised land of God's own presence. Elisha's return across a parted Jordan is a return to an Israel so like Egypt that it needs the continued service of God's spokesman. Elie Wiesel comments on Elisha's last request of Elijah. Is this an acceptable request of a loyal follower—to be greater than one's teacher? Why does Elijah not respond in anger to this vainglorious request? As Wiesel sees it, both Elijah and Elisha see the humanity of the moment of their parting and yet see beyond this moment to its larger meanings. Restating the older prophet's final words, Wiesel writes:

> CROSSING INTO THE WILDERNESS AND FREEDOM, ELIJAH EXPERIENCES HIS OWN EXODUS FROM A LIFE OF HARD DUTY AND THREAT TO THE PROMISED LAND OF GOD'S OWN PRESENCE.

You want your powers to be twice as great as mine? If you see me go away, if you know how to look, how to participate in all events, if you know how to face pain and despair and go beyond them, and if later you will be capable of telling about them, your wish will be granted: you will have my powers and yours as well.

And you will need them. I am your master but you are the survivor. I thought I was alone, and I was—and still am—but now you are with me and you too will

be alone, you already are. You will speak and you will need great strength and good
fortune to make yourself heard. . . . And yet, the fire that will carry me away will not
stay with me; it will stay with you.[1]

This story of transition invites us to ponder how we mentor those who follow us. How do we prepare them for the challenges ahead, giving them the strength and confidence to claim the presence of God's power in their lives? In the end, the giving of God's power is a mystery that no human can control. Nonetheless, this story is about the pivotal point in life when a student recognizes and claims her or his authority and when a teacher recognizes the time to bless and release the student.

RESPONSIVE READING
PSALM 16 (RCL, BCP)
PSALM 16:5-11 (BCP ALT.)
PSALM 16:1-2, 5, 7-8, 9-10, 11 (RC)

This psalm is a song of trust in God's faithfulness. Perhaps it is the song of those in danger at this moment, Elijahs who after regaining their footing confess God's presence even in danger, a presence that will bring blessing. It is a song that comes from long experience that has led to growing trust: even in trouble God has not abandoned me, and I can claim this hope and the larger goodness of life and God's purposes even now. This is a song we have to grow into.

PSALM 77:1-2, 11-20 (RCL ALT.)

This psalm opens with the psalmist in deep anguish, refusing to be comforted, except by God's action here and now. The psalmist looks to the past for evidence of Yahweh's mighty and loyal presence. The memory of the exodus, especially the crossing of the Red Sea, closes the psalm, leaving the next move to God. Perhaps the anguish and anxiety of this psalm underlie the final request of Elisha. The mighty Elijah departs. O God, how will we see your hand in the future?

SECOND READING
GALATIANS 5:1, 13-25 (RCL, BCP)
GALATIANS 5:1, 13-18 (RC)

This text is one of the emancipation proclamations of the early church. Paul opens it with the powerful statement, "For freedom Christ has set us free.

Stand firm, therefore, and do not submit again to a yoke of slavery" (v. 1). The verb of the last clause can also be translated "do not be subjected to" or "loaded down with" (*enechō*). As Hans Dieter Betz comments, "Both meanings recall the imagery of cruel subjection of the slaves under their masters, and the heavy burden of suppression which the enslaved have to bear."[2] What has enslaved the people? One is a master who has served a good and useful purpose in the past. The other is a master whom none should ever serve.

The first master is, as verses 2-12 make clear, the law. In particular, Paul refers to circumcision and other laws that distinguish Jews from Gentiles. Paul does not mean that the laws of God mean nothing, for he refers to the law positively in verse 14, and the law has served well in the past (see 3:15—4:7). But for Paul, the Spirit and life by the Spirit have replaced the law. Paul seems to be saying that the underlying principle of the law—love of God and of one another—the principle demonstrated by Jesus Christ, is what characterizes living by the Spirit. This kind of life means voluntary love and service to one another, not self-absorption and self-indulgence.

The second master from whom Christians have freedom is the flesh. Paul is not mounting a Platonic argument against the body and for the spirit. The catalog of "works of the flesh" in verses 19-21 includes works that involve much more than just the body. The flesh refers to the life that has nothing to do with God's desires for humankind, in particular, with love for one's neighbor.

Taking the place of both of these masters is the Spirit, whom Paul sees as our guide. What, then, does Paul mean by our new freedom? The NEB translates verse 25 in a way that is helpful: "If the Spirit is the source of our life, let the Spirit also direct our course." Let me tell a little parable that will hopefully make things clearer. Last fall, I planted a Leland cypress in my backyard. This tree came tied to a long stake. But when I planted it, I realized that the stake was too short, and the tree was hobbled. The stake had served the tree up to a certain point, but the tree now needed to be liberated from that stake so that it could rely on the strength from within its own trunk to be the tree it is and one day to produce the cones it has been created to produce. For Paul, the law is much like the stake, an outer rule applied to our lives, in many ways restricting our lives. But the Spirit is the divine sap flowing freely from within and creating in us a new life lived out of loving generosity. Spirit-enlivened and -led followers of Jesus *will*, as a matter of course, produce the fruits nourished by the Spirit, and not because of obedience to the law. Spirit sap means Spirit fruit.

A SERMON ON THIS TEXT MIGHT LOOK AT PAUL'S UNDERSTANDING OF FREEDOM THAT CHALLENGES MANY OF US WHO HAVE LEARNED TO UNDERSTAND FAITHFULNESS AS OBEYING THE RULES.

A sermon on this text might look at Paul's understanding of freedom that challenges many of us who have learned to understand faithfulness as obeying the rules. Perhaps rigid adherence to rules, what Paul describes as a heavy yoke, has killed the S/spirit of some in our churches and homes. Paul is in no way antinomian. But he speaks of a freedom that is about spaciousness in life, not strict rule-abiding. How do we learn new, freer ways that open us and our communities to fresh and vigorous Spirit-life? How do we factor in the maturing of our children as we teach them a larger loyalty to God than "simply" to a list of rules?

THE GOSPEL
LUKE 9:51-62 (RCL, BCP, RC)

Our text opens what some scholars call the "travel account" of Luke. The powerful opening verse provides an important context for the next chapters. According to the Synoptic Gospels, Jesus leaves Galilee for Jerusalem for the first and only time in his ministry. Jerusalem is linked with Jesus' destiny and with the mystery of his being "taken up" (v. 51), a reference to Jesus' ascension (see Acts 1:2, 11, 22 for similar wording), implying all that

> THE DEAD WHOM JESUS HOPES TO RAISE ARE THOSE WHO NEED THE GOOD NEWS OF GOD'S REALM, NOT A FINAL RESTING PLACE WITHIN THE EARTH.

precedes the ascension as well. Jesus "set his face to go to Jerusalem," Luke writes (v. 51), describing Jesus as single-minded in his determination. The disciples are indignant when Samaritan villagers reject Jesus, and they are eager to try out their new powers (9:1-6, 10) in ways reminiscent of Elijah's fiery judgments (see 2 Kgs. 1:10, 12). But not even the rejection of these villagers throws Jesus off his stride. He is on his way! It seems that Jesus is prepared to experience rejection without curses and without retaliation. He instead rebukes the disciples, perhaps for their quick willingness to condemn and destroy. In this brief scene, we see Jesus fully committed to his course and yet tolerant of others, even when they reject his presence.

In verses 57-62, we hear some of the exchanges Jesus has with potential disciples who join him "along the road" (v. 57). To one person who promises to follow Jesus anywhere, Jesus warns of the peril and discomfort of the road. Even wild animals have homes, but Jesus and those who travel with him will know homelessness along the way, for certainly other villagers will refuse to take them in, and then there are the realities of life on the move that mean camping out in the middle of nowhere. To two potential followers who claim Jesus as Lord, but have things they must take care of first, Jesus points out the priority of his journey. His words seem harsh and heartless. Leave a dead father without my presence at the burial? Leave without saying good-bye to my family? Why, even Elijah allowed Elisha time to say his farewells.

Jesus' words remind me of my father, up at 4:00 on the morning before one of our cross-continental family trips, doing the final packing, already feeling the burdens of the journey, and without his usual cheer. He was determined to get a half day's drive in before the heat began to rise and we stopped for breakfast on the first of what would be three or four days' driving. Jesus is feeling the urgency of his last journey and the burdens before him. The dead whom Jesus hopes to raise are those who need the good news of God's Realm, not a final resting place within the earth. And the seed that the one who plows the earth will soon sow is none other than the life-giving Word of God (see Luke 8:4-15). This journey will concern immense and pressing life-and-death matters. And Jesus makes this point clear with his sharp replies. This is the other side of the reality of following Jesus. Yes, my burden is light, and my yoke easy, but . . . !

This text challenges all of us who hear it, for it calls those of us who follow Jesus to leave the predictable and treasured elements of our lives to accept sacrifice, surprise, and unexpected fellowship. There is a paradox in what Jesus is calling for: standing firm in new ways that call followers to be on the move. In his study of Celtic spirituality, Ray Simpson, the founder of the interdenominational community of Aidan and Hilda, a body of believers on many continents, writes of the tradition of Celtic monks who traveled far from their communities in answer to God's leading.[3] Simpson claims that "Celtic Christians have retained this ability to sit loose to the ties that bind, and to follow their inspirations."[4] The tradition of journey epics in Irish lore—for example, the ninth- or tenth-century epic of Brendan's Atlantic voyage—opens the motif of the journey to many levels of interpretation: the journey of the disciples who preach the good news of Jesus in distant places; the journey of the individual pilgrim learning to follow Jesus (like the disciples learning not to call down fire on the Samaritans); the journey of followers who leave behind what is dear but no longer living in order to make room for what is vibrantly alive.

THIS TEXT CHALLENGES ALL OF US WHO HEAR IT, FOR IT CALLS THOSE OF US WHO FOLLOW JESUS TO LEAVE THE PREDICTABLE AND TREASURED ELEMENTS OF OUR LIVES TO ACCEPT SACRIFICE, SURPRISE, AND UNEXPECTED FELLOWSHIP.

This Lukan text also invites us to consider what the geography of this journey means. In the opening verses of this text, we learn that Jesus of Galilee is traveling to Jerusalem. Virgilio Elizondo, parish priest and founder of the Mexican-American Cultural Center in San Antonio, comments that to the elitist Jews of Jerusalem, Galilee was just a backwater region of Jews too ignorant to study the law, let alone pronounce it properly, and too lax to follow the law, some of them too accommodating of non-Jews. Elizondo writes of God's choice of a Galilean and his band of Galilean followers to bring the good news of a new kingdom to the very center of power, Jerusalem, where Jesus would confront structures of power that resist the kingdom:

> As his Galilean followers were called to go with him, so today his followers are likewise called to go with him and in him to the Jerusalems of today's world....
>
> Fidelity to Christ means to stay with him on his way to Jerusalem; to depart from that way would be infidelity.... Conformity to the ways of the world would be a betrayal to the way of Christ, which is that of confrontation with the ways of the world.[5]

Are we the Galileans, rejected but specially chosen to carry the good news to places of power? Or are we those who find it hard to welcome "outsiders" with their urgent message that upsets our sense of the right way of doing things?

Notes

1. Elie Wiesel, *Five Biblical Portraits* (Notre Dame, Ind.: University of Notre Dame Press, 1981), 66–67. The italics are in Wiesel's text.

2. Hans Dieter Betz, *Galatians: A Commentary on Paul's Letter to the Churches in Galatia*, Hermeneia (Philadelphia: Fortress Press, 1979), 258.

3. Ray Simpson, *Exploring Celtic Spirituality: Historic Roots for Our Future* (London: Hodder & Stoughton, 1995), 45–49.

4. Ibid., 46.

5. Virgilio Elizondo, *Galilean Journey: The Mexican-American Promise* (Maryknoll, N.Y.: Orbis Books, 1983), 104. Elizondo likens the Jerusalem Jews' image of Jews from Galilee to U.S. Anglos' image of Mexican Americans (pp. 50–53).

SIXTH SUNDAY AFTER PENTECOST

FOURTEENTH SUNDAY IN ORDINARY TIME /
PROPER 9
JULY 8, 2007

REVISED COMMON	EPISCOPAL (BCP)	ROMAN CATHOLIC
Isa. 66:10–14 or	Isa. 66:10–16	Isa. 66:10–14c
2 Kgs. 5:1–14		
Ps. 66:1–9 or	Psalm 66 or 66:1–8	Ps. 66:1–3, 4–5, 6–7,
Psalm 30		16, 20
Gal. 6:(1–6) 7–16	Gal. 6:(1–10) 14–18	Gal. 6:14–18
Luke 10:1–11, 16–20	Luke 10:1–12, 16–20	Luke 10:1–12, 17–20
		or 10:1–9

FIRST READING

ISAIAH 66:10–14 (RCL)
ISAIAH 66:10–16 (BCP)
ISAIAH 66:10–14c (RC)

This text occurs in the section of Isaiah often identified as Third Isaiah, the oracles of those who sought to encourage the returned exiles, who had

THE PROPHET PLAYS WITH THE IMAGE OF THE FLOWING MILK OF THE MOTHER, NOW THE RIVER OF PROSPERITY FLOWING FROM EVERYWHERE TO JERUSALEM AT GOD'S BEHEST.

expected such a glorious return but instead found poverty and conflict. It would be best to read all of the verses that develop the image of the rebirth of Jerusalem and her inhabitants, beginning with verse 7. In verses 7–9, the prophet speaks of God the midwife, helping Mother Jerusalem to give birth to a new reality. What God has in mind for this city is so extraordinary that even birth must be made more miraculous: birth before labor and without pain.

Our assigned text begins after this birth scene with the call to joy and consolation. Why? Because birth is fraught with threat and uncertainty for both mother and child, and this birth is successful. And so comes the invitation to the newly born to be nourished and satisfied at the breast of Mother Jerusalem. Once again there will be new life, and even festivity and play, in this old ruined city. Imagine Mother Jerusalem playing with her children on her lap.

In verse 12, the prophet plays with the image of the flowing milk of the mother, now the river of prosperity flowing from everywhere to Jerusalem at God's behest. This image of joyful abundance ascends to an even higher level when God decides that playing the role of midwife for this new city is not enough. In verse 13, God *becomes* the mother, comforting, nursing, renewing the beloved city.

This text is a remarkable passage, not only for the moving image of God as midwife and then mother, but also for the joy that speaks to all of us who encounter times in our lives and world when we are wondering whether we will survive some process of birth that seems fragile and uncertain. God delivers us safely. God holds us in loving arms, breast overflowing with the milk of new life.

2 KINGS 5:1-14 (RCL ALT.)

This text gives us a glimpse into the life of a nation other than Israel where God is at work. In verse 1, we read that God has given victory to Aram, enemy of Israel, and now works to heal this nation's top commander, Naaman. God's dealings with the nations of the world have a mysterious life of their own, not fully explained in the sacred texts of Israel. In our story, God's wisdom and healing are not lodged with the top brass of Aram or Israel, not even with the kings of both nations. God's presence and purpose reside with the lowly—first with the Israelite slave girl who knows of Elisha, then with the servants who accompany Naaman on his quest for healing, and finally with the backwater prophet who ignores court etiquette, sending his servant to communicate with Aram's great commander. Only Naaman's servants, who have long experience with powerlessness and humility, are able to persuade their master to entrust his life to Elisha and Elisha's God. This story raises any number of questions: about God's calling to nations that we consider our enemies; about the unexpected resources for God's word in our communities and nation; about whom we seek for wisdom versus for flattery and what we see as the respect due us.

RESPONSIVE READING

PSALM 66:1-9 (RCL)
PSALM 66 OR 66:1-8 (BCP)
PSALM 66:1-3, 4-5, 6-7, 16, 20 (RC)

This responsive reading is a hymn of praise and thanksgiving to God, whose power surpasses all other powers and yet is mobilized on behalf of God's people. This psalm does not draw on the tender imagery of Isaiah 66, but it gets at the same commitment and passion in the life of God and for God's beloved. When the seventy disciples return to Jesus with reports of their triumph over demons, Jesus' reply echoes this psalm's sense of God's power to deliver us from all forces of destruction.

PSALM 30 (RCL ALT.)

This psalm is a song of thanksgiving for healing. But the experience of a personal earthquake is still so recent and real that the psalmist has not yet forgotten its wrenching or the sense of God's hiddenness. With stark honesty, the psalmist honors the time of weeping and dismay, even if the time of joy now calls for dance and thanksgiving. What a model for all of us in our suffering and healing. This is the song of all Naamans as well as all followers of Jesus, who, like Paul, rejoice in healing and new life.

SECOND READING

GALATIANS 6:(1-6) 7-16 (RCL)
GALATIANS 6:(1-10) 14-18 (BCP)
GALATIANS 6:14-18 (RC)

Often in spring my husband and I pore over seed and plant catalogs as we plan our summer vegetable garden and flowerbeds. The opening image in this reading is all about planning the gardens of our lives. This passage warns the followers of Jesus to choose the seeds they will sow carefully, for there are two seed companies, Flesh (later called World) and Spirit, and they will yield substantially different results at God's end-time harvest. Paul is not arguing against physicality and for a higher life of the mind/spirit. Rather, he compares life given energy and direction by the Spirit with life without this energy and direction.

As our text proceeds, Paul outlines some of the evidence that we are indeed planting seeds from the Spirit Seed Company. First, he mentions "not grow[ing] weary in doing what is right" (v. 9), for example, "work[ing] for the good of all, and especially for those of the family of faith" (v. 10). In commenting on this advice, John Chrysostom writes that Paul envisions a "way of life that comes from grace [and] takes the whole land and sea as the table of mercy, even while it also shows the greater care that is due toward one's household."[1] Loving *all* our neighbors as ourselves (5:14) is essential, even if our love is also to recognize the special bonds of family.

> LOVING *all* OUR NEIGHBORS AS OURSELVES IS ESSENTIAL, EVEN IF OUR LOVE IS ALSO TO RECOGNIZE THE SPECIAL BONDS OF FAMILY.

The second sign of Spirit seeds permits Paul to restate a key theme of Galatians as a whole: refusing to bow to legal requirements, like that of circumcision, that do not recognize the role of Jesus Christ as freedom giver (vv. 12-15). The third sign is living our lives in the "new creation" that God has brought into existence through the work of Jesus Christ. For Paul, living in the new creation means being dead to the old creation, that is, the world and flesh.

Paul closes this text with a blessing of peace upon "those who will follow this rule" (v. 16). Most likely, "this rule" refers to loving one's neighbor, the foundational commandment that Paul quotes in 5:14, as well as to "the law of Christ" in 6:2, probably the example of Jesus in living out this commandment. Many scholars have tried to explain both Paul's sense of welcome freedom from the law and his sense of the law as something positive in the Christian's life. Clearly, Paul does not believe that the law is unimportant, as 5:14 indicates. On the other hand, he disagrees with law that denies the all-encompassing love of God demonstrated in Jesus Christ and draws boundaries between people or leads to a life that seems more about restriction than freedom. The positive and negative sides of the law for Paul come together in his unique understanding of life in the new creation. Paul sees this new life as flowing from and, therefore, reflecting the Spirit. It is not life lived by checking off the dos and don'ts of life, a rote discipline. In this way, Spirit-life is freedom from the law, even if it is also living out the law as Jesus lived it: love for God and for neighbor. (For another pertinent gardening parable, see the comments on the second reading for the Fifth Sunday after Pentecost, above.)

THE POSITIVE AND NEGATIVE SIDES OF THE LAW FOR PAUL COME TOGETHER IN HIS UNIQUE UNDERSTANDING OF LIFE IN THE NEW CREATION.

THE GOSPEL

LUKE 10:1-11, 16-20 (RCL)
LUKE 10:1-12, 16-20 (BCP)
LUKE 10:1-12, 17-20 OR 10:1-9 (RC)

In a passage that echoes the commissioning of the twelve disciples (Luke 9:1-6), this text tells of the commissioning of "seventy others" (10:1). The mission of Jesus is burgeoning within Jesus' own lifetime, moving beyond the initial twelve disciples, a sign of the future spread of the church. These seventy "others" are sent out in twos—perhaps for moral support, perhaps in keeping with the biblical injunctions requiring more than one witness for testimony (Num. 35:30; Deut. 19:15). Jesus first lets these thirty-five pairs know the significance of their mission.

REBECCA J.
KRUGER GAUDINO

They are laborers in a harvest seeking yet other laborers, for the fields are full of ripe grain. Here Jesus refers to the end-time harvest when God gathers all God's people (for instance, Isa. 27:12; Matt. 13:30; Luke 3:17). This work is urgent, and it carries risk. Jesus shifts images as he compares the seventy to lambs sent into the midst of wolves. Doing God's work is not going to be easy in a world that may attack God's emissaries. As Jesus says, these seventy are going ahead of Jesus, to the places he intends to travel (10:1), but by the time we reach verse 16, the seventy go instead of Jesus, or *as Jesus*.

The following instructions comprise the handbook of these early missionaries. Rather than asking the seventy to equip themselves well to meet the challenges ahead, Jesus tells them to leave behind purse, bag, and sandals. In many ways, these instructions call upon the seventy to remain open to life. They are not to come thickly padded with supplies—a credit card for all eventualities, a rucksack full of food, and all-terrain sandals. They will travel light and depend on those whom they meet, as well as upon God, for their needs. In so doing, they will come to know the poverty and/or the wealth of those they encounter. They will walk the paths of the people and know the very land from which they must draw their living—fertile and lush, or rocky and harsh. To be open is to know and to be known.

WHILE THE GREETING OF PEACE IS COMMONPLACE, THESE SEVENTY GIVE NOT JUST A GREETING BUT PEACE ITSELF.

While the seventy are to press on to their destinations and to forgo greetings and news along the way, they are not to make short shrift of courtesy upon arrival. In fact, they must give extravagant greetings at the homes they enter. While the greeting of peace is commonplace, these seventy give not just a greeting but peace itself. This gift appears to be an active sign of God's presence, for it resides where it finds welcome and returns from where there is no welcome.

The handbook continues. The seventy are to be satisfied with the home in which they are first welcomed, and they are to "eat what is set before you; cure the sick" and proclaim the nearness of God's Realm (vv. 8-9). In their vulnerability and poverty, the seventy permit those with whom they reside to give of their own lives. Here the seventy are learning firsthand about the mutuality of God's Realm, accepting gifts from others, giving what they have to share. In their example, they flesh out what God's peace means not only in their own vulnerability and openness, but also in their acts of power and words of good news. This peace is not the *Pax Romana*, enforced by garrisons and weapons. It is the freely offered gift of God that proclaims God's love and welcome but accepts rejection. Jesus instructs the seventy to protest the lack of welcome in towns that turn them away. They may not impose God's presence and Realm, but they must nonetheless warn the people and proclaim the nearness of this Realm.

The last verses of this lesson allow us to learn what happened with this important early mission. Verse 17 says it all: "The seventy returned with joy, saying, 'Lord, in your name even the demons submit to us!'" Jesus' response underlines their success. The submission of demons, Satan's falling from heaven, the treading of snakes and scorpions—all speak of the incredible power of Jesus' new followers. They have successfully confronted the enemy—those powers of destruction that oppose God's coming rule. But Jesus' next words of advice to the seventy are knowing: don't let your great powers go to your head, but rejoice in the gift of life that God has given you.

This passage reminds me of a cookbook that has sat on my kitchen shelf for about fifteen years, *Extending the Table: A World Community Cookbook*, by Joetta Handrich Schlabach. Commissioned by the Mennonite Central Committee, it is in reality a devotional book, for throughout its pages are stories of the "others" who have traveled far and wide bringing God's peace

JESUS' NEW FOLLOWERS HAVE SUCCESSFULLY CONFRONTED THE ENEMY—THOSE POWERS OF DESTRUCTION THAT OPPOSE GOD'S COMING RULE.

to the world. In the foreword to this unique cookbook is the story of two North Americans traveling to the Argentine Chaco,

sitting under a tree and talking with Salustiano Lopez, a Toba Indian church leader. Our interest was to seek his counsel on how North American mission and service organizations should work in the years ahead. We asked how, in Argentina or neighboring countries, *he* would begin to share the gospel with other indigenous people who do not have churches among them. He paused for a moment, and then responded, "I would go and eat their food." He began to weep, and the missionary couple who were our translators wept with him. Nancy and I were also overcome with his simple but powerful response. We knew that these forty-year missionaries and their colleagues had acknowledged the dignity of the indigenous people of the Chaco by eating their food, sleeping in their houses, and learning and recording their languages.[2]

A deeply moving prayer from the Canadian First Nations people opens the "Breads" section of this cookbook:

You have come from afar
and waited long and are wearied:
Let us sit side by side
sharing the same bread drawn from the same source
to quiet the same hunger that makes us weak.
Then standing together

let us share the same spirit, the same thoughts
that once again draw us together in friendship and unity and peace.[3]

Perhaps this text's vision of mission could help many of us hesitant about sharing our faith know how we might join these early "others" in this sharing. As Jesus says, the harvest seeks more laborers. In this model of mission, we as Christians are called to live out the good news of God's Realm by first admitting our own neediness (that is, not going about padded and protected) and then identifying with the people with whom we hope to share the good news, bringing Christ to them as guest first: the one who accepts and eats their food in thanksgiving. This openness to others may then create the opportunity for healing and finally proclaiming. What the seventy accomplish is dictated by the people whom they approach and their needs. This mission is not a one-size-fits-all mission applied to people like jam to a piece of toast. From our own vulnerability, we come to know the humanity of others and to build the trust that invites others to reveal that which needs healing (as we reveal our needs) and to create the space for profound conversation about the Ultimate.

WE ARE PART OF GOD'S GREAT GARDENING, SOWING AND REAPING ACROSS THE SEASONS UNTIL THAT GREAT SEASON WHEN THE FINAL HARVEST WILL BE GATHERED.

Another approach to this text might be to look at the vision of our participation in the harvest according to Luke and Paul. According to Luke, Jesus' seventy are called to help with God's harvest. Paul advises the Galatians to choose carefully the seed they will sow, for it will influence the harvest God will find in their lives. These two visions of the Christian life point to our participation in the overarching plans of God. We are never alone but always part of the long line of gardeners who have toiled faithfully. We are the evidence of the sowing and harvesting of others. Now we harvest what others have sown and plant for the future. We are part of God's great gardening, sowing and reaping across the seasons until that Great Season when the final harvest will be gathered.

Notes

1. John Chrysostrom, *Interpretatio Omnium Epistularum Paulinarum*, ed. F. Field (Oxford: Clarendon, 1849–1862), 4:97, quoted in *Galatians, Ephesians, Philippians*, ed. Mark J. Edwards, Ancient Christian Commentary on Scripture, New Testament, vol. 8 (Downers Grove, Ill.: InterVarsity Press, 1999), 98.

2. Paul Longacre, foreword to Joetta Handrich Schlabach, *Extending the Table: A World Community Cookbook* (Scottdale, Pa.: Herald Press, 1991), 7.

3. *Prières d'Ozawamick*, source untraced, in *With All God's People: The New Ecumenical Prayer Cycle*, comp. John Carden (Geneva: WCC Publications, 1989), 223.

SEVENTH SUNDAY AFTER PENTECOST

FIFTEENTH SUNDAY IN ORDINARY TIME /
PROPER 10

JULY 15, 2007

REVISED COMMON	EPISCOPAL (BCP)	ROMAN CATHOLIC
Deut. 30:9-14 or Amos 7:7-17	Deut. 30:9-14	Deut. 30:10-14

Ps. 25:1-10 or
Psalm 82
	Psalm 25 or 25:3-9	Ps. 69:14, 17, 30-31,
		    33-34, 36, 37 or
		    Ps. 19:8, 9, 10, 11

Col. 1:1-14	Col. 1:1-14	Col. 1:15-20
Luke 10:25-37	Luke 10:25-37	Luke 10:25-37

FIRST READING

DEUTERONOMY 30:9-14 (RCL, BCP)
DEUTERONOMY 30:10-14 (RC)

This reading comes from the second covenant ceremony held as the twelve tribes prepare to enter Canaan. Moses reminds the people that they must obey God's commands in order to know the blessings of God. Scholars understand Deuteronomy to have been shaped by the exiles in Babylon, and this chapter certainly evidences this influence. Thus, we have different layers of memory behind our reading: memories of slavery in Egypt and the desert wanderings that followed, and memories of the loss of Jerusalem and the long years of anguish in Babylon. Just

TURNING TO GOD WITH ALL ONE'S BEING HAS IMPLICATIONS FOR LIVING WITH ONE'S NEIGHBORS AS WELL.

as Moses wonders what future lies ahead for the children of those who will enter Canaan, the exiles wonder what future lies ahead for them as they long for the golden days of Israel.

Moses promises God's delight in the people when they obey his commandments "because you turn to the LORD your God with all your heart and with all your soul" (v. 10). Moses refers to the call to this God-focused life as a commandment

126

THE SEASON
AFTER PENTECOST
─────────────
REBECCA J.
KRUGER GAUDINO

in its own right (v. 11) that is neither distant nor hard to grasp. Moses gets at a fundamental principle underlying all the commandments that can become a part of daily speech and thought. As much of Deuteronomy implies, turning to God with all one's being has implications for living with one's neighbors as well.

AMOS 7:7-17 (RCL ALT.)

In this passage set around 750 B.C.E. during the reign of Jeroboam II of Israel, Amos proclaims his third vision of God's judgment against the Northern Kingdom at the Bethel sanctuary. God has measured Israel with a plumb line and found the people to be out of line or warped. Earlier in this book, Amos has described Israel as a nation marked by false worship, injustice, and lack of compassion. With the third vision, God warns the people that destruction is near.

Preaching about this passage affirms God's role in the affairs of nations. No temple, no "king's sanctuary" (v. 13), can protect a nation and people from the plumb line of a God who cares how people worship God and treat the poor. A nation must not forget love of God and love of neighbor. This passage is also about an ordinary person—without the "proper" credentials—who accepts the role of prophet and carries it out with dignity and dedication. Not even the nation's priest(s) can silence someone with a higher claim to authority: "The LORD took me from [teaching kindergarten] . . ." (v. 15). What might a modern-day Amos from somewhere far from our community envision and proclaim to us? Who among us is called to be Amos who sees with new eyes and proclaims God's words in new symbols and media for today's world? This reading invites us to consider the ever-evolving role and message of prophecy in our own midst.

> WHO AMONG US IS CALLED TO BE AMOS WHO SEES WITH NEW EYES AND PROCLAIMS GOD'S WORDS IN NEW SYMBOLS AND MEDIA FOR TODAY'S WORLD?

RESPONSIVE READING

PSALM 25:1-10 (RCL)
PSALM 25 OR 25:3-9 (BCP)

This psalm is a prayer for God's loving guidance. The psalmist prays for forgiveness as well as instruction that leads those who love God to right paths and keeps them within God's careful watch and protection. As in Deuteronomy, covenant keeping is linked with the blessings and protection of God (v. 10).

PSALM 69:14, 17, 30–31, 33–34, 36, 37 (RC)

This response is a plea for deliverance from "deep waters" (v. 14). The psalmist waits for God to hear and answer, "for the LORD hears the needy" (v. 33). The psalmist trusts that God will answer and moves to a call for praise from all creation. This response is the prayer of those who have fallen by the hands of enemies and await the intervention and ministrations of God (and God's faithful).

PSALM 19:8, 9, 10, 11 (RC ALT.)

This reading concerns the Torah and its life-giving qualities. It would be good to add verse 7 to this reading, as it clearly identifies the "law of the LORD" or Torah. While Christians have tended to understand Torah faithfulness as deadening legalism, largely because of misreadings of Paul, this stance does not jibe with our reading. The law is reviving, giving joy and wisdom. Sweet and precious, it leads to "great reward" (v. 11). Surely the understanding that turning one's whole being to God is sweet revival underlies Moses' words in Deuteronomy 30 and Jesus' "right answer" in Luke 10.

PSALM 82 (RCL ALT.)

In this response, we hear God speaking before the divine council, charging its members with injustice and cruelty. They have permitted wickedness to prevail so that the vulnerable suffer and chaos has broken out in earth's macrocosm. Failed and false gods that they are, these members of the council will now die. The psalm ends with a call to God to "judge the earth; for all the nations belong to you!" (v. 8). Only God has proven God's self as protector and caretaker of the world. This psalm lays out some of the charges that God, through Amos, brings against the Northern Kingdom.

SECOND READING
COLOSSIANS 1:1-14 (RCL, BCP)

The opening section of Colossians reads much like a standard letter of the time: opening salutation and thanksgiving. The sentiments sound pretty and nice: be strong, patient, and wise. Nothing particularly noteworthy. And then we hit verse 13: "He has rescued us from the power of darkness and transferred us into the kingdom of his beloved Son." With one verse, we readers are rescued from the quiet drone of nice and transferred to an ancient landscape of turmoil and rescue. Paul speaks in the language of epic, of heroes journeying into kingdoms clouded by death and evil, searching for a beloved, and leading that beloved to safety. Not just one beloved has been rescued; rather, all of us in a mass rescue have been brought into a new kingdom of life and hope, the kingdom of Jesus Christ. More than this, the great epic of rescue from the despairing tyranny of "the power of darkness" (v. 13) has brought us into a new inheritance. We share in the kingdom of Jesus Christ because we have been forgiven of all that would have disallowed our belonging.

Only when we understand this underlying epic story does the rest of this reading come to life. The history of our past rescue (our "redemption," v. 14—an allusion to our rescue from slavery) gives profound meaning to the earlier nice words. Why do we have faith, love, and hope? Why do we bear the fruit of this faith, love, and hope? Because we are amazed at, cannot forget, the rescue that moved us from despair to new possibility. Why should we worry about living lives that evidence "spiritual wisdom and understanding" (v. 9)? Because we are ever grateful to "God our Father" (v. 2) for mounting this rescue, for caring what happened to us, and for incorporating us into a new kingdom and family with many resources. And the instruction to be strong and patient—isn't that just the Stoic response to life? No. In our inheritance, we are granted "all the strength that comes from [God's] glorious power" (v. 11), the incredible power mobilized in our rescue.

> WE SHARE IN THE KINGDOM OF JESUS CHRIST BECAUSE WE HAVE BEEN FORGIVEN OF ALL THAT WOULD HAVE DISALLOWED OUR BELONGING.

When I read this segment of Colossians, I think of my grandparents who were rescued from the Ukraine after the Russian Revolution. As Mennonites, they had suffered greatly at the hands of the Bolsheviks, the Mensheviks, and the bandits who took advantage of the chaos. My grandfather in particular never forgot this rescue and the new life that opened up for him and his family as they emigrated to Canada and began again. For the rest of his life, he voted for the political party that oversaw his and his family's rescue, and he did his part to help those whom he understood to be the "underdogs," as he called them. The fruits of gratitude, loyalty, new energy, love, and patience marked much of his life because of this rescue. You could say that he became a Good Samaritan because he understood what it meant to be trapped in despair and then to discover hope and decide that hope was something he could give others.

COLOSSIANS 1:15-20 (RC)

Scholars have speculated that this text was one of the early church's first hymns about Jesus Christ. It is packed with repeated words that echo huge ideas, with prepositional phrases that locate Jesus everywhere, and with mysterious language that calls to mind ancient texts about Woman Wisdom. The high Christology in this text identifies Jesus as "the image of the invisible God," the one in whom "all the fullness of God was pleased to dwell" (vv. 15, 19). No effort is made to clarify this mystery of Jesus' relationship to both humans and God. Rather, the mystery continues in language that describes Jesus as foremost and supreme: "before all things" (v. 17), "the head of the body," "the beginning," having "first place in everything" (v. 18). One word that appears twice is *firstborn*, or *prōtotokos*: Jesus is "firstborn of all creation" (v. 15) and "firstborn from the dead" (v. 18). While scholars tell us that *prōtotokos* can signify preeminence rather than standing within a family, for the church who believes Jesus' incarnation made and makes all the difference for the future of humankind, this term holds great promise. It boldly links the preeminent Christ with the humble family of humankind. All that the firstborn has done for creation and new creation has also been done for the "saints and faithful brothers and sisters in Christ in Colossae," who share in the grace and peace "from God our Father" (1:2). Luke's lesson about the Good Samaritan is a story about neighbors called to live out Torah in line with Jesus' proclamation of the Realm, but Paul and those who write in his name use the language of family to describe the new social unit created by Jesus Christ the firstborn, who acts out of the authority of the firstborn in ancient family systems to reconcile and save his family.

THE GOSPEL
LUKE 10:25-37 (RCL, BCP, RC)

The story of the Good Samaritan follows a passage in which Jesus thanks God for revealing God's self and power to the seventy disciples while "[hiding] these things from the wise and the intelligent" (10:21). Then Jesus turns to his own disciples, blessing them for seeing and hearing what even prophets and kings have had difficulty understanding. At this very moment, a scholar of the Torah—one of the learned and well-respected who needs help seeing and hearing—stands up "to test Jesus" (v. 25) with a question about inheriting everlasting life. Like many a savvy professor, Jesus turns the tables on this man: "What is written in the law? What do *you* read there?" (v. 26). The lawyer answers with a combination of Deuteronomy 6:5 (the Shema) and Leviticus 19:18—love of God and love of neighbor. Jesus bids the lawyer to follow the law's instruction. But the scholar wants "to justify himself" (v. 29), perhaps to prove that he has followed the law. Seeking a definition of his neighbor, he as a Jew no doubt expects a definition in line with the purity laws. In essence, he expects to discover the limits to the phrase "my neighbor."

The professor, however, shifts the domain of the discussion from "Who is my neighbor?" to "What is love of my neighbor?" Jesus tells the story of a man beset by bandits. Most likely the fallen man is a Jew, or so this Jewish audience will assume. We then hear about a priest and a Levite, two students of the Torah who would know all about loving their neighbors. Seeing the fallen man, the two learned men, however, do not see his place in their lives or God's life. Like the lawyer, they have trouble recognizing the call of God's Realm. Perhaps they fear contamination by a dead body (Num. 5:2; 19:2-13; Lev. 21:1-3), although Robert C. Tannehill reports that the Mishnah permits even a high priest to take care of a neglected body.[1] Perhaps they fear bandits. In the end, only the Samaritan truly sees and hears and is moved to act. Jesus holds up an outsider who also knows the law but whom observant Jews would consider a practitioner of a false Judaism as one who truly demonstrates love.

Preaching on this text invites us to speak about love that crosses boundaries and takes risks. If, indeed, the priest and Levite fear contamination, they do so because of laws that have as their intent the protection of Israel's holiness before a holy God. But at what point does the quest for holiness violate God's commands to love? Certainly all of us in our own communities have regulations intended to safeguard our community. At what point does our allegiance to these laws jeopardize the lives and well-being of our fallen neighbors? Or is it possible that loving God and loving neighbor are at some point incompatible? If the purity laws lie in the background of this story, then Jesus questions laws that purport to honor God while dishonoring God's creation.

Another way to preach about this text is to look more fully at the despised Samaritan. While Jesus does not fill in any brushstrokes about this man's life, or the reality of Samaritans in general, he does not need to. All in his audience understand the basic distrust and hatred between these communities, with the Samaritans cast as apostate. It is interesting, then, that the one who has experienced the prejudice and resentment of observant Jews is the one who finds compassion within himself for the fallen man, probably a Jew. This tale is the story of one who has been rejected and yet has somehow been able to transform this hurt into compassion. Perhaps this man can teach us what it means to understand our own hurts to such an extent that we can respond to our enemies with compassion.

> IF THE PURITY LAWS LIE IN THE BACKGROUND OF THIS STORY, THEN JESUS QUESTIONS LAWS THAT PURPORT TO HONOR GOD WHILE DISHONORING GOD'S CREATION.

A third way to consider this text is to reflect on the ways our own eyes and ears are closed to signs of God's Realm, in particular to God's encompassing love. Jesus seems to be saying that we need to look among those whom we despise for signs of God's presence and power. I think of Ghaffar Khan, also known as Badshah Khan and the Frontier Gandhi, who raised up, among the Pashtun peoples (some of whom today are part of the Taliban) the one and only nonviolent army this earth has known: 100,000 men and women pledged to nonviolence and community service. He and his nonviolent Muslim soldiers helped to win the liberation of India from the British Empire and thereafter protected the homes of Hindus during the violent partition of India and Pakistan.[2] I think of my grandfather, hated in Russia because he was perceived as a non-Russian, placed in prison during the Russian Revolution, put before firing squads—and yet becoming a helper of the dispossessed in Canada, with special compassion for First Nations people. I think

> JESUS SEEMS TO BE SAYING THAT WE NEED TO LOOK AMONG THOSE WHOM WE DESPISE FOR SIGNS OF GOD'S PRESENCE AND POWER.

of Cho Wha Soon, a Korean minister who in the 1970s and 1980s entered the struggles of her Korean sisters who, because the West wants to purchase cheap goods, worked in horrible conditions in textile and electronics factories.[3]

A student of Soon, Henna Han, comments that "doing theology is more a matter of foot than of heart and brain."[4] It seems that Jesus might say that heart and brain are important—may you be filled with the love for and knowledge of God—but be sure to get those feet moving, for they take you to the highways and byways of life. There we may learn from those we look down upon how to live out the two essential commandments of Luke 10:27.

Notes

1. Robert C. Tannehill, *Luke*, Abingdon New Testament Commentaries (Nashville: Abingdon Press, 1996), 183.

2. To learn more about Ghaffar Khan, read Eknath Easwaran, *Nonviolent Soldier of Islam: Badshah Khan, A Man to Match His Mountains*, 2nd ed. (Tomales, Calif.: Nilgiri Press, 1999).

3. Read Cho Wha Soon's story in *Let the Weak Be Strong: A Woman's Struggle for Justice*, ed. Lee Sun Ai and Ahn Sang Nim (New York: Crossroad, 1988).

4. Hanna Yeogumhyun Han, "Rev. Cho Wha Soon: A Mother Apostle" (paper, Yale Divinity School, April 2, 1987), quoted in Letty M. Russell, introduction to Soon, *Let the Weak Be Strong*, 3.

EIGHTH SUNDAY AFTER PENTECOST

SIXTEENTH SUNDAY IN ORDINARY TIME / PROPER 11

JULY 22, 2007

REVISED COMMON	EPISCOPAL (BCP)	ROMAN CATHOLIC
Gen. 18:1-10a or	Gen. 18:1-10a	Gen. 18:1-10a
Amos 8:1-12	(10b-14)	
Psalm 15 or Psalm 52	Psalm 15	Ps. 15:2-3, 3-4, 5
Col. 1:15-28	Col. 1:21-29	Col. 1:24-28
Luke 10:38-42	Luke 10:38-42	Luke 10:38-42

FIRST READING

GENESIS 18:1-10a (RCL, RC)
GENESIS 18:1-10a (10b-14) (BCP)

This story of Abraham and Sarah's hospitality to God is a marvelous companion piece to the story of Mary and Martha (please see more comments below in my discussion of the Gospel reading from Luke). In Genesis, we have a narrative about the mystery of Presence. How do we make sense of the three men/the LORD/the "they" who seem to speak as a chorus to Abraham and Sarah? Clearly, Jewish doctrine does not permit any trinitarian assumptions. This reference probably has more to do with the idea of a divine council, God accompanied by other numinous beings. Certainly verse 22 separates Yahweh from the other two men, even if in our reading the three speak as one.

> HERE WE HAVE THE GUEST, THE ONE RECEIVING THE FRUITS OF HOSPITALITY, BECOME THE HOST, THE ONE WHO GIVES THESE FRUITS.

The more interesting feature of this narrative is its assumption that this mysterious and overwhelming Presence is at home in our homes. God comes visiting. Hebrews 13:2 warns, "Do not neglect to show hospitality to strangers, for by doing that some have entertained angels without knowing it." Abraham and Sarah's hospitality is considerable, as is the honor these two hosts show the three visitors. Only after the lengthy preparations are done and the guests are enjoying the results does God come forth with the reason for this visit. The BCP reading goes on to include God's promise to Sarah and Sarah's delicious laughter at the thought of knowing "pleasure" (*'edenah*—related to the Hebrew "Eden") while an old woman. While Sarah at first denies her laughter, her name for Isaac later admits the laughter God has brought her (21:6). Here we have the guest, the one receiving the fruits of hospitality, become the host, the one who gives these fruits.

AMOS 8:1-12 (RCL ALT.)

This Sunday's reading comprises Amos's fourth vision of destruction for the Northern Kingdom. It begins with the visual symbol of Israel's destruction: "a basket of summer fruit" (v. 1). This ripe fruit has been picked. The harvest season has come. And Amos informs all those at the royal sanctuary of Bethel that their harvest, their end, is also near. The Temple itself will be no sanctuary, no place of comfort for Israel, because the Temple hymns will become wailings in the midst of destruction.

The reading then outlines the indictment that God brings against Israel: greed that leads the people to dishonor the Sabbath and to steal from the poor. For these practices, the whole land will tremble as if it has become the land of the Nile, Egypt, land of toil and slavery, flood and drought. The movement of the sun itself will be unhinged from its usual place in creation. And merriment will become the time of dirges. More than all this destruc-

> GOD HAS NOT BEEN HOSTED IN THE LIVES OF THE PEOPLE AND THE NATION, AND GOD RETREATS FROM ISRAEL, NO LONGER GUEST, NO LONGER HOST.

tion is the famine that Amos says God will send upon the land. But it will not be "a famine of bread, or a thirst for water, but of hearing the words of the LORD" (v. 11). God's dismay at the injustice and false worship of Israel leads to a time when God seems to give up on Israel, withdrawing the life-giving word from the people.

This passage is a difficult text for preaching because of its unrelieved message of doom. That Amos mounts his criticism of and prophecy against Israel at the royal temple is a clear sign of the audience the prophet seeks for his oracles: the wealthy and the powerful. He is preaching not to the choir but to a people increasingly complacent in their sense of economic and political security. Faced with Amaziah, the Bethel temple's priest, who has ordered him to leave the temple and the land (7:10-13), Amos responds with this vision of great destruction. Will his oracle wake up Israel, shake it from its sleep of complacency?

The Gospel lesson from Luke teaches us more about love of God and of neighbor. Son of David and Messiah Jesus shares the hospitality of Mary and Martha. But in this text we see a temple for which God provides no protection, and we see a land abandoned by the presence of God's Word. God has not been hosted in the lives of the people and the nation, and God retreats from Israel, no longer guest, no longer host.

RESPONSIVE READING
PSALM 15 (RCL, BCP)
PSALM 15:2-3, 3-4, 5 (RC)

While the readings from Genesis and Luke are about the Divine visiting human homes, this response is about those who are welcome in God's tent and on God's "holy hill" (v. 1). In other words, whom does God welcome? The answer is in many ways a description of what it is to love God and one's neighbor: truth telling, no slander, no mistreatment of friends and neighbors, honor of God-fearers, oath keeping, no usury, no acceptance of bribes. The final line of this poem promises that those who abide by these instructions "shall never be moved" (v. 5). The one who is God's guest is the one who never leaves, always abides in, God's presence, his or her daily life suffused with this presence.

PSALM 52 (RCL ALT.)

This response provides a word of hope that the Amos reading does not. It opens as an indictment of those who harm the godly through treacherous words and deeds and who rely on their own wealth to protect them. To those who are dedicated to their own acquisition and to the destruction of others, the psalmist promises God's retribution. They will be uprooted, torn from their homes. But the righteous will survive because they trust in God alone and root themselves in the soil of God's own house.

SECOND READING
COLOSSIANS 1:15-28 (RCL)
COLOSSIANS 1:21-29 (BCP)
COLOSSIANS 1:24-28 (RC)

For a discussion of the Christ hymn, Colossians 1:15-20, please see the Roman Catholic second reading for the Seventh Sunday after Pentecost, above. Verse 21 opens with the assertion that Jesus reconciled with God all those estranged from God. Paul is the "servant [*diakonos*] of this gospel" (v. 23), letting the world know about "the word of God," what Paul also describes as "the mystery" (vv. 25-26) hidden for ages, now revealed in Jesus Christ. Paul identifies "the riches of the glory of this mystery" as "Christ in you, the hope of glory" (v. 27). And Paul's assignment has been to make these riches known to the Gentiles.

Paul calls on this fledgling church to "continue securely established and steadfast in the faith, without shifting from the hope promised by the gospel that you heard" (v. 23). Plant yourself firmly in your faith and the gospel news, he encourages the Colossian church. One of the words Paul uses, "established," or *themelioō*, has to do with constructing the foundations of buildings. The Colossians' peace with God and hope in Jesus Christ rest on the secure foundation of their faith. With this image of immovability and fixedness comes another image that speaks of change and growth. While Paul calls on all to be "securely established," he also speaks of presenting "everyone mature in Christ" (v. 28). Here the word "mature," or *teleios*, means "having brought to an end" or "having completed" a project, in this case, learning the wisdom that Paul teaches. Paul describes life as a follower of Christ with these two seemingly discordant images. While being a follower of Christ means establishing oneself in the faith and gospel of Jesus, it also means a lifetime of growing in and learning about the mystery of Jesus Christ, who has labored on our behalf, who abides within us, and who is the end point to which we move—in other words, being "mature in Christ." We see the beginnings of this process in the story of Martha and Mary, who welcome Jesus into their home and then begin to learn what it means to be in relationship with Mystery revealed in their very living room.

> THE COLOSSIANS' PEACE WITH GOD AND HOPE IN JESUS CHRIST REST ON THE SECURE FOUNDATION OF THEIR FAITH.

THE GOSPEL
LUKE 10:38-42 (RCL, BCP, RC)

The story of Mary and Martha and their guest Jesus is a hard story for women. Too often, we women have been expected to roll up our sleeves in the kitchen—and then to be told—by Jesus, no less—that we women have "chosen" wrongly! It's just one more kick in the teeth. As an Italian poet reflecting on this story writes in Martha's voice:

> "Listen, if I sat around on my salvation
> the way [Mary] does, who'd keep this house together?"[1]

How can this story be good news for all women, including those who have put in countless hours chopping, peeling, baking, and washing up?

It's helpful to remember that this pericope follows the story of the Good Samaritan. In many ways, it is another lesson in what it means to love God and neighbor. The whole discussion of love is set within the larger story of Jesus' journey and the hospitality that he and his followers either receive or do not receive and that which they give. The previous village that Jesus hoped to enter turned him away (9:53), and since that experience Jesus has sent his followers to yet other villages, instructing them how to accept hospitality and how to respond to rejection. For "whoever listens to you listens to me, and whoever rejects you rejects me, and whoever rejects me rejects the one who sent me," Jesus comments (10:16). Jesus' visit to the village of Mary and Martha opens with promise, for Martha "welcome[s Jesus] into her home" (v. 38). Jesus experiences hospitality in this village, thanks to Martha.

But then the story turns to Mary, who sits listening to Jesus. Martha disappears into the garden, the kitchen, the guest room—wherever guestly work needs to be done. It seems Jesus' arrival has caught her unprepared, and we learn that she is "distracted by her many tasks" (v. 40). The Greek word for "distracted" (*perispaō*) means "pulled or dragged away." In other words, perhaps Martha would rather be sitting with Jesus, but her long list of duties

THIS MUCH WORKED-OVER STORY IS BY NO MEANS TELLING US THAT ACTS OF HOSPITALITY ARE UNIMPORTANT OR THAT MEAL PREPARATION IS A LESSER DUTY.

pulls her away from enjoying his company. Being forthright, Martha points out to Jesus what seems to her a lopsided work arrangement: Mary sitting here enjoying herself, me slaving away in the kitchen. "Tell her then to help me," she demands (v. 40). Recognizing her anxiety, Jesus states that "only one thing" is needed: "Mary has chosen the better part, which will not be taken away from her" (v. 42).

The first thing that needs saying about this much-worked-over story is that it is by no means telling us that acts of hospitality are unimportant or that meal preparation is a lesser duty. Luke is full of stories about meals: picnics, banquets, even the institution of a ritual meal that commemorates Jesus' self-giving. And behind the scenes of most of these meals are, no doubt, women like Martha "manning" the ovens and chopping boards. The Old Testament story also emphasizes the importance of the singular act of hospitality, when God and two mysterious companions drop in on Abraham and Sarah. After what must have been several hours of preparation, a lunch of roasted calf, milk and curds, and fresh bread arrives. Nowhere do we read any complaints from God about all this fuss! Hospitality is a significant act of love for both God and neighbor, as all the acts of hospitality in Luke emphasize time and again. Some scholars have wondered whether Luke privileges word (or preaching) over service (*diakonia*, "the work," v. 40). But Luke as a whole does not downplay service, instead pointing out instances of *diakonia*: the grateful who serve Jesus, whether Peter's mother (4:39) or the women who provide for Jesus and his band (8:3); and Jesus who describes himself as "one who serves" (22:26-27; cf. 12:37). This *diakonia* is the service that the early church more fully fleshes out to involve serving the Eucharist as well as preaching and caretaking before these duties are separated and ranked.

So if Jesus is not dissing Martha for her service, what do his comments mean? The first word that really stands out in Jesus' reply to Martha is the word "chosen": "Mary has chosen . . ." (v. 42). In other words, Jesus is open to the choices of women. He does not expect women to run for the kitchen when he enters the door. Mary sits at Jesus' feet, listening and learning. It seems that Jesus is saying that there is room for Martha to join him as well. He permits choice and will not undercut Mary's decision by ordering her to the kitchen.

What, then, does Jesus mean by the "one thing" that alone is needed and "the better part" that Mary chooses? These two phrases seem to be equated. The one thing is what Mary has chosen. And here that one thing is the point of hospitality itself: the interchange between guest and host. In the Genesis story, for example, we infer all the work involved in preparing God's lunch, but at a certain point, this work pauses, and God enjoys lunch while Abraham respectfully remains at attention before God, and Sarah stands within earshot, even if within the tent. The work is done. Now the interchange begins, and important it is, for God has significant news for Sarah. But with Martha we do not hear of a pause in the work. The list of duties truly pulls her away from her guest. Martha's focus becomes her work rather than her guest. And Jesus implies that this focus is Martha's choice.

This reading is not a lesson on preparing a simple meal—Abraham and Sarah don't. But it is a lesson on finding time for the Guest. Read this way, this story becomes a window on all of our lives as many of us fill our days with truly important work but have not yet figured out how to balance this work with other important duties, or better yet, privileges. Where does time with the Holy One fit in our lives? Where does time with guests from God fit?

> JESUS PERMITS CHOICE AND WILL NOT UNDER-CUT MARY'S DECISION BY ORDERING HER TO THE KITCHEN.

Jeanne Stevenson Moessner offers more insight into this story. As she sees it, Mary and Martha together provide a model for how anyone—parent, counselor, pastor, teacher—called to give of her- or himself to others can do so in life-giving ways. Moessner writes of the Good Shepherd as one model in Scripture that exemplifies the lone individual responsible for the good of others. But in the story of Mary and Martha, she asserts, we learn that to be caregivers we need also to be care receivers. We are not to be alone in the world, operating out of our own font of energy. Rather, we are interconnected beings, in need of welcome and nurture for our own selves. Only after recognizing our interrelatedness can we truly begin to love God and love neighbor as ourselves.[2]

When Jesus recognizes Martha's anxiety and overwork, he invites her to receive his care and ministration. In other words, he invites Martha to be Mary and receive the care and nurture that she needs. Jesus' implied invitation is in harmony with any number of other meal settings in which Jesus the guest becomes Jesus the host, the one who has received and now gives. Martha offers hospitality to Jesus. Now Jesus offers to return this honor. While the Greek word for "guest" or "stranger," *xenos*, does not appear in this reading, it certainly captures the thinking of Luke, for *xenos* means not only guest but also host. Jesus comes to play both roles. And we are invited to do the same in our lives in the way we love God and neighbor—seeking and permitting care for ourselves in order that we may give out of a fullness of our own being. If we only give and give and give, we soon find ourselves filled with resentment and weariness. So may all of us Marthas learn to be Marys and both receive and give out of the nourishment of God's love.

ONLY AFTER RECOGNIZING OUR INTERRELATED-
NESS CAN WE TRULY BEGIN TO LOVE GOD AND LOVE
NEIGHBOR AS OUR SELVES.

Notes

1. Giuseppe Gioacchino Belli, "Martha and Magdalene," *Sonnets of Giuseppe Belli*, trans. Miller Williams (Shreveport: Louisiana State University Press, 1981), quoted in *Divine Inspiration: The Life of Jesus in World Poetry*, ed. Robert Atwan, George Dardess, Peggy Rosenthal (New York: Oxford University Press, 1998), 209. As the title of this poem indicates, nineteenth-century writer of satirical verse Belli, like many other Christians, assumed that the Mary of "Mary and Martha" was Mary Magdalene. This understanding rests on the conflation of John 11:2 with Luke 7:36-50 and then the assumption that the Luke 7 story concerns Mary Magdalene.

2. Jeanne Stevenson Moessner, "A New Pastoral Paradigm and Practice," in *Women in Travail and Transition: A New Pastoral Care*, ed. Maxine Glaz and Jeanne Stevenson Moessner (Minneapolis: Fortress Press, 1991), 198–209.

NINTH SUNDAY AFTER PENTECOST

SEVENTEENTH SUNDAY IN ORDINARY TIME /
PROPER 12
JULY 29, 2007

REVISED COMMON	EPISCOPAL (BCP)	ROMAN CATHOLIC
Gen. 18:20-32 or	Gen. 18:20-33	Gen. 18:20-32
Hos. 1:2-10		
Psalm 138 or	Psalm 138	Ps. 138:1-2, 2-3,
Psalm 85		6-7, 7-8
Col. 2:6-15 (16-19)	Col. 2:6-15	Col. 2:12-14
Luke 11:1-13	Luke 11:1-13	Luke 11:1-13

FIRST READING

GENESIS 18:20-32 (RCL, RC)
GENESIS 18:20-33 (BCP)

Verses 16/17-19 would be a helpful preamble for this reading. Because Abraham has been chosen to be a blessing to all the nations, and because he is to guide his family in God's ways, God decides to reveal the future of Sodom and Gomorrah to this man. In other words, God determines that it is appropriate to speak with Abraham, a man of blessing for all, about the people who live near him. And so God introduces the matter to Abraham in verse 21. Verse 22 contains one of the few scribal emendations (*tikkun sopherim*) in the Hebrew Bible. The original text read, "The LORD remained standing before Abraham," a reading that ancient scribes did not think bespoke divine sovereignty, and so the emended reading has Abraham standing before the Lord. But what if this story is all about the ways in which God seeks our mind on matters, queries our stances, invites our responses and arguments?

Abraham shows himself no milquetoast as he approaches God and asks a question that gets at the heart of divine justice: "Will you indeed sweep away the righteous with the wicked?" (v. 23). In other words, is collective guilt and punishment your way, O God? With this question, Abraham embarks on a daring discussion with the Almighty. "Far be it from you to do such a thing, to slay the righteous with the wicked, so that the righteous fare as the wicked! Far be that from you! Shall not the Judge of all the earth do what is just?" (v. 25). If God is offended, we do not hear about it. Instead, God makes a proposal: fifty righteous found for the lives of all. And so begins the bargaining for the survival of the citizenry of two cities. Abraham tentatively steps forward, like a man cautiously checking whether the ice will hold under his weight: "Let me take it upon myself to speak to the Lord, I who am but dust and ashes" (v. 27); "Oh do not let the Lord be angry if I speak" (v. 30); "Oh do not let the Lord be angry if I speak just once more" (v. 32). But step forward Abraham does, and he manages to bargain God down to ten righteous for the lives of all.

Scholars speculate about the setting in which this conversation was first composed and assert that it was composed later than Genesis 19:1-28 and is perhaps exilic or postexilic, especially given its concern about collective guilt. Abraham offers a different concept, that of the righteous few whose lives are redemptive for the many (a theme that Second Isaiah develops). But whatever the setting of this text's composition, Abraham certainly redirects God's attention from guilt to righteousness, from the many to the few. Unfortunately, not even ten righteous can be found in these cities, or so the rest of the story implies. Still, today's text is remarkable for its vision of human initiative with the Divine. God is intimately involved in life here on earth—hearing the outcry, coming to see what the truth is, considering avenues of proceeding. God seems to meet God's match in Abraham, also involved in the affairs of those near him, perhaps arguing out of a sense of solidarity with humankind, but certainly out of a sense of what is "properly" divine: justice that considers guilt and innocence in new ways. God has expectations of humanity, and Abraham has expectations of God. And neither refrains from the honest talk that lays these on the table, attempts to reach new understandings, and moves forward with the relationship, no matter what.

> GOD IS INTIMATELY INVOLVED IN LIFE HERE ON EARTH—HEARING THE OUTCRY, COMING TO SEE WHAT THE TRUTH IS, CONSIDERING AVENUES OF PROCEEDING.

HOSEA 1:2-10 (RCL ALT.)

Hosea was a prophet from the Northern Kingdom during its last tumultuous years. Assassinations, unwise political alliances, wars, social injustice, indifference to Yahweh—all marked the character of Israel, according to Hosea. The prophet's oracles are powerful, probably because they often speak of Israel's falling away from Yahweh in terms of one of the most intimate human relationships, that of husband and wife. With this metaphor, the prophet gets at the infidelity of Israel while also communicating the passion of God at being forgotten and abandoned. But this metaphor for us today, especially as Hosea develops it, also raises concerns. The images of the pure male and the sinful, promiscuous woman are stereotypical. Moreover, the language of God concerning women is sometimes violent (for example, 2:3). And the children in our passage are forced to bear in their very names the consequences of their parents' failed relationship and Israel's failure. The metaphor of God as husband, Israel as wife is powerful and at times beautiful, but it is also limited. What a daring (foolhardy?) move to use our human relationships, in all their despairing and sometimes violent failings, as an analogy for God's relationship with Israel.

What then can we touch on in this story that is helpful? We find a God who claims intimacy with us and who speaks in terms of all the strong emotions that would lead a human spouse to terminate a relationship. But in these few words of anger, God quickly moves to compassion and even renames the children of Hosea and Gomer (perhaps include 2:1ff. in your sermon to alert listeners to this change). It seems that God cannot let us go, cannot cast us out. Hosea attempts to make real the great harm that has come to the intimate relationship of God and humankind and the great, steadfast love of God in the face of the agony of knowing the lightness with which we humans often treat this relationship. Do we understand this pain?

> WE FIND A GOD WHO CLAIMS INTIMACY WITH US AND WHO SPEAKS IN TERMS OF ALL THE STRONG EMOTIONS THAT WOULD LEAD A HUMAN SPOUSE TO TERMINATE A RELATIONSHIP.

RESPONSIVE READING

PSALM 138 (RCL, BCP)
PSALM 138:1-2, 2-3, 6-7, 7-8 (RC)

This psalm speaks of the relationship of trust between God and human in a personal profession of faith that can also be interpreted as communal. The psalmist extols a God who is ready and able to help, who hears the cries of those in need and then acts to save. One might say that this relationship of trust is the relationship of Abraham with God. While it does not comment on the daring courage of humans before God, it does speak of the resilience of the human-divine relationship that leads through thick and thin to praise and thanksgiving.

PSALM 85 (RCL ALT.)

This psalm is a postexilic psalm about the returned exiles. While the psalm celebrates the forgiveness of sins and the withdrawal of God's wrath, it also recognizes the continued need of the people for further renewal and salvation. The vision that draws the people can be found in verses 10-13, where many of the theologically powerful words about God are gathered: steadfast love, faithfulness, righteousness, peace. The returned exiles imagine a life replete with these divine qualities to such an extent that the land itself comes to rich new life. But life is not yet there. This psalm is the prayer of those who recognize their need and call out for full restoration.

SECOND READING

COLOSSIANS 2:6-15 (16-19) (RCL)
COLOSSIANS 2:6-15 (BCP)
COLOSSIANS 2:12-14 (RC)

Our reading, like the Colossians reading two Sundays ago, finds its energy in its last verses. Verse 15 provides a cinematic moment that is so much more than cinema. It is reminiscent of the triumph scene in *Ben Hur*: "[God] disarmed the rulers and authorities and made a public example of them, triumphing over them in it." In explaining the historical references of this verse, scholars point to ancient victory marches in which the conquering general rode in a chariot into the royal city, followed by columns of defeated captives, stripped (as the Greek word translated "disarmed" actually means) of their arms and warrior's clothing. While we may be uncomfortable with this language of war, this analogy was true to life for the peoples of the ancient world, and it continues true for many today. It speaks of another kingdom, another realm beyond that of Rome's tyranny.

The reason the writer of Colossians turns to this intense image of warfare is that the Christians in Colossae were apparently facing a new threat. Scholars are unsure what this threat was, but it seems to have involved doctrine and practice. Were the Christians in Colossae influenced by Gnosticism, mystery religions, or some form of philosophy? We simply do not know. But verses 16-19 seem to indicate that these Christians were being told to submit to rigid rules. And so the person writing them reminds them that God has won a tremendous victory over all the things that try to rule over them in place of God. The writer says, "Remember that God has already won this victory." Verse 8 says, in essence, "Be careful or you will be taken captive by other forces that are not of Christ. Don't give up ground that has already been won. Don't become a prisoner of war once again."

Instead, our letter writer urges these Christians to remember and claim their baptism, which symbolizes God's victory in their lives. The phrase "putting off" in verse 11 ("putting off the body of the flesh") is the very same used in verse 15 to describe what God does to the forces of evil: God strips them, disarms them. But in this verse the baptized have been stripped of their bondage to evil. The ancient baptismal practice of disrobing and then donning new robes explains this second reference to stripping.

To preach on this text is to remind the church that the followers of Jesus have left behind captivity to old, deathly ways of living. We have been raised up to a new life. And nothing and no one should be permitted to lead us off as captives to other authorities and rules and systems of thought that bind us, reduce us, and deprive us of our standing as the baptized—those who "have received Christ Jesus the Lord" (v. 6). The vision of verses 6-14 is that of unity—of being within Christ who is within us—of drawing our nourishment and energy for growth and fullness from Christ, of finding our forgiveness and life through him and with him. This reading calls on us to claim our liberty, our source of power and life, and to be discerning about where and to whom we give our allegiance.

THIS READING CALLS ON US TO CLAIM OUR LIBERTY, OUR SOURCE OF POWER AND LIFE, AND TO BE DISCERNING ABOUT WHERE AND TO WHOM WE GIVE OUR ALLEGIANCE.

THE GOSPEL
LUKE 11:1-13 (RCL, BCP, RC)

This Sunday's Gospel lesson appears within the sequence of stories and teachings that have dealt with loving God and neighbor, a sequence that appears within the larger journey section of Luke that itself looks at the hospitality that Jesus receives from and gives to those whom he meets. Today's lesson picks up the theme of love and hospitality and looks at it from the perspective of the acceptance and generosity that God shows to visitors. In other words, what kind of relationship can those who love God expect with God? The lesson opens with Jesus in prayer with God and moves to the disciples' question about how they may speak to and with God. Jesus presents them with an example of prayer.

WHAT JESUS TEACHES IN THIS LESSON IS THAT WE FOLLOWERS MUST ASK FOR WHAT WE SEEK. MORE THAN THIS, WE MUST BE UNRELENTING IN OUR ASKING, UNEMBARRASSED IN OUR SEEKING.

It begins with the intimate term of address for God, "Father," but then speaks of the hallowing of God's name. What an odd combination, the intimate with the Ultimate. From there, it moves to a sense of God's cosmic presence and purpose with the revolutionary call for God's kingdom to arrive. The next petitions evidence what this coming means: daily nourishment (physical and spiritual bread), release from guilt and hopelessness in forgiveness, and the power to resist evil. What a world we would live in were these petitions fully in place in our world

144

THE SEASON
AFTER PENTECOST

───────

REBECCA J.
KRUGER GAUDINO

today! It is for this fullness of the kingdom that Jesus bids his disciples pray. A bold prayer, indeed.

Perhaps Jesus sees these followers glance at each other as if wondering at the grandness of this prayer that brings together both the universal and the local/personal. "Isn't this a bit much for us to pray?" they may be wondering, for Jesus moves right into a parable of a friend who, at midnight, comes looking for bread for a newly arrived visitor. Despite the late hour, the wakened friend, Jesus asserts, will get up and bring bread to the door, if not for friendship's sake, at least because of the persistence of the petitioner. Jesus then moves into a powerful saying about prayer that instructs his followers to ask, search, and knock, for those who do so will receive what they seek. He even promises the Holy Spirit, yet ungiven to his followers, to those who request this gift.

What Jesus teaches in this lesson is that we followers must ask for what we seek. More than this, we must be unrelenting in our asking, unembarrassed in our seeking. Our attentiveness and diligence in asking have something to do with God's provision of the things that Jesus bids us request: the Realm of God in our midst, our nourishment, our unburdening, our endurance and strength in times of struggle.

BOTH OUR LUKE AND GENESIS TEXTS OFFER US A VISION OF THE HUMAN/DIVINE RELATIONSHIP THAT IS TOUGH AND FLEXIBLE AND TO A GOD WHO IS OPEN TO THE BEST OF OUR ARGUMENTS AND THE MOST PERSISTENT OF OUR PETITIONS.

While other New Testament passages teach us that God already knows our needs and desires, this passage teaches that we may advocate with clarity and specificity for our needs: three loaves of bread, an egg or some fish, as Jesus' examples say.

In the relationship of love and loyalty that we establish with the God whom we address as "Father" or "Mother," we find generosity and openness to our voice. God hosts our prayers, takes them seriously, responds to them. Our thoughts, dreams, hopes, and needs make up a part of the conversation that we bring to God. In Jesus' eyes, they are our work and responsibility. So knock on the door of the Friend, yes, even in extreme and unlikely times and situations. Tug on the cloak of the Father/Mother busy with household matters.

This lesson dovetails nicely with the reading from Genesis in which God invites Abraham into a consultation about Sodom and Gomorrah. Genuinely interested in Abraham's response to God's plans for these nearby cities, God listens attentively to Abraham's bold questions and intercessions for both friend and foe (see commentary on the first reading, above). Both our Luke and Genesis texts offer us a vision of the human/divine relationship that is tough and flexible and of a God who is open to the best of our arguments and the most persistent of our petitions. An Anglican minister and poet, George Herbert (1593–1633), spent many hours of his ministry contemplating this at times rough-and-tumble relationship. When he neared his death, he handed over a manuscript of poems entitled *The Temple* in which we find record of his reflections. His first poem on prayer gets at the open and enduring human/divine relationship:

> Prayer the Church's banquet, Angels' age,
> God's breath in man returning to his birth,
> The soul in paraphrase, heart in pilgrimage,
> The Christian plummet sounding heav'n and earth;
> Engine against th'Almighty, sinners' tower,
> Reversed thunder, Christ-side-piercing spear,
> The six-days world transposing in an hour,
> A kind of tune, which all things hear and fear;
> Softness, and peace, and joy, and love, and bliss,
> Exalted Manna, gladness of the best,
> Heaven in ordinary, man well dressed,
> The milky way, the bird of Paradise,
> Church-bells beyond the stars heard, the soul's blood,
> The land of spices; something understood.[1]

Seeking, insisting, advocating, wounding, transforming—Herbert gets at a relationship that takes in the fullness of our being as we present ourselves before a God who wants this fullness—of heart, mind, soul, and body, of honesty and straighforwardness, of passion and exaltation.

Note

1. George Herbert, "Prayer (1)," in *George Herbert: The Complete English Poems*, ed. John Tobin (New York: Penguin Books, 1991), 45–46.

THE SEASON AFTER PENTECOST:

PROPERS 13 THROUGH 22

GARY E. PELUSO-VERDEND

Ordinary Time is a span of the church year during which lectionary preachers often consider preaching topically rather than from the lectionary. The following ten Sundays offer a preacher several "both-and" options: using the lections, there are several recurring topics that could be worked into a fitting, powerful series of sermons. Chiefly, those topics are the Christian community and stewardship, keeping time, doing justice, and witnessing. Actually, all of these topics could fall under the one heading of stewardship, with practices in regard to keeping time, doing justice, and witnessing viewed as expressions of Christian stewardship.

At its core, stewardship refers to a way of living that sees life in all its parts as held in trust from God. As Christians, we know ourselves to be stewards of God's gifts rather than owners. Thus, in this understanding of being human, Christians present a radical alternative to the image of human beings as owners, as consumers, and as devotees of mammon. Although we are not "in the Garden," our fundamental responsibility before God is still "to till and to keep," to take good care of the Earth and of the people whom God has entrusted within our relationship circles. Both the Earth and people, including our most intimate relations (for instance, parents, children, spouses), belong to God and not to us. Christian stewards orient their resources of time, energy, attention, and money toward preparing to receive the reign of God. This active reception is expressed through engaging in acts of mercy and justice and in witnessing to the peace and justice-making activity of God in the world.

Many congregations conduct their annual stewardship campaigns during the fall. The lections from these ten Sundays offer the opportunity for the preacher to prepare the congregation to think about stewardship and to evaluate the community's stewardship practices in a deep and broad manner. Yes, stewardship practice and education must include our relationship with money and possessions; a yearly stewardship campaign can be part of that practice and education. But Christian stewardship practice and education are really a constituent dimension of being a Christian and deserve far greater attention than most congregations give. These ten Sundays provide a wonderful opportunity to give attention to stewardship.

The Gospel texts provide the foundation for stewardship preaching, with great assistance coming from the other readings for each Sunday. The lections will cover portions of Luke 12–17. Jesus and the disciples are already on the way to Jerusalem, already on the way toward the cross. Luke takes much of chapters 12–16 to address issues of possessions, anxiety, wealth, Sabbath keeping, and what time it is. Luke helps us view the meaning of Christian life with the cross in focus; and that focus affects, often in upsetting ways, how we treat our possessions, how we spend our time, and how we relate to our families. In Luke, we will encounter a rich farmer who tries to act as an owner rather than a steward and fails to act justly and for the sake of the community with the wealth that he mistakes as his own (12:13-21); a dishonest steward who nonetheless has something to teach us about resolute action (16:1-3); and the rich man who knows Lazarus but who cannot treat Lazarus as a human being (16:19-31). We will be instructed twice that household stewardship must yield to the demands of the reign of God, once when Jesus says he came to bring divisions within households (12:49-56) and once when he asserts that whoever does not *hate* family cannot be his disciple (14:25-33). The contemporary icon of the Christian family will find no support in these texts. The meaning of keeping Sabbath will be tied to liberation of the oppressed and the celebration of freedom from bondage (13:10-17). And Christians will be instructed to allow the reign of God to transform attitudes toward family, possessions, and party invitations and seating, as well as their stance toward how they should spend their ordinary time—to wait attentively, seek the lost, and trust the power of God (12:32-40; 14:1, 7-14; 15:1-10; 17:5-10).

> CHRISTIAN STEWARDS ORIENT THEIR RESOURCES OF TIME, ENERGY, ATTENTION, AND MONEY TOWARD PREPARING TO RECEIVE THE REIGN OF GOD.

> THE CONTEMPORARY ICON OF THE CHRISTIAN FAMILY WILL FIND NO SUPPORT IN THESE TEXTS.

The other readings that the lectionary shapers chose for these Sundays are strong selections, rich and interesting texts. There is one powerful set of lections on sin, which can be viewed as teachings on what happens when stewards attempt to act as owners, when creatures confuse themselves with the Creator (Sixteenth

Sunday after Pentecost/Twenty-fourth Sunday in Ordinary Time/Proper 19). Then there is Philemon 1–21, arguably Paul's most engaging rhetorical presentation in his extant letters, which could be the basis of several sermons all by itself. But this text on what should be done in regard to a runaway slave also provides a powerful example from the early church of the change in household relations that being a Christian demands. The preacher will find great support for stewardship themes from many of the first and second readings. Texts from Amos, Isaiah, Hosea, and Jeremiah connect Sabbath keeping with just economic practices. Selections from Hebrews open windows into a persecuted community that was struggling to stay together and whose members were tempted to revert to former religious practices. We overhear their exhorter reminding

> IF WE LISTEN TO ECCLESIASTES CLOSELY AND TAKE SERIOUSLY HIS CLAIM THAT LIFE IS EMPTINESS, HE MAY MAKE US SQUIRM. GET USED TO THAT FEELING.

them who they are, what time it is, and who all is counting on them to finish the race. Texts from 1 and 2 Timothy express the need for courageous witness, both within the Christian community and outside the community when the government takes on the trappings of deity.

The lessons for these Sundays begin with the preacher from Ecclesiastes questioning the meaning of life. If we listen to him closely and take seriously his claim that life is emptiness, he may make us squirm. Get used to that feeling. Jesus' words in these six chapters almost assuredly will make hearers squirm. In writing the following pages and trying to take all these texts seriously, I know that I squirmed a lot!

A NOTE ON METHOD

Back in college and seminary, I was taught to work on texts for sermons by producing first an exegesis (what the text says) and then, through employing a hermeneutical method, an interpretation of what the text might mean for today. Over time, I have lost confidence in this method. I will not go into all the reasons here; but one of the major reasons I do not work with texts this way anymore is that I know that I am always interpreting, that I am always using my imagination to try to discern what the texts might have meant to the first hearers and readers and what these texts might mean to the community who will be hearing the text today. So I look for the elements in the texts that might stir imaginations: metaphors and images; drama and tension; plot twists; and, very important, points of view. I use these as access points into the world of the text and then, from this imaginative point of view, look around at my world and my communities and ask where the analogous points of contact might be. Sure, history and word studies and sociocultural work are very important in helping to know what I am looking at. But with those tools, I am increasingly trying to find connection points between the spiritual imagination expressed through the text and what taking that imagination seriously might mean for the communities I serve as a preacher.

TENTH SUNDAY AFTER PENTECOST

Eighteenth Sunday in Ordinary Time / Proper 13

August 5, 2007

Revised Common	Episcopal (BCP)	Roman Catholic
Eccl. 1:2, 12-14; 2:18-23 or Hosea 11:1-11	Eccl. 1:12-14; 2:(1-7, 11) 18-23	Eccl. 1:2; 2:21-23
Ps. 49:1-12 or Ps. 107:1-9, 43	Psalm 49 or 49:1-11	Ps. 90:3-4, 5-6, 12-13, 14, 17
Col. 3:1-11	Col. 3:(5-11) 12-17	Col. 3:1-5, 9-11
Luke 12:13-21	Luke 12:13-21	Luke 12:13-21

First Reading

ECCLESIASTES 1:2, 12-14; 2:18-23 (RCL)
ECCLESIASTES 1:12-14; 2:(1-7, 11) 18-23 (BCP)
ECCLESIASTES 1:2; 2:21-23 (RC)

Ecclesiastes is a biblical example of wisdom literature, writing devoted to reflection on experience, oriented toward contributing to the practical task of living well. Explicitly or implicitly, the writers of wisdom literature are asking, what is the meaning of life? The voice of Ecclesiastes, also known as the Preacher or Qoheleth, answers in 1:2: there is none; life is emptiness. The remainder of the book is a collection of variations on this theme. All of life is empty, vanity, a chasing after wind.

Where, existentially, does one have to be in order to judge that all of life has no more substance than vapor (Heb.: *hebel*)? Verses 12-14 identify the author with an unnamed king in Jerusalem. Tradition identifies this king as Solomon, but most scholars date this book hundreds of years later than Solomon. Regardless of the actual historical setting, these verses help to set the author's frame: a king on a throne, who has the opportunity to do great things, to command armies and build monuments, looks back upon all of his efforts and declares them empty. The very act of philosophizing is an unhappy burden God has laid on human beings.

For this author, philosophy and learning lead not to enlightenment but to a deep, empty darkness, to unrefreshing sleep and to waking despair.

As Christians, we may have difficulty staying within the author's framework or taking his point of view seriously. We may want to categorize and context him immediately as depressed, cranky, or a jaded voice from the Other Testament. But grant him this fundamental point: all mortals die, our lives end, our works are passed along to another generation. Death robs all life of meaning—this *is* one logical conclusion one might draw. In the Gospel lesson for today, Jesus also understands that death creates a crisis of meaning for humanity, but he draws a different conclusion: death can drive us to look for the meaning of life beyond what we can accumulate, possess, or build.

> FOR THIS AUTHOR, PHILOSOPHY AND LEARNING LEAD NOT TO ENLIGHTENMENT BUT TO A DEEP, EMPTY DARKNESS, TO UNREFRESHING SLEEP AND TO WAKING DESPAIR.

HOSEA 11:1-11 (RCL ALT.)

The prophet Hosea's life was a living allegory of the relationship between God and Israel, with Hosea playing the role of God, who alternates between righteous anger and forgiving compassion. God called Hosea to marry Gomer the prostitute (1:2-3). Gomer had three children; Hosea may or may not have been the father. Gomer left him, just as the people of Israel (Northern Kingdom) left God to worship Baal. Hosea, following God's command, makes a public show of taking her back. Hosea's treatment of Gomer is an outward and visible sign akin to God's compassion for Israel.

Here in chapter 11 the metaphor changes from marriage to mothering; but the focus on God's compassion remains. We might even say that the attention to compassion intensifies. "When Israel was a child, . . . it was I who taught Ephraim to walk. . . . I bent down to them and fed them. . . . I will return them to their homes" (vv. 1, 3, 4, 11).

The other part of this story, of course, is why Israel so needed God's compassion. Hosea prophesies against idolatry, against Israel's turn toward the Baals (playing the prostitute), the fertility gods associated with seasons and the harvest and the natural order. While God's compassion triumphs over God's anger—at least in this passage—the anger is nevertheless strong. God reminds the people that it was God who called them up from Egypt (v. 1); and to an Egyptian-like bondage in a foreign land they shall return (v. 5).

RESPONSIVE READING
PSALM 49:1–12 (RCL)
PSALM 49 OR 49:1–11 (BCP)

A balladeer or troubadour, harp in hand, invites the whole world to listen to his wisdom. Verses 5–9 assert that we will all die; no amount of wealth can ransom us from the grave. The balladeer's refrain is found first in verse 12: "Mortals cannot abide in their pomp; they are like the animals that perish." Because this verse is repeated and sums up the author's perspective, I would recommend including this verse in the reading.

If one reads the whole psalm, one will hear echoes of Qoheleth: wealth cannot ransom a life.

PSALM 107:1–9, 43 (RCL ALT.)

The psalmist expresses thanksgiving for God's compassion. In contrast to the Hosea text that expresses compassion from God's point of view, the vantage point in this psalm is that of human beings who give thanks for their experience of God's compassion. (In fact, it is noteworthy how often in the lections the psalmist's point of view is very different from the point of view expressed in the first reading.) Throughout the psalm, the author invokes experiences of affliction from which God compassionately delivers people, as well as images of affliction that God brings on the wicked. In verses 1–9, the author conjures images of desert wandering, hunger, and thirst, and then God's deliverance. Verse 43 is included in the reading, it seems, because of the counsel for the wise to "give heed to these things."

PSALM 90:3–4, 5–6, 12–13, 14, 17 (RC)

One of my favorite hymns, "O God, Our Help in Ages Past," is based on this psalm. That hymn focuses on God's greatness, in contrast to human mortality, and celebrates God as "our eternal home." The psalm is much more of a lament than that hymn, however. This psalm is a lament rising from a people who feel the *weight* of their mortality, who feel as significant to God as mowed grass. The psalmist pleads for God's anger to cease and God's compassion to flow.

SECOND READING

COLOSSIANS 3:1-11 (RCL)
COLOSSIANS 3:(5-11) 12-17 (BCP)
COLOSSIANS 3:1-5, 9-11 (RC)

We do not know who wrote Colossians. Tradition ascribes the letter to Paul, and some scholars continue to argue for Pauline authorship. Other scholars see phrases from Paul's writing woven together by a new editor with a different theology. Regardless of the *author's* identity, however, he is intent on conveying a new identity, a Christ-centered identity to his readers or hearers.

Christian identity is radically different from the pagan, Gentile identity the author sketches of his audience's "before" life. He believes that Christians have been raised with Christ, now live in Christ, and will be revealed in glory with Christ. The author creates dramatic movement, a sense of "before" and "now," with contrasting words: below and above; died and raised; hidden and revealed; strip off and clothe. He sees a radical break between their old selves and their new selves in Christ. The new life involves shedding the old as one changes clothes—no, tosses out the old wardrobe and buys all new (3:9-14). From emotions to thoughts, from speech to social standing, everything has changed with those who are "in Christ."

> FROM EMOTIONS TO THOUGHTS, FROM SPEECH TO SOCIAL STANDING, EVERYTHING HAS CHANGED WITH THOSE WHO ARE "IN CHRIST."

The Episcopal version of this lection adds verses 12-17. These verses extend the metaphor of changing clothes referenced in verse 9. It is a beautiful text to use in a wedding ceremony, with the special clothes of the day serving as a visual illustration of new life in Christ. And the virtues and spiritual gifts named here—compassion, kindness, humility, meekness, patience, forbearance, forgiveness, love, peace—are, from a Christian point of view, a "stylish outfit" for any Christian, most befitting of expressing a Christian's identity.

THE GOSPEL

LUKE 12:13-21 (RCL, BCP, RC)

The staging in this text is common in Luke: someone asks a question or passes on his or her news to Jesus (for instance, Pilate's murder of some Galileans, 13:1); Jesus responds with a teaching that reorients and reframes the listeners' attention; then he tells a parable.

Jesus and his disciples are on their way to Jerusalem. A man commands Jesus to act, saying, "Tell my brother to divide the family inheritance with me." We do not know anything more about the situation. Was the "someone in the crowd" a younger brother whose older brother refused to abide by the injunction in Deuteronomy 21:17 to give his younger brother a third of the estate? Perhaps, but Luke does not care. He uses the question as an occasion to express Jesus' teaching about greed. Jesus refuses to play judge (see also v. 57: "Why do you not judge for yourselves what is right?"). He frustrates the crowd, who would have loved to overhear his answer to this drama. Who is not attracted to the gossip generated by someone else's family arguing about money, especially an inheritance? Rather than buying into his listeners' perspective, Jesus changes the framework. He turns to the whole crowd and issues a warning regarding greed: "For one's life does not consist in the abundance of possessions" (v. 15). The text seeks to reorient our attention from what we think we are owed to the relationship between life and wealth.

Then follows the parable of the rich fool or the rich farmer. The farmer is blessed with a harvest so large that his barns cannot handle it. As Brandon Scott suggests, a harvest so unexpectedly large signals a miracle.[1] Something about the reign of God is afoot. God has abundantly provided for the whole community. The farmer does not notice God's hand at all, however; he mistakes the community's wealth, of which he should be a steward, for his own. In typical Lukan fashion, the man carries on an inner dialogue (as does the unjust steward and the prodigal son, to name two others) in which he elevates his own self to the highest position in the narrative. The man's conclusion is that he now

> THE TEXT SEEKS TO REORIENT OUR ATTENTION FROM WHAT WE THINK WE ARE OWED TO THE RELATIONSHIP BETWEEN LIFE AND WEALTH.

has plenty for himself and that he must tear down his present barns and build all-new, larger ones. Think of contemporary neighborhood teardowns of $400,000 houses in order to build big-foot starter mansions with oodles of custom closets to hold all of the owner's stuff!

PUTTING THE TEXTS TOGETHER

With this parable, Luke joins with the other texts for today in expressing the fact that all mortals die. There is a text in Ecclesiastes (6:1-2) with a striking parallel to the parable of the rich farmer: "There is an evil that I have seen under the sun, and it lies heavy upon humankind: those to whom God gives wealth, possessions, and honor, so that they lack nothing of all that they desire, yet God does not enable them to enjoy these things, but a stranger enjoys them. This is vanity; it is a grievous ill." But notice the different point of view. Luke's Jesus parts company with the voice of Ecclesiastes at the close of this lection: "So it is with those who store up treasures for themselves but are not rich toward God" (Luke 12:21). Jesus' answer to Qoheleth's problem is to reframe what wealth means and what kind of wealth is ultimately meaningful. Qoheleth—and perhaps we ourselves—are disappointed that meaning cannot be found in accumulating wealth. Jesus in Luke does not regret that there is no meaning inherent in accumulating wealth and possessions. There is another kind of wealth, being rich in God, stewarding God's abundance on behalf of the whole community, that survives death and therefore sets the meaning of life on an indestructible foundation.

What is the meaning of life? The Preacher judges that death swallows wisdom, wealth, and accomplishments into nothingness. Jesus judges that the horizon of death should orient our attention to sharing wealth in the community and living life trusting in God's abundance. The author of Colossians adds another viewpoint, complementary to Luke's: As Christians, we have already died in Christ. We ought, therefore, to live as he lived, because we live in him. The fact of our living in Christ means that we can and should strive to put on the wardrobe of virtues that belong to Jesus, such as compassion, kindness, and love. Combining this perspective with the Luke text, one might conclude that these texts call the Christian community to live life as the resurrection community, a community that strives to be "rich toward God."

> JESUS JUDGES THAT THE HORIZON OF DEATH SHOULD ORIENT OUR ATTENTION TO SHARING WEALTH IN THE COMMUNITY AND LIVING LIFE TRUSTING IN GOD'S ABUNDANCE.

There is a great opportunity in these texts to connect directly to that which is dear to our hearts: our possessions and our relationship with our possessions. If ever there was a society that has demonstrated the desire to build bigger barns to hold all of our stuff, it is us! A very powerful sermon would result if the preacher could establish a point of view from within the bigger barns in which her or his parishioners might live. After all, we all must die, even in order to live.

Note

1. Bernard Brandon Scott, *Hear Then the Parable: A Commentary on the Parables of Jesus* (Minneapolis: Fortress Press, 1989), 132–40.

ELEVENTH SUNDAY AFTER PENTECOST

NINETEENTH SUNDAY IN ORDINARY TIME /
PROPER 14
AUGUST 12, 2007

REVISED COMMON	EPISCOPAL (BCP)	ROMAN CATHOLIC
Gen. 15:1-6 or Isa. 1:1, 10-20	Gen. 15:1-6	Wisd. of Sol. 18:6-9
Ps. 33:12-22 or Ps. 50:1-8, 22-23	Psalm 33 or 33:12-15, 18-22	Ps. 33:1, 12, 18-19, 20-22
Heb. 11:1-3, 8-16	Heb. 11:1-3 (4-7) 8-16	Heb. 11:1-2, 8-19 or 11:1-2, 8-12
Luke 12:32-40	Luke 12:32-40	Luke 12:32-48 or 12:35-40

Note the power arrangements in the Genesis, Hebrews, and Luke texts in regard to who has the power to initiate saving action. The timing of events is completely in the God's hands. The power that we have is to decide whether to trust or not and, based on our trust in God, to decide where to focus our attention and how we will wait.

FIRST READING
GENESIS 15:1-6 (RCL, BCP)

It will be particularly difficult for us in the twenty-first century West to get inside of this passage. One reason for our difficulty is the very fact that Abram had a vision, not to mention his response to that vision. The text begins by telling us that Abram receives a vision from God. Most people I know would either dismiss the vision on some alleged rational grounds or be blown away by having had a vision. Not so with Abram. In the vision, God tells Abram that his "reward shall be very great" (v. 1). Abram pushes for more information! What will be the reward? Abram also complains or at least reminds God that his current heir is "a slave born in my house" (v. 3). No reward yet. God assures Abram that he will have heirs of his own DNA, takes him outside, shows him the stars, and tells him that he will enjoy a like number of heirs. Then follows an iteration of the line so famous because of its use first in Paul's letters and then in the sixteenth-century Protestant Reformation: "And he believed the LORD; and the LORD reckoned it to him as righteousness" (v. 6). But if one reads the next few verses, Abram is again pushing for more information and some demonstration that God will bring about what was promised (v. 8). God promises Abram the land. Abram does not merely believe but asks for some evidence that what God says is true. So Abram is not simply a passive recipient.

The other problem we may have with this text is that our sense of time is much different from that of a less technologically advanced and wealthy world. We in the West, particularly in the United States, driven by technological innovation and demanding instant gratification, may have difficulty with the concept of fulfillment deferred from one generation to the next. Abram received a promise but did not see the promise fulfilled. Generations to come tried to live according to the promise but also died without fulfillment.

> THIS GENESIS TEXT CHALLENGES US, AS THE PEOPLE OF GOD, TO TAKE A LONG VIEW TOWARD TIME AND WHAT IT MEANS TO WAIT ON GOD.

Millennia later, the people to whom the author of Hebrews wrote believed that the promises were finally on the verge of fulfillment; but even they died without God's reign coming fully in the way they expected. In today's world, we want everything *now*. This Genesis text challenges us, as the people of God, to take a long view toward time and what it means to wait on God.

ISAIAH 1:1, 10-20 (RCL ALT.)

The great Assyrian Empire is on the move, on its way to devouring the Northern Kingdom, Israel. Isaiah receives his prophetic call to speak to the people and the powers of Judah, the Southern Kingdom. In this passage, the prophet addresses Judah by imaging it as Sodom and Gomorrah, destroyed because of their inhospitable and wicked behavior. In phrase after phrase, Isaiah shreds the belief that worshiping God can be disconnected from doing justice. Right ritual alone does not sustain the world. Said differently, Isaiah emphasizes that acting justly in everyday social and economic relations, fulfilling the Torah by doing good to neighbor, is the

> IN PHRASE AFTER PHRASE, ISAIAH SHREDS THE BELIEF THAT WORSHIPING GOD CAN BE DISCONNECTED FROM DOING JUSTICE. RIGHT RITUAL ALONE DOES NOT SUSTAIN THE WORLD.

behavior that sustains good order in Judah. In the world of the ancient Near East, Isaiah's understanding of the nature of the universe was radically different from conventional thought and practice. Does not the priests' work of marking time and sustaining the sacrificial system on behalf of the king and the people sustain the hierarchy that holds up the heavens and the earth? The seasonal cycle of festivals, sacrifices, and rituals—do not these provide the foundations on which the world rests? Isaiah's answer: no. Sacrificing animals and keeping festivals do not sustain the relations between heaven and earth. Rather, the people are to "cease to do evil, learn to do good; seek justice, rescue the oppressed, defend the orphan, plead for the widow" (vv. 16-17).

In contrast to the Genesis lection, where *belief* is counted as righteousness (and Abram is given a gracious amount of credit considering his level of trust), in this text righteousness must be expressed through *just treatment of the neighbor*, as judged especially by the treatment of the least powerful members of society.

WISDOM OF SOLOMON 18:6-9 (RC)

The Wisdom of Solomon is a pseudepigraphic book, meaning that it is attributed to a famous person but is clearly from another era. Scholars believe that Wisdom was written by an Alexandrian Jew in the first or second century C.E. The author recasts biblical narrative from a wisdom perspective, emphasizing the need to pursue wisdom through following the Torah, God's providence and forethought evident in the great events of their history, and the need to trust in God and God's timing. The author is particularly confident that God will protect those who are righteous and faithful and will punish those who are not (see 1:1-4).

In today's text, the author is in the midst of his commentary on the exodus narrative. He interprets the Passover night in which God's messenger killed the Egyptian children and passed over the Hebrew households as a demonstration of God's providential care for the righteous and punishment of the unrighteous. Consider in particular verse 8: "For by the same means by which you punished our enemies you called us to yourself and glorified us."

RESPONSIVE READING

PSALM 33:12-22 (RCL)
PSALM 33 OR 33:12-15, 18-22 (BCP)
PSALM 33:1, 12, 18-19, 20-22 (RC)

The first eleven verses command the congregation to praise God, who made all that is through God's word. Justice, righteousness, and steadfast love are named as God's attributes as well as the qualities God loves in people. In verse 11, the point of view shifts to Israel, "the nation whose God is the LORD" (v. 12). Verses 13-19 then shift the congregation's attention up to heaven where the LORD is seated on the throne and sees all the people and all their deeds. But God's eye is particularly fixed on the righteous, on those who fear God. The author also twice connects the people's hope and God's steadfast love (vv. 18, 22).

PSALM 50:1-8, 22-23 (RCL ALT.)

The choice of this psalm reflects its connection in thought to the Isaiah passage. This psalm opens with an image of God summoning all the world to assemble as a court before God passes judgment. The judge declares that God has no need of sacrifices for two reasons: all the animals already belong to God; God does not need to eat and drink! The only sacrifice that counts for anything with God is a sacrifice of thanksgiving from "those who go the right way" (v. 23).

SECOND READING

HEBREWS 11:1-3, 8-16 (RCL)
HEBREWS 11:1-3 (4-7) 8-16 (BCP)
HEBREWS 11:1-2, 8-19 OR 11:1-2, 8-12 (RC)

These verses read like a sermon on the refrain "by faith" (Gk.: *pistei*). In fact, the book "to the Hebrews" is best read as an extended exhortation to a community tempted to disperse because difficult times had arrived and they had not yet received the promised fulfillment. Throughout the discourse, one of the chief messages is to have faith and to act faithfully. Here in chapter 11, the preacher layers example on top of example of biblical ancestors who lived in faith. The writer assembles the "great cloud of witnesses" referenced in chapter 12, the heavenly cheerleading squad that serves to inspire the community to finish the race, to carry on faithfully all the way to the finish line. Never mind that one could poke holes in some of the exhorter's examples! Here in Hebrews, the exhorter seeks to inspire and encourage; counterevidence, such as Abram's need for more information and evidence, can be overlooked.

TO LIVE WITH THE ASSURANCE OF THINGS HOPED FOR IS TO CONTINUE TO STEWARD THE PROMISE ENTRUSTED TO THE PEOPLE OF GOD OVER MANY GENERATIONS.

It is worthwhile to pause on the preacher's famous definition of faith as "the assurance of things hoped for, the conviction of things not seen" (v. 1). The first clause, the assurance of things hoped for, relates to the belief expressed throughout Hebrews that the exhorter's community stands at the threshold of fulfilled time. Patriarchs and matriarchs, every generation of God's people, journeyed closer to this moment, but the preacher's people are at the threshold of the city prepared by God (see especially vv. 13-16). Generations have lived in faith, acting with assurance that the hoped-for future would come to pass. The present community is exhorted to stand in the tradition of their ancestors, to hang on and live in the same assurance for yet a little while longer. To live with the assurance of things hoped for is to continue to steward the promise entrusted to the people of God over many generations, passed off like a baton in a race, from one generation to the next, and now nestled in the hands of the exhorter's community.

The second clause, "the conviction of things not seen," refers to the cause of the assured outcomes: God. Faith has a reason: God. As the invisible word created the visible world, so the same Cause of the world's foundation is the Cause who will bring about the city "without foundation," for which the present community is to wait faithfully. The faith the community holds is faith in God and God's promises.

THE GOSPEL

LUKE 12:32-40 (RCL, BCP)
LUKE 12:32-48 OR 12:35-40 (RC)

Biblical time is God's time. Human beings do not have time. We do not spend time. We cannot save time. We live in time as fish live in water, and all time belongs to God. Human beings are called to act as good stewards of the time God gives to us.

"What time is it?" Many, many biblical texts imply this question and its consequent correlate, "Based on our understanding of what time it is, what then shall we do?" In this text, Luke's answer continues the teachings on wealth from earlier in the chapter: it is time to detach from possessions (vv. 32-34) and to wait attentively and alertly (vv. 35-40)—this is especially true for the community's leaders (vv. 41-48).

Verses 32-34, along with verses 22-31, parallel portions of Matthew 6 ("Do not be anxious"). Some scholars of the Roman Empire refer to the decades around the events and writing of the New Testament as an Age of Anxiety. One can find philosophical prescriptions for anxiety in both classical and biblical intertestamental literature. In a world where social structures are changing, people tend to be particularly anxious. It is a human tendency to want to hang on to what we know and what we have. When our world is threatened, anxiety results. Anxious people create and grasp on to security blankets of their own making: possessions, doctrines, ways of living peculiar to one time or place that become absolutes.

> LUKE SEEMS PARTICULARLY CONCERNED ABOUT HIS COMMUNITY'S RELATIONSHIP WITH WEALTH AND THE DISTRACTION FROM THE REIGN OF GOD THAT WEALTH REPRESENTS.

The New Testament communities certainly were troubled by anxieties, perhaps especially the anxieties generated by living into their new lives as Christians when the rules and roles were in the process of being defined. Whatever Jesus' words meant to his first hearers, the communities to which the Gospels were written lived decades later. How does the passage of forty or fifty years or more affect the answers to the questions about what time it is and how the community should act? The demographics of Jesus communities likely changed over that time. Luke's community, for instance, may have included more people of means than Jesus' first hearers. Luke seems particularly concerned about his community's relationship with wealth and the distraction from the reign of God that wealth represents. He includes more teaching on wealth and the poor than Matthew or Mark. In Luke, as in Matthew, Jesus' counsel to counter anxiety is to focus on waiting actively for the reign

IN A WORLD WHERE THE SON OF MAN OR THE REIGN OF GOD MIGHT BREAK IN AT ANY MOMENT, THE FAITHFUL COMMUNITY RESPONSE IS TO WAIT ACTIVELY AND ATTENTIVELY.

of God. The community's members should prepare themselves to receive God's reign by detaching from their possessions, by giving alms, and by making purses fit for heaven. Attachment per se is not bad. If we attach to that which cannot be taken from us and cannot be destroyed, then anxiety has no food.

But what it meant to remain attentive will have changed as the first century progressed. It is hard, is it not, for an individual to remain attentive for a few hours—sometimes even a few minutes? It takes great discipline to cultivate attentiveness in order to remain attentive to that which is important for days, weeks, months, or years. How much more difficult is it for a *community* to cultivate active, attentive waiting for *decades*? We saw how the exhorter in Hebrews struggled to keep his community focused.

Luke provides two interesting, very different examples of waiting. In the one example, the hearer is asked to wait as a slave waits for the master to return from the wedding banquet. There is great, positive anticipation, and the slave knows the master will return—that is not in doubt. The reward for the slave's attentive waiting is that the master will serve the attentive slave. In the other example, hearers are warned to wait as if for a thief in the night, for the surprise visitor. Note the strong, even startling contrast between the two images: waiting for a master, with positive anticipation; keeping vigil to thwart a thief, an image that emphasizes suddenness and the need to be alert. The former image allows Luke to emphasize the wonderful result: the master will serve the slave. The latter image focuses listeners on waiting actively for an event, the timing of which is beyond their control; for who can time when someone will break into their home? In a world where the Son of Man or the reign of God might break in at any moment, the faithful community response is to wait actively and attentively.

The Roman Catholic text includes verses 41-48. Peter, speaking on behalf of the "leadership team," asks whether this teaching is for all the disciples (the host of folks traveling to Jerusalem with Jesus) or for the leadership team particularly. Jesus' response begins with "Who then is the faithful and prudent manager whom his master will put in charge of his slaves . . . ?" He is addressing the leadership. The household steward is to know and follow the master's teaching in his treatment of the household. If he gets caught doing otherwise, the consequences will be severe (v. 46).

PUTTING THE TEXTS TOGETHER

If we adopt the biblical perspective on time, then human beings are stewards of the time God has given to us. Time belongs to God, not to us. Each Christian community will be held responsible for how we use the time God has entrusted to us.

The Christian community is always somewhere along the way, somewhere on the journey of God's people that began with Abram and Sarai and continues even today. It is cliché but also true: life for Christians is about the journey, for the arrival of the destination—the reign of God—is in God's hands. The author of Hebrews thought his community was on the cusp of receiving the fulfilled promises. Today, we still live on that cusp.

We are joined to God's community of promise through faith, which is a gift from God. We also have responsibilities in the way we use the gift of faith. We must make decisions regarding what we attend to and what time we think it is. The Isaiah text could serve as a reminder that it is always time to act justly. God's people will always be judged by how we treat

EACH CHRISTIAN COMMUNITY WILL BE HELD RESPONSIBLE FOR HOW WE USE THE TIME GOD HAS ENTRUSTED TO US.

our most vulnerable neighbors. Watching for opportunities to treat a vulnerable neighbor justly, whether by giving alms or by advocating for the poor, is one way to remain faithful and attentive to the Bridegroom's return.

TWELFTH SUNDAY AFTER PENTECOST

TWENTIETH SUNDAY IN ORDINARY TIME / PROPER 15
AUGUST 19, 2007

REVISED COMMON	EPISCOPAL (BCP)	ROMAN CATHOLIC
Jer. 23:23-29 or Isa. 5:1-7	Jer. 23:23-29	Jer. 38:4-6, 8-10
Psalm 82 or Ps. 80:1-2, 8-19	Psalm 82	Ps. 40:2, 3, 4, 18
Heb. 11:29—12:2	Heb. 12:1-7 (8-10) 11-14	Heb. 12:1-4
Luke 12:49-56	Luke 12:49-56	Luke 12:49-53

These texts are full of difficult words. If a congregation is a collection of individuals each hoping to hear a word of comfort and solace in the midst of afflictions, these texts may be hard to hear! If a congregation has attuned its life to those who suffer and is looking for hope in the midst of or on the other side of their pain, however, read on.

FIRST READING
JEREMIAH 23:23-29 (RCL, BCP)

Jeremiah was one of the classical prophets who was active in Judah and Jerusalem at the time of the Babylonian siege (ca. 587 B.C.E.) and until his death in Egypt. He was called to be a prophet while just a youth (1:6ff.). His prophecies, some of which were dictated to his scribe Baruch and were collected into the book that bears his name, are characterized well in these lines from his call: "I appoint you over nations and over kingdoms, to pluck up and to pull down, to destroy and to overthrow, to build and to plant" (1:10).

In Jeremiah 23, the prophet condemns two groups of leaders, kings and prophets, who serve themselves rather than God and who tell and act on lies. Verses 1-4 deride kings who shepherd poorly. From verse 9 through the end of the chapter, the author turns to false prophets. Verse 23 opens the lection for today with a mocking or sarcastic tone: "Do these so-called prophets think that I reside in only one place and that they are hidden from me as they tell lies in my name? Do they think they can tell their lies and I don't see and hear?" The implication of this charge is that these so-called prophets knew the truth and intentionally deceived their hearers with lies that suited someone's ears and purposes. Jeremiah issues his word from God, which instructs the people how to discern between which prophecies are God-given and which are false, misrepresentations of God's will. Listen to these two very different attributes of a true prophecy: "What has straw in common with wheat? . . . Is not my word like fire . . . and like a hammer that breaks a rock in pieces?" (vv. 28-29). There are two images in this passage, one that nourishes

> THE WORD OF GOD WILL BE RECOGNIZED, IN JERE-MIAH'S CONTEXT, NOT BY HOW MUCH COMFORT IT OFFERS BUT BY HOW IT BURNS UP AND BREAKS DOWN THE HOUSE OF LIES.

and one that jars. God's true word is like wheat that nourishes rather than like inedible straw. But God's word is also like fire, which destroys and purifies, or like a hammer, which can be used either to build a house or break a rock. Given the context in Jeremiah of prophets preaching comfort and well-being with the dust of invading armies on the horizon, we should think destruction and breaking here. The word of God will be recognized, in Jeremiah's context, not by how much comfort it offers but by how it burns up and breaks down the house of lies.

For the preacher who also wishes to be the spokesperson for God's truth, the challenge is to keep *nourishing* and *breaking* in relationship. I mean this two ways. First, to keep the work of nourishing and the work of breaking in relationship with each other. When a "reality" has been built on lies, that falsehood often needs to be burnt up or hammered down in order to make room for truth. And the preacher who plays the angry prophet may be blinded by her or his own anger and neglect the nourishing work of truth. Therefore, it is also important for preachers to stay in relationship with their congregants as they attempt the difficult, prophetic work of pulling down *and* building up.

JEREMIAH 38:4-6, 8-10 (RC)

The Roman Catholic reading tells a story about Jeremiah that would also be a useful adjunct to the Revised Common Lectionary choice because this story illustrates a potential consequence of relating God's fiery and pounding word—hearers will get very angry! Three of King Zedekiah's counselors approach the king and accuse Jeremiah of bringing harm to the people and undermining the morale of the remaining soldiers battling the Babylonian siege-works. Zedekiah gives his tacit permission for his counselors to kill Jeremiah. The men seize Jeremiah and lower him into the king's son's well to die of exposure or hunger. Then Ebed-Melech, an Ethiopian eunuch in the king's service, saw what the men had done. He told Zedekiah as if Zedekiah did not know and authorize this deed. Perhaps because he could no longer participate in Jeremiah's destruction and publicly keep Jeremiah's blood off his hands, Zedekiah now assertively orders the eunuch to draw Jeremiah up and bring him into the safety of the king's household.

Telling the truth has consequences when a people is living on a foundation of lies.

ISAIAH 5:1-7 (RCL ALT.)

What an interesting rhetorical vehicle—use an allegorical love-song format to communicate a message of doom and betrayal! The allegory portrays God as a vineyard builder and owner and Israel as the vineyard. The owner acted according to good farming practices and expected a good grape harvest. He planted and cultivated in all the right ways, expecting an outstanding harvest and a fine wine. The vines produced only wild grapes, however. Therefore, the owner will tear down the protective hedge (the city walls) and the vines (Israel and Judah) will be trampled. Why? God "expected justice, but saw bloodshed; righteousness, but heard a cry!" (v. 7).

In order to help the congregation hear this text, the reader should note aloud the changes of voice between third and first person. In verses 1-2, the balladeer (Isaiah) opens, singing of his beloved (God) in the third person. In verse 3, the voice changes to God speaking directly to the people. Then in verse 7, the song moves back to the balladeer's voice, singing of God in the third person.

RESPONSIVE READING
PSALM 82 (RCL, BCP)
PSALM 40:2, 3, 4, 18 (RC)

Psalm 82 presents another interesting rhetorical device to present a message complementary to the other texts for this Sunday. In this psalm, God calls together a council of all the gods, perhaps meaning the gods worshiped by all the peoples of the earth—the gods, that is, who were the ultimate legitimation for the statutes of other nations, statutes that justify enslavement and exploitation of the many by a few. One might imagine one living entity on a throne surrounded by lesser thrones on which sit mute statues. Right judgment will entail justice for the weak and protection of the lowly from the wicked (vv. 3-4). God lectures these puppet gods, informing them that they shall all "die like mortals" (v. 7).

The Psalm 40 variation is included because of its tie to the Jeremiah story of being left in the well to die and then being rescued: "He drew me up from the desolate pit, out of the miry bog" (v. 2).

PSALM 80:1-2, 8-19 (RCL ALT.)

The choice of this psalm is clearly linked with the Isaiah text; both employ the image of the vineyard, with the people being the vine. The point of view here is radically different from that of the Isaiah text, however. There, the point of view is God's disappointment in his beloved vineyard. Here, the psalmist cries for God to save the vineyard and expresses no understanding of why calamity has befallen the people. The psalmist reminds God that God brought this vine up from Egypt and carefully planted and cultivated it. The author cries in distress because the vine is under attack. What a difference point of view makes!

As an aside, it may be worth noting that grapevines are propagated through taking cuttings and planting them in new soil. That is how Fertile Crescent cuttings made their way to Italy and Spain, and how French grapes found homes, at least as a hybrid with native plants, in California. It is a powerful image: a people picked up from one place (Egypt) and planted in a new place (the Promised Land), with the intent that the vine could flourish in this new place. It is an image that has held power for the Jewish people and for the Christian people for many centuries.

SECOND READING
HEBREWS 11:29—12:2 (RCL)
HEBREWS 12:1-7 (8-10) 11-14 (BCP)
HEBREWS 12:1-4 (RC)

What a powerful set of choices and themes the lectionary writers offer preachers in these texts! The Revised Common Lectionary focuses on the "great cloud of witnesses" and the faithfulness of these witnesses in the midst of trials, persecution, and suffering. The Book of Common Prayer lectionary picks up at the "cloud of witnesses," turns attention to Jesus, "the pioneer and perfecter of our faith," and then moves back to the importance of enduring discipline in order to "share holiness."

If one looks at the full sweep of these texts, one can see a very dramatic movement with the listeners' attention shifting from the cloud of witnesses, to the present hearers, to Jesus. Imagine a race, staggered over time, that no one can finish until the last of the participants has entered ("so they would not, apart from us,

168

THE SEASON
AFTER PENTECOST
───────────
GARY E. PELUSO-
VERDEND

be made perfect," 11:40). Near the starting line (11:29-39), the writer assembles a cloud of witnesses, from persons who did great things in history by faith to martyrs for the faith. Note the variety of witnesses included, from Rahab to David, and from the fiery furnace trio and Daniel in the lion's den to martyrs and suffering relatives in stories told in 2 Maccabees (which indicates that the exhorter's audience knew these stories). Then, in 12:1 the exhorter "makes it plain" to his hearers. Like runners who have trained with weights, it is time now for this congregation to lay them aside, for it is time to run the race. Sin is also a weight that must be laid aside, even suffered and trained (disciplined) out. Keep your eyes focused, he tells them, on Jesus, the lead runner, the pioneer and perfecter of the faith. Then the focus shifts briefly to Jesus, who "for the sake of the joy that was set before him endured the cross" (v. 2). But quickly the exhorter, who is worried that tough times are driving community members from the community and into isolation and spiritual death, reminds them to "endure trials for the sake of discipline" (v. 7).

> LIKE RUNNERS WHO HAVE TRAINED WITH WEIGHTS, IT IS TIME NOW FOR THIS CONGREGATION TO LAY THEM ASIDE, FOR IT IS TIME TO RUN THE RACE.

This reading expresses the antithesis of the health-and-wealth gospel. Look ahead to 12:16 and remember Esau's shallow exchange: his belly for his life. In Hebrews, we find the opposite of immediate gratification, individualism, and even eudaemonism (the belief that life is ultimately about being happy). Living life as God intended, in faith and truth, will involve suffering.

THE GOSPEL
LUKE 12:49-56 (RCL, BCP)
LUKE 12:49-53 (RC)

In this text, Jesus echoes what John the Baptizer said of him, that he will baptize with the Holy Spirit and with fire (Luke 3:16). This is a fire text. This lection is one of those texts that shreds those mental pictures of the pastoral Jesus, gently walking the flowered slopes of the Galilean countryside, or portrayed only as the compassionate shepherd returning the lost sheep to the fold, carried upon his shoulders. "I came to bring fire. . . . What stress I am under. . . . I have come to bring [not peace but] division." Division at the deepest level: father versus son, mother versus daughter, mother-in-law versus daughter-in-law. Here is one of the two places in the lections over these ten Sundays in which Jesus overthrows household

> EARLY CHRISTIANITY WAS NOT TOLERANT OR SYNCRETISTIC. WITH SO MANY EVERYDAY PRACTICES AND BEHAVIORS NEEDING TO BE REVISED, BOUNDARIES WERE CONSTANTLY BEING TESTED AND REDRAWN.

mores (the other is 14:26 [Twelfth Sunday after Pentecost/Twenty-third Sunday in Ordinary Time/Proper 18]). This is truth as fire and truth as hammer.

To deal with such a text for our own day, it may be helpful to imagine the situation in Luke's congregation to which this text spoke. Unless the reader is from a so-called non-Christian country or comes from a family that is not Christian in background or culture, it may be hard to imagine the division that declaring Jesus to be the Messiah, the Savior of the world, caused in either Jewish or (more likely for Luke's first readers) Gentile households. The demands of Christian community life were strong. Mores governing everything from table behavior to marital relations to the meaning of family and neighbor had changed. Jesus' teachings nullified the Mediterranean patronage system. If there were household or imperial deities

> A RIGHT USE OF THIS TEXT TODAY WILL INVOLVE AN INTENSE DEBATE WITHIN CHRISTIAN CONGREGATIONS IN REGARD TO HOW OUR FAMILY PRACTICES HELP US OR HINDER IN ACTING AS CHRISTIAN COMMUNITIES.

of any sort, they were set aside. Early Christianity was not tolerant or syncretistic. With so many everyday practices and behaviors needing to be revised, boundaries were constantly being tested and redrawn. Often, boundaries were tightly drawn in order to cast out the old pagan ways and to live with newly formed Christian practices. To bring Jesus home was to stir conflict and division. The experience of twentieth-century Christian converts in India may be akin to the family experience of the first century. Converts sometimes found themselves without village or family.

Let us assume that the situation in Luke's congregation was akin to this scenario. That still leaves us with the question, why did Jesus say he brought division and fire (or why did Luke say that Jesus said these things)? Remember that Jesus and the disciples are on the way to Jerusalem. Jesus is teaching constantly about the reign of God as the community's highest good, a reign in which imperial and patronage relationships are void. Any obstacle to receiving the reign of God is to be cast aside, whether that obstacle be wealth, self—or family. Apparently, to be attached to family as primary obligation is to be disqualified as a citizen of God's reign.

This text is also a powerful reminder of both the importance and the power of declaring what time it is (vv. 54-56). It is a power that the preacher has and should use with the utmost care. How do we use this text today? Is it time to stir division or to make peace? Consider the differences that time and context might make in regard to interpreting this text. The original audience was a Christian community, and the households in that community, in the Roman Empire. The meaning of sword, fire, and division in that context was significantly different from that of today. Take this text within our present era and in a U.S. context, in which we experience renewed conflicts between Islam and the West and between Islam and

Christianity, conflicts that are driven by nations and national leaders as well as by groups and movements. Is Jesus being rightly used by those persons who seek to kindle the fire through sword and the courts? I do not think these texts could be used to justify laws that divide or national behaviors that drive wedges between peoples and religions. A right use of this text today will involve an intense debate within Christian congregations in regard to how our family practices—at table, in the raising of our children, in marriage and singleness—help us or hinder us in acting as Christian communities.

PUTTING THE TEXTS TOGETHER

One of the common denominators in these lections is that telling the truth and deciding who is telling the truth often divide people. It was the case in Jeremiah's day as in the days of the other classical prophets: speaking truth to power either causes or reveals division. Why? Because part of being in power is defining both what is real and what time it is; and we human beings tend to make those determinations based on what serves our narrow interests. Our current day is by no means the first time in history when this is so! A contemporary comedian who satirizes the day's news and newsmakers coined the term *truthiness*, meaning that in today's parlance, public words that pass for truth are too often mushy and questionable. Real truth often divides and evokes anger from those who live in and with lies. It is always time to speak in a truthful manner, a way that burns away the straw and the dross, the lies and the ways of life built on lies. It is not good to isolate the need for truthful speech and actions from the needs for compassion and community; sometimes we are afraid to speak of truth for fear of evoking anger or even violence against ourselves. Neither is it good to allow truthiness to go unchecked. Truth, spoken in love, nourishes even as it tears down in order to build on a solid foundation. Truthiness neither nourishes nor can endure over time.

> IT IS ALWAYS TIME TO SPEAK IN A TRUTHFUL MANNER, A WAY THAT BURNS AWAY THE STRAW AND THE DROSS, THE LIES AND THE WAYS OF LIFE BUILT ON LIES.

The truth, Luke tells us, is that there is a value higher than family: the reign of God. The truth is that sometimes our family ties skew our understanding of stewardship by too narrowly defining "us." If we utilize our resources by first determining what is best for "me and mine," we are beginning at a false point. The exhorter in Hebrews reminds his hearers that "us" includes a great cloud of witnesses. Jesus in Luke challenges everyone from his leadership team the crowds to expand their idea of "us" until it is as broad as the table at the messianic banquet.

THIRTEENTH SUNDAY AFTER PENTECOST

TWENTY-FIRST SUNDAY IN ORDINARY TIME /
PROPER 16
AUGUST 26, 2007

REVISED COMMON	EPISCOPAL (BCP)	ROMAN CATHOLIC
Isa. 58:9b–14 or Jer. 1:4–10	Isa. 28:14–22	Isa. 66:18–21
Ps. 103:1–8 or Ps. 71:1-6	Psalm 46	Ps. 117:1, 2
Heb. 12:18–29	Heb. 12:18–19, 22-29	Heb. 12:5-7, 11-13
Luke 13:10-17	Luke 13:22-30	Luke 13:22-30

In the last four to five decades, the American church has focused on a sense of loss in regard to Sabbath. The church once enjoyed an unofficial establishment with the state supporting at least some of the church's calendar, especially at Christmas and on Sundays. Then that state support waned as Sunday closing laws gave way to entertainment, commercial, and leisure activities. Movie theaters competed with youth groups on Sunday night. Soccer, hockey, traveling baseball teams, the Sunday *New York Times*, and dozens of other attractive leisure pursuits won converts from Sunday worship. Sabbath keeping has been romanticized by such sentence stems as, "Ah, remember the day when we didn't have to compete with . . . ?" However, the lections offer a different understanding of Sabbath from the one we think we have been losing. Sabbath keeping for the people of God is more about liberation and the stewardship of God's time than about a list of prohibitions.

FIRST READING
ISAIAH 58:9b–14 (RCL)

Scholars speak of three Isaiahs. One was active during the Assyrian destruction of the Northern Kingdom (chaps. 1–39). A second worked during the end of the exile (chaps. 40–55). A third prophesied during a period of postexilic restoration (chaps. 56–66).

Second Isaiah gives us a lengthy list of if-thens: great benefits will accrue to the people if they act justly, if they rebuild the city on a foundation of justice. They will be made like never-failing waters, they will be a watered garden, known as the repairer of the breach, as those who restored streets in which to live. This people who sat in the darkness of exile, who were cut off from their land, who feared assimilation by their captors, could not contemplate life after exile. They were going home. They would need to rebuild their city and the culture of their people. Isaiah helps the leaders to envision how future generations will know them, the good name they will have—*if* they rebuild Jerusalem on a foundation of justice.

One key behavior that evidences justice is keeping the Sabbath. Today, I suspect that if non-Jews were asked what it means to "keep the Sabbath," most people would say something like "taking a day to rest." Alternatively, they might express annoyance that they live in states that still uphold at least remnants of Blue laws, for instance, liquor stores closed on Sundays. In Isaiah's world, keeping the Sabbath was primarily an expression of faith in God's abundance. Every living being rests on the Sabbath because God has made enough for everyone. Therefore, keeping the Sabbath means to refrain from any sort of commercial gain, "not going your own ways, serving your own interests, or pursuing your own affairs" (v. 13). This behavior is ordered not for the sake of the prohibition but for the sake of every living creature enjoying a day of regal rest. Sabbath keeping, then, is a very important expression of acting justly, one day a week during which every strata of society is to enjoy God's blessings and abundance.

> SABBATH KEEPING IS A VERY IMPORTANT EXPRESSION OF ACTING JUSTLY, ONE DAY A WEEK DURING WHICH EVERY STRATA OF SOCIETY IS TO ENJOY GOD'S BLESSINGS AND ABUNDANCE.

ISAIAH 28:14-22 (BCP)

This text comes from First Isaiah and is full of powerful images of judgment upon Israel's corrupt, lying leaders. Isaiah addresses scoffers "who rule this people in Jerusalem" (v. 14), who have built a house of lies and have "made a covenant with death" (v. 15). God, however, is laying a cornerstone in Zion named "One who trusts will not panic" (v. 16). Only this cornerstone and the buildings set upon it, it seems, will withstand the fury to come. With justice and righteousness serving as a plumb line, the measure by which a wall is determined to be straight and thus can stand or crooked and thus must be corrected or torn down, Isaiah prophesies God's "decree of destruction" (v. 22): God will destroy the house of lies with hail and downpour. One hears echoes of Jeremiah 23 from last week in regard to God's disdain for lying leaders. There will be no hiding from this destruction, "for the bed is too short to stretch oneself on it, and the covering too narrow to wrap oneself in it" (v. 21).

Is there a more consistent biblical message than this, a message that is found often in both Testaments, that a civilization built on anything but justice, as determined by treatment of the most vulnerable members of society, cannot endure?

ISAIAH 66:18-21 (RC)

Third Isaiah proclaims a vision of restoration and of a new order. "Survivors" shall go to all the nations and do two activities: they shall declare God's glory among the nations; they shall bring the diaspora home. The latter action is vividly envisioned: horses, chariots, litters, mules, camels—any form of travel but walking. First-class transportation will be provided!

The vision is not of a simple restoration of the way things were. There will be a new order, for priests and Levites will be drawn from these exiles.

JEREMIAH 1:4-10 (RCL ALT.)

This text is one of the classic call stories in the Bible. Note the form. God appoints and calls. Jeremiah objects that he is not fit for the role: "Truly I do not know how to speak, for I am only a boy" (v. 6). God counters the objection. First, God promises to be present with Jeremiah. Second, as an expression of divine presence, God touches Jeremiah's mouth and tells him that his mouth is now full of God's words. As the saying goes, God equips the called (rather than necessarily calling the equipped). Could anyone, without God's power, endure such a calling "over nations and over kingdoms, to pluck up and to pull down, to destroy and to overthrow, to build and to plant" (v. 10)?

RESPONSIVE READING
PSALM 103:1-8 (RCL)

This is a praise psalm, with both a subjective and an objective dimension. The subjective dimension in verses 1-5 praises the benefits of God given to human beings: forgiveness, healing, redemption, completion, satisfaction, renewal. The preacher might compare the if-then conditional benefits named in the Isaiah 58 reading with those mentioned here (for instance, "If you pursue justice, then . . ."). The objective verses 5-8 sing of God's attributes: working justice for

174

THE SEASON
AFTER PENTECOST
―――――――――
GARY E. PELUSO-
VERDEND

the oppressed; self-revealing; merciful and gracious; slow to anger; abounding in steadfast love.

PSALM 46 (BCP)

The psalmist's refrain is that "God is our refuge." Verb after verb conjures tumult and instability in the world ("change," "shake," "roar," "tremble," "uproar," "totter," "melt," "desolation") and is contrasted with God's strength, steadfastness, safety, and presence. In the midst of all the tumult: "Be still, and know that I am God!" (v. 10). The preacher might connect this set of images with the Isaiah 28 text, which contrasts the fate of a house of lies with God's cornerstone.

PSALM 117:1, 2 (RC)

This is a two-verse psalm of praise that opens and closes with "Hallelujah!"

PSALM 71:1-6 (RCL ALT.)

The lectionary writers clearly chose this psalm for its fit with the Jeremiah call text. The psalmist seems to be besieged by hostile forces. Be my refuge. Don't let me be shamed. Save me from the wicked and the cruel. I've depended on you all my life, and you "took me from my mother's womb" (v. 6). In like manner, Jeremiah would plead his case to God because of the negative consequence of fulfilling his call: he developed many enemies who did not like a prophet they could not control.

SECOND READING
HEBREWS 12:18-29 (RCL)
HEBREWS 12:18-19, 22-29 (BCP)
HEBREWS 12:5-7, 11-13 (RC)

Most modern commentators date Hebrews late in the chronology of canonical New Testament books. They cite its radically different Christology and theology as evidence of lateness. One can make good sense of the text, however, by understanding it as written to a community, near Jerusalem, before the Roman destructions of the city and the Temple. The community is tempted to return to temple practices, especially putting their faith back into the temple sacrificial system. The exhorter of Hebrews attempts to help his troubled people remain true to the understanding of Jesus as perfect high priest and perfect victim, whose perfect sacrifice atoned for all sin and ended the efficacy of the temple sacrificial system.

Regardless of dating and location, the exhorter employs a typological approach to Scripture throughout his sermon, often contrasting the covenant, teachings, and sacrificial system given through Moses (the type) with the superior covenant, teachings, and sacrifice that ends all sacrifices given in and accomplished through Jesus (the archetype). His entire orientation is really toward the present and the near future: all of history has led up to this moment in time, to this place, to this people (who may be "the assembly of the firstborn who are enrolled in heaven," v. 23). The Sinai event was a type of the Zion event, Moses was a type of Jesus, the shaking of the earth then was a type of the shaking of the earth's foundations that is to come about when the congregation receives "a kingdom that cannot be shaken." In each case, the "real thing" is more powerful than the type. The contrast has been developed throughout the entire sermon. In the verses leading up to 12:29, the tension reaches a climax (some commentators believe the exhortation per se ends with 12:29, with chapter 13 coming from another hand). The only adequate response, claims the exhorter, is to continue to gather for worship, "with reverence and awe," for "our God is a consuming fire" (vv. 28, 29).

> THE EXHORTER OF HEBREWS ATTEMPTS TO HELP HIS TROUBLED PEOPLE REMAIN TRUE TO THE UNDERSTANDING OF JESUS AS PERFECT HIGH PRIEST AND PERFECT VICTIM, WHOSE PERFECT SACRIFICE ATONED FOR ALL SIN AND ENDED THE EFFICACY OF THE TEMPLE SACRIFICIAL SYSTEM.

The person who reads this passage to the congregation would do well to set it up in some way. Most of Hebrews is *not* a well-known Scripture for lay Christians. What is the meaning of this contrast between the Sinai event and the anticipated Mt. Zion event? Or what is the consequence of not heeding the voice that calls from heaven? These were huge questions for the community to which this exhortation was given. What meaning could these questions possibly have for a contemporary congregation?

The recognition of and appreciation for contemporary Christian-Jewish relations might also frame how this passage is preached. This is a supersessionist text for the first century, for one of the main arguments the author is making is that Christ's sacrifice has superseded the temple sacrificial system. The author pleads for a wall of separation between the community's former lives and practices and their present. Contemporary Christians need not continue this supersessionism, however. After all, Judaism itself has not relied on the temple sacrificial system for over 1,900 years! Also, it is not necessary for today's Christian communities to maintain their identity by showing how different we are from Jewish communities.

The Roman Catholic variation deals with the text and the theme that the other lectionaries addressed last Sunday: a reminder that discipline and suffering are important, even essential experiences if a community wishes to be a holy people. (See the Twelfth Sunday after Pentecost/Twentieth Sunday in Ordinary Time/Proper 15, above.)

THE GOSPEL

LUKE 13:10-17 (RCL)

The Revised Common Lectionary is using a section of Luke that has no parallel in the other Gospels. This story is particularly interesting because it is evidently a literary construction. The story reads more like a script played out on the stage of the listener's imagination than a telling of a historical event. I am not meaning to say that something like this story did not happen. But Luke's staging is evident.

As the story begins, Jesus is teaching in a synagogue on the Sabbath. "And just then there appeared . . ." As if a spotlight now illumines a previously dark section of the stage, this woman is now the focal point of Jesus' and the hearer's attention. She does not ask for healing, but Jesus calls her over and heals her, an act of compassion in regard to the woman, an act of provocation in regard to his critics. Shift audience attention to the critics. Then the synagogue leader, addressing the crowd rather than Jesus, admonishes the crowd that work is forbidden on the Sabbath. The leader speaks with the *crowd* and tells them not to come for healing on the Sabbath, rather than speaking with Jesus and telling him not to do healing work on the Sabbath. Is the synagogue leader demonstrating a sign of respect for Jesus' power or attempting to shame him by not speaking with him directly? In either case, he can stop Jesus if he cuts off Jesus' supply of sick people! Back to Jesus. Jesus' retort begins in the plural: "You hypocrites!" Was Jesus now speaking to more than one leader? Was he speaking to those in the crowd swayed by the leader's admonition? Or was he speaking to the members of Luke's community who questioned the legitimacy of doing good works on the Sabbath? In any case, Jesus makes a powerful *kal vehomer*, from the light to the heavy or from lenient to strict, argument: "If this is the case, how much the more so is that the case." Thus: "If you will loose an animal from a manger to let it drink on the sabbath, how much the more ought I to set free on the sabbath a child of Abraham whom Satan kept bound for eighteen years" (vv. 15-16; we are not told how Jesus knew she was crippled for eighteen years). One of the reasons for keeping Sabbath is to be reminded of the glorious freedom of the children of God, to be liberated from work one day in seven.

ONE OF THE REASONS FOR KEEPING SABBATH IS TO BE REMINDED OF THE GLORIOUS FREEDOM OF THE CHILDREN OF GOD, TO BE LIBERATED FROM WORK ONE DAY IN SEVEN.

Jesus extends freedom from work to include freedom from suffering. The scene concludes with Jesus' opponents (plural) shamed and the "entire crowd" cheering "the wonderful things that he was doing."

Luke's staging allows the preacher several entryways into the text, each doorway representing a different point of view. We have the crowd who watched the drama of the healing, heard the synagogue leader admonish them not to come for healing on the Sabbath, listened as Jesus rebuked the prohibitionist stance of their leaders, and rejoiced at all the good Jesus did. We have the bent-over woman who, unlike the woman in another story who reached out to touch the hem of Jesus' garment, did not seek healing but was picked out by Jesus and healed after eighteen years of constant suffering. We have the synagogue leader(s) and Jesus' other critics, representing a prohibitionist view of Sabbath keeping. And we have Jesus, taking advantage of any opportunity to liberate a suffering person from Satan's bondage either through his healing or through his teaching.

LUKE 13:22-30 (BCP, RC)

The Episcopal and Roman Catholic Lukan reading clashes with our contemporary mind-set. In a democratic culture, in which we propound ideals such as rights and benefits for all and "You get what you deserve," here is a saying regarding the few who will be saved. "Strive to enter by the narrow door." Jesus does not directly answer the question, "Will only a few be saved?" However, his answer seems to indicate that people will be surprised by who is saved: the diaspora gathered (echoes of the Isaiah 66 text for the day); the last being first and first last.

Note that this text does not tell us which specific behaviors or virtues prepare a person for entering the narrow door and which specific behaviors and dispositions will get one labeled as an "evildoer." The preacher might highlight that Jesus is on his way to Jerusalem—and his suffering there represents his own narrow gate, perhaps. But the text does tell us that to the extent that having a seat at the Messiah's banquet is in human control at all, it is necessary to "strive." The Greek for "strive" is the root of the English word *agony*. Entering that narrow gate is an energy-intensive activity, even painful. Being acquainted with Jesus socially is insufficient: "We ate and drank with you, and you taught in our streets" (v. 26). The lectionary shapers' choice of the Hebrews text suggests that a disciplined life, marked by corrective suffering, is at least part of the agony necessary to gain passage through the narrow door.

Whatever salvation by grace through faith means, if one looks to these Lukan words, it cannot mean a passive acceptance. Faithful living into the reign of God involves active striving.

Putting the Texts Together

THE SEASON
AFTER PENTECOST

GARY E. PELUSO-
VERDEND

What is the meaning of Sabbath for today's Christian communities? The Revised Common Lectionary texts suggest a more nuanced answer than following a list of personal "thou shalt nots." Keeping Sabbath is not simply about time off. It is not about personal indulgence. Keeping Sabbath is a means of participating in the freedom of the children of God, freedom from want, freedom from commercial gain, freedom from self-interest, freedom from the need to accumulate more stuff. We *hear* much more about the need to adopt "an attitude of gratitude" and an abundance rather than a scarcity mentality than we keep before ourselves the inspiration to *live* with gratitude for abundant life in Christ.

> KEEPING SABBATH IS A WEEKLY REMINDER OF GOD'S HOUSEHOLD ECONOMICS IN WHICH ECONOMIC JUSTICE IS A FOUNDATIONAL VIRTUE OF ANY SOCIETY AND IN WHICH THE VALUE OF LIBERATION FOR THE BOUND TAKES PRECEDENCE OVER NORMAL PROHIBITIONS.

Keeping Sabbath is also a weekly reminder of God's household economics in which economic justice is a foundational virtue of any society and in which the value of liberation for the bound takes precedence over normal prohibitions. In today's 24/7/365 globalized and commercialized economy, keeping Sabbath thus understood will involve striving that rises to the level of agony. We Christians have little external support for Sabbath stewardship. It is not easy to be a good steward of time, money, energy, and attention in a world that never sleeps or rests, in which faith in the global economy sometimes crosses over into idolatry.

FOURTEENTH SUNDAY AFTER PENTECOST

TWENTY-SECOND SUNDAY IN ORDINARY TIME/
PROPER 17
SEPTEMBER 2, 2007

REVISED COMMON	EPISCOPAL (BCP)	ROMAN CATHOLIC
Prov. 25:6-7 or Sir. 10:12-18 or Jer. 2:4-13	Sir. 10:(7-11) 12-18	Sir. 3:17-18, 20, 28-29
Psalm 112 or Ps. 81:1, 10-16	Psalm 112	Ps. 68:4-5, 6-7, 10-11
Heb. 13:1-8, 15-16	Heb. 13:1-8	Heb. 12:18-19, 22-24a
Luke 14:1, 7-14	Luke 14:1, 7-14	Luke 14:1, 7-14

Stewards may be called to account at any point for the goods entrusted to them. Good stewards will be able to provide an accurate accounting. What if we viewed our very self as one of the items on the list for which we must give an account to God? We should be able to give an accurate accounting, thinking of ourselves neither too highly nor too lowly.

How do we assess our own importance? In traditional Western theology, from Augustine onward, sin has been closely connected with pride, an inflated estimate or expression of oneself. Some contemporary theologians, influenced by feminist interpretation and women's experience, remind us that some of us seriously undervalue our lives. The texts for today address more of the inflated-ego perspective than the undervalued framework. Whether we underestimate or overestimate our importance (often as a reflection of how we think someone else sees us or our community), however, the texts remind us that the value of human life is derived from God.

FIRST READING

PROVERBS 25:6-7 OR SIRACH 10:12-18 (RCL)
SIRACH 10:(7-11) 12-18 (BCP)

Both the Proverbs text and the Sirach passage deal with the sin of pride, here meaning an excessive estimate of or expression of self. The preacher has a choice in regard to the level at which to address the text. One could use the Proverbs text, which speaks of pride more on a microlevel (personal behavior at a dinner party). Or one could use the Sirach text, which, while it also addresses interpersonal behavior, deals with pride on a macrolevel (the actions of kings and nations). The Lukan text for the day includes Jesus' critique of guests and hosts at a dinner party. If the preacher chooses to expound directly on the Lukan text, then she or he may want to include the Proverbs reading.

In Proverbs, pride takes the form of choosing one's own position of prominence at a gathering of notables. If one oversteps one's station, one could be "put in one's place," that is, shamed. While this text speaks of "standing" in the presence of the king, rather than an explicit reference to appropriate banquet behavior, the advice here is complementary to that found in Luke: allow a superior to elevate you rather than assume that you are more significant to your host than you may be.

The author of Sirach values human life *in relationship with* God; pride is an expression of trying to value human life *apart from* God. From the author's perspective, human beings do nothing that is unrelated to God. In chapter 10, he uses several expressions of human mortality: governments are in God's hand; success is in God's hand; human beings are dust and ashes, whose bowels decay while still alive and who will eventually be eaten by worms and wild animals! Then follows verse 12: "The beginning of human pride is to forsake the Lord" Sin is a departure or separation from God. The consequence of sin and pride is overturning, like spading over soil. Verses 14–17 describe that destruction in large, revolutionary terms that echo the Magnificat (Luke 1:52). Rulers and nations have been cast down, plucked up, overthrown, removed. In their places, the humble and lowly have been planted and seated.

> IN PROVERBS, PRIDE TAKES THE FORM OF CHOOSING ONE'S OWN POSITION OF PROMINENCE AT A GATHERING OF NOTABLES.

The authors of both of these texts would concur with the writer of Proverbs 16:18: "Pride goes before destruction, and a haughty spirit before a fall."

SIRACH 3:17-18, 20, 28-29 (RC)

This text expresses essentially the same thoughts as the Revised Common Lectionary and Book of Common Prayer selections from Sirach. An additional vivid expression of the life-sapping consequence of pride is given in verse 28: "When calamity befalls the proud, there is no healing, for an evil plant has taken root in him."

JEREMIAH 2:4-13 (RCL ALT.)

In this reading, God accuses the people of apostasy, another version of attempting to live life apart from God. The powerful images used in verse 13 sum up the passage: the people have abandoned a foundation of living water in exchange for hewing their own cisterns that cannot hold even rainwater. Verse 4 opens this text with another angle, a damning image and consequence of apostasy: "[Your ancestors] went after worthless things and became worthless themselves." Human beings are created in God's image. If, however, human beings take up with other so-called gods, then human beings will be degraded into the image of those gods, which are nothings.

> HUMAN BEINGS ARE CREATED IN GOD'S IMAGE. IF HUMAN BEINGS TAKE UP WITH OTHER SO-CALLED GODS, THEN HUMAN BEINGS WILL BE DEGRADED INTO THE IMAGE OF THOSE GODS, WHICH ARE NOTHINGS.

The text's movement begins with God expressing incredulity to the people that they have made such a stupid choice, exchanging a real God for worthless idols. Ancestors, priests, rulers, and prophets all conspired in this stupidity. Therefore, God accuses the people of their apostasy, pronounces judgment that will be meted out beyond this generation, and then mocks the people for their evils.

RESPONSIVE READING
PSALM 112 (RCL, BCP)

Psalm 112 is an acrostic psalm, meaning that each line of the text utilizes successive letters in the Hebrew alphabet. One could read this text as the positive opposite of the accusations God made in the Jeremiah text. There, the focus was on the consequences of idolatrous and unrighteous living. Here, the psalmist attends to the demonstrations of and rewards for righteous living: the righteous delight in the commandments and are steadfast, gracious, generous with money, fearless, just. The righteous are also wealthy and happy; they have good names and will be well remembered by their many descendents.

PSALM 68:4-5, 6-7, 10-11 (RC)

Scholars question the integrity of this psalm. It is not obviously a single unit. In light of the other texts for today, the preacher using these verses might focus on two ideas. First, notice the attributes of God: father of orphans, protector of widows, provider of homes for the desolate, liberator of prisoners, home of the people. Second, note that righteousness would then consist of living by these attributes.

PSALM 81:1, 10-16 (RCL ALT.)

The lectionary writers chose this psalm because it parallels the Jeremiah text and the contrast between a people abandoning God's living water and putting trust in human-made cracked cisterns. The contrast in the psalm is between what God can do for the people ("Open wide your mouth and I will fill it" (v. 10), like a bird feeding its young) and how they forfeit all good in order to go their own way. God *wants* to treat the people royally, feeding with the finest wheat and even bringing sweetness from the most unlikely places—a rock, of all things!

SECOND READING
HEBREWS 13:1-8, 15-16 (RCL)
HEBREWS 13:1-8 (BCP)

Commentators often note that 1 Corinthians 13:4-7 is one of the only, if not the only, definition of love in the Bible. One could argue that Hebrews 13:1-7 also approximates a definition of love, however. "Let mutual love continue," begins the author. Then follows a series of proffered demonstrations of what mutual love means: show hospitality, remember the imprisoned and the tortured, honor marriage, keep free of the love of money, trust in God, imitate the faith of your leaders. Recall from the commentary for previous weeks that the exhorter who wrote Hebrews believed his community stood at the threshold of fulfilled time. Every significant event from Abraham through the perfect sacrifice of Jesus, the perfect high priest, had led them to this point. The whole cloud of witnesses has gathered, waiting together with the earthly congregation for the final step in their journey to the renewed Jerusalem. The drama! What are they to do as they wait? Show mutual love in the concrete ways the author recommends.

This is another text that responds to the implied question, what time is it? It is time to love, to praise God for Jesus' unchanging teaching and once-for-all sacrifice (vv. 8-15), and to do as much good as you can (v. 16).

HEBREWS 12:18-19, 22-24a (RC)

See the second reading for the Thirteenth Sunday after Pentecost (Twenty-second Sunday in Ordinary Time/Proper 17), above.

THE GOSPEL

LUKE 14:1, 7-14 (RCL, BCP, RC)

Scholars have noted for many years that Jesus, in numerous ways, acted and argued like a Pharisee. If one asks whether he behaved more like a Sadducee, a Pharisee, an Essene, or simply one of the "people of the land," for the most part, one would have to answer, "Pharisee." It is much more historically accurate, productive for preaching, and less anti-Semitic in outcome to treat Jesus' disputes with the

> JESUS SAW GUESTS CHOOSING PLACES OF HONOR FOR THEMSELVES, PRESUMING TO KNOW THEIR IMPORTANCE IN THAT PARTICULAR COMMUNITY OR THEIR IMPORTANCE TO THE HOST.

Pharisees as conflicts within a community and a tradition rather than as Jesus' efforts to destroy the tradition and its adherents.

This text is a case in point. The previous verses, 13:31ff., report that some Pharisees came to Jesus to warn him that Herod sought his life—hardly the behavior of a group *completely* bent on Jesus' destruction. Luke 14:1 tells us that Jesus is invited by a leader of the Pharisees to share the Sabbath meal at his home. The leader wanted Jesus to be part of their conversation and table fellowship. Again, not an invitation that suggests complete mutual condemnation!

Clearly, however, there were significant tensions between Jesus and at least some of the Pharisees. The issue of how to keep the Sabbath, which came up previously (Luke 13:10-17), is raised again in verses 2-6 (not included in today's pericope). Then Luke's attention turns to a dispute regarding banquet manners, in one way of thinking. Interpreting these verses from a broader framework of meaning, this text challenges hearers to assess how they evaluate their own self-worth.

Jesus saw guests choosing places of honor for themselves, presuming to know their importance in that particular community or their importance to the host. In language closely attuned to today's Proverbs text, Jesus first addresses the guest. By means of a parable, he invites them to imagine being at a wedding banquet where they overestimated their own importance in the host's eyes. Overpromoting themselves would result in their being shamed when the host publicly asked them to move down—a very big deal in a shame-and-honor culture.

Then our attention is turned to the host. Jesus has corrective instructions for him, too—which means that Jesus has now criticized the pretensions of everyone at the dinner other than those who are serving them. He instructs the host not to invite the kinds of guests who are currently at table. Rather, invite the outcasts, the poor, the infirm—all those who cannot repay.

Jesus' challenge to the conventions regarding Sabbath dinner invitations strikes at the heart of what hospitality means. The Greek word for hospitality, *philoxenia*, means "love of the stranger." Hospitality that comes to mean mutual, reciprocating dinner invitations to friends and family is often an enjoyable way to spend time and resources but does not really express biblical hospitality. Jesus challenges conventional hospitality with a vision of the hospitality of the messianic banquet. For Jesus, banquet behavior fitting for the reign of God ought to affect dinner invitations even now. Theologians talk about Christian communities participating in the reign of God through proleptic events, through events that anticipate and in some small way even help to bring about the kingdom. There is nothing proleptic about returning the favor of a dinner invitation to a friend or a neighbor who previously invited you. But there is proleptic power when a Christian community opens its table to those who are outcasts and strangers.

THERE IS PROLEPTIC POWER WHEN A CHRISTIAN COMMUNITY OPENS ITS TABLE TO THOSE WHO ARE OUTCASTS AND STRANGERS.

PUTTING THE TEXTS TOGETHER

There are at least two streams of thought in these texts on which the preacher could expound. First, there is the issue of pride. As mentioned at the outset of these lessons, pride as sin, even as original sin, is a concept deeply rooted in Western Christian theology. Feminist theologians, writing from the perspective of women who have been robbed of their selves by oppressive social structures or who have otherwise sacrificed their selves for the sake of others, have rightly challenged the equation of pride and sin. Others, influenced by contemporary schools of self-psychology, might argue for the goodness of pride and the positive connection between pride and self-esteem. Christians adhere to these and any number of positions. But the theme that is repeated often in these texts is this: the value of any human life is determined in relationship with God. God is the author of our lives. God endows us with value that no human power can add to or steal. Human beings are made in the image of God and, as such, have inviolate value. This is the source of self-esteem. Consequently, when we depart from God, when we disconnect ourselves from God,

HUMAN BEINGS ARE MADE IN THE IMAGE OF GOD AND, AS SUCH, HAVE INVIOLATE VALUE. THIS IS THE SOURCE OF SELF-ESTEEM.

we diminish our ability to see the image of God in us and we are debased. We might express this disconnect through either undervaluing or inflating ourselves. In either case, the image we create apart from God is a false image. Individuals participate in creating idolatrous disconnects. So do communities and congregations. So do nations. The ground of all authentic life is God.

This is why right worship and right attention are so absolutely and fundamentally important. We are shaped by that to which we attend, by that to which we give our consciousness and presence. We are shaped into the form of whatever or whomever we worship. As creatures, we were made for worship. That attribute can be deformed, but it cannot be erased. We will either worship rightly or be deformed through worshiping idols. In order to know the image of God, in our communities and in ourselves, and to be equipped to be good stewards of that image, in ourselves and in others, we will want to pay our best attention to how we worship.

Second, note what Jesus does in his instructions both to the guests and to the hosts. He extends kingdom practices into the present time. It is not okay to live today according to warped and disordered social rules, waiting passively for the day that God will usher in the kingdom, the great banquet, and set everything right. "In the meantime," writes the author of Hebrews, "love one another; let me outline how." "In the meantime," said Jesus to guests and host, "live by kingdom manners now." It is already time to live according to the practices of the kingdom that we pray to come "on earth as it is in heaven."

FIFTEENTH SUNDAY AFTER PENTECOST

TWENTY-THIRD SUNDAY IN ORDINARY TIME /
PROPER 18
SEPTEMBER 9, 2007

REVISED COMMON	EPISCOPAL (BCP)	ROMAN CATHOLIC
Deut. 30:15-20 or Jer. 18:1-11	Deut. 30:15-20	Wisd. of Sol. 9:13-18b
Psalm 1 or Ps. 139:1-6, 13-18	Psalm 1	Ps. 90:3-4, 5-6, 12-13, 14-17
Philemon 1-21	Philemon 1-20	Philemon 9-10, 12-17
Luke 14:25-33	Luke 14:25-33	Luke 14:25-33

Each of the day's texts, even the familiar "clay in the potter's hand" (Jer. 18:6), is premised on the idea that our choices matter. Human beings are agents. We are not "free agents" in the sense used in professional sports; but we are meaning-making, decision-making, choosing agents. And our choices matter. Through our choices, we choose life or we choose death. The biblical texts for today present multiple angles on the theme "We make choices, and our choices matter." Our choices result in life or in death.

These texts are also premier "cost of discipleship" texts. Choosing life is costly in terms of obedience, whether that obedience is to the Torah or to Christ's assertion that those who do not hate their family and relinquish all of their possessions cannot be his disciple.

FIRST READING

DEUTERONOMY 30:15-20 (RCL, BCP)

Moses is nearing the end of his final discourse with the descendants of those with whom he escaped from Egypt a generation back. They are on the frontier of the Promised Land, which Moses will glimpse before he dies but will not enter. He has just talked through twenty-nine chapters' worth of history and law and instruction on how God's people must live. With these fifteen verses, he reaches the dramatic climax. While we moderns may be daunted by the sheer volume of do's and don'ts, Moses does not see the Torah as a burden at all. What God requires of them is "not too hard . . . , nor is it too far away" (30:11). In fact, God's commandment is "in your mouth and in your heart" (v. 14). These expressions of how intimate and immediate the law is to the people echo the new covenant announced in Jeremiah 31:31-34. Such powerful images: you do not need to make an arduous trip to heaven or across dangerous seas to retrieve the commandments; they are readily available in the community's mouth and heart.

At the climax of the discourse (vv. 15-20), one can hardly imagine a speech in which a people is offered a clearer choice: "life and prosperity, death and adversity." The choice is framed in parallel ways. First, there is a simple if-then: if you love God by following God's commandments, then you will live long and prosper. If you serve other gods, you will die. Second, God calls all of heaven and earth to witness to the deal that God proffers again, the ultimate choice between life and death that God has set before them. Moses then urges the people to "choose life so that you and your descendants may live" (v. 17).

> ONE CANNOT READ MOSES' DISCOURSE WITHOUT KNOWING THE HAPPY-TRAGIC ROLLER COASTER THAT WOULD BE ISRAEL'S LIFE IN THE COMING CENTURIES.

We might note that scholars believe this discourse was written well after the fact of the conquest, well after the people had failed to follow the commandments, worshiped other gods, and suffered both the consequence of their being a minor people (in terms of power) whose land lay in the crossroads of mighty empires and the consequence of their ethical, moral, and spiritual failures. In other words, one cannot read Moses' discourse without knowing the happy-tragic roller coaster that would be Israel's life in the coming centuries.

The preacher may note that this text presents one of the distinct differences between the way Judaism is understood by Jews and a Pauline Christian take on Judaism, a framework that claims following the commandments apart from Christ is impossible.

WISDOM OF SOLOMON 9:13-18b (RC)

These verses are an excerpt of a long prayer in praise of Wisdom personified. Scholars have drawn connections between the way Wisdom is described by this author (identified as Solomon) and the way the *logos* is described at the outset of John's Gospel ("In the beginning was the *Logos* . . ."); with Sophia as a feminine manifestation of deity; and with Sophia's relationship to the Holy Spirit.

In the excerpt, the author asserts through a rhetorical question that only through the gift of heaven-sent wisdom can anyone understand what is the will of God. Verse 15 seems to express a Platonic anthropology, of mind and spirit trapped in and darkened by mortal flesh.

As Christians, we might be disposed to connect this text to the revelation of God in Jesus Christ and the giving of the Holy Spirit. If we want to understand the text in a more original context, however, then we will tie the giving of wisdom to the giving of the commandments, that "other" great revealed truth in the biblical witness. In Judaism, the commandments are neither burdensome nor impossible to keep. Rather, the Torah is a glorious revelation from God to God's people that shows the people how to live.

JEREMIAH 18:1-11 (RCL ALT.)

God tells Jeremiah to go down to the potter's house, where God will give a word to him. Jeremiah watches the potter shape and reshape the clay on the wheel, "as seemed good to him." God then molds Jeremiah's understanding through making plain a parable: God is the potter, the people are the clay, and God can shape and reshape the people "as seems good to him." There is a crucial difference between clay and the people, however; the text does not express this difference explicitly, but it is certainly implied. Christian hymnody and piety, as in "Have Thine Own Way, Lord," focus on the pliable nature of clay in the potter's hands and urges Christians to yield. But there is something more here. Unlike inanimate clay, the people can choose. In fact, *God's actions with the clay are made in response to the people's choices.* The "clay" thus profoundly affects its own destiny! The people can rebel or repent, be evil and turn to good or be good and turn to evil. In any case, God will reshape the clay as a consequence of the people's actions, a consequence of how they use their God-given agency. God has purposes and intents for the people, but their actions can actually change what God does with them. Our choices matter.

> GOD WILL RESHAPE THE CLAY AS A CONSEQUENCE OF THE PEOPLE'S ACTIONS, A CONSEQUENCE OF HOW THEY USE THEIR GOD-GIVEN AGENCY.

RESPONSIVE READING
PSALM 1 (RCL, BCP)

Psalm 1 is a poetic version of the "Choose life" theme (see the Deuteronomy text, above), an expression of the premise that God's law gives life. The poem expresses the contrast between those who delight in God's law and those who are wicked. Those who delight in the law are like fruit trees planted alongside a stream. The wicked are like chaff blown off by the wind.

PSALM 90:3-4, 5-6, 12-13, 14-17 (RC)

This psalm was also used on the first Sunday in this series (see Tenth Sunday after Pentecost/Eighteenth Sunday in Ordinary Time/Proper 13, above). As I mentioned above, this psalm is a plea to God, voiced by a people with an intense sense of their mortality. Does the psalmist wonder whether God has forgotten the difference between a divine sense of time and a human sense, the difference that mortality makes in being human? Mortals cannot wait forever; our hourglass eventually runs out. Hear the sense of uselessness in the images the psalmist uses to express the sense of the people: blown dust, mown grass, evaporated dreams. In the second part of this reading, the psalmist pleads with God to change the people's condition—to grant wisdom, compassion, gladness, favor, and prosperity.

PSALM 139:1-6, 13-18 (RCL ALT.)

Reading this psalm as a whole leads to a different interpretation of the selected verses than if one reads only the selected verses. Verses 19-24 indicate that the psalmist is being sorely persecuted. He wants God to destroy the wicked enemies and to search his own thoughts to show that there is no wickedness in him. In the context of the final verses, the selected verses could be read as attributing to God profound powers of creation, discernment, and presence, as well as invoking God to use those powers to see the wicked and eliminate them. That fuller context presents a very different reading of this psalm than the selected verses by themselves. In the liturgical contexts I can recall when this psalm has been read, the emphasis has been solely on the care of God for the individual, the God of all creation who also created me, the God from whom we cannot flee and, wherever we go, whose "right hand shall hold me fast" (v. 10). Interpreting the psalm in the fuller context may help the preacher romanticize these verses less and link them to either the Deuteronomy text or the Jeremiah text. Yes, God shapes and molds like a potter. Yes, God wills life for the people, and the people's choices affect whether God will need to remake them into something else and whether life or death is the consequence.

> YES, GOD WILLS LIFE FOR THE PEOPLE, AND THE PEOPLE'S CHOICES AFFECT WHETHER GOD WILL NEED TO REMAKE THEM INTO SOMETHING ELSE AND WHETHER LIFE OR DEATH IS THE CONSEQUENCE.

SECOND READING

PHILEMON 1-21 (RCL)
PHILEMON 1-20 (BCP)
PHILEMON 9-10, 12-17 (RC)

The letter to Philemon is a wonderful example of moral suasion. It is a rhetorical jewel. Onesimus is a slave in Philemon's household and has run away. He comes to Paul, who is in prison. Paul sends Onesimus back to Philemon with this letter. There is no doubt what Paul expects of Philemon. He will not command compliance with his request, though he knows he could (vv. 8-9). But he leaves no question in regard to what the right action is: act as a Christian rather than an imperial citizen, set Onesimus free, treat him as a brother in Christ rather than as a slave.

Paul is in prison, perhaps in Ephesus. Onesimus, whose name means "useful" or "beneficial" (it was a common practice to name slaves after activities or physical attributes or even mythic figures), had run away from Philemon's household and made his way to Paul. Paul has sent Onesimus back with the letter to Philemon—but not to Philemon alone. Other persons are named individually, as is "the church in your house" (v. 2). This letter is to be read publicly in the *ecclesia*, the gathered assembly. A public rather than only a private reading adds to the suasive power! In verses 4-21, the "you" is singular, meaning that Paul is putting Philemon on the spot in the hearing of the whole church!

Can you imagine being Philemon and either reading this letter aloud to your community or hearing it read aloud with the whole community present, then turning down Paul's request? Paul reminds Philemon that he owes his life to Paul (v. 19), uses humor, and expresses how important Onesimus has become to him. Paul's humor comes through in all the plays on the meaning of Onesimus's (beneficial, useful, of service) name; see verses 11, 13, and 20. Verses 11 and 20 surely would have evoked smiles and chuckles. The word that is translated as "heart" in these verses (vv. 7, 12, 20) is not *kardia* but *splanchna*, often translated "bowels" or "compassion." Paul is expressing very deep feeling for Onesimus. In verse 12, Paul calls Onesimus his "heart." In verse 20, with the combination of the direct play on Onesimus's name (in the word "benefit") and Paul's request of Philemon to "refresh his heart," Paul may well be asking both for Onesimus's freedom from slavery and freedom for Onesimus to return to Paul.

PAUL MAY WELL BE ASKING BOTH FOR ONESIMUS'S FREEDOM FROM SLAVERY AND FREEDOM FOR ONESIMUS TO RETURN TO PAUL.

Paul does not butt heads with imperial law head-on in this letter. But on Christian principles, he does a masterful job of subverting the imperial order as he lays out for Philemon's church a practical theological application of the life-giving difference that being a Christian makes.

The Gospel
LUKE 14:25–33 (RCL, BCP, RC)

The choice given in Deuteronomy is between following the command-ments that lead to life and disobeying and choosing death. Make your choice. Then you, according to Jeremiah, are clay in the potter's hands; the potter may remake your community if you have chosen badly. Becoming a Christian gives an identity that replaces the matrix of your household and larger social relationships. These are some of the messages in the texts leading up to today's Gospel.

Jesus is Jerusalem-bound. In Luke, Jesus addresses crowds, disciples, and apostles. In this passage, he turns to speak to the great crowd who followed him. One won-ders what happened at the end of these words. We note that the Gospel writers often let us know that the people rejoiced after a miracle; but aside from the rich ruler who declined to give up everything (Mark 10:17-22) and the disciples in John who dropped away after Jesus called himself the bread of life and told people to eat his flesh (John 6:35-52), we are not informed how the crowd received his words on the cost of discipleship.

Matthew's version (10:37-38) of these words in regard to Jesus and family is easier to swallow. "Whoever does not *love* me more than . . ." Surely, we can still love our children and our spouses and our parents and yet love Jesus more. Here in Luke, however, Jesus chooses a more charged word, at least as far as our culture is con-cerned. "Whoever comes to me and does not *hate* father and mother, wife and chil-dren, brothers and sisters, yes, and even life itself . . ." (v. 26). Commentators often seek to soften the impact of the word "hate" by judging that it is just another way of saying "love less." Hmm. Okay, let us assume that Mark was the first Gospel and Matthew and Luke used Mark, some collection of sayings, and their own materials in order to write their Gospels. Mark does not contain a ver-

IN ORDER TO PUT THE VALUE OF THE REIGN OF GOD FIRST, THE REIGN OF THE PATRONAGE SYSTEM, THE REIGN OF FAMILY RELATIONS THAT CREATES CLEAR BOUNDARIES BETWEEN "THEM" AND "US" MUST BE BROKEN.

sion of this saying, so we can move him to the side. It is possible that Matthew and Luke each started with a different version of this saying within the tradition each received. But one could assume that either (a) Matthew and Luke used the same source (what scholars call "Q," a collection of sayings) and one changed the source to read either "love me more" or "hate"; or (b) Luke read Matthew and changed the wording to "hate." In the latter two scenarios, either the sayings source used the word "hate" or Luke chose the word. The odds are that Luke chose this word and did not mean to say "love less."

Why "hate"? We wonder about Luke's audience. If they are predominantly Gentile and more urban than many of Jesus' original hearers, they may also have been ensconced in the Roman patronage system and attached to household hierarchy and extended family relationships above all else. In order to attach to Jesus and the reign of God he proclaimed, Jesus' hearers would first need to detach from their possessions, from *all* that possesses them, including their most intimate and entangled relations. The word "hate" may be hyperbole that functions as a wake-up call, a slap in the face, a bracing sheet of cold water. In order to put the value of the reign of God first, the reign of the patronage system, the reign of family relations that creates clear boundaries between "them" and "us" must be broken. Whoever does not hate . . .

Putting the Texts Together

In today's texts, we are faced with the repeated call to choose and a variety of reminders that the choices we make matter. The choice between life and death: follow the commandments and choose life. If we choose against God, as clay in the potter's hands, we may be reshaped. Or the choice between upholding a patronage system that includes treating other persons as possessions and realigning community relationships based on everyone in the Christian community being brothers and sisters in Christ. The choice is between merely seeking some tangible benefit from Jesus that we can fold into our lives as they are, which is what the crowd does, and "hating" all attachments that prevent us from embracing the reign of God, which is what disciples do.

SIXTEENTH SUNDAY AFTER PENTECOST

SEVENTEENTH

TWENTY-FOURTH SUNDAY IN ORDINARY TIME/
PROPER 19
SEPTEMBER 16, 2007

REVISED COMMON	EPISCOPAL (BCP)	ROMAN CATHOLIC
Exod. 32:7-14 or Jer. 4:11-12, 22-28	Exod. 32:1, 7-14	Exod. 32:7-11, 13-14
Ps. 51:1-10 or Psalm 14	Ps. 51:1-18 or 51:1-11	Ps. 51:3-4, 12-13, 17, 19
1 Tim. 1:12-17	1 Tim. 1:12-17	1 Tim. 1:12-17
Luke 15:1-10	Luke 15:1-10	Luke 15:1-32 or 15:1-10

How do we talk about sin in the church these days? If the congregation's conversation about sin and forgiveness, judgment, and mercy is a little thin, this would be a good Sunday to enrich it! These passages contain several of the classic ecclesial texts on sin and forgiveness. Aside from the reference at the outset of Psalm 51 stating that this is a psalm of David after he had sinned with Bathsheba, the preacher will find little in these texts to confirm the popular connection between sin and sex. Rather, sin is connected with idolatry (putting another god before God) and apostasy (denying the truth that you know).

Unfortunately, the Hebrew Bible texts focus on judgment due the sinner while the New Testament texts highlight forgiveness. The preacher will want to be careful not to reinforce Marcion's heresy, which still lives in the church: the God of wrath in the Old; the God of love in the New.

FIRST READING

EXODUS 32:7-14 (RCL)
EXODUS 32:1, 7-14 (BCP)
EXODUS 32:7-11, 13-14 (RC)

In last Sunday's assigned lections, the first reading was the "Choose life" text from Deuteronomy. For today, the lectionary committee serves up one of the most notorious accounts of choosing death over life from the days of Israel's encampment at Sinai: a scene from the golden calf story.

This particular scene is one movement in a tragedy (many people die) but with a decidedly comic staging. God plays the trickster. The Lord says to Moses, "*Your* people, whom *you* brought up out of the land of Egypt, have acted perversely" (v. 7). After expressing more righteous indignation, God concludes his pronouncement with, "Now let me alone, so that . . . I may consume them; and of you I will make a great nation" (v. 10). One can imagine God turning the divine backside toward Moses and making a "talk to the hand" dismissive gesture before resolutely folding his arms and setting his face away from Moses.

Moses stakes his ground and in solidarity with his people reminds God whose people these are and what the consequence would be of acting on this consuming anger. "Why does your wrath burn hot against *your* people?" (v. 11). He then makes his argument for why God should repent from this decision. For his case, he imagines two negative consequences if God follows through on his feelings. First, the Egyptians will laugh and claim victory. Second, God made a promise to the patriarchs regarding their descendants. As a result of Moses' argument, God repents.

> ONE CAN IMAGINE GOD TURNING THE DIVINE BACK-SIDE TOWARD MOSES AND MAKING A "TALK TO THE HAND" DISMISSIVE GESTURE BEFORE RESOLUTELY FOLDING HIS ARMS AND SETTING HIS FACE AWAY FROM MOSES.

Have you ever watched an hour-long crime drama in which the detectives seemingly have the crime solved by the first commercial break? "Too easy," you say to yourself. That response is the appropriate audience response to God's telling Moses, "You are right. I was wrong. I repent of what I said." After all, the following verses explain that "Moses' anger burned hot" (v. 19) and he himself did much of what God had threatened to do! This story reads like a setup. God set up Moses to take the responsibility of disciplining the people. Why did God bait Moses? Perhaps it is because leaders cannot pass off the difficult work of dealing with sin to anyone else. No real leader gets to be simply the innocuous version of Santa Claus with which we live in the United States, bringing good gifts regardless of whether the people are "naughty or nice." Remember, choices matter; and God's communities must be accountable communities. Any human community will be troubled by sin. Period. Leaders must learn to deal with sin in ways that do not allow communities to destroy themselves. No, leaders do not need

> THOSE CALLED INTO LEADERSHIP AMONG GOD'S PEOPLE WILL FIND THEMSELVES IN MOSES' SPOT, NEEDING TO HOLD PEOPLE ACCOUNTABLE FOR FAILING TO LIVE UP TO THE HIGH CALLING OF THE PEOPLE OF GOD.

to let their anger burn as hot as Moses did. Here, as Doug Adams, a professor of Christianity and the Arts at Pacific School of Religion, says, Moses is a mirror for identity rather than a model for morality.[1] Those called into leadership among God's people will find themselves in Moses' spot, needing to hold people accountable for failing to live up to the high calling of the people of God.

JEREMIAH 4:11–12, 22–28 (RCL ALT.)

This text is akin to the Exodus text for the day. It is full of images to communicate God's righteous judgment against a sinful people—but without the trickster humor of the Lord-Moses exchange. In this text, the prophet relates a vision of the day of judgment. That day is on the other side of a tipping point. There will come a day when it will no longer be possible to repent. In that day, God will say, "My people . . . are skilled in doing evil, but do not know how to do good" (v. 22). Image upon image of desolation is piled up—of quaking mountains; of eerie, lifeless, quiet Earth returned to primordial chaos; of waste and void.

RESPONSIVE READING
PSALM 51:1–10 (RCL)
PSALM 51:1–18 OR 51:1–11 (BCP)
PSALM 51:3–4, 12–13, 17, 19 (RC)

Some churchgoers do not want to talk of sin in church. I recall the letter the church staff received after a Sunday service during which we used a classic prayer of confession. "I have worked too hard on my self-esteem to let this language of sin back into my life," was the gist of the complaint. But for others of us, this psalm continues to function as a classic, perhaps even *the* classic, confessional psalm in the church. There is power in the repetition of the plea to be made clean: have mercy; wash me; cleanse me; purge me; create in me a clean heart and a right spirit; give me joy. In return, the author offers up a confession of guilt and a contrite spirit.

This psalm is linked to the testimony in the epistle that Jesus Christ saves sinners and to the Gospel for the day in regard to God's joy when the lost are found.

PSALM 14 (RCL ALT.)

This psalm is a companion for the Jeremiah text, which relates visions of destruction, consequences of sin, and a time in which repentance is no longer possible. The psalmist, in verses 2–3, pictures God's judgment of humankind akin to the judgment that produced the great flood: "They have all gone astray, they are all alike perverse." A difference may be that the psalmist focuses God's sight on leaders "who eat up my people as they eat bread . . . [and] would confound the

SECOND READING
1 TIMOTHY 1:12-17 (RCL, BCP, RC)

The author, in Paul's voice (some scholars do not think Paul was the author of this letter, but for the sake of simplicity, I will refer to the author as Paul), testifies in a form that, like Psalm 51, functions as a classic or an archetype in the church's life—in the last several centuries, for the evangelical churches especially. Many evangelical Christians discern in this story a classic conversion narrative, an archetype that one expects to hear often in the testimonies of evangelical Christians. Note the structure: thanksgiving (v. 12) and doxology (v. 17) provide bookends. Paul's past life is reduced to his evil character (v. 13), which was overcome by the grace, hope, and love of God given through Jesus Christ (v. 14). All the credit for the author's conversion of character and role goes to God, who took him as the "foremost sinner" to make an example of him—how great the mercy of God to save such a person! The implied conclusion the reader should reach is, "If Jesus Christ can save the foremost sinner, how much more can he save me?"

> THE IMPLIED CONCLUSION THE READER SHOULD REACH IS, "IF JESUS CHRIST CAN SAVE THE FOREMOST SINNER, HOW MUCH MORE CAN HE SAVE ME?"

That is the desired effect of testimony. It points to the power of God to save. And it functions as encouragement for others to frame the meaning of their lives similarly to the one giving testimony. It is one thing to offer such testimony in the midst of a supportive congregation that views it as something of a rite of passage from childhood into adult faith. It is quite another, however, to offer such testimony as part of a larger confession that might bring one into conflict with imperial authorities—which is the situation Paul is in as he writes.

THE GOSPEL
LUKE 15:1-10 (RCL, BCP, RC ALT.)
LUKE 15:1-32 (RC)

All three lectionaries include verses 1-10, which set up the story of the prodigal son, or the Father's love, or the unrepentant elder brother—depending on the angle from which we read.

The staging in verses 1-10 is, again, striking. Tax collectors and sinners drew near to hear Jesus. The scribes and Pharisees expressed their disdain for the company Jesus welcomed. They refer to him as "that guy" or "that thing"; *houtos* is an

197

SIXTEENTH
SUNDAY AFTER
PENTECOST
───────
SEPTEMBER 16

expression of contempt. We start with Jesus' religious brothers utterly disagreeing with the company he is keeping.

There are at least two points of view that the preacher may find profitable in approaching this text. First, let us see what Jesus is doing with the images of those who search for the lost. In Jesus' day, his critics may have seriously objected to both images, shepherd and woman. True, the text does not say a *shepherd* went in search of the lost sheep, but Jesus cast his hearers into the role of a shepherd. We know that shepherds were held in low esteem in Jesus' day. And by today's standards, so were women. So the staging is that Jesus' religious brothers disapprove of his compan-

> FIRST JESUS' RELIGIOUS BROTHERS DISAPPROVE OF HIS COMPANIONS AND THEN JESUS USES TWO OFFENSIVE IMAGES, SHEPHERDS AND WOMEN, TO DESCRIBE GOD'S ACTION IN REGARD TO THE LOST!

ions, and then Jesus uses two offensive images, shepherd and woman, to describe God's action in regard to the lost!

Can we still feel the offense? Probably not in regard to shepherds. Most of us would have no opinion of shepherds. Consider this: from the late nineteenth and into the twentieth centuries, how many country churches in the United States installed a stained-glass window of Jesus the Good Shepherd, with that one sheep yoked across his shoulders, the shepherd who leaves the ninety-nine in search of the one? Hundreds, at least. But far fewer, I am certain, portray the woman with the lamp, bent low, brushing every inch of a dirt floor in search of that day's wage on which the family's food depended. Why more shepherds than women? I would bet the choice of image has to do with conventional understandings of who God is: male. Even contemporary congregations miss that Jesus was saying, "God is like the woman who . . ." The images of God, or the Christ, as "like the woman who" may continue to disturb.

The other point of view would be to imagine what Jesus thought was the fitting way for his critics to respond to the lost, whether the lost whom they sought out themselves or the lost who gathered around Jesus while he spoke. Surely Jesus thinks his brother Pharisees ought to respond to the lost like the friends and neighbors in the parables of the lost sheep and the lost coin, who are called together to rejoice that the lost has been found. In fact, if one reads through the prodigal son parable, as in the Roman Catholic lectionary, what is the conclusion? "We had to celebrate and rejoice, because this brother of yours was dead and has come to life; he was lost and has been found" (v. 32). The correct response to Jesus' work with sinners is to join with the angels in heaven and throw a party! The grumbling and disdain of the scribes and Pharisees, who refer to Jesus as "that guy," are clearly echoed in the words of the elder brother who cannot rejoice and refers to his brother as "this son of yours" (v. 30).

Jesus is like the one who goes out after the sheep. Jesus is like the woman who searches for that coin. Jesus is the one who finds the lost and then calls out to the neighbors (the scribes and Pharisees—his brothers) to rejoice with him and with the "angels of God," a phrase that is a circumlocution for saying "God." Jesus rejoices and God rejoices. Who wants to oppose Jesus or his God in their joy?

We might wonder who were the people in Luke's congregation who refused to rejoice when sinners were welcomed. We might also imagine the ways that congregations today continue to be scandalized by this God who sends our leaders out as shepherds and women in search of the lost and who brings sinners to our doors. Do we rejoice or grumble?

PUTTING THE TEXTS TOGETHER

There is quite a range of vision and expression in today's texts—from the anger of Moses in reaction to the golden calf after-orgy, to the no-hope-for-repentance day prophesied by Jeremiah, to the elegance of the "create in me a clean heart" sinner-psalmist, to the lost-and-found testimony of Paul to the congregation Timothy pastored, to Jesus's spinning of parables so that his Pharisaic brothers might rejoice with the once-lost, rather than demonstrate by their disdain and disapproval that they themselves are in need of being found.

THE LOST MAY ALSO INCLUDE THOSE WHO REFUSE TO PARTICIPATE IN GOD'S JOY WHEN SINNERS COME HOME.

The Timothy and Luke lections work well together. Both address the topic of the God who seeks the lost and who joyfully exercises the power to save. Both look to Jesus as the Savior of the lost. Still, these texts beg the question of what it means to be lost. In the Exodus text, the lost are those who, in their grasping anxiety, fashioned gods for themselves. In Jeremiah, the lost are those who once had the power to repent and to turn from their oppression of society's most vulnerable but could no longer; the time of consequence had arrived. In Luke, the lost may be the outcasts, all those whom the purity party among the Pharisees labeled unclean. But the lost may also include those who refuse to participate in God's joy when sinners come home.

These are powerful texts, if the congregation has a framework in which to understand what it means to be lost or, for that matter, only if they have an understanding of sin. Joy at discovery is meaningless if no one is lost. And grace is meaningless if no one participates in sin.

Note

1. See Douglas Adams, *The Prostitute and the Family Tree: Discovering Humor and Irony in the Bible* (Louisville: Westminster John Knox Press, 1997).

SEVENTEENTH SUNDAY AFTER PENTECOST

TWENTY-FIFTH SUNDAY IN ORDINARY TIME /
PROPER 20
SEPTEMBER 23, 2007

REVISED COMMON	EPISCOPAL (BCP)	ROMAN CATHOLIC
Amos 8:4-7 or Jer. 8:18—9:1	Amos 8:4-7 (8-12)	Amos 8:4-7
Psalm 113 or Ps. 79:1-9	Psalm 138	Ps. 113:1-2, 4-6, 7-8
1 Tim. 2:1-7	1 Tim. 2:1-8	1 Tim. 2:1-8
Luke 16:1-13	Luke 16:1-13	Luke 16:1-13 or 16:10-13

These texts address themes of stewardship in at least two ways. The first-reading texts, the psalms, and the Gospel all speak about the right use of money, sometimes by describing wrong uses that God will condemn. In terms of the way God judges a society, there is hardly any value that God looks at with greater attention than the way that wealth is made and used. A second perspective on stewardship, found in the Timothy and Gospel readings, is the understanding that the people of God owe their first loyalty to the reign of God, a loyalty that no earthly ruler can rightly claim and that no Christian should give except to God. Stewards need to know to whom they are ultimately accountable, as well as for what they will be held responsible.

FIRST READING
AMOS 8:4-7 (RCL, RC)
AMOS 8:4-7 (8-12) (BCP)

In the Bible, business is never "just business." God cares deeply about the character of all transactions between human beings. The Lord expects the people to act justly and pays close attention to how those with more power act toward the less powerful. Once again, the first-reading texts connect business practices, justice, faith, and judgment.

200

THE SEASON
AFTER PENTECOST
────────────
GARY E. PELUSO-
VERDEND

Amos's words were surely poorly received by his intended audience. Amos is a Judean who made his living as a shepherd and "a dresser of sycamore trees" (7:14). He treks from Judah north to preach impending doom to those who are enjoying their prosperity with nary a puffy cloud on the horizon, let alone a thunderhead.

Akin to several of the prophetic texts from earlier in these Ordinary Time Sundays, Amos speaks against the economic violation of the poor. He also connects practicing justice and keeping the Sabbath and exposes the disdain, in disposition if not in practice, of the powerful for the Sabbath.

God's standard of justice, regularly expressed by the classical writing prophets, is focused on how well the society in general and the leaders in particular treat the poor and the powerless. In this text, Amos observes that, rather than Sabbath being a time of rest for all and of the rebalancing of economic injustice, sellers cannot wait for Sabbath to end and the selling to begin again. Their transactions are rife with injustice: using measures too small, weights too heavy; passing off chaff as nourishment; devaluing the life of the poor. Amos informs his audience that God is paying attention and is keeping an account: "Surely I will never forget any of their deeds" (v. 7).

> GOD'S STANDARD OF JUSTICE IS FOCUSED ON HOW WELL THE SOCIETY IN GENERAL AND THE LEADERS IN PARTICULAR TREAT THE POOR AND THE POWERLESS.

JEREMIAH 8:18—9:1 (RCL ALT.)

This text presents the preacher using the Revised Common Lectionary an alternative point of view to that given in the Amos text. The Amos text expresses the point of view of a southern prophet called to bring words of judgment to his northern cousins. Jeremiah, no stranger to the Lord's call to preach judgment, speaks his words as an insider, as "one of us." He compassionately identifies with his people. In this text, Jeremiah laments. His words are full of pathos and pain, of unrequited longing, as in verse 20: "The harvest is passed, the summer is ended, and we are not saved." While there may be a healing tree resin in Gilead (a balm in Gilead) and healers who know how to use it, "the health of my poor people" (v. 22) is unaffected and remains awful. Two plus two is not adding up to four. Whatever timeline and expectations of deliverance the people have in mind are wrong.

Amos preaches powerful, memorable, faithful words of judgment. In today's Jeremiah text, as well as elsewhere in that book, Jeremiah does the same, with the addition of compassion for the people who will suffer because of their leaders' unrighteous behavior: "O that . . . my eyes were a fountain of tears, so that I might weep day and night" (9:1).

Amos and Jeremiah present two compelling alternative biblical views for a preacher vis-à-vis a congregation. When God's word of judgment must be spoken, is it spoken by the preacher playing the role of an insider or an outsider?

RESPONSIVE READING
PSALM 113 (RCL)
PSALM 113:1-2, 4-6, 7-8 (RC)

To what does the Supreme Monarch of the universe pay attention? Verses 1-6 urge the congregation to "praise the LORD" and place the Lord as far away from the earth as a poet can imagine. God is not in heaven but above the heavens, looking "far down on the heavens and the earth." And from that infinitely removed perch, to what does God pay attention? God pays attention to the poor and the barren. God lifts the poor, causing them to sit with princes, and gives children to barren women.

PSALM 138 (BCP)

This psalm also is a psalm of praise. After praising the Lord and predicting that "all the kings of the earth" shall praise God (v .4), the psalmist lifts up three ideas. First, akin to Psalm 113, "The LORD is high, but regards the lowly" (v. 6). God pays close attention to the lowly, but "the haughty" are only specks in God's sight. Second, verse 7 ("Though I walk in the midst of trouble, you preserve me against the wrath of my enemies") echoes Psalm 23:4, as well as other testimonies of deliverance. Third, verse 8 is neither pure confession of faith nor pure anxious plea to God but both at the same time. On the one hand, the psalmist confesses, "The LORD will fulfill his purpose for me." But he concludes with a plea to the Lord: "Do not forsake the work of your hands."

PSALM 79:1-9 (RCL ALT.)

Images of devastation in Jerusalem, the beloved city, are piled up like the bodies the author sees. The psalmist pleads for God to stop the judgment on and the destruction of the psalmist's people. The Temple is defiled. Bodies lie everywhere. There are not enough living persons to bury the dead. Consequently, one sees animals feeding on the remains of God's children. The psalmist pleads with God to turn God's anger toward the "nations that do not know you."

In the early twenty-first century, these images may evoke pictures from Baghdad, Darfur, Kigali, Monrovia, or perhaps even New Orleans in the days following

Hurricane Katrina. "It looks like a war zone" is a phrase that seems to be used increasingly to describe devastation, whether human or natural in origin.

A popular folk theology becomes manifest during disasters. It might be expressed as a question: "What did we do to deserve this?" It might be expressed as a conclusion: "We deserved this," or "We did not deserve this," or perhaps, "We deserved this, but now enough already!" Using this psalm gives the preacher an opportunity to address such questions.

SECOND READING
1 TIMOTHY 2:1-7 (RCL)
1 TIMOTHY 2:1-8 (BCP, RC)

It is popular to read this text as an affirmation of rulers. That, I believe, is a misreading. The author does call Christians to pray for rulers *for a specific reason that has nothing to do with divine support of the empire.* The author commends the practice of praying for rulers in order that Christians can go about God's work in peace.

It may be difficult for the preacher to help the congregation get behind our current practices and move into the world of this text, especially if the congregation is comprised of persons who drive about town with "We support our president" bumper stickers and who otherwise feel enfranchised by whoever represents them in the current administration in Washington. Such positive connections with the government would have been foreign to the experience of the author's audience in Timothy.

Let us assume that 1 Timothy was written late in the first century C.E. Christians had experienced at least one, if not two, systematic persecutions. Certainly, some of the community lived through Emperor Nero's persecutions. Depending on how late the letter was written, it is possible that Trajan's persecutions (mid-90s C.E.) were fresh memories. In any case, think of your council or board chair disappearing one night, or your confirmation teacher imprisoned, or pressures put on you either to turn over the names of your congregation to Imperial Security or to forfeit your freedom or your life. Now receive the author's words: make thanksgivings for everyone, including kings; God desires that everyone will be saved "and come to the knowledge of the truth" (v. 4). Pray even (or, rather, especially) for the godless emperor in order that we Christians may live in peace (v. 2).

THE AUTHOR CLAIMS A MEDIATOR ROLE FOR JESUS AND TESTIFIES TO THE CONGREGATION THAT IT IS THIS MESSAGE THAT GOD CALLED HIM TO PROCLAIM TO THE GENTILE WORLD.

Does the author go further? While asking for prayers for the emperor in order that Christians may live in peace, does he also imply that an imperial role belongs not to Caesar but to Jesus? "There is also one mediator [*mesitēs*] between God and humankind, Christ Jesus" (v. 5). The chief priest in the Roman cult, which was sometimes the emperor, was the *pontifex maximus*, the main "road" between the gods and humankind. Among the roles of the *pontifex maximus* was mediation between the gods and humankind for the sake of the peace. The author claims this mediator role for Jesus and testifies to the congregation that it is this message that God called him to proclaim to the Gentile world. Christ, and not Caesar, is the universal Mediator and Savior.

The Gospel
LUKE 16:1–13 (RCL, BCP, RC)
LUKE 16:10–13 (RC ALT.)

I have been reading biblical texts in preparation for preaching for almost thirty years. Few texts in the lectionary cycle make me groan when their Sunday arrives like this text does! Is there a more twisted parable, difficult to understand either as Jesus' first audience may have heard it or in the way that Luke has situated it in his Gospel's context? That said, the preacher would do well to wrestle with this text until it yields its blessing!

The preacher has two exegetical choices: to try to discern the parable per se and imagine its meaning for Jesus' audience, or to examine the parable in a canonical frame of reference, exploring what Luke was doing with this parable for his own community. Either approach could yield a biblically faithful sermon.

I will follow Brandon Scott's reconstruction of the parable and its possible meaning for Jesus' hearers.[1] Scott sees this as one of the accounting parables that expresses the rules that govern the reign of God, rules that often subvert or twist conventional rules. The characters in this parable do not act as the audience would expect them to behave. Thus, the audience will experience strong cognitive dissonance, or at least "Huh?" moments, several times before Jesus is finished, leaving them open to a different way of thinking and being.

Start with the rich man. Jesus' audience would likely be disposed to dislike the rich man. At first, those feelings are confirmed: the rich man, probably an absentee landlord, hears a charge against a manager and, without investigating, summons that manager in order to dismiss him. In the end (v. 8), however, rather than punishing the steward as expected, the rich master compliments him for his shrewd action. The steward faced a crisis; the master admired the steward's response.

Shift to the manager. The hearers are told that he was a poor steward, that he squandered or wasted the master's property. He is also lazy; one can imagine the disdain that an audience of people who work from dawn past dusk would have for a man who claims to be too weak to dig and too proud to beg! But like the prodigal son who "came to himself" and made a prudent response that put a roof back over his head and food in his stomach, the steward did what was necessary. He went to each of the master's debtors and asked them to rewrite the bill. Did that difference come out of the master's pocket? Maybe some of it did; but much if not all of it would have come from the steward's own commission. There was an amount owed to the master and an amount the steward would take in commission, often set by the steward. The steward's shrewd action was to take money from his own pocket to cover whatever revenues due his master that he had squandered. Certainly, Jesus is not commending the entire scenario to his hearers: go ahead and exploit the master's absence, squander his goods, and when you are called to account, forgo your own commission in order to make the books balance. Rather, as the master commended the steward for his resolute action in the face of a crisis, so Jesus commends resolute action by those facing the crisis of the coming reign of God.

> AS THE MASTER COMMENDED THE STEWARD FOR HIS RESOLUTE ACTION IN THE FACE OF A CRISIS, SO JESUS COMMENDS RESOLUTE ACTION BY THOSE FACING THE CRISIS OF THE COMING REIGN OF GOD.

In addition to admiring resolute action in the face of a crisis, Luke seems determined to tell his readers something about the relationship between being a faithful disciple and using money rightly on this side of the kingdom's advent. The steward becomes an example of dealing prudently with money—something else is more important than mammon! In the steward's case, that something was where he would live after the master threw him out. In verses 10-13, Luke draws out three contrasts that he believes disciples of Jesus must understand: one must be faithful in little in order to be faithful in much; one must be faithful with mammon in order to be faithful with true riches; one must demonstrate that one can be faithful with another's goods in order to be entrusted with his or her own. In each comparison, money represents the inferior side of the equation but also an essential matter in a Christian's life. Perhaps Luke is

> LUKE DOES NOT WANT HIS CONGREGATION TO ATTACH TO MONEY AS HE BELIEVED THE PHARISEES HAD SUCCUMBED TO MONEY'S TEMPTATIONS.

saying that using money prudently is practice for being entrusted with real wealth. Hear the inversion of contemporary, and perhaps ancient, conventional thinking. Money is real. Whenever we hear someone in the church say, "Well, in the real world . . . ," we know that money is not far away! In Luke, however, money is but game pieces in preparation for handling real wealth, treasure in heaven associated with the reign of God. Luke teaches his congregation to learn to use money wisely as practice for the day when they are entrusted with real wealth. Luke does not want his congregation to attach to money as he believed the Pharisees had succumbed to money's temptations (see v. 14). Perhaps he believed that practicing stewardship with money in preparation for real stewardship would habituate the congregation to treat money with light fingers.

Putting the Texts Together

Arguably, one of the strongest desires in today's world is to make money and participate in the global economy. We know this desire has been strong for generations in Europe and North America. Every day we read something more about the rapidly expanding economies of India, China, and other Southeast Asian nations—and the people's desire to partici- pate in that rising sea of wealth. We lament how far behind much of Africa and Central and South America are from full participa- tion in the global economy; and we mea-

> CULTIVATE THE PRACTICE OF PLAYING WITH MONEY, LUKE SAYS, IN PREPARATION FOR HANDLING REAL WEALTH.

sure their misery by reporting how many dollars, or cents, the average worker makes per day. So we in North America desire to make money, and many of us hope and pray that others will have the opportunity to make more money and be able to participate in the global economy.

Today's texts more than remind us that there is something more important than making money. They instruct us, maybe even command us, to avoid the idolatry of money. Biblical authors do not condemn making money. Folks like Amos condemn accumulating wealth at the expense of keeping others poor and making money the focus of our lives so strongly that Sabbath—as a day of freedom from servitude for all of God's creatures and of enjoyment of God's abundance—is disdained. Luke does not condemn making money, but he does condemn idola- trous attachment to money. Cultivate the practice of playing with money, he says, in preparation for handling real wealth. For Luke, like the author of 1 Timothy, looks to the horizon and sees neither the empire nor the global economy as the defining force of the world. Rather, the author of 1 Timothy sees Christ reign- ing over Caesar. And Luke sees the in-breaking reign of God and anticipates a messianic banquet invitation that will go to those without money and those who have learned to handle money as good stewards yet who could give it all up at a moment's notice for the sake of entering the banquet hall.

Note

1. Bernard Brandon Scott, *Hear Then the Parable: A Commentary on the Parables of Jesus* (Minneapolis: Fortress Press, 1989), 255–66.

EIGHTEENTH SUNDAY AFTER PENTECOST

TWENTY-SIXTH SUNDAY IN ORDINARY TIME/
PROPER 21
SEPTEMBER 30, 2007

REVISED COMMON	EPISCOPAL (BCP)	ROMAN CATHOLIC
Amos 6:1a, 4-7 or Jer. 32:1-3a, 6-15	Amos 6:1-7	Amos 6:1a, 4-7
Psalm 146 or Ps. 91:1-6, 14-16	Psalm 146 or 146:4-9	Ps. 146:7, 8-9, 9-10
1 Tim. 6:6-19	1 Tim. 6:11-19	1 Tim. 6:11-16
Luke 16:19-31	Luke 16:19-31	Luke 16:19-31

One of the biblical concerns about wealth is that it can become insulation and an anesthetic or intoxicant. The wealthy can insulate themselves from the consequences of their actions and from the poor. They can become anesthetized to the pain in a social system or even in their neighbors. Both Amos and Jesus in Luke address persons who have the means to help others but do not care.

Our desires can lead either to our being sensitive to the plight of the poor or to the deadening of our compassion. The author of 1 Timothy counsels attention to desires, especially the desire for godliness. Pay attention to what you desire, for your desires will lead you to be attracted to whatever is necessary to fulfill them.

FIRST READING

AMOS 6:1a, 4-7 (RCL, RC)
AMOS 6:1-7 (BCP)

In rhetoric we speak of "the jeremiad," but we don't say, "he Amosed me." Perhaps we should. Amos, you may recall, begins his prophecies by condemning the actions of nations far away and then, one by one, bringing the judgment closer to home. "For three transgressions . . . and for four, I will not revoke the punishment" is the rhetorical refrain that Amos employs to proclaim God's judgment on the nations, creeping up upon Judah and then Israel. Condemnation comes to (in order) Damascus, Gaza, Tyre, Edom, Ammon, and Moab (now we are to the cousins), then to Judah (from whence Amos came), and finally to Israel (1:3—2:6ff.). As we saw in last week's lection, Amos's judgment on the rich and the leaders in Israel is unblinking. That withering tone continues in this week's texts.

The picture Amos paints is one of detached decadence, of wealthy people dedicated to comfort and leisure and willfully ignorant of the wrath to come. Hear Amos's snapshots of the behaviors he condemns. He takes aim at those who are "at ease" and "secure," "lie on beds of ivory," "lounge," "eat lambs," "sing idle songs," "drink wine from bowls," and "anoint themselves with the finest oils." All this sounds much like a contemporary spa. The wealthy and the leaders are on vacation at the spa, luxuriating in all that their wealth can afford them, rather than grieving over the ruin of the people! These people do not see the trouble in which the nation lives; thus, the shock of the day of the Lord will be hardest on them. They will be the "first to go into exile" (6:7). These folks are about to be "Amosed."

> THE PICTURE AMOS PAINTS IS ONE OF DETACHED DECADENCE, OF WEALTHY PEOPLE DEDICATED TO COMFORT AND LEISURE AND WILLFULLY IGNORANT OF THE WRATH TO COME.

JEREMIAH 32:1-3a, 6-15 (RCL ALT.)

Once again, in contrast to the unrelenting judgment that was Amos's mission to prophesy, Jeremiah is called to display some explicit act of hope. The hopeful action described in this text is one of the most remarkable demonstrations of hope in the Hebrew Bible.

The year is about 587 B.C.E. Nebuchadnezzar has laid siege to Jerusalem. Jeremiah was under house arrest in King Zedekiah's palace, the victim of the king's displeasure because he had prophesied the siege of Jerusalem and the capture and exile of the king to Babylon. In a vision, Jeremiah receives an instruction from God that when his cousin Hanamel comes to him with the offer to purchase a field, "for the right of redemption by purchase is yours" (v. 7; see Lev. 25:25-28), Jeremiah should do it. Now, Jeremiah is under house arrest for prophesying the coming exile and the futility of resisting the Babylonians—seemingly not the best time to put money into land! But here comes God's word, and then Hanamel with the offer of purchase, to "buy it for yourself" (v. 8). The contemporary mantra for real estate purchases, "location, location, location," was not the operative rule in Israel. Today's scholars debate the extent to which Israel practiced Jubilee, the every-fiftieth-year forgiveness of debts and return of lands to their original tribal allotments. But there certainly were Israelites who held the belief that the Lord is the landowner who gives the land and the people are but tenants (Lev. 25:23).

208

THE SEASON
AFTER PENTECOST

──────────

GARY E. PELUSO-
VERDEND

We see an extension of this belief here: the Lord gave the land to the people of Israel; the Lord is taking the land from the people to punish them for their sins. But the story will not end with punishment. One day, the Lord will again restore the people to the land. What better demonstration of that hope than to purchase land *now*?

Jeremiah is the perfect person to make that purchase. He is the prophet of doom who foretells the coming exile, whom the king's counselors first try to murder and whom the king then keeps under house arrest for his prophecies. His stance toward this administration and the war is well known. His hope, however, just like his prophetic voice, is grounded not in the administration and its might but in the God who is Lord of all administrations, the God who is also Lord over all the lands of all the nations. So, publicly, with many witnesses present, Jeremiah buys Hanamel's land. The silver is weighed out.

> ONE DAY, THE LORD WILL AGAIN RESTORE THE PEOPLE TO THE LAND. WHAT BETTER DEMONSTRATION OF THAT HOPE THAN TO PURCHASE LAND *NOW*?

The deeds are signed, with one deed to remain publicly visible and the other to be preserved in an earthenware jar, for the people will return to this land. Jeremiah might not survive the war and the exile (indeed, we do not think he did survive), but the hope survives Jeremiah. Purchasing that piece of property symbolizes the hope of a renewed people with a new covenant and a new lease from God on the land *at the very moment* that the only bit of the future that is clear is the fact that Jerusalem is in very deep trouble.

RESPONSIVE READING

PSALM 146 (RCL, BCP)
PSALM 146:4-9 (BCP ALT.)
PSALM 146:7, 8-9, 9-10 (RC)

This psalm complements either of the first readings. God, and not any human ruler, is the basis and giver of life. In an era of partisan politics, ruthless actions of the powerful, and unbridled violence by those without power, hear these words: do not trust in princes, in mortals. "When their breath departs, they return to the earth; on that very day their plans perish" (v. 4). In contrast, God is creator of all that is, lover of the righteous, and redeemer of all who have been wronged. The psalmist goes on to outline what God pays attention to—the oppressed, the hungry, the blind, the bowed down, the strangers, the orphans, the widows—and how those in power treat such. Amos and Jeremiah prophesy judgment because of what the rulers did and failed to do. The psalmist outlines God's program for which all rulers will be held accountable.

PSALM 91:1-6, 14-16 (RCL ALT.)

It is difficult to tie this psalm with these texts, aside from the common expression of confidence in God's plan. Jeremiah buys land as a hostile army waits to take his city. In Psalm 91, the images are of God as protector—of the faithful. The faithful will not be harmed, even if people are dying to the right and to the left (vv. 7-8). The images are powerful and are used in hymnody: fortress, deliverer, mighty eagle, shield. But God is not portrayed as the protector of everyone. Rather, God is fortress, deliverer, fierce eagle, and shield for those "who live in the shelter of the Most High," those "who love me, . . . who know my name" (vv. 1, 14). This psalm reads as a testimony from one inside the circle of protection.

SECOND READING

1 TIMOTHY 6:6-19 (RCL)
1 TIMOTHY 6:11-19 (BCP)
1 TIMOTHY 6:11-16 (RC)

In the psychology of the ancient world, there is an intimate and intense bond between desire and attention. Human beings are motivated to satisfy their desires. They seek out the objects, the ideas, the relationships to fulfill what they desire. Said differently, one will pay attention to the environment, seeking out and being drawn to that which looks as if it can satisfy the desire. It follows, then, that if one is to live a good life (whatever the content of that goodness is), one must order and train one's desires. Rightly ordered and trained desires will lead one to a good life. Disordered desires, however, will lead one to attend to and be attracted to that which leads to perdition. While the word *crave* comes from a different root than the word *craven*, one might say that a life of unexamined, undisciplined desires is a life of craving (begging) that leads even to a craven (cowardly) life. This thought finds expression in verse 9: "But those who want to be rich fall into temptation and are trapped by many senseless and harmful desires that plunge people into ruin and destruction."

This passage (I would recommend using the full verses 6-19, which provide a much richer context for preaching than verses 11-19 alone) from 1 Timothy is focused on rightly ordering desires. Specifically, diminish the desire for money and increase the desire for godliness and contentment. Contemporary advocates

> RIGHTLY ORDERED AND TRAINED DESIRES WILL LEAD ONE TO A GOOD LIFE. DISORDERED DESIRES WILL LEAD ONE TO ATTEND TO AND BE ATTRACTED TO THAT WHICH LEADS TO PERDITION.

of the health-and-wealth gospel get no help here. The author corrects anyone who believes that "godliness is a means of gain" (v. 5). Real gain is achieved when godliness is paired with contentment, detachment from desires other than for sufficient food and clothing as well as godliness. We do not *deserve* a designer kitchen or a five-dollar coffee or a dinner out "because I am worth it." Rather, we deserve godliness because we were made for it. In order to desire godliness, we must free our attention from seeking wealth, the author asserts. Note that it is "the love of money," the desire for money, the attachment to money that is the "root of all kinds of evil," not money per se.

Right desire will lead us to attend to "righteousness, godliness, faith, love, endurance, gentleness" (v. 11). Then in verse 12, we see the author's reason why Christians cannot afford to waste their attention pursuing disordered desires. Christians must "fight the good fight of the faith" (v. 12). Christians are in a battle against the empire. The author recalls Jesus before Pilate, adhering to the truth while speaking to the governing authorities, making "the good confession." Jesus, and not Caesar, is the "King of kings and Lord of lords" (v. 15). To fight the good fight, Christians must discipline their desires and pay attention to godliness and eternal life, "to which you were called and for which you made the good confession" (v. 12).

The Gospel
LUKE 16:19-31 (RCL, BCP, RC)

Wealthy people do not come off well in this Sunday's texts. In Amos, the wealthy are anesthetized in regard to coming destruction. In Timothy, the author addresses the disordered desires of the rich or would-be rich who substitute the love of money for the love of godliness. In Luke's Gospel, he tells the story of the rich man, traditionally known as Dives, and Lazarus.

The focus of this story is not really on Dives and Lazarus but rather on Dives's brother whom Dives cannot save but who might be saved if they heed the story's warning. The audience, we might say, is the main character in this story. That is also the case with the so-called parable of the prodigal son, which might also be named the parable of the elder brother who refused to rejoice. Set within the context of chapter 16, this story, with Dives as the message bearer, is directed toward the Pharisees (see verse 14 on the Pharisees as "lovers of money") and those in Luke's community who represent the Pharisees' perspective as "lovers of money."

After two verses that set up the initial tension between rich Dives and poor Lazarus, who lives at Dives's gate (and, one would imagine, was visible to Dives every time he left his home), both men die and find themselves with reversed fortunes for all eternity. Lazarus did not earn his fate but received compensation for misfortune and misery that were beyond his control. Dives, however, finds himself tormented in Hades as the consequence of his own actions, or as a consequence of his inaction in regard to Lazarus.

Dives's first response to his condition is as self-absorbed as the life he lived. He calls to Abraham to release Lazarus with some water to cool his burning tongue. The fact that Dives knows Lazarus's name means that he knew the name of the man he passed every day and to whom he would not give even his table crumbs. The nerve! Abraham addresses Dives with the same term with which the father in the prodigal son parable addresses his elder son, "child" or *teknon*, and tells him that it is not possible for anyone to cross the divide. Note that Abraham says, "Those who might want to pass from here to you

> LAZARUS DID NOT EARN HIS FATE BUT RECEIVED COMPENSATION FOR MISFORTUNE AND MISERY THAT WERE BEYOND HIS CONTROL.

cannot do so" (v. 26), perhaps implying that Lazarus would have done this deed of mercy were it allowed. Dives, by contrast, is incapable of compassion for Lazarus, even in death. But he does muster some compassion for his brothers. After he learns that his torment cannot be relieved, he asks Abraham to employ Lazarus as a messenger (again with no regard for Lazarus other than as someone to do his bidding) to his five brothers to warn them in order that they may avoid his fate. Abraham denies this request also. There will be no Dickensian ghosts of Christmas past, present, and future to warn his brothers. Abraham holds firmly to the position that the brothers have Moses and the prophets, who are sufficient to convince the convincible to live their lives with compassion for the poor. From the audience's perspective, however, they also have this story to add to their warnings. Dives, who could not reach his brothers via Lazarus, has reached his brothers through the telling of the story.

Let us turn to the audience. If the Pharisees represent for Luke "lovers of money," then they are the brothers. However, repositioning this story in the context of Luke's congregation—and contemporary congregations—adds another dimension to the story. Assuming that the parable is authentic to Jesus, scholars debate what the final verse might have meant prior to Jesus' resurrection. But the context of Luke's congregation, and our own, is on the other side of Jesus' resurrection. For Christian congregations, we have both Moses and the prophets, as well as the

> AS A CONTEMPORARY AUDIENCE OF THIS STORY, WE ARE THE BROTHERS WHO, BY MEANS OF THIS STORY, HAVE BEEN REMINDED OF WHAT GOD REQUIRES OF US—AND WARNED NOT TO FOLLOW DIVES.

one who has risen from the dead! Yet we still struggle with the right use of wealth in Christian communities. In the story, the brothers cannot be warned. But, in fact, in telling the story at all, Jesus is warning the brothers to pay attention to the Torah in regard to right treatment of the poor. As a contemporary audience of this story, we are the brothers who, by means of this story, have been reminded of what God requires of us—and warned not to follow Dives.

PUTTING THE TEXTS TOGETHER

The author of 1 Timothy reminds us that the love of money, and not money itself, is the root of much evil. Throughout the centuries of human experience with trade and commerce, humanity has found it difficult to have wealth yet not become possessed by it or love it. Here again, the practice of stewardship is important. Acting as stewards rather than owners can function like a riverbank that helps to keep our desires flowing powerfully where they belong. Or, to change the metaphor, remembering that we are stewards rather than owners can raise speedbumps for us when we have taken a questionable road in pursuit of "more."

An explicit message in 1 Timothy and an implicit message in Amos are that communities need to pay attention to their desires. The contemporary church would do well to develop a vocabulary of attending to desires. Created as we are in the image of God, we are born to desire God and to care for one another. Disordering of desires can lead to worshiping things other than God and turning others into means to our self-interested, self-absorbed ends.

These texts also contain two messages of hope on which a preacher could expound. The Jeremiah text includes one. What a powerful action, to purchase a piece of property as a massive army is breaking down the city's defenses. This is hardly a "buy low and sell high" transaction! Jeremiah's investment, on which he did not live to see a return, was a strong signal of trust in God's promises as well as in there being a future for his people in the promised land. How many opportunities for such hopeful signs might we make in our day? Working in development for a seminary, I have come to admire people with wealth who are determined to invest in ways that give hope. Sure, there may be plenty to critique in the way that Bill Gates or Warren Buffet or other very wealthy people have made their money. But when they take that wealth and invest in projects that may turn out to be the earthen jars containing the deeds to life for millions of people, they should also be given credit as persons who give hope.

> JEREMIAH'S INVESTMENT, ON WHICH HE DID NOT LIVE TO SEE A RETURN, WAS A STRONG SIGNAL OF TRUST IN GOD'S PROMISES AS WELL AS IN THERE BEING A FUTURE FOR HIS PEOPLE IN THE PROMISED LAND.

The other message of hope is found in Luke. Despite Abraham's claim in Jesus' story that those who did not listen to Moses and the prophets would not listen to one raised from the dead, we who listen to this story today can still heed the story, and with even more encouragement; for we have Moses, the prophets, *and* Dives and the risen Lord. What a tremendous blessing! Unlike Dives who got the message too late that he would suffer the negative consequence of "the chain [he] forged in life" (to quote Jacob Marley in Dickens's *A Christmas Carol*), it is not too late for us.

NINETEENTH SUNDAY AFTER PENTECOST

TWENTY-SEVENTH SUNDAY IN ORDINARY TIME /
PROPER 22
OCTOBER 7, 2007

REVISED COMMON	EPISCOPAL (BCP)	ROMAN CATHOLIC
Hab. 1:1-4; 2:1-4 or	Hab. 1:1-6 (7-11)	Hab. 1:2-3; 2:2-4
Lam. 1:1-6	12-13; 2:1-4	
Ps. 37:1-9 or Lam.	Ps. 37:1-18 or	Ps. 95:1-2, 6-7, 8-9
3:19-26 or Psalm	37:3-10	
137		
2 Tim. 1:1-14	2 Tim. 1:(1-5) 6-14	2 Tim. 1:6-8, 13-14
Luke 17:5-10	Luke 17:5-10	Luke 17:5-10

Lections in recent weeks have referred often to wealth, money, and possessions. Today's lections turn our attention to a less material set of issues, issues such as courage, vision, faith, and testimony. In the context of reading today's Gospel, the reader might recall the teachings that followed the parable of the unjust steward: only those who are faithful in little will be given more. Apparently, this teaching applies to faith, too.

FIRST READING

HABAKKUK 1:1-4; 2:1-4 (RCL)
HABAKKUK 1:1-6 (7-11) 12-13; 2:1-4 (BCP)
HABAKKUK 1:2-3; 2:2-4 (RC)

Scholars know very little about the person Habakkuk. The book of Habakkuk has the feel of a composite work, divided between a complaint-answer dialogue (covering the verses included in today's lection), five woes (2:6-20), and a psalm-like prayer (chap. 3). The complaint dialogue in today's lection may be dated in the decade before or after 600 B.C.E.

What is the complaint that Habakkuk has for God? He accuses God of turning a deaf ear and a blind eye toward injustice and violence. Violence and injustice have become so endemic that social structures, including the law, have broken down. One imagines contemporary war zones or, from the perspective of the poor and powerless, court systems in many countries. The righteous continuously lose to the wicked and "judgment comes forth perverted" (1:4). Habakkuk questions whether God is working for justice. Thus, his complaint raises the question of theodicy: given all this injustice that apparently goes unpunished, how can we say that God is just?

The RCL reading pauses at 1:4, picking up at chapter 2. The BCP and the RC editors decided to include God's response to this first complaint. Now, it is unclear who the perpetrators of violence are that Habakkuk believes God should handle. Commentators lean toward understanding the perpetrators as persons within Israel. Then 1:5-6 means that God is using the Chaldeans (neo-Babylonians) as instruments of justice. Social breakdown within Israel will be punished by God's use ("I am rousing the Chaldeans") of a foreign people.

None of the lectionaries includes 1:12-17, but the preacher will want to look at these verses in order to understand the context of 2:1-4. It is unclear what 1:12-17 means, other than that Habakkuk is dissatisfied with God's first reply. Does Habakkuk return to his first complaint and restate it, amplifying his viewpoint in regard to how the wicked devour the righteous and go unpunished? Or, in these verses, is Habakkuk adding a complaint in response to God's reply about the Chaldeans? After all, the way God describes the Chaldeans, they will destroy the wicked and the righteous equally—hardly justice for the righteous. "The enemy brings all of them up with a hook; he drags them out with his net, he gathers them in his seine" (1:15). Habakkuk is not seeing God's justice yet.

> IN THE MIDST OF SOCIETY-DESTROYING VIOLENCE, GOD'S WORD THAT HABAKKUK RECEIVES AND IS TO BROADCAST IS: "LIVE BY FAITH."

Boldly, Habakkuk positions himself at a watchpost and waits to see God's answer, which does come. God commands Habakkuk to write down a vision, to write it on tablets large enough for a runner to see while running—in today's terms, think at least as large as a church signboard or perhaps as large as a billboard that a cruising motorist can see. God assures Habakkuk that justice will be done. But the focus of this text is how to live while the people wait for that day: "The righteous shall live by their faith" (2:4). So in the midst of society-destroying violence, God's word that Habakkuk receives and is to broadcast is this: "Live by faith." A demanding word by which to live, then or now.

LAMENTATIONS 1:1-6 (RCL ALT.)

Tradition attributes Lamentations to Jeremiah. Based on several factors, including style, some modern scholars do not believe Jeremiah authored this book.

216

THE SEASON
AFTER PENTECOST
───────────
GARY E. PELUSO-
VERDEND

However, one can imagine Jeremiah, who delivered God's words of judgment and had deep compassion for his people, or a Jeremiah-like community of people, trying to make sense of the terrible things they had endured by writing the acrostic poetry of Lamentations.

In this text, poetic images tumble forth, all portraying physical, emotional, and spiritual devastation. Jerusalem is like a widow, a princess now taken captive, an abandoned lover, a friend betrayed, an imprisoned slave, a family member assimilated into the captor's people. No one comes to visit her for the religious festivals. Even her rulers abandoned her. And all of this happened as due punishment for her sins. "The Lord has made her suffer for the multitude of her transgressions" (1:5).

RESPONSIVE READING

PSALM 37:1-9 (RCL)
PSALM 37:1-18 OR 37:3-10 (BCP)

Psalm 37 is an acrostic psalm, following the letters of the Hebrew alphabet. This structure will frustrate the reader or hearer looking for a line of logic. Rather, the logic pattern resembles a daisy, with pedals that are variations of and circle back around to a common theme: trust in the Lord. The psalm reads akin to a hymn with a refrain. Do not fret or envy the ways of the wicked; trust in the Lord. God will act and vindicate your cause; trust in the Lord. While the wicked might prosper for a time, the meek will inherit the land; trust in the Lord.

The message of this psalm complements the text from Habakkuk: the righteous will live by their faith.

PSALM 95:1-2, 6-7, 8-9 (RC)

This liturgical psalm opens with praise of God as the procession enters a sacred space (vv. 1-6). Then, in light of this reminder of who God is, the people are reminded that they are "the people of his pasture, the sheep of his hand" (v. 7). It follows, then, that the people are reminded to listen to the shepherd's voice. In contrast to the trusting way his people should act toward God, the psalmist recalls the incident at what became known as Masseh and Meribah (Exod. 17:1-7), where the people's thirsty anxiety spilled into testing God. Again, the message is to trust in God.

LAMENTATIONS 3:19-26 (RCL ALT.)

The reading picks up in the midst of yet another acrostic (this one with each letter of the twenty-two-letter Hebrew alphabet used three times). The author first sinks to his nadir: he compares his pain and homelessness to wormwood and gall. Gall is a poison herb; wormwood is not poison but fouls whatever liquid it touches. Taken together, the words connote a stinking, rotten, poisonous mess of a life. But the author then willfully directs his mind to attend to something else: the "steadfast love of the LORD" (v. 22). If he thinks not of his portion of land in Israel but rather that the "LORD is my portion" (v. 29), then he has hope.

PSALM 137 (RCL ALT.)

In a workshop many years ago, I heard biblical scholar and chronicler of biblical humor Doug Adams remark that the Bible is not "a model for morality but a mirror for identity."[1] Biblical stories often cannot conclude with the command "Go thou and do likewise." Here, in this classic psalm of exile (introduced to my generation by the haunting Don McLean song) and desire for retributive justice (which McLean did not include in his musical rendering) we have a mirror for identity. Walter Brueggeman believes that the theme of exile is one that resonates around the world today, across cultures and demographics. The experience of feeling displaced is pandemic.[2] If that interpretation is correct, then this psalm provides an important mirror for today's church.

The psalm contains three movements. In the first (vv. 1–4), the people remember Zion, weep, and decide that they cannot sing to God from this foreign land. Then (vv. 5–6) they remind themselves of the ultimate importance of remembering Jerusalem, which becomes more and more difficult to do as years pass and as the generation who once lived there dies, leaving only those who were born in exile. The psalmist concludes with an indictment of Edom, who conspired against Judah, and of Babylon, who besieged Judah, murdered and destroyed, and drove any but the weakest into exile. The psalmist looks forward to the day when Babylon is paid back, including when it's "little ones [are dashed] against the rock" (v. 9).

SECOND READING
2 TIMOTHY 1:1–14 (RCL)
2 TIMOTHY 1:(1–5) 6–14 (BCP)
2 TIMOTHY 1:6–8, 13–14 (RC)

This letter reads as words of encouragement and instruction from a mentor to his mentee. I want to bracket the question of authorship and will reflect on the text by calling the author "Paul" as a convenience. Timothy is presumed to be the same man mentioned in Acts 16, who had a Jewish mother and a Gentile father and became one of Paul's traveling companions.

What was the situation Timothy was facing? It was something daunting enough that Paul perceives Timothy is recoiling from it. Paul is concerned that Timothy has become timid or cowardly in his faith. Listen to Paul's line of thought:

- "I am grateful to God—whom I worship with a clear conscience, as my ancestors did" (v. 3);
- "I am reminded of your sincere faith, a faith that lived first in your grand-mother . . . and your mother" (v. 5);
- "I remind you to rekindle the gift of God that is within you" (v. 6);
- "God did not give us a spirit of cowardice" (v. 7);
- "Do not be ashamed . . . of the testimony about our Lord" (v. 8);
- "But I am not ashamed, for I know the one in whom I have put my trust" (v. 12).

Paul goes on to explore further the contrast between faith and cowardice, between strength in grace that allows Christians to suffer with Christ and weakness that leads to denial of who Christ is.

THE GOSPEL
LUKE 17:5-10 (RCL, BCP, RC)

It is particularly important to pay attention to the context Luke sets for the apostles' plea, "Increase our faith!" In the preceding four verses, Jesus has warned the disciples to guard against causing someone else to stumble and commands them to rebuke an offender and to forgive an offending brother seven times a day, if the brother shows repentance each time. So it makes great sense that the apostles would cry, "Increase our faith!" Who would want to be the cause of another's falling or would like to countenance a consequence worse than a miller's version of cement overshoes and "swimming with the fishes"? "Increase our faith!" Who has the strength of faith to *rebuke* a member of the community seven times in a day? Well, some folks may be strong in this way. But who has the strength to *forgive* that community member as many times as they sincerely ask to be forgiven? "Increase our faith!"

> IT IS HARD TO SEE JESUS' REPLY AS ANYTHING BUT HARSH. HE IMPLIES THAT THE CURRENT ANALOGICAL SIZE OF THEIR FAITH IS SOMETHING LESS THAN A MUSTARD SEED.

Note that in verse 1 Jesus addresses the "disciples." In verse 5 he speaks to the "apostles." Typically, "disciples" refers to a larger group than the "apostles," which refers more narrowly to the Twelve. If that distinction holds here, then the staging may mean that the apostles are understood as the community's leaders, whether in Jesus' day, Luke's day, or our own.

The community leaders, not wanting to fail in their roles, say to Jesus, "Increase our faith!" Again, a very reasonable request, given Jesus' demands of his apostolic leadership. It is hard to see Jesus' reply as anything but harsh. He implies that the current analogical size of their faith is something less than a mustard seed. Ouch! If they had even a mustard seed worth of faith, they would be able to uproot a mulberry tree and "plant" it in the ocean. At least this hyperbole is less than the saying in Matthew (17:20) and Mark (11:23) that a mustard seed worth of faith is strong enough to move a mountain.

The next verses, 7–10, do not relieve this sense of diminishment—at least not on a surface reading. In verse 7, Jesus addresses the group as if they know what it is like to be the master, the farmer who has enough means to own a slave. That slave is both field hand and kitchen help. When the slave comes in from the field, the owner does not think the slave's work is done. The slave must move on to his next task: preparing dinner for his master. Then, when the master has finished, the slave may eat. All is right with the chain of being and the order of the world. But then Jesus abruptly inverts his listeners' point of view. Now that he has them thinking from the master's perspective, he puts them in their place. The apostles, and their successors in Luke's community, are slaves. When they have finished all that they were ordered to do, they have only fulfilled their duty. Those who would like to view themselves as the master must rather think of themselves as "worthless slaves [who] have done only what we ought to have done."

To our contemporary ears, this parable is thoroughly counterintuitive. Hierarchy! This is no way to treat volunteers! This is no way to treat your clergy or your leadership team! Indeed, how many wounded leaders and wounded congregations do you know where the expectations of congregations (read: masters) for their leaders are never-ending, where salaries are as small as mustard seeds, and where praise and other rewards are as hard to find as a slave's reward in this parable?

PUTTING THE TEXTS TOGETHER

So, now that we are offended as well as diminished, what are we to do? Well, we may now be prepared to receive faith! Jesus' gospel is the power of life. In order to receive that life, we—as individuals and communities—must be prepared to receive. As long as we believe ourselves to be self-sufficient, we are not receptive. Therefore, the gospel is often working on us in one of two ways to render us receptive. When we have inflated ourselves and come to think more of ourselves than we ought, we are told to lose ourselves in order to save our lives. In this case, to be rendered receptive, we must be "put in our places," moved down the table at the banquet, reminded that we live in a servant mode and are not masters ourselves. On the other hand, there are those who have been so diminished by some unjust system or action that they do not think they are worthy of God's love. Those persons need to be rendered receptive to God via another path. When we are beaten down by society, oppressed by the hand of another, victimized by systems that keep us low in order that someone else might live an exalted life, kept away from the table because we are unclean, then by the power of God through the gospel we are lifted from the dirt and set free, we are raised from lowly estate and set on thrones, we are given our lives.

In either case, Jesus seeks to give the church life, Jesus seeks to give us our lives. The power of life is not resident in us. The power of life is God, and we access the power of God through faith. As Paul in 2 Timothy says, accessing that power through faith allows us to stand firm when attacked, to offer the good confession when challenged, to suffer for the sake of Christ.

In the Star Wars movie *The Empire Strikes Back*, Luke Skywalker crashes into the planet Dagobah, where he meets his mentor, Yoda. Yoda is trying to teach him to access and rightly use, for good, the power of the Force. When Luke decides to leave the planet before his training is complete because he senses his friends are in danger, Luke tries to levitate his ship out of the muck into which he had crashed. He is unable. Then Yoda closes his eyes and raises his hand, and the ship floats up from the slime and is set gently onto solid ground. An amazed Luke mutters, "I don't believe it." Yoda's reply: "That is why you failed." It was not Luke or Yoda who was the power to lift that ship. It was the Force.

IN ORDER TO RECEIVE THAT LIFE, WE—AS INDIVIDU-ALS AND COMMUNITIES—MUST BE PREPARED TO RECEIVE. AS LONG AS WE BELIEVE OURSELVES TO BE SELF-SUFFICIENT, WE ARE NOT RECEPTIVE.

As stewards of the lives God has given to us rather than as owners, when we are thinking rightly, we know that faith is a powerful gift from God, for through faith, we are given access to grace, which is the very life of God. Even a small faith in a great God can have great results.

"Lord, increase our faith!"

Notes

1. Adams subsequently published this thought in *The Prostitute in the Family Tree: Discovering Humor and Irony in the Bible* (Louisville: Westminster John Knox Press, 1997).

2. Walter Brueggeman, *Cadences of Home: Preaching among Exiles* (Louisville: Westminster John Knox Press, 1997).

THE SEASON
AFTER
PENTECOST:

DAVID SCHNASA JACOBSEN

To many of us the end of the church year may seem like an afterthought. By October, the standard church timetable has reasserted itself. Sunday school is now back on track and, perhaps after a summer break, the regular schedule of congregational committee meetings has resumed. In the face of this, the changing leaves of fall remind us of the regularity of it all. Some things this time of year seem to go like clockwork. In our church practice and in the seasons of nature itself, the expected, ordinary cycle of life has returned.

The season after Pentecost is known as "Ordinary Time." In one sense, the name is apt. Unlike the main liturgical cycles of Advent to Christmas and Lent to Easter, the season after Pentecost does not have the same festal zing that the more christologically oriented cycles do. While some preachers of a thematic bent will find the less-coordinated lections in this part of the church calendar disconcerting, Ordinary Time does offer its own homiletical opportunities—especially as the long season after Pentecost draws to a close.

Among readings from the Hebrew Bible, there is a greater variability that allows preachers to attend to voices not often heard. The last few weeks of this season after Pentecost offer opportunities to preach on texts not otherwise frequently featured in the lectionary. For those who follow the alternative, semicontinuous readings of the RCL, there are also moments for considering short sermon series on a given Hebrew Bible book. Either way, the staples of Sunday proclamation are enriched by biblical books that are often given short shrift. God's people benefit from hearing the less-familiar voices of Hebrew Bible figures such as Ruth, Haggai, Habakkuk, and Malachi. Thanks to them, Ordinary Time can be truly extraordinary.

The epistle readings offer their own opportunities. Again, the end of the calendar features readings from texts we don't often consider: the Pastoral Epistles and some of the more obscure Deutero-Pauline texts. Since some of these appointed texts also focus on matters eschatological, preachers find an opportunity to consider "endings" and what they might mean to a people who in an age of terror and war are perhaps more open than usual to reflecting on the nature of faith in the face of chaos. Perhaps by gaining a better sense of "endings," this Ordinary Time can be truly extraordinary.

The Gospel of Luke adds to the seasonal richness we've described. Although some have accused Luke of embodying a "theology of glory," this part of the Lukan cycle, here at the very end of Year C, helps us to see Luke's understanding of the gospel as it relates to the cross. Early on in these final weeks of Year C, we encounter healing stories, parables, and controversy with religious authorities—yet all of these familiar texts take place in the long Lukan travel narrative that began back in Luke 9:51. Back then, Jesus set his face toward Jerusalem, toward his coming passion. The cross, therefore, casts its shadow across all these familiar Lukan texts and invites us to consider Luke's Jesus in a more cruciform, less "glorious" way. This way of the cross leads us right up to the Reign of Christ Sunday, when Jesus' final conversation at the end of the season takes place paradoxically among two crucified thieves. Maybe Luke's Jesus can also make this Ordinary Time extraordinary.

Perhaps, then, this season is worth a second look. What seems familiar and routine may not be so at all—especially when you consider it from a new perspective. Ten years ago I moved to Canada after living several years in Tennessee. One of the first things I noticed when I moved to Ontario is how spectacular the fall can be. Up here, I am regularly captivated by the early, technicolor fall that helped me experience the season as if for the first time. The leaves yield their customary green color earlier than I remembered in the States, bringing with them a characteristic change in the air: the crisp mornings signaling that transformation is afoot. Yet the falling orange, yellow, and red leaves also reveal that the change in the season, while beautiful, is costly and fragile. Maybe that is as it should be. Fall is beautiful—but beautiful *because it dies*. A pressed leaf between sheets of wax paper is a nice memory for a scrapbook. However, a true experience of the fragile splendor of fall encompasses both transformative vision *and* death. And that, as these largely uncoordinated readings in Ordinary Time will show us, can be truly extraordinary.

TWENTIETH SUNDAY AFTER PENTECOST

Twenty-eighth Sunday in Ordinary Time /
Proper 23
October 14, 2007

Revised Common	Episcopal (BCP)	Roman Catholic
2 Kgs. 5:1-3, 7-15c or Jer. 29:1, 4-7	Ruth 1:(1-7), 8-19a	2 Kgs. 5:14-17
Psalm 111 or Ps. 66:1-12	Psalm 113	Ps. 98:1, 2-3, 3-4
2 Tim. 2:8-15	2 Tim. 2:(3-7) 8-15	2 Tim. 2:8-13
Luke 17:11-19	Luke 17:11-19	Luke 17:11-19

First Reading

2 KINGS 5:1-3, 7-15C (RCL)
2 KINGS 5:14-17 (RC)

The fact that this text deals with a miraculous healing of a foreign leper makes it a helpful pairing with today's Gospel lection. Yet its homiletical value is found in the way it deals with the healing of the powerful. In the end, the story attributes their healing not to their own considerable powers, but to an inscrutable God whose prophetic word is captive neither to kings nor to commanders.

From the beginning, Naaman, a commander of the Arameans, is described as a mighty warrior. He has the favor of his king and victories under his belt. But the text offers a strange footnote that foreshadows this miracle story's outcome. Naaman's many victories had actually been given *by the Lord* (v. 1). Then comes a twist. This powerful and influential warrior suffers from leprosy.

So whence will healing come for the well-heeled leader? Chain-of-command types might expect such things to happen from the top down. Yet in this text, healing bubbles up from "below." A young girl serving in the commander's household who had been taken captive after a raid into Israelite territory tells of a prophet/healer in Samaria.

So what does commander Naaman do with this inside information from his lowly servant? He opts for working the system from the top down. Naaman's Aramean king sends a letter to the Israelite king on Naaman's behalf. Israel's king interprets the letter as power politics. In frustration he blurts out the crucial question: "Am I God, to give death or life, that this man sends word to me to cure a man of his leprosy?" (v. 7). The narrative tacitly answers his rhetorical question. Though he and the unnamed king of Aram are both royalty, they cannot heal—despite Naaman's top-down assumptions.

The prophet Elisha learns of the royal correspondence and sends his own letter. Elisha invites Israel's king to send Naaman to someone who can really get the job done. Yet in the end, Elisha actually refuses to come outside to heal the commander. He merely passes on the healing word to him. Naaman complains that Elisha has not shown him due deference, even while he holds in his hands "power gifts" of horses and chariots for his would-be healer.

> AS GOD'S PEOPLE, WE ARE CALLED TO PUT OUR TRUST NOT IN PRINCES, BUT IN A LITTLE WORD, PERHAPS EVEN RELAYED ONLY BY SERVANTS.

Yet with those who serve under Naaman pressing him on, the commander reluctantly accedes to Elisha's relayed message. Naaman washes in the lowly Jordan seven times, according to the prophet's word, and is healed. The commander in his new, nubile skin then confesses faith (v. 15c).

We live in a world where healing is marketed, yet so little is delivered. It is tempting, amid the great alarm of global terrorism, to turn everything over to presidents, generals, and powers-that-be. What is needed, however, is more than tanks, GDP numbers, and the latest technology can provide. As God's people, we are called to put our trust not in princes, but in a little Word, perhaps even relayed only by servants. Although few among us possess the power of a Naaman, we are, as first-world Christians, powerful enough that we need to be disarmed by God's healing Word—especially in times like these. Maybe there we can begin to find our healing, too.

RUTH 1:(1–7) 8–19a (BCP)

Ruth's beautiful narrative allows preachers to consider the relationship between foreigners, hardship, and blessings. In a xenophobic time like ours, it may just be a means for preaching a gospel word.

The narrative begins with a once-upon-a-time feel. A famine comes upon the land and a certain man, Elimelech; his wife, Naomi; and his two sons settle in Moab, where food is more plentiful. Eventually, Elimelech dies. Naomi, now his widow, is dependent on her two sons who have married two Moabite women, Orpah and Ruth. After ten years, her two sons die. Now Naomi and her two Moabite daughters-in-law are not only widows but have no means of support in their patriarchal society.

In the midst of this Job-like situation, Naomi learns that times were better back in Judah. She decides to return to her homeland in the hope that she might still find a life for herself there. When her two Moabite daughters-in-law decide to accompany her home, she tries to talk them out of it. Orpah and Ruth would have better chances among their own people, Naomi argues; they can at least return to their mothers' homes and hope for another marriage. Besides, Naomi is too old to beget more sons for her daughters-in-law (although scholars question whether the law of levirate marriage would even apply in this case). Orpah agrees with Naomi's assessment and kisses her good-bye. But Ruth is different. Though Ruth herself would be a foreigner among Naomi's people, she professes deep loyalty to Naomi *and her God.*

Preachers revel in a beautiful story like this. Yet preachers preach more than feelings of affection. There is profound loss in this story. If it is about love, it is about love in the face of death. Yet there is more here. The text presupposes an active God. Does the initial famine display divine displeasure with the judges' rule (v. 1)? Does the Lord's giving of food in verse 6 betoken a divine change of heart? Do Naomi's circumstances indicate that God has taken issue with her as she thinks in verse 13b? Clearly the story of Ruth and Naomi takes on issues such as foreigners, hardship, and blessing within a wider theological horizon. The story treats the problem of theodicy and plays it out in the remarkable relationship of two women: one from Judah, the other from Moab. Given the fact that the marriage of foreign women becomes an issue elsewhere in the canon (for instance, Ezra and Nehemiah), Ruth's presence in the Bible is unusual. Given the fact that Ruth eventually makes possible a lineage that leads to King David himself, its place in the canon becomes strangely indispensable. This is a theological mystery worth preaching.

> THERE IS PROFOUND LOSS IN THIS STORY. IF IT IS ABOUT LOVE, IT IS ABOUT LOVE IN THE FACE OF DEATH.

JEREMIAH 29:1, 4-7 (RCL ALT.)

This lection describes Jeremiah's letter to exiles in Babylon. The prophet, who had long talked about his people's coming judgment at the hands of the Babylonians, now writes a letter to the exiled leaders, advising them to get used to life there. They are to have children there and expect that their return home is not imminent (seventy years). Yet this is not merely practical advice. The exiles should pray for the welfare of the city.

> THE HUMILIATION OF EXILE AND THE LOSS OF FAITH IN KING AND TEMPLE WOULD HAVE MADE JEREMIAH'S RECOMMENDATIONS HARD TO FOLLOW.

Contemporary preachers need to hold at least two issues in view. First, Jeremiah was asking the exiled community to go against the grain. Taking Jeremiah's advice was tantamount to losing their identity altogether. The humiliation of exile and the loss of faith in king and Temple would have made Jeremiah's recommendations hard to follow. The idea that they should do what they can, even *pray* for the city's welfare, would have seemed impossible. Babylon was the city that laid low every promise they based their lives on. Second, Jeremiah makes it a point to phrase his prophecy ("Thus says the LORD," v. 4) as more than mere command. In fact, his words echo the language of creation's blessing in Genesis 1. The exiles are to "multiply" in Babylon (v. 6). The word choice is telling and eminently preachable. The exiles will discover and experience God's creative blessing . . . even in Babylon.

RESPONSIVE READING
PSALM 111 (RCL)

This psalm is an acrostic; that is, every line begins with a successive letter of the Hebrew alphabet. James Luther Mays argues that the lines of Psalm 111 correspond to different moments in salvation history.[1] The psalm uses language that reminds one of exodus (v. 4), calls to mind the provision of food in the wilderness (v. 5), and points to the giving of the Promised Land (v. 6). Yet this God is not all about salvation, but also about law: verses 7–10 focus on this part of the divine economy, too. This explains the shift to wisdom language at its conclusion.

PSALM 113 (BCP)

This psalm is a wonderful choice for this day liturgically, especially given its resonance with the Gospel lection. Psalm 113 represents one of the five *Hallel* praise psalms used in conjunction with the Passover liturgy. Psalms 113 and 114 were sung before the meal; 115–118, afterward. The key question to ask when reciting them is what they are praising God *for*.

This psalm answers the question in the way it is structured. First, there is a summons to praise. In verses 2–4 there is a choral response that locates this God above nature and history. In verses 5–6 a question is raised about what kind of God this is who is seated on high, transcendent above all things. The answer ensues in verses 7–9. This is God who, though high and lifted up, "raises the poor from the dust," "lifts the needy from the ash heap," and "gives the barren woman a home." In short, this God, though above all, comes down to us.

PSALM 98:1, 2–3, 3–4 (RC)

Psalm 98 is a hymn of praise that many scholars link with the liturgical enthronement of Yahweh. Although much of the lectionary text recalls God's mighty acts of salvation for the people of Israel in the past, the thrust of the whole psalm is forward into the future. God, who has remembered the covenant in the past, is coming to reign in justice and equity. This coming manifestation of God's kingship evokes both a "new song" (v. 1) and a call to worship now for the whole cosmos (vv. 4-9).

PSALM 66:1-12 (RCL ALT.)

This responsive reading represents most of a thanksgiving psalm. The lectionary's portion corresponds to the community praise that leads to the subsequent individual thanksgiving in verses 13-30. After an opening call to praise and response, verses 5-7 then recall the ground for the praise, specifically the exodus story as the paradigm of God's saving deeds. What connects this psalm to its associated Hebrew Bible lection in Jeremiah is the way in which it integrates an experience of pain and testing into that thanksgiving in verses 8-12. This God who saves does so in light of profound experiences of loss and suffering.

Second Reading

2 TIMOTHY 2:8-15 (RCL)
2 TIMOTHY 2:(3-7) 8-15 (BCP)
2 TIMOTHY 2:8-13 (RC)

The second reading belongs to the Pastoral Epistles. This designation is significant in at least two ways. First, our text's authorship is probably pseudonymous. It was likely written to a later generation in the name or spirit of Paul, not by Paul himself. Although some scholars have argued for an earlier date and thus the possibility of Pauline authorship, most place the letter in the context of an emergent institutional life of the early second-century church. Second, as a pseudonymous "pastoral" letter, its audience is probably not just Timothy, a companion of Paul's, but pastors more generally.

The fact that 2 Timothy does talk about Paul and his "departure" toward death (4:6-8) makes this letter an epistolary "testament." Here a pseudonymous Paul invokes his experience before his death and exhorts pastors like Timothy to endure in the faith even in the face of suffering. Other noncanonical testaments written in the name of significant biblical figures (for instance, Moses, the Twelve Patriarchs, and so forth) do something similar. This places 2 Timothy in a literary tradition that helps us understand the text. The author invokes a memory of Paul on his deathbed because those about to die see the future and its perils more clearly than the rest of us. Paul's authority, conveyed pseudonymously, encourages readers to greater faithfulness.

This testament makes for interesting preaching. The writer begins by exhorting the young pastor to faithfulness. The reasoning moves from common examples to general principle. Like soldiers, athletes, and farmers, pastors have necessary work to focus on yet also hope for reward despite the suffering (vv. 3-7). Underlying this exhortation is an understanding of the gospel that, while different from Paul's, echoes his nonetheless. We are to remember Jesus Christ, descendant of David and yet raised. However much its proclaimers may be chained in suffering, the Word itself cannot be restrained. The idea is reiterated in the hymnic saying the writer quotes in verses 11-13. Its structure is fascinating: if we do X, Christ will do Y. In verses 11-12, the structure sounds legalistic.

> JUST WHEN WE THINK THAT OUR WORK, SUFFERING, AND PERSEVERANCE ARE ALL-IMPORTANT, WE STUMBLE ON THE GOSPEL TRUTH THAT UNDERLIES EVERYTHING.

Yet verse 13 breaks that structure: "If we are faithless, he remains faithful—for he cannot deny himself." Just when we think that our work, suffering, and perseverance are all-important, we stumble on the gospel truth that underlies everything. Of course, the writer uses that truth in verses 14-15 to make it possible to appeal to those who would mislead others in their "wrangling over words." Nonetheless, for all of 2 Timothy's subsequent attempts to regulate the life of the church in a time of controversy, verse 14 still evokes a memory of the gospel Paul preached (Rom. 3:3-4a).

Preachers might reflect on this tension homiletically. Suffering is no doubt part of the life of faith. In fact, it may even be necessary to endure suffering for the sake of the gospel. As our churches become more and more disestablished, this fact becomes clearer every day in our budgets, our numbers, and our relations to the powers-that-be. Nonetheless, lest we be tempted to turn endurance into a work, a gospel word of grace comes through. Even when we are faithless—and a church in our situation has been and will be—God in Christ is nonetheless faithful. That's what *helps* us to persevere. This gospel is the only foundation our broken-down churches have.

THE GOSPEL
LUKE 17:11-19 (RCL, BCP, RC)

The first thing to note about our Gospel text is its location in the Lukan travel narrative. The story of the ten lepers occurs "on the way to Jerusalem" (17:11). Luke as narrator reminds us of the great turn that took place in 9:51, where Jesus "set his face to go to Jerusalem" and anticipates Jesus' arrival in all of its conflict and subsequent passion. Consequently, even healing stories take place in the looming shadow of the cross. Luke is giving us an interpretive frame for a story that is 100 percent cleansing, yet tragically only 10 percent healing/thanksgiving.

The second thing to be noted is the story's setting in Jewish Scriptures and identity.[2] The cultural and legal details in Luke's story give his narrative a helpful and relevant "local color." The ten lepers "keep their distance" from the approaching Jesus in accordance with the law (Lev. 13:45-46). Jesus' command to show themselves to the priests also corresponds to Torah. Just as the onset of leprosy was not confirmed without priestly observation, so also any healing was not complete without the priest recognizing and ritualizing it (Lev. 13:2-3; 14:2-32).

The third thing to note is that this lection is a story. Stories don't just reflect statically on a theme but possess a dynamic movement. Consequently, we cannot merely reduce it to some sermonic nugget but must appreciate instead the purposive unity of its unfolding form. One problem here is that scholars are not in agreement about the form of Luke 17:11-19. Some

LUKE IS GIVING US AN INTERPRETIVE FRAME FOR A STORY THAT IS 100 PERCENT CLEANSING, YET TRAGICALLY ONLY 10 PERCENT HEALING/THANKSGIVING.

debate whether our text is a miracle story, a legend, or perhaps a pronouncement story. The confusion may result from the fact that the story has its own agenda. It begins with a miracle, yet the focus does not remain there. The miraculous is almost assumed on the way back to Jesus, where matters of gratitude, identity, and salvation are discussed. Instead of allowing us to get hung up on miracles, the unfolding story guides us elsewhere. Only one of the ten lepers returns, and only after he "sees"

THE CONTRAST BETWEEN THE THANKFUL OUTSIDER AND THE UNGRATEFUL INSIDERS TRAGICALLY HEIGHTENS THE IMPORTANCE OF JESUS HIMSELF AS ONE WHO CAUSES A SAMARITAN TO GLORIFY GOD.

that he was healed. Furthermore, when he does come back, it is for the sake of fall-on-your-face worship, thanking Jesus. Only then do we learn a crucial bit of information from the narrator: this grateful leper was a despised Samaritan. What started off as a typical miracle story has taken an unusual turn.

Jesus then pursues the story's real agenda with three rhetorical questions (vv. 17-18), which contrast the response of this Samaritan with the other nine, presumably Jews. The point is made with the third question: "Was none of them found to return and give praise to God except this foreigner?" Then verse 19 concludes the story: faith (in Jesus) has made him well. Strangely, in this miracle story the miracle recedes in importance while the contrast between the thankful outsider and the ungrateful insiders tragically heightens the importance of Jesus himself as one who causes a Samaritan to glorify God (vv. 15, 18).

Two homiletical emphases emerge from the unfolding narrative. Healing is not a work, but a gift to the grateful and ungrateful alike. Jesus' word in verse 14 sends all ten lepers on their way to "cleansing." Their changed condition does not hinge on their act of thanksgiving to Jesus, nor is it revoked for ingratitude. We who preach should remember that there is even here an astounding "wideness in God's mercy." Second, Luke's narrative emphasizes faith, "seeing," and "making well." New Testament scholar Robert Tannehill puts it this way: "The context of the story implies that Jesus' final words to the Samaritan . . . refer to a salvation which includes but goes beyond healing."[3] In this way, Jesus' phrase "Your faith has made you well" means something more than the magical thinking that slick-haired faith healers sell like snake oil on TV. This story leads preachers past the televised gimmickry of the miraculous spectacle of the individual on stage to a "being made well" that includes Jesus' tragic insight about the other nine and restoration of the outsider in salvific relationship. Among some of those living with HIV/AIDS there is such a double-sided sense of miracle. Who could have conceived years ago that a cocktail of drugs might make it possible to undo the immediate death sentence that the disease once was? Yet even today that miracle does not necessarily change the dynamics of neighborhoods and families, for whom the persistent public misperception of a so-called gay disease opens up rifts of separation between neighbors, church members, or even blood relatives. Of course, in that awful mix of healing *and* separation, other new communities occasionally emerge. In some places, those rejected in their disease and partial healing are made well with others undergoing the same treatment. Their new life with the help of medications too often continues to be tragic, yet even in such small communities people with HIV/AIDS sometimes discover themselves being made well.

> JESUS' PHRASE "YOUR FAITH HAS MADE YOU WELL" MEANS SOMETHING MORE THAN THE MAGICAL THINKING THAT SLICK-HAIRED FAITH HEALERS SELL LIKE SNAKE OIL ON TV.

Notes

1. James L. Mays, *Psalms*, Interpretation (Louisville: John Knox Press, 1994), 356f.

2. The issue of Jewish and Gentile identities in the entire work of Luke-Acts is central to the development of the narrative as a whole and is treated more fully in a work I coauthored with New Testament scholar Günter Wasserberg, *Preaching Luke-Acts* (Nashville: Abingdon Press, 2001).

3. Robert C. Tannehill, *The Narrative Unity of Luke-Acts: A Literary Interpretation*, vol. 1 (Philadelphia: Fortress Press, 1986), 119.

TWENTY-FIRST SUNDAY AFTER PENTECOST

TWENTY-NINTH SUNDAY IN ORDINARY TIME /
PROPER 24
OCTOBER 21, 2007

REVISED COMMON	EPISCOPAL (BCP)	ROMAN CATHOLIC
Gen. 32:22-31 or	Gen. 32:3-8, 22-30	Exod. 17:8-13
Jer. 31:27-34		
Psalm 121 or Ps.	Psalm 121	Ps. 121:1-2, 3-4,
119:97-104		5-6, 7-8
2 Tim. 3:14—4:5	2 Tim. 3:14—4:5	2 Tim. 3:14—4:2
Luke 18:1-8	Luke 18:1-8a	Luke 18:1-8

FIRST READING
GENESIS 32:22-31 (RCL)
GENESIS 32:3-8, 22-30 (BCP)

The power of the story of Jacob's wrestling at the Jabbok comes from the wider Jacob narrative. Jacob is at the ford of the Jabbok in 32:22-31 for a reason. He's getting ready to come to terms with his brother, whom he tricked out of his birthright years (and a few chapters) ago. Earlier, in 32:3-8, Jacob sends gifts ahead to his brother with hopes of placating Esau after all these years. In the meantime, Jacob hedges his bets by splitting up his family and property. Just in case Esau is not up for an Oprah-like reconciliation moment, he makes sure that only half of his family and goods would be affected by a potential fraternal revenge attack.

Consequently, there is more than a little confusion at the Jabbok's ford. Jacob prepares to meet his brother, though he really should prepare to meet his God. In fairness, the narrative is less than clear here. Genesis says Jacob wrestled with a "man" (v. 24). However, the story's liminal location at the river at night (think vampires, or better, trolls under a bridge) and the strange words and actions there seem to tease mystery out of the scene. On one level, Jacob may just be wrestling with his brother—Esau is no doubt on Jacob's mind in Genesis 32. Yet on another level, the text invites us to consider that this wrestling opens up a transcendent moment. How do we know? Jacob is transformed by the encounter. He tries to secure a name from the mysterious midnight wrestler (remember Esau in the womb in Genesis 25:22, 26?) but this time walks away with a limp and a blessing. Jacob even gets a new name—Israel—which is itself revelatory. As if that's not enough, the narrative signals further its transcendent dimension. Jacob confesses that he has seen God "face to face."

Of course, invoking the transcendence of God at such a key fraternal moment does not give the narrative a one-way ticket out of the world of brotherly scammers and scammees. If you go beyond the scope of today's lection, you'll discover a key quote from Jacob/Israel. When he is in fact reconciled with his brother in 33:10f., Jacob/Israel says to Esau, "For truly to see your face is like seeing the face of God."

Preaching this text narratively could be a bit like peeling away the layers of an onion. One could start with Jacob and Esau and the unease Jacob feels about his impending fraternal meeting. Yet in such liminal moments, is it not also true that the difficulties we wrestle with are *more* than they seem? Perhaps in the gathering light, Jacob wrestles long enough to discover that his "issues" are not really just with his brother, but with his covenant God. In this way, a good narrative sermon could open up to a transcendence capable of renaming us and reconciling relationships in ways we cannot merely scheme and manage. Of course, we need to be ready for what such transformation entails. We may find ourselves walking away from such transformative events with both a blessing *and a limp*. Preaching that holds both the blessing and the limp together (just as it holds together cross and resurrection) will prove more powerful and profound.

> A GOOD NARRATIVE SERMON COULD OPEN UP TO A TRANSCENDENCE CAPABLE OF RENAMING US AND RECONCILING RELATIONSHIPS IN WAYS WE CANNOT MERELY SCHEME AND MANAGE.

EXODUS 17:8-13 (RC)

The story treats a battle with the Amalekites, a nomadic people who may have been a traditional enemy of Israel. The fact that the instruction to hold up the rod during the battle comes from God seems to indicate that divine engagement is key. Nonetheless, God's people only overcome the Amalekites when Moses holds the rod aloft (sometimes with assistance) and, presumably, when it's in view. This might indicate some magical thinking about either the rod or its connection with personages like Moses. Nonetheless, the (textually unsure) closing explanation in verse 16 offers a metaphoric frame for the text. Somehow the rod functions like a "banner" of divine presence, making victory over the Amalekites possible.

JEREMIAH 31:27-34 (RCL ALT.)

The lection comes from the "Book of Consolation," Jeremiah 30–31. This hopeful section represents an important shift in Jeremiah's prophecy. Now that Judah faces imminent exile, Jeremiah can finally articulate a hope for his people.

Verse 27 envisions the sowing of a new people and their reunification with Israel in days to come. The hope is grounded in a God who watches over them. Just as God watched over the plucking up and breaking down of God's people (the words recall the substance of Jeremiah's call back in 1:10), God will do the same as they are built and planted. This hopeful vision sets right the words of the people's proverb:

> IN CONTRAST TO SINAI, A COVENANT THAT GOD'S PEOPLE BROKE, GOD INTENDS TO "CUT" A NEW COVENANT WITH ISRAEL AND JUDAH BY WHICH THE LAW WILL BE INTERNALIZED.

now those who sin will pay the price themselves, instead of subsequent generations. Yet all this merely sets up the contours of the new covenant God is establishing (vv. 31-34). In contrast to Sinai, a covenant that God's people broke, God intends to "cut" a new covenant with Israel and Judah by which the law will be internalized. In the end, this covenant will rest on divine forgiveness—the only way out of exile and back into covenant relationship with God.

Christian preachers will be tempted to treat this text in light of the Christian meaning of "new covenant," which is altogether foreign to this text. Preachers would be better off reflecting theologically on the divine commitment to reengage God's people, even as exile and death loom. That word needs no supersessionist "old" covenant as a foil; it is one that can still be spoken evangelically today.

RESPONSIVE READING

PSALM 121 (RCL, BCP)
PSALM 121:1-2, 3-4, 5-6, 7-8 (RC)

This responsive reading belongs to the psalms of ascent (Psalms 120–134). One theory is that they were sung in connection with pilgrimages to Jerusalem. If so, it provides a fascinating context for understanding Psalm 121 in particular. Perhaps the language of "lifting up my eyes to the hills" refers to a pilgrim seeing Jerusalem on the horizon. The language, therefore, could represent a dialogue between a pilgrim longing to depart and a priest who offers a benediction for the pilgrim's way. Apart from that theory, the psalm expresses a profoundly confident faith that resonates with power even today. The repetition of the imagery adds to the step-like effect ("my help" in verses 1-2, "slumber" in verses 3-4, and so forth), evoking in verse a movement toward a destination within the context of a trusting relationship with God.

PSALM 119:97-104 (RCL ALT.)

This responsive reading is one eight-verse unit from a twenty-two-unit acrostic psalm that meditates on God's law and life. Acrostic psalms begin each line with a successive letter of the Hebrew alphabet. Psalm 119 distinguishes itself acrostically by having all eight lines of each of its twenty-two units begin with a successive letter of the alphabet. The accomplishment of such poetry may be mind numbing to us when we read it, but its rhetorical force may just be meditative. The psalmist loves the law and understands that such meditative dwelling on it brings with it divine relationship and an examined life worth living.

Our eight verses are typical of this meditative effect. The psalmist uses synonyms of the word *law* throughout in order to aid reflection (for instance, "commandment," "decrees," "precepts," "word," "ordinances," and so forth). But the focus is not on the law as pure external reality. It is the object of the psalmist's "meditation" and love (v. 97). The psalmist's relationship with the law produces wisdom and understanding (vv. 98-99). As a result, the psalmist is empowered to keep the law and to hold back from evil (vv. 100-101). Consequently, the word of the law (far from being a burden-some taskmaster as sometimes portrayed in Christian circles) is sweeter than honey to the mouth (v. 103). Because the beautiful sense of the psalmist's relationship to the law is so wonderfully portrayed here, this reading makes a marvelous match with the RCL alternative first reading for this day, especially Jeremiah 31:31-34.

SECOND READING
2 TIMOTHY 3:14—4:5 (RCL, BCP)
2 TIMOTHY 3:14—4:2 (RC)

This section of 2 Timothy is important today. Quite often 3:16 ("All scripture is inspired by God . . .") is bandied about by those who would advo-cate fundamentalist views of Scripture. Those who love the Bible for what it is, however, receive it as God's gift and thus read it thankfully in context and with the care of studied discernment. Here, such a text also calls forth preachers' best exegetical care.

The first context to consider is that laid out in last week's exegesis. Second Timothy 3:16 did not drop down from dogmatic heaven but is part of a pastoral epistle designed to invoke memories of the apostle Paul for the pastoral life of a later generation in conflict. Because of the testamentary feel of this letter, the writer uses Paul's suffering and death as a way of understanding the calling of Timothy and other pastors to preach the gospel in later times of suffering and opposition. In this section, the writer reminds Timothy of what he has learned and believed and exhorts him to hold to it (vv. 14-15). Here, then, Paul invokes the Scriptures as "inspired by God" and "useful for teaching" so that all who are God's might be "equipped for every good work" (vv. 16-17).

Yet by invoking Scripture in this way, the writer offers words that need to be understood in context. When the writer says "inspired," he may not mean it in the sense we think of—especially in today's world where the language of "inspiration" has become so technical. The word in Greek means something like "God-breathed." The point here is not to argue for the Scriptures' perfection, but to emphasize their *usefulness*. One last consideration should also give us pause. When the writer here talks about Scripture, its referent is not the New Testament, but the Hebrew Scriptures alone. At this point in history, there is no New Testament canon to speak of.

> THE WORD INSPIRED IN GREEK MEANS SOMETHING LIKE "GOD-BREATHED." THE POINT HERE IS NOT TO ARGUE FOR THE SCRIPTURES' PERFECTION, BUT THEIR *USEFULNESS*.

Naturally, the writer's guidance is still helpful. His argument is not about the perfection of the Scriptures, but about their usefulness—especially for pastors charged with preaching the Word in difficult times. So it is with gospel preaching in any time. The good news would be nice enough if it always eventuated in a big circle where everyone held hands and sang "Kum ba Yah." The reality of gospel preaching, however, is different. It entails, as the writer points out, carrying out one's ministry "fully," even in the face of suffering. Those of us charged to preach the gospel in the face of the claims of jingoistic nationalism that holds too little regard for others, a breathless consumerism that lurches from one credit-card minimum payment to the next, and a cultural narcissism that reduces all of life to one's own "habits of the heart," may just benefit from such a word. It may not always be what North Americans are itching to hear, but it may just be something as gracious and challenging as the gospel: a divine breath of fresh air . . . and useful, too.

THE GOSPEL
LUKE 18:1-8 (RCL, RC)
LUKE 18:1-8a (BCP)

As with most parables, preachers need to come to terms with material that has been redacted. Jesus' parabolic teaching (18:2-5) is framed by uniquely Lukan theological material (18:1, 6-8).

Parables turn tedious when preachers turn them into allegories or moralistic examples. While the widow is to be admired for her perseverance, Christian interpreters should be loath to assume that the unjust judge could ever be a divine "figure." The unjust judge pretty much agrees that he is no exemplary figure (his soliloquy in verse 4b echoes almost word for word the narrator's judgment about him in verse 2!) but only gives in because the widow is wearing him out. A parable is like a moving metaphor that teases out truth. It offers neither moral examples nor allegorical figures for God.

In fact, Luke as redactor reinforces our embarrassing parable by framing it with a discontinuous rhetorical trope: from the lesser to the greater. In other words, if an unjust judge can be goaded by a lowly widow to give in and do right, how much more can God the Judge (who is righteous, good, and loving) be counted on to deliver the justice that God's own chosen ones desire (vv. 7–8a). Theologically, what Luke offers us is no allegorical or moralistic identity with parabolic characters, but the *discontinuity* of faith. It is, moreover, precisely this discontinuity between unjust judges and God that makes divine justice so trustworthy.

In light of this surety of hope in God's eschatological justice, the real question is not whether God will deliver, but whether the Son of Man will come at the end of everything and still find faith on earth. What is in play here is not the God who is the object of our "How long, O Lord?" prayers, but the faith that is requisite for such prayer and, indeed, animates it. In other words, how does Luke's discontinuous, parabolically faith-full prayer and action survive against Luke's own tragic backdrop of injustice and unrealized hope?

In his book *Death in the Haymarket*, historian James Green includes the story of Lucy Parsons, who together with her labor leader husband, Albert, had participated in several strikes and labor actions in late nineteenth-century Chicago that ended in a tragic bombing in Haymarket Square.[1] Lucy, like her husband, had helped to organize workers to realize the promise of an eight-hour workday in the days when robber barons and the captains of industry

THEOLOGICALLY, WHAT LUKE OFFERS US IS NO ALLEGORICAL OR MORALISTIC IDENTITY WITH PARABOLIC CHARACTERS, BUT THE DISCONTINUITY OF FAITH.

seemed to hold all the power. After the Haymarket bombing, Lucy's husband, along with several other labor leaders, were unjustly executed for conspiring in the bombing solely because of their organizing activity and speeches—none of them was deemed to have actually been involved in the planning of the event, nor was the actual bomber ever named or arrested. In the face of such injustice, Albert's widow, Lucy, went on to live her life toward hope. Because the labor movement and the tragic bombing happened at the beginning of May, eventually the story of the Haymarket became famous in the international labor movement, which is why so many nations around the world celebrate May 1 as Labor Day. How ironic that though this event took place in late nineteenth-century America, the United States is one of the few countries that doesn't recognize a May Labor Day even now! Yet Lucy never lost sight even when her nation forgot. Even as an aged widow in 1937, she continued to speak with fervor at the memorial service on the fiftieth anniversary of her husband's unjust execution. And yet in the remaining three and a half years of her life, she could look back with more than just regret, for in 1938 Congress mandated the eight-hour workday in the Fair Labor Standards Act.

What is it that keeps people like Lucy going in the face of injustice and adversity? We human beings are a stubborn, persistent lot—that is true enough. Yet surely there is more at work in such situations than our own meager resources. Those of us who confess faith in a God of justice must surely believe in the great discontinuity between God and us, what is and what will be. For it is in our crying, our tears, and our prayers that the ground of our hope is revealed. It is faith, the very gift that empowers us to keep on keepin' on. Martin Luther King Jr. put the view of such divinely wrought, faith-full, prayer-full action rather nicely: "The arc of the moral universe is long, but it bends toward justice."[2]

> THOSE OF US WHO CONFESS FAITH IN A GOD OF JUSTICE MUST SURELY BELIEVE IN THE GREAT DISCONTINUITY BETWEEN GOD AND US, WHAT IS AND WHAT WILL BE.

Notes

1. The story, which is much larger than Albert and Lucy's described above, is amply retold in Green's book, *Death in the Haymarket: A Story of Chicago, the First Labor Movement and the Bombing That Divided Gilded Age America* (New York: Pantheon, 2006).

2. Martin Luther King Jr., "Our God Is Marching On," in *A Testament of Hope: The Essential Writings and Speeches of Martin Luther King, Jr.*, ed. James M. Washington (San Francisco: HarperSanFrancisco, 1986), 230. The use of the word *arm* for *arc* in Washington's transcribed text may be a misprint.

TWENTY-SECOND SUNDAY AFTER PENTECOST

Thirtieth Sunday in Ordinary Time /
Proper 25
October 28, 2007

Revised Common	Episcopal (BCP)	Roman Catholic
Jer. 14:7-10, 19-22 or Sir. 35:12-17 or Joel 2:23-32	Jer. 14:(1-6) 7-10, 19-22	Sir. 35:12-14, 16-18
Ps. 84:1-7 or Psalm 65	Psalm 84 or 84:1-6	Ps. 34:2-3, 17-18, 19, 23
2 Tim. 4:6-8, 16-18	2 Tim. 4:6-8, 16-18	2 Tim. 4:6-8, 16-18
Luke 18:9-14	Luke 18:9-14	Luke 18:9-14

First Reading

JEREMIAH 14:7-10, 19-22 (RCL)
JEREMIAH 14:(1-6) 7-10, 19-22 (BCP)

Jeremiah 14 makes for an interesting pairing with the day's Gospel lection, mostly by way of contrast. Whereas in Luke, the tax collector's regretful prayer is heard and he heads home "justified," the people's prayer of lament in verses 7-9 is not accepted by God in verse 10. The people respond with yet another attempt to move God by asking questions (v. 19), confessing guilt (v. 20), and appealing to God's own name (v. 20). In the end, despite the negative response of verse 10, all they can do is rely on God's mercy. Yet the silence at the end of chapter 14 is deafening. Assuming that 15:1-9 represents the conclusion to this unit in Jeremiah, the answer is not positive in the least.

> HOW DO WE GO FORWARD WITH GOD IN THE FACE OF BOTH CATASTROPHE AND DIVINE SILENCE? MORE IMPORTANT, HOW DOES GOD GO FORWARD WITH US?

Hebrew Bible scholar William Holladay argues that our text represents a kind of counter-liturgy in the mode of lamentation.[1] While we see that Jeremiah conforms to most of the normal elements of a lamentation (description of problem in verses 1-6, prayer of confession in verses 7-9, divine response in verse 10, and later, confession of trust in God in verse 22), the prophet's use of the form only highlights the divine refusal to accept it. Formally, the lament assumes God's heart can be moved to show mercy. In this text, where the issue is also the question of judgment and exile in Babylon, the relationship is too far gone for the old liturgical formulae. As such, it stands in stark contrast. We may celebrate God's yes to the tax collector in Luke, but it only has evangelical power because God can also say no—as God does indeed through the prophet Jeremiah here.

Preachers may want to consider such a text as a way of wrestling with some of the more difficult questions around theodicy. While the equation of experiences of drought and war as divine judgment may be theologically problematic, the strange silence of God in the face of the lament's end in verses 19-22 is poignant and theologically provocative for today. How do we go forward with God in the face of both catastrophe and divine silence? More important, how does God go forward with us? Here preachers will need to be more than exegetes of Scripture alone, but together with conflicted prophet Jeremiah (note his weeping in verses 17-18), theologians of the Word in solidarity with God's people.

SIRACH 35:12-14, 16-18 (RC)
SIRACH 35:12-17 (RCL ALT.)

Sirach is a book of wisdom, likely committed to writing prior to the Maccabbean period. As a book of wisdom, most of its material takes the form of proverbs. Unlike the book of Proverbs, however, the material is arranged more poetically so that connections between the proverbial forms are smoother and more unified.

This particular text in chapter 35 focuses on giving to God and how it should be regarded (vv. 12-13). Special emphasis is given to avoiding gifts that are offered in bad faith (for instance, bribery in v. 14) or are the result of exploitative relationships with the poor (v. 15). Indeed, since God is the one who champions the orphan and the widow (vv. 16ff.), God is sure to hear their supplications. As such, any gift offered as a "dishonest" sacrifice will surely not influence God's impartial judgments.

JOEL 2:23-32 (RCL ALT.)

Joel is a prophet from the postexilic, Persian period when the Temple had been rebuilt and the cult and priesthood had once again become central to Judah's life. The first part of Joel, featuring the figure of the locusts for an advancing northern army, calls Joel's people to repentance in order to avert total calamity (2:12-17). With the people's favorable response to Joel's call to repentance, God promises to remove the northern army (v. 20) and there ensues a joyous announcement, which is our lection. With verse 23, Joel paints a picture of a renewal of the land that shall once again be ample in grain, wine, and oil. In light of this, God's people will once again praise God and not worry about their shame (vv. 26-27). Afterward shall come the Day of the Lord, which is at once great and terrible. God's Spirit shall be poured upon all the people. The people's enemies will be decisively defeated, even while those who faithfully worship God will be saved (vv. 28-31).

Preaching such a text takes great imagination and care. Like apocalyptic language, it moves back and forth between symbolic and concrete realities. Because it is a historical product, we cannot turn it into future prediction. To the degree that it describes hope in the very shadow of suffering and looks forward to a new day when God will level distinctions among God's people (vv. 28-29), however, it offers a powerful homiletical opportunity for visionary preaching.

> PREACHING SUCH A TEXT TAKES GREAT IMAGINATION AND CARE. LIKE APOCALYPTIC LANGUAGE, IT MOVES BACK AND FORTH BETWEEN SYMBOLIC AND CONCRETE REALITIES.

RESPONSIVE READING

PSALM 84:1-7 (RCL)
PSALM 84 OR 84:1-6 (BCP)

This responsive reading stands in stark contrast to its paired Hebrew Bible lection from Jeremiah 14. Whereas the prophet speaks of divine absence and thirst, the psalmist envisages a kind of longing that waits for something assured and is therefore empowering. Many scholars think Psalm 84 would have been sung for one of the pilgrimages to Jerusalem. The first four verses look forward to being present at the Temple and celebrate the shelter it offers even to the most vulnerable of creatures. With that, verses 5-7 describe the way of pilgrims toward Zion. Though the pilgrimage is arduous, God's strength is sufficient to make it a place of "springs" and "early rains." From there the psalm turns to pray for the king. It may well be that scholars like Artur Weiser are right when they point out that this pilgrimage was part of a celebration in which the king was reconnected with Yahweh's enthronement.[2] With the final verses, the psalmist turns eyes toward a return home. This God met in the Temple is a "strength and shield" even as the pilgrim leaves the sacred precincts.

PSALM 34:2-3, 17-18, 19, 23 (RC)

This psalm is a thanksgiving by form, and yet it embodies something of a wisdom perspective on life. As such, the psalm begins with a brief hymn of praise

(34:2-4, in this versification). What follows is a narrative of the psalmist's experience, which in turn sets up in the final portion of the psalm, the didactic wisdom material, from which most of today's responsive reading actually comes. A profound sense of trust in God's justice is articulated in this section: God's eyes are on the righteous and God's face is against evildoers. Lest the reader assume, however, that God's engagement is merely about vengeance, verse 19 qualifies that engagement: "The LORD is near to the brokenhearted, and saves the crushed in spirit."

PSALM 65 (RCL ALT.)

Psalm 65 is a psalm of thanksgiving (perhaps composed after a period of drought) that reorients our awareness of ourselves in creation "God-ward." The psalm begins in verses 1-4 with reflection on who we are in the presence of God: sinners who can trust God to forgive. In the presence of such a God, we can give thanks, because God has brought us near. In verses 5-8, the psalm then turns to who this God is. This God is one whose deeds of salvation are borne out in nature *and* history. From there, it is possible in verses 9-13 to understand God's gift in "visiting the earth" with timely spring rains. Although God's "wagon tracks overflow with richness" (v. 11b), this is not just any god riding a chariot through the heavens and leaving a verdant trail of fertility and growth. This is none other than God in Zion to whom "praise is due."

SECOND READING
2 TIMOTHY 4:6-8, 16-18 (RCL, BCP, RC)

With this final lectionary reading from 2 Timothy in Year C, we see the culmination of the exegetical issues we have been highlighting over the last few weeks. Here the writer uses the story of Paul's imprisonment, his suffering, and the prospect of his death to bring home the need for faithful pastoral ministry on the part of Timothy and all who would read this pastoral epistle. As an epistolary testament, the letter allows the writer to explore how this great apostle's death gives occasion to reflect on how subsequent generations might also keep faith.

IF THE WRITER WISHES TO SET UP PAUL'S FAITHFULNESS AS IN ANY SENSE EXEMPLARY, HE MUST ALSO CONTEND WITH THE ABSOLUTE GRACIOUSNESS OF THE TRADITION OF PAUL'S GOSPEL.

The writer sets out the situation with great feeling. In the first person he has Paul describe himself as "being poured out as a libation" (v. 6). As if the reference to death might not be clear enough, he adds in the second half of the verse that the time of his departure is at hand—departure being in all likelihood a metaphor

242

THE SEASON
AFTER PENTECOST
─────────────
DAVID SCHNASA
JACOBSEN

for his death. He then fleshes out what has brought him to this point with images from athletic competition: he has "fought the good fight, . . . finished the race, . . . kept the faith" (v. 7). He looks forward, staying with the athletic metaphor, to the "crown of righteousness" (v. 8), the laurels that all receive who long for the Lord's appearance on the last day.

Yet if the writer wishes to set up Paul's faithfulness as in any sense exemplary, he must also contend with the absolute graciousness of the tradition of Paul's gospel. In verses 16-18, he therefore also recalls that in his suffering, everyone deserted him . . . except for the Lord. If Paul is portrayed as having persevered, it is only because the Lord gave him strength, "so that the message might be fully proclaimed" (v. 17). In the end, Paul is portrayed as no longer speaking of his perseverance, but of doxology. Even the great apostle is heard here concluding his personal reminiscence of suffering and endurance in praise to the one who will save him for the heavenly kingdom: "To him be the glory forever and ever. Amen" (v. 18).

Within this form we see powerful homiletical possibilities. Those charged with preaching the gospel walk a fine line. On the one hand, gospel preaching does not exempt from suffering. To the contrary, it is a way of suffering that calls for perseverance. Nonetheless, for all its moral seriousness, that perseverance can never lose sight of the truth that its power is not intrinsic to who we are. Rather, what underlies such pastoral commitment is a profound sense of divine grace. And in the end, even in our best moments, we are left in hapless gratitude: *soli Deo gloria*, to God alone be the glory.

THE GOSPEL
LUKE 18:9-14 (RCL, BCP, RC)

With one of his more familiar parables from Luke, Jesus continues the ostensible topic of prayer (recall 18:1-8) but with quite a different focus. Here the parable of the Pharisee and the publican sets the prayers of two representative figures side by side and uses the surprising outcome of the story to tease out a difficult evangelical truth. Preachers would be wise not to weaken the parable by reducing its figures (the Pharisee and the tax collector) to melodramatic stereotypes, nor by hedging its very strange outcome. Therefore, we begin its homiletic interpretation here by ensuring that we don't veer into allegory or moralism but stay with the parable in all its gospel strangeness.

JESUS CHOOSES A PHARISEE FOR THIS PARABLE TO HEIGHTEN PARABOLIC INCREDULITY, NOT TO INDULGE IN A STEREOTYPE THAT WOULD ONLY FEED SOME LESS-THAN-CHRISTIAN DESIRE FOR THEIR COMEUPPANCE.

First, we need to consider the figures of the Pharisee and the tax collector. It would be a mistake to read Luke's Pharisees as if they were Matthew's or a mere stereotype for legalism. If there is any group that is closest to Luke's very Jewish Jesus, it is the Pharisees. When Jesus tells the parable here, his hearers and Luke's readers probably do not expect such a markedly negative outcome. We contemporaries may want to dress the Pharisees in the melodramatic garb of the ill-intentioned Simon LeGree. This would do a disservice, however, to the Pharisees themselves and to the rhetorical force of Jesus' parable. Jesus chooses a Pharisee for this parable to heighten parabolic incredulity, not to indulge in a stereotype that would only feed some less-than-Christian desire for their comeuppance. The tax collector as a figure also needs some homiletic care. He is not the publican with a heart of gold. A tax collector is unclean because he is a hated collaborator. Tax collectors work *with* the Roman authorities, use less-than-scrupulous methods to secure revenue for the empire, and subsist off a kind of commission at the point of payment. Tax collectors are not merely "misunderstood"; they are on the wrong side religiously, politically, and economically. If we misrepresent the figures of the Pharisee and the tax collector, we mitigate the shocking impact of Jesus' parable. It's not about taking the "not so nice but righteous" down a peg and making those who deep down are not so bad a little nicer. The parable is about the justification of the ungodly (although Luke's view of justification is definitely not the same as Paul's—please note, for example, the absence of the cross in our pre-passion lection—Luke is using the term "justified" in verse 14 in just such a provocative way). We should not lessen the scandal by indulging our twenty-first-century stereotypes about either one.

This brings us to the problem of hedging the parable's outcome. By having Jesus tell the parable in the way he does, Luke actually heightens the scandal of a justified tax collector. In chapter 19, Luke will have Jesus come to the house of another toll collector, Zacchaeus. As a response to this gift, Zacchaeus repents with some extravagance. But in our text, Jesus pronounces a tax collector justified *and there is not even a hint of repentance.* When you compare this text even to other portions of Luke, it should cause pious people of any age and epoch concern. There is no moralism in the parable itself.

Nonetheless, the parable does more than simply portray two representative figures at prayer. In fact, Luke uses the prayers themselves to reveal important truth about the figures. Both use language steeped in Jewish tradition. The Pharisee's prayer is a prayer of thanksgiving. Though its language sounds strange to us in that it compares the Pharisee to other people, it may have legitimate precedents in Jewish tradition.

> JESUS PRONOUNCES A TAX COLLECTOR JUSTIFIED *and there is not even a hint of repentance*. THIS SHOULD CAUSE PIOUS PEOPLE OF ANY AGE AND EPOCH CONCERN.

Although Luke gives us other clues about the Pharisee's attitude (he stands apart by himself all his thanksgivings begin with "I"), much of the prayer's content does not veer too far from the tradition. Likewise, the tax collector's prayer has roots in the Jewish tradition. His humble language and attitude are reminiscent of both the Psalms and other noncanonical Jewish sources. The fact, however, that this prayer is uttered by the hated collaborator is what is strange about our text. As a result, Jesus' pronouncement of him as "justified" is, despite the excesses of the Pharisee's very Jewish prayer, still shocking. Preaching that wishes to convey something similar to hearers today will need to do so without papering over this problem.

In her short story "The Lame Shall Enter First," Flannery O'Connor tells of a widowed father, Sheppard; his grieving son, Norton; and an older boy named Rufus Johnson.[3] Sheppard meets Rufus as part of his Saturday volunteer work as a counselor at a reformatory for wayward youth. Sheppard recognizes an intelligence in Rufus that makes him think the boy is redeemable, even though Rufus is outwardly bitter and struggles to come to terms with a misshapen foot that causes him to limp. In an effort to overcome what Sheppard perceives as his own son, Norton's, self-absorbed grief, and out of a desire to save Rufus from himself, Sheppard brings Rufus into his home. Over time, it becomes clear that Rufus is not about to be reformed by the secular do-gooder, Sheppard. The police show up at Sheppard's door on more than one occasion while Norton, Sheppard's own son, begins to deal with his grief in increasingly strange ways. When Rufus begins spouting Bible verses to Sheppard's grieving son, Sheppard becomes more disconcerted, yet tries not to show that he has lost faith in his secular project of redeeming Rufus from himself. Toward the end, when Sheppard gives up his quest and finally looks for an opportunity to be rid of his young houseguest, the police show up at his door again, this time with Rufus in tow. Sheppard lets the police take Rufus off his hands, but not before Rufus indicts Sheppard and tells him "he ain't right." Rufus the ruffian Bible quoter with the bad foot knows that God will accept him, for the lame shall enter first. But, says Rufus to Sheppard, you are nothing more than a "big tin Jesus." In O'Connor's troubling story, there is a powerful reversal and a painful recognition. Try as we may, we cannot redeem others, much less ourselves. There is only one who can save, and we can only throw our sinful selves at the feet of this one's inscrutable mercy. We "ain't right," and only God can make us so.

> THERE IS ONLY ONE WHO CAN SAVE, AND WE CAN ONLY THROW OUR SINFUL SELVES AT THE FEET OF THIS ONE'S INSCRUTABLE MERCY. WE "AIN'T RIGHT," AND ONLY GOD CAN MAKE US SO.

Notes

1. William Holladay, *Jeremiah 1*, Hermeneia (Philadelphia: Fortress Press, 1986), 422, 427ff.

2. Artur Weiser, *The Psalms*, Old Testament Library, trans. H. Hartwell (Philadelphia: Westminster Press, 1962), 568.

3. Flannery O'Connor, *The Complete Stories* (New York: Noonday, 1991), 445–82.

REFORMATION DAY /
REFORMATION SUNDAY

OCTOBER 31 / NOVEMBER 4, 2007*

REVISED COMMON
Jer. 31:31–34
Psalm 46
Rom. 3:19–28
John 8:31–36

FIRST READING
JEREMIAH 31:31–34

See the first reading for the Twenty-first Sunday after Pentecost (Twenty-ninth Sunday in Ordinary Time/Proper 24).

RESPONSIVE READING
PSALM 46

This famous psalm, well known as the inspiration for Luther's hymn "A Mighty Fortress," holds a special value for this day. It exudes a sense of confidence in God. It is not the breezy confidence of superficial praise choruses; it is a hard-won confidence that is birthed in difficulty. Though the psalm begins with a confession that God is our "refuge and strength," verses 2–3 give the crucial context. Using cosmic mythological imagery of shaking mountains and foaming sea, the psalmist helps us understand this first psalm among the so-called "songs of Zion" as a word of trust spoken in crisis. With verses 4–5, the psalm shifts into a

*If transferred to the Twenty-third Sunday after Pentecost (Thirty-first Sunday in Ordinary Time / Proper 26)

vision of Zion itself. The streams refer to the myth of a river that flows from the center of the cosmos (compare Isa. 33:21; Ezek. 47:1-12; Rev. 22:1-2). This is, in other words, where God has chosen to dwell. As such, when in verse 6 the nations (their enemies) are in an uproar and totter like the mythological mountains of the opening verses, it is the voice of their God that causes them and all the earth to "melt." Though war may be the chosen tool of nations, God makes "wars to cease" by breaking bows, shattering spears, and burning shields. As such, to "be still and know that I am God" is no mere act of apophatic mysticism, but a realization that God is indeed God, despite our warring human ways. God is indeed the one who is "with us" in the very face of danger.

SECOND READING
ROMANS 3:19-28

The pericope straddles two key portions of Paul's argument in Romans. With 3:19-20, Paul concludes a longer section on the universality of sin. Basing his argument on Jewish Scripture (especially Psalm 143:2), Paul places both Jew and Gentile within the same horizon. The law, says Paul, exists to give knowledge of sin. In this way "every mouth" is "silenced, and the whole world . . . held accountable to God" (v. 19). With the subsequent verses, Paul then shifts his argument to talk about what righteousness really is. Righteousness is God's and is given as a gift in Jesus Christ through faith. God's way of accomplishing this is through Christ, whom God put forward as a sacrifice of atonement (the Greek reference here in verse 25 may be to a "mercy seat"; it is not the word for the propitiation of an angry god) that is effective through faith. If so, a righteousness of God that is a gift through faith means that there is no room for boasting (vv. 27-28.) about works at all.

> WHEN REFORMATION DAY BECOMES MERELY AN OCCASION TO BASH OTHERS, IT SEEMS TO PRESUPPOSE THAT SOMETHING MORE THAN CHRIST'S OWN CRUCIFIXION BECOMES NECESSARY FOR "WINNING THE DAY."

The text is important for preaching on Reformation Day, but preachers will want to watch out for at least a few problems. It is sometimes tempting on such days to turn Paul's opponents into rank legalists and to apply an analogy to contemporaries in other denominations in order to turn them into "foils." The rhetorical form of Paul's text here is a diatribe. New Testament scholar Paul Achtemeier notes that while the term *diatribe* has a negative connotation in English, as an ancient rhetorical form it represents a conversational way of working through what a speaker wishes to say.[1] As part of the argument, the speaker anticipates objections as a means of clarifying and distinguishing what is said. When Reformation Day becomes merely an occasion to bash others, it seems to presuppose that something more than Christ's own crucifixion becomes necessary for "winning the day." Perhaps preachers should follow the model of Paul, who takes pains to argue that God's promises to the Jews are still good (Romans 9–11). Some commentators theorize that Paul's letter to the Romans is, after all, written to a mixed Jewish- and Gentile-Christian community. If so, Paul's words are meant not to divide, but to unite; not to triumph over, but to converse.

Nonetheless, there is something scandalous about this gospel Paul announces and that we celebrate on Reformation Day. All *are* liable to judgment (v. 19), and yet all in Christ Jesus are given righteousness as a gift. The fact that Paul uses the language of divine righteousness to talk about justification means that God's righteousness is infinitely more than merely conforming to an external norm; rather, as Achtemeier points out, it is a matter of relationship.[2] God doesn't simply have a change of mind about sin as if now there were a Plan B. No, God's righteousness is revealed in doing what it takes to open a relationship with a humanity mired in sin. Faith is not a requirement to get in, nor a new human work, nor a matter of choice. Rather, says Achtemeier, faith *is* the relationship that God's righteousness opens up and enables for us. That, of course, as revealed through the cross of Christ, should be sufficient scandal. We need add no others to the cross itself on Reformation Day. Perhaps this is why Lucas Cranach's famous painting in the Stadtkirche in Wittenberg shows what it does. One sees in the picture a crowd gathered in church and, up front, Martin Luther preaching. Yet the preacher merely points—for pictured right between preacher and congregants is Christ crucified himself. What a graphic relationship between those people in the scene! One suspects that for Luther, that alone would be scandal enough.

> GOD'S RIGHTEOUSNESS IS REVEALED IN DOING WHAT IT TAKES TO OPEN A RELATIONSHIP WITH A HUMANITY MIRED IN SIN.

THE GOSPEL
JOHN 8:31-36

This lection focuses more on the issue of freedom as it relates to the gospel. While the signature phrase "The truth shall set you free" is perhaps overly familiar, the text offers provocative ways of thinking about what it means to preach the gospel of Jesus Christ on this day. In fact, the text offers us a theological ground for thinking about freedom in a challenging way.

With John, it is always important to place the dialogue of a given pericope in a broader literary context. John may be the most explicitly theological of all the

Gospels. Nonetheless, readers benefit from understanding what is said within some sort of concrete horizon. In this case, the almost chapter-long discussion between Jesus and some Jewish leaders is a dialogue that becomes increasingly vituperative. The text immediately preceding our lection, however, reports that many of those hearing Jesus "believed" (8:30). The question arises, then, who it is who believes and just what do they believe.

In 8:31, the reader's trust in the narrator's evaluation of "many" of Jesus' hearers in verse 30 begins to be undermined. Although some scholars consider the statement in verse 31a to be a gloss, it can be read in context as a question about how it is that some have believed in Jesus. This is indicated in part by the past perfect form of the verb used to describe "the Jews *who had believed in him*" (v. 31). It is explicated more fully as Jesus confronts some of his hearers in the unfolding narrative. Since a lack of understanding tends to drive a lot of the discussion in John's Gospel narrative (for instance, Nicodemus, the Samaritan woman), this should be no surprise.

In the case of our lection, the misunderstanding has to do with freedom and what it means to call people "descendants of Abraham." Jesus asserts that those who believe in him, by "continuing [Gk: remaining/abiding] in his word," will be his disciples, know the truth, and thereby be set free (vv. 31-32). The misunderstanding arises among some of the Jews "who *had*

> JESUS' OFFER OF FREEDOM PRESUPPOSES A KIND OF "CONTINUING" FAITH THAT CALLS FORTH AMONG BELIEVERS A COMING-TO-FREEDOM FROM SIN.

believed in him" when they assert that they need no such freedom. As descendants of Abraham, they are not now nor ever have been, in their view, slaves to anyone. In other words, to be Abraham's descendant is to be free already (v. 33). On one level, their assertion about Abraham's offspring through the centuries seems strange. One thinks of slavery in Egypt, the humiliation of Babylonian exile, not to mention the fact that, as they speak, these particular Jews are under Roman occupation. Yet there is also a deep theological thread within Judaism that may explain their answer. Despite being in such abject historical situations, the Jews have continued to worship God and have thus refused to be slaves of any human master. Yet Jesus clarifies his statement by pushing the discussion yet further. Jesus is not speaking of such forms of slavery as his hearers imagine, but a slavery *to sin* (v. 34). This kind of freedom comes from the Son, a freedom that no slave can grant because slaves, unlike sons, don't "continue/remain/abide" in the household.

In essence, Jesus' offer of freedom presupposes a kind of "continuing" faith that calls forth among believers a coming-to-freedom from sin. Such freedom cannot be guaranteed by a traditional, Abrahamic parentage. Such freedom, instead, comes from believing in the Son as a means of "continuing/remaining/abiding" in the Father's household. Apart from the Son, there is no possibility of being freed from sin. In fact, it is only by continuing in the Son's Word and being his disciple that we will even "know," not intellectually, but salvifically, the truth that sets us free.

The language of bondage and sin runs deeply in Reformation Day faith. On Sundays when the Brief Order is used for confession of sins and pardon in many Lutheran churches in North America, the language of the prayer is sobering: "We are in bondage to sin and cannot free ourselves." At the same time, this strange view conflicts with our heady Western conception of freedom as something that can be purchased (think of the promises of freedom wrapped up in a car commercial, for example, or as something that we have to buy either with our own blood or with the blood of others in war). Reformation faith calls us first of all to disabuse ourselves of notions of freedom like this. To be a church "*reformata, semper reformanda*" (reformed and always reforming) means to keep returning to and abiding in a Word that first reveals our slave status for what it is. Being old Abraham's physical patrimony can't guarantee it. Yet neither can the newest Lexus. And as for our war-making capacities in the world, does anyone feel freer today than when the war on terrorism began a few years ago? The light of the gospel is grace and, as John reminds us from chapter 1 on, truth. Yet living in the light of grace and truth is both jarring *and* freeing—hence the opposition among some of Jesus' people and many of ours today. This side of our illusions, it is difficult to hear.

> OUR HEALING IS LESS AN ACT OF THE PROMETHEAN WILL AND MORE THE RECOGNITION OF A PAINFUL AND YET JOYFUL TRUTH: A TRUTH IN JESUS CHRIST THAT SETS US FREE FOR GOD AND NEIGHBORS.

Yet there is another side to this Reformation text. This difficult truth that refuses to harbor *our* illusions of freedom is nonetheless profoundly liberating. Sometimes you even find it among groups that go by the oxymoronic name "self-help." I say oxymoronic because one such group, AA, begins the first of its twelve steps with a profound cry of bondage and hope. In the first step, the person struggling with alcoholism admits that he or she is a slave to the bottle and learns to rely day by day on a higher power in the process of being freed from addiction. We in Christ should at least see the glimpse of truth that resides there. Our healing is less an act of the Promethean will and more the recognition of a painful and yet joyful truth: a truth in Jesus Christ that sets us free for God and neighbors.

Notes

1. Paul Achtemeier offers an insightful excursus on the diatribe form in his commentary *Romans*, Interpretation, ed. James L. Mays (Atlanta: John Knox, 1985), 73–76.

2. The discussion here is based on Achtemeier's helpful summary and proposal of the issue of righteousness in Romans and its relationship to the language of justification and faith in *Romans*, 61–66.

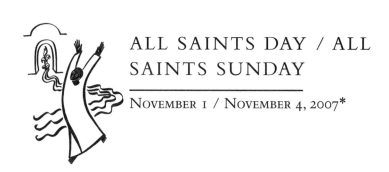

ALL SAINTS DAY / ALL SAINTS SUNDAY

November 1 / November 4, 2007*

Revised Common	Episcopal (BCP)	Roman Catholic
Dan. 7:1-3, 15-18	Sirach 44:1-10, 13-14 or Sirach 2:(1-6), 7-11	Rev. 7:2-4, 9-14
Psalm 149	Psalm 149	Ps. 24:1-2, 3-4, 5-6
Eph. 1:11-23	Rev. 7:2-4, 9-17 or Eph. 1:(11-14) 15-23	1 John 3:1-3
Luke 6:20-31	Matt. 5:1-12 or Luke 6:20-26 (27-36)	Matt. 5:1-12a

FIRST READING

DANIEL 7:1-3, 15-18 (RCL)

This lection frames material for the dream visions that make up the lion's share of Daniel 7. Our verses bracket a vision of four beastly kingdoms (Dan. 7:4-14), which most scholars link to the Babylonian, Median, Persian, and Greek empires.

This background also aids us in understanding the wider context of this whole book. Daniel joins together legendary material about Jewish characters set in the Babylonian court in chapters 1-6 with an apocalypse in chapters 7-12. The visionary material about four kingdoms helps us to date Daniel to the second century B.C.E. Like most apocalyptic literature, Daniel is pseudonymous. It presents material associated with an ancient personage or time and uses visions to "foresee" a

---

*If transferred to the Twenty-third Sunday after Pentecost (Thirty-first Sunday in Ordinary Time / Proper 26)

future that has already or largely already taken place. By telling stories and visions of ancient venerable figures, it attempts to comfort persons in extreme situations by placing their suffering within a transcendent framework—in this case, the persecutions of the Jews under the Seleucid king Antiochus IV Epiphanes. The visionary material shows something of the beastly nature of human power and helps to relativize four empires: they are just "one damn thing after another" and beastly aberrations that come rightly under the judgment of God in good time.

Our lection has an even more specific agenda, however. In 7:1-3, the vision is placed in its narrative context: Daniel in King Belshazzar's court in ancient Babylon. As in many apocalyptic texts, the seer writes down what he dreams, thinking it may be helpful later. Although Daniel proved himself adroit at interpreting dreams for King Belshazzar in the legend of chapters 1-6, he here has a terrifying vision in a dream of four beasts arising out of the sea. The sea is the place of primordial chaos. Although Israel's creation stories in Genesis characteristically underplay mythic conflict, there lurk elsewhere in the canon several traditions that describe the sea as a mythic force (Isa. 27:1; 51:9-10; Ps. 74:13-14) working contrary to the divine will. The four beasts may hearken back to the legendary material of 2:31-45, where Daniel interprets a dream, again with reference to four kingdoms.

> By telling stories and visions of ancient venerable figures, Daniel attempts to comfort persons in extreme situations by placing their suffering within a transcendent framework.

The fearfulness of the dream visions for Daniel is treated in 7:15-18, where the seer acknowledges he is "troubled" by them. In this case, however, the ace dream interpreter of Belshazzar's court requires the help of a heavenly attendant, probably an angel, to interpret what he has seen. But along with the summary we've already surmised—four bestial empires, one after another—comes an important revelation that is the primary disclosure for this lection: "But the holy ones of the Most High shall receive the kingdom and possess the kingdom forever" (v. 18). Through divine aid, dreamer Daniel learns that these four kingdoms fall so that the kingdom will be *given* to the "holy ones."

> For us who try to manage life under the empire, there is still truth in the idea that we receive God's kingdom only as a gift.

The problem of who Daniel's "holy ones" are has vexed scholars. Some are quick to say that the holy ones are a figure for the people. John J. Collins, however, says that the "holy ones" are most likely angels *who represent the people in heaven*.[1] The idea is that on the mythic heavenly level, events transpire that in turn have an impact below. Either way, God's people hear the end of this angelic interpretation of Daniel's dream vision in a powerful way. Kingdoms come and kingdoms go. One day, however, God will rightly judge them all. Then the kingdom will be given to the "holy ones," the people's angelic representatives in heaven.

Preachers will need to tread carefully here. Most of us in North America are not under persecution. Disestablished mainliners may be annoyed by our disappearing place in the culture, but we are hardly persecuted. The Christian right in the United States fancies itself persecuted. But it actually controls the executive, the legislative, and now perhaps even the judicial branches of the U.S. government. Does that sound persecuted to you? So talking about the kingdom in Daniel's way may require us to acknowledge first our complicity with bestial powers. Remember: our stock markets feature raging bulls and bears, and there's hardly a pastor around (with the exception of some Catholic colleagues) without a pension's worth of stake in the bestial outcome on Toronto's Bay Street or New York's Wall Street. Even with that caveat, however, Daniel has a word for us on All Saints Day. For us who try to manage life under the empire, there is still truth in the idea that we receive God's kingdom only as a gift. True, it may be a painful gift that also requires letting go of privilege. Yet it is nonetheless a gift—and one that no empire can give to anyone.

SIRACH 44:1-10, 13-14 (BCP)

This reading features one of the more famous quotes in ancient literature, "Let us now sing the praises of famous men . . ." (44:1). Apart from its androcentrism, the text offers positive possibilities for preaching. Here "famous men" means people whose piety in the subsequent five chapters of Sirach is recalled and whose character is celebrated as central to Israel's life and history.

SIRACH 2:(1-6) 7-11 (BCP ALT.)

This lection represents the bulk of a seventeen-verse poem on trusting God. Sirach belongs to the genre of wisdom literature, so naturally the poem focuses on individual action and motivation with respect to God. The beginning of the poem, verses 1-6, reflects on being tested and thus acting wisely. In the end, the basis for trust and wise action is the nature of the Lord (vv. 7-11). A person being "tested" can trust God and persevere because "the Lord is compassionate and merciful . . . forgives sins and saves in times of distress" (v. 11).

REVELATION 7:2-4, 9-14 (RC)

This vision of the 144,000 in Revelation represents the faithful martyrs with a number (12 x 12 x 1000) indicating their redeemed completeness. The seal with which they are sealed (vv. 2-3) is reminiscent of the idea in the Hebrew Bible that God preserves God's own not *from* tribulation, but *through* it. These ideas are important when we think about "the saints" on this day. They are not saints because they rise in pristine purity into our stained-glass windows and statuary, but because they keep faith, with God's help, in the midst of the muck. With Revelation, however, it is just as important to realize the dynamics of such visionary texts. Apocalyptic texts are not allegories in which everything can be linked one-to-one to something else. Preachers are wise to try to understand how visions like this one do more than "say" something and actually "do" something. In this case, we have the vision of the 144,000 in the context of a throne-room vision.[2] In light of this, the outcome of the text is all the more striking. The vision moves toward a disclosure of those "robed in white" (vv. 13f-14) and appends to it a striking visionary promise of divine grace, guidance, and compassion (vv. 16-17). In this vision, sainthood is less about us, and more about a God who guides "to springs of the water of life" and "wipe[s] away every tear from their eyes." It is not that the saints have no tears or thirst, but that God's promise gives grace to get through them.

> IT IS NOT THAT THE SAINTS HAVE NO TEARS OR THIRST, BUT THAT GOD'S PROMISE GIVES GRACE TO GET THROUGH THEM.

RESPONSIVE READING
PSALM 149 (RCL, BCP)

This responsive reading starts off in the same way as many of the other hallelujah psalms grouped at the end of the psalter. The opening verse offers a call to praise. The people here are "the assembly of the faithful" who are to be glad in their "Maker" and "King." After describing the dancing and music such praise entails, the reason for praise is given: the Lord takes pleasure in the people and adorns the humble with victory.

The psalm takes an odd turn at the point where the results of such praise are envisioned. The assembly is to have the praise of God "in their throats" and "two-edged swords in their hands" (v. 6). The reason for this strange juxtaposition of praise and violence becomes clear in verses 7-9. They are to be empowered by such praise to execute God's vengeance on the nations, their nobles, and kings.

All Saints Day can be a wonderful moment for recalling the life of God's people in the face of great conflict and tribulation. Given the violence here, however, perhaps we who would read Scripture and sing its songs need to be clear that the temptation of our own "will to power" can complicate the way we use such texts today.

PSALM 24:1-2, 3-4, 5-6 (RC)

The psalm, probably sung in connection with the procession of the ark, begins with a powerful theological affirmation. This world is God's because God founded it, conquering the very watery forces of chaos in the process (vv. 1-2). In light of this, a question goes up at the point of processional entry. Who shall ascend and stand in such a holy place? The answer is ethical: those with clean hands and pure hearts will receive blessing and vindication (vv. 3-6). With that, the ark now comes and enters the sanctuary, thus embodying not only the entrance but also the acknowledgment of the Lord's kingship.

SECOND READING

EPHESIANS 1:11-23 (RCL)
EPHESIANS 1:(11-14) 15-23 (BCP ALT.)

Ephesians probably does not belong to the list of authentic Pauline letters. Still, it embodies many Pauline ways of thinking and writing. This particular lection is part of an ornate thanksgiving, which, just as in the authentic Pauline letters, becomes an occasion for connecting with the local "saints" (1:1) and summing up themes that will dominate the letter.

On this All Saints Day, it's useful to note that the writer's vision for the community begins (v. 11) and ends (vv. 22-23) in Christ. Although the sometimes florid language can be confusing (verses 15-23 represent a breathless single sentence in the Greek!), it seeks to relate the lives of the Ephesian saints to the reality given and being formed in the resurrection and ascension of Christ. As such, verses 11-12 focus on our purpose: as God's saints we are destined to live for the praise of Christ's glory. How do we know? The writer refers back to when the Ephesians first heard the gospel, believed, and were marked with the seal of the Holy Spirit (probably a baptismal reference). This was merely the down payment of what they will be and receive (vv. 13-14). The writer's words about the community seem a little

> HERE'S THE HOMILETICAL KICKER: THIS SAME CHRIST WHO IS NOW OVER ALL IS ALSO THE HEAD OF THE *CHURCH*, WHICH IS HIS BODY AND THE PLACE OF HIS REPRESENTATIVE FULLNESS.

vague compared with other authentic Pauline letters, but he or she does not pause there for long. The Ephesians' love and faithfulness are reasons for giving thanks and interceding for their increase in wisdom, revelation, and enlightenment. In other words, the goal is that the Ephesian saints understand more deeply what God in Christ is up to (vv. 15-19). Its basis is the Christ with whom the writer began in verse 11. The power of which the author writes is the same by which God resurrected Christ and seated him on high (vv. 20-22a). But here's the homiletical kicker: this same Christ who is now over all is also the head of the *church*, which is his body and the place of his representative fullness (vv. 22b-23). While this should never be a cause for ecclesial pride (Christ is, after all, still the head), the word invites us into the middle of mystery. In the church—which still lives in trial, tribulation, and even brokenness—Christ *is* still present.

REVELATION 7:2-4, 9-17 (BCP)

See the first reading for All Saints Day, above.

1 JOHN 3:1-3 (RC)

The text uses Johannine ways of thinking to bridge together issues of who we are and who we are "to be," the latter understood both eschatologically and ethically. John the elder's goal is to reaffirm the tradition of "what we know" while also holding out the possibility that we don't "know" everything yet. For the author, our identity as God's children is itself an act of divine love, a conferral of identity that cannot be gainsaid (v. 1a). Drawing on the theme of not recognizing Christ in John's Gospel, John the elder says that the reason others fail to see us that way is analogous to Jesus' experience (v. 1b). With that, the writer speaks boldly in the indicative and yet shifts paradoxically into the future tense: "Beloved, we are God's children now; what we will be has not yet been revealed" (v. 2a). In other words, it does not detract from our present belief in that identity to say that not everything is realized already. Yet John the elder can say a little more about this future: at that revelation, we will be "like him" and see him as he is (v. 2b). The idea here seems to be something like a theosis motif: although we are now God's children, we are becoming more and more like Christ until that final revelation takes place. Until then, we have the same task as all those have who prepare to see God (think cultically here): to purify ourselves (v. 3b). Yet please note that even this task is rooted in "hope." To the degree that we are being purified in anticipation, it happens because of the one in whom we hope.

> TO THE DEGREE THAT WE ARE BEING PURIFIED IN ANTICIPATION, IT HAPPENS BECAUSE OF THE ONE IN WHOM WE HOPE.

LUKE 6:20-31 (RCL)
LUKE 6:20-26 (27-36) (BCP ALT.)

The context for our lection is the early part of Jesus' ministry. It commenced with his inaugural hometown sermon in 4:16-30. Jesus announced his purpose by reading Isaiah's words about preaching good news to the poor and release to the captives. While the hometown folk liked his familiar prophetic words, it didn't take long for Jesus' first sermon to go awry. The hometown crowd turned on him, thus setting a characteristically tragic tone for his early ministry. Although they wanted to toss Jesus off a cliff, he managed to pass through them unscathed (4:30).

Two chapters later this Jesus has been busy healing, preaching, getting in trouble with religious leaders, and choosing the Twelve. In 6:20, Luke describes Jesus as lifting up his eyes to them to begin teaching his newly formed disciples. While his words no doubt have them in mind, there are still others present who are hoping for a little healing for themselves, too (vv. 18-19). So when we read Luke's Sermon on the Plain, it is best to understand it as words for the disciples, yet words also for others who might wish to follow Jesus.

> WHEN WE READ LUKE'S SERMON ON THE PLAIN, IT IS BEST TO UNDERSTAND THEM AS WORDS FOR THE DISCIPLES, YET WORDS ALSO FOR OTHERS WHO MIGHT WISH TO FOLLOW JESUS.

Two features immediately jump out with the opening section of the Sermon on the Plain. First, all of the sentences are in the second-person plural: blessed are y'all (or youse, if you live in Southwest Ontario). Jesus is not so much interested in personal virtue or piety as in social condition. Tellingly, his disciples have become "poor" in order to follow him (5:11, 28). In this proclamation, therefore, the promise of his inaugural sermon has thus come to pass. Second, the four blessings in Luke (vv. 20-23) are accompanied by four woes or curses (vv. 24-26). Again, the Lukan Jesus has an agenda here. From the beginning, the figures of the early part of Luke's Gospel have anticipated both good news *and* conflict (for instance, Simeon in 2:34f-35). In fact, this split of blessings and woes especially hearkens back to Mary's own prophetic words in the Magnificat: "He has filled the hungry with good things, and sent the rich away empty" (1:53; see 6:21a, 25a). Jesus' sermon is thus a continuation of his ministry with those who do and *might* follow him. To them, he promises in his own tragic, conflicted way both blessings and curses as well as an opposition that takes the form of hatred, exclusion, and defamation about which his disciples should nonetheless rejoice.

> JESUS' SERMON IS A CONTINUATION OF HIS MINISTRY WITH THOSE WHO DO AND *might* FOLLOW HIM.

Afterward, Luke's Jesus goes beyond blessings and woes to teach concretely what the conflicted, tragic life of discipleship looks like (vv. 27-31) and, more important, what it's based on (vv. 32-36). For Jesus, discipleship is about loving enemies. The very people because of whose rejection Jesus blesses his disciples in his fourth beatitude (vv. 22-23) should be the object of the disciples' love. Jesus piles example upon example to make it clear. In fact, Jesus himself eventually exemplifies the ethic in its fullness on the cross (Luke 23:24). Yet Jesus is not interested in leaving us with impossible examples of heroic sainthood in his teaching on discipleship. Subsequently, in verses 32-36, he begins to explore the motivation for that love. By doing so, Jesus sets the "golden rule" on an even higher "plain." One could interpret "doing unto others as you would have them do unto you" as just another ethic of reciprocity: I'll scratch your back in the hope you'll scratch mine.

> JESUS' DIFFICULT WAY IS NOT ABOUT HEROIC SAINTLY STRIVING, BUT FOLLOWS FROM DIVINE PARENTAL MERCY, FROM THE VERY GOD WHO IS KIND TO THE "UNGRATEFUL AND THE WICKED."

Jesus compares such a truncated view of that ethic to what "sinners" do (vv. 33-34). However, the kind of love he's talking about goes higher still, in fact, all the way to the Most High (v. 35). Here we finally arrive at the pinnacle of Jesus' difficult discipleship ethic. We might expect to find there the likes of Mother Teresa and Albert Schweitzer, whose saintly hagiographies we retell on All Saints Day because they inspire yet strangely keep us at an impossible distance. Jesus, however, is not interested in saintly heroism. In fact, the ground of his "Most High," tragic, conflicted discipleship ethic is this: "Be merciful, just as your Father is merciful" (v. 36). Jesus' difficult way is not about heroic saintly striving, but follows from divine parental mercy, from the very God who is kind to the "ungrateful and the wicked" (v. 35).

In his book *Bury the Chains*, Adam Hochschild retraces the developments in the eighteenth- and nineteenth-century British Empire that led to the abolition of slavery and its connection to the international sugar trade.[3] It started with twelve unlikely men, many of them Quakers, one of them a Tory member of Parliament, one of them Anglican Thomas Clarkson, meeting in a London printer's shop in May 1787. Over several decades, others joined the twelve in the struggle, including a freed slave named Olaudah Equiano, whose published story about his experiences helped galvanize the movement. Although no one prior to their time ever would have heard of newsletters, political buttons, and consumer boycotts, we would not either had it not been for their innovative and persistent methods of getting people on board. Of course, it wasn't easy. On the one hand, low-cost sugar was becoming an important staple in everyday life in the empire—and the slavery on which it depended was nearly invisible to consumers in England. On the other hand, the limited democracy of the time was built more on cobbling together various parties' "interests" in order to get things done. No one in the white British Empire had a vested interest to see the abolition of slavery until this movement started. How did it happen? The movement was one of the first to conclude that political change could be organized and effected on the basis of something that is as new to the powers-that-be today as it was during the British Empire or even Jesus' day: not on reciprocity, surely not on self-interest, but on the incalculable basis of compassionate mercy. Hochschild describes his religious Quaker and Anglican activists, who had received so much scorn and resistance for their efforts, this way: "But they also shared a newer kind of faith. They believed that because human beings had a capacity to care about the suffering of others, exposing the truth would move people to action."[4] We who live in the shadow of the suffering of the cross should understand. What wondrous love is this? A love born of divine mercy and a love that then shares mercy . . . come what may.

MATTHEW 5:1-12 (BCP)
MATTHEW 5:1-12a (RC)

Preachers will want to be careful not to turn beatitudes, which are blessings, into something they are not. Beatitudes are not exhortations ("Let us all be more like peacemakers in our daily lives") or commands ("Therefore, be as meek as you can, I say!"), but something quite different. Three features may be especially useful from a homiletical point of view. First, these blessings are given to groups of people, not individuals. All of the subjects in the Greek are plural. So we ought not imagine these blessings as advocating a kind of private, individual virtue, but a shared lot or community vocation. Second, these

> WE OUGHT NOT IMAGINE THESE BLESSINGS AS ADVOCATING A KIND OF PRIVATE, INDIVIDUAL VIRTUE, BUT A SHARED LOT OR COMMUNITY VOCATION.

blessings are grounded ultimately on an eschatological hope or promise: "Blessed are those who mourn, for they *will be comforted*" (v. 4, emphasis mine). Most of us know that the poor in spirit, the mourning, the meek seem to have no outward sign of blessing in the present. Their hope clearly lies not in their own saintliness or virtue, but in a God who can be trusted with a different future called the kingdom of heaven, the conferral of which specifically brackets the third-person beatitudes in verses 3 and 10. Third, Matthew's agenda in listing these third-person beatitudes becomes a bit clearer by the final one, whose telling phrase is suddenly expressed in the second-person plural: "Blessed are *you* when people revile you and persecute you . . ." (v. 11). For ten verses Jesus is handing out blessings to this person and that person. At the end, however, he hands one to all of "you." As with many such blessings, we may not always want to be in such an awful state that we need them in the first place. On All Saints Day, however, we may take comfort in

DAVID SCHNASA
JACOBSEN

knowing how God helps us keep faith, not because of our virtue, but because of God's coming righteous reign in the midst of our shared need and vision. Jesus announces this day a God who blesses us troubled saints in the future perfect.

Notes

1. John J. Collins, *Daniel*, Hermeneia (Minneapolis: Fortress Press, 1993), 312–18.

2. I treat the homiletical impact of the throne-room vision of this lection on my Web site at http://www.wlu.ca/~wwwsem/dsj/apocarchive.html. Just follow the link listed on that page for Rev. 7:9-17. For further information about how I approach the problem of preaching apocalyptic texts in the New Testament, see my book *Preaching in the New Creation: The Promise of New Testament Apocalyptic Texts* (Louisville: Westminster John Knox Press, 1999).

3. Much of the summary here comes from the introduction to Adam Hochschild's *Bury the Chains: Prophets and Rebels in the Fight to Free an Empire's Slaves* (New York: Houghton Mifflin, 2005), 1–8.

4. Ibid., 366.

TWENTY-THIRD SUNDAY AFTER PENTECOST

THIRTY-FIRST SUNDAY IN ORDINARY TIME /
PROPER 26
NOVEMBER 4, 2007

REVISED COMMON	EPISCOPAL (BCP)	ROMAN CATHOLIC
Isa. 1:10-18 or Hab. 1:1-4; 2:1-4	Isa. 1:10-20	Wisd. of Sol. 11:22—12:2
Ps. 32:1-7 or Ps. 119:137-144	Psalm 32 or 32:1-8	Ps. 145:1-2, 8-9, 10-11, 13, 14
2 Thess. 1:1-4, 11-12	2 Thess. 1:1-5 (6-10) 11-12	2 Thess. 1:11—2:2
Luke 19:1-10	Luke 19:1-10	Luke 19:1-10

FIRST READING

ISAIAH 1:10-18 (RCL)
ISAIAH 1:10-20 (BCP)

This first chapter of Isaiah is largely programmatic for the entire book, especially the part known as First Isaiah, chapters 1–39. While not every part of this chapter can be dated to the Assyrian period, the issues here have an impact on the development of the Isaianic corpus as a whole. We might liken this first chapter to the overture played at the beginning of a work. Its themes are telling of what comes.

The indictment of the people's liturgical life in Judah is sharp. The leaders of the people the prophet likens to those of Sodom and Gomorrah. As such, their many sacrifices, their burnt offerings, are not enough. Burning incense and observing sacred calendars are also insufficient. The Lord is not even sure about their prayers. What God desires is obedience.

WHEN THE WEALTHY CONTROL EVERYTHING, TRAMPLE THE POOR, AND STILL THRONG TO WORSHIP, IT IS TIME TO TAKE STOCK.

Their bloodstained hands at worship undermine what they are trying to say and do liturgically. The prophet, speaking for God, points out what is needful: "Seek justice, rescue the oppressed, defend the orphan, plead for the widow."

Preachers should not assume that the text is a blanket indictment of all things liturgical. In fact, the text presupposes liturgy, the availability of the Temple and its means of grace. What is questioned is the way liturgy and life can become disjointed. When the wealthy control everything, trample the poor, and still throng to worship, it is time to take stock. The Lord is "the Holy One of Israel" (v. 4) and as such will not be mocked.

With this word of warning also comes an opportunity for God's people. It may be hard to imagine turning blood-crimson hands into pure, white innocence (v. 18). Yet the promise still holds from God's side, sounding almost Deuteronomistic in character (v. 19). Then comes the programmatic warning in verse 20—failure to do so will mean that the people shall be devoured by the sword. This prophesied defeat will be God's wrath, a means for purging the people.

The homiletical possibilities of this text are daunting. Isaiah speaks a difficult word here, one spoken to a people who will one day experience exile. Yet lurking within that is a strange word of grace. God speaks the warning, not because it is destiny, but because God's goodness is still sufficient, even now, to permit a new way forward (v. 19). Even at the beginning of the difficult chapters of First Isaiah, the prophet can still say that God's people can yet "eat the good of the land" (v. 19b).

WISDOM OF SOLOMON 11:22—12:2 (RC)

This text purports to be a compilation of King Solomon's reflections on wisdom. In reality, the book was produced in all likelihood in the Hellenistic period. Many scholars link it, in fact, to the Jewish community in Alexandria, which shared a lot of the questions, issues, and Hellenistic perspectives that color its treatment of Jewish history.

In the material immediately prior to the lection for this Sunday, the writer reflects on the fate of the Egyptians in the exodus story and uses it as an occasion to reflect on God's punishment as it relates to God's mercy. God is indeed slow to punish, in part because the world from God's perspective is so small, "like a speck that tips the scales" (11:22). Yet God loves all that God has made and therefore does not fully show God's punitive might in all its fullness. God's way, rather, is to correct and to warn so that the wicked might change (12:1-2).

HABAKKUK 1:1-4; 2:1-4 (RCL ALT.)

We don't know much about the prophet Habakkuk. However, his words about the righteous living "by faith" (2:4) have had an important impact on the Christian tradition. This brief book from the Minor Prophets treats issues of theodicy. In all likelihood, its context is the rise of the Babylonian Empire. Here, the

Babylonians (Chaldeans) have just defeated Egypt and turned Judah into a vassal. The theodicy problem that vexes the prophet is this: If the Chaldeans were turned loose on God's people to judge them (Habbakuk may have been a contemporary of Jeremiah), how is it that this instrument of God against God's people is worse than they are? Is not the punishment worse than the crime? How can such a state of affairs be squared with God's righteousness?

The lection for the day features two portions of Habakkuk's work. The first, 1:1-4, contains the superscription for the work along with the prophet's complaint. How can God stand by idly when such injustice is done (1:2-4)? Juxtaposed with that is a later part of Habbakuk's prophetic vision, which represents the second half of today's lection. Habakkuk indicates he will keep watch until God answers his complaint (2:1). The Lord then addresses the prophet. God wants him to write the vision plainly, big enough so someone who

PREACHERS MAY WISH TO REFLECT ON HOW DIVINE VISION SPONSORS, ENABLES, AND STRENGTHENS FAITH—EVEN IN THE FACE OF THE POWERFUL WHO WOULD TRUST ONLY IN THEMSELVES OR IN THEIR OWN POWER.

is running can read it. There is still a vision from God; it is true and can be trusted. Even when the waiting seems long, Habakkuk trusts that it will happen. The proud (the Chaldeans), though powerful, do not have a "right spirit." But the righteous live by their faith; that is, they trust God for the vision and "live" doing so, even when it seems long in coming.

This text is an important one for theological developments centuries later in early Christianity. Its homiletical power should not merely be emptied, however, by turning Christian faith into a flattened fulfillment of Habakkuk's prophecy. Instead, preachers may wish to reflect on how divine vision sponsors, enables, and strengthens faith—even in the face of the powerful who would trust only in themselves or in their own power. Along with Habbakuk, we may just find words such as these are still worth waiting and watching for. In this way, we don't merely reduce Habakkuk's text to a proof text but allow it to enlarge Christian homiletical vision today.

RESPONSIVE READING

PSALM 32:1-7 (RCL)
PSALM 32 OR 32:1-8 (BCP)

The connection of this psalm to the Isaiah text is strong. If the Isaiah text focuses on the external aspect of sin, forgiveness, and repentance, Psalm 32 is its internal counterpart. The psalm begins with beatitudes that set the terms of what follows. Blessed are those who are forgiven *and who are honest about themselves before*

God (vv. 1-2, emphasis mine). The personal narrative of the psalmist is then laid out in verses 3-5. Could there be a connection here between sin and disease? Perhaps, but the point is that the psalmist understood silence about his sin to be deadly, and honesty in confession as an occasion for forgiveness and transformation. The final portion of the psalm then breaks out of personal narrative and into a more didactic feel (vv. 6-11). It draws out of the heartfelt experience of the previous section and advises others with almost a kind of wisdom tone. It is no wonder that this psalm, so full of personal candor, has been especially beloved in both synagogue and church, where it has received special place by being numbered among the seven penitential psalms.

PSALM 119:137-144 (RCL ALT.)

This responsive reading offers an apt pairing with the alternative reading from Habakkuk above. Whereas the Hebrew Bible lection speaks of a cry for justice and the promise of divine answer, the psalmist continues his epic acrostic meditation on the law (see the RCL alternative psalm for the Twenty-first Sunday after Pentecost, above), which, though offered in personal difficulty (vv. 139, 141a, 143a), nonetheless underlines the psalmist's commitment to keeping the law come what may. What the psalmist does pray for, however, is important: understanding (vv. 144b). In this, both the prophet Habakkuk and the psalmist are one.

PSALM 145:1-2, 8-9, 10-11, 13, 14 (RC)

In Hebrew, Psalm 145 is also an acrostic or "alphabetic" psalm. Each line begins with a successive letter of the Hebrew alphabet (although the Hebrew *n* may be missing here). The idea with acrostics is to convey something of the comprehensiveness of the theme treated: everything from A to Z about God, our King. The psalm starts with a personal expression of praise (vv. 1-3) and shifts to a recalling of God's mighty acts (vv. 4-7). A classic statement about God's loving nature follows (vv. 8-9). The God it praises is "gracious and merciful, slow to anger and abounding in steadfast love." Then follows a general statement about God's responsive people, whose existence bears witness to what God has done (vv. 10-13a). Yet the psalmist is not done. In 145:13b, an important shift in thought happens. This God, who is of such great splendor and love, this God who reigns and will reign forever, is known chiefly for this: "The LORD upholds all who are falling, and raises up all who are bowed down" (v. 14). This God is known not solely for acts of ongoing creative love, but also for redemptive action for the sake of the weakest. In this, God's kingship is known most decisively. It is on this basis that the psalm concludes with a ringing endorsement of the Lord's justice (vv. 17-21).

SECOND READING

2 THESSALONIANS 1:1-4, 11-12 (RCL)
2 THESSALONIANS 1:1-5 (6-10) 11-12 (BCP)
2 THESSALONIANS 1:11—2:2 (RC)

The authenticity of 2 Thessalonians as a letter from Paul's own hand is disputed. While many important English-language commentators have asserted its Pauline authorship, many other scholars have pointed to the shifts in thinking and writing style that this letter represents.

Our text begins with Paul's familiar greeting (vv. 1-2) and shifts immediately into the equally familiar thanksgiving (vv. 3-4). The focus of the thanksgiving is key to interpreting the rest of our lection for the day and for the whole of the letter: the writer thanks God for the growth of the Thessalonians' faith and love for one another in the face of persecutions—a reality about which the writer boasts among other churches. Beneath this thanksgiving

GOD WILL REPAY NOT ONLY THE THESSALONIANS' PERSECUTORS FOR THEIR ACTIONS, BUT THE CHURCH FOR ITS AFFLICTIONS AS WELL.

lurk some important theological questions. How are the people of God to understand their suffering in persecutions in relation to a loving God and in the horizon of the end-time teachings that Paul had articulated before in 1 Thessalonians 4–5?

The writer's answer in verses 5-10 draws on typical apocalyptic thinking. Their steadfastness in affliction is a sign, or evidence, of God's judgment to make them worthy of the kingdom. Because God is just, what the Thessalonians suffer will be "repaid." The word "vengeance" in verse 8 really means a repayment or recompense—in other words, God will repay not only the Thessalonians' persecutors for their actions, but the church for its afflictions as well. This is not to say that the church somehow earns its coming salvation in the face of affliction, but it does offer "evidence" that they are the elect and will be "repaid," even as their persecutors are "repaid" negatively. The time of this vengeance is linked specifically to the revelation (*apokalypsis*) of the Lord. Then what is now hidden will be revealed. While "eternal destruction" is the consequence for those who do not know (usually, the Gentiles) or obey God, that punishment is described specifically as being "separated from the presence of the Lord" (v. 9), not annihilation.

It is this conception of the coming judgment that grounds the writer's prayer in verses 11-12. The prayer is not a general one, but specific to this persecution and hope. The prayer asks God to continue to do this work among them by grace in the face of their affliction and its connection to eschatological realities and hopes.

This is why chapter 2, which is the doctrinal focus of the letter, begins the way it does. Here the writer sees a need to correct an earlier misunderstanding (or perhaps a false prophecy in the community). In 1 Thessalonians Paul pointed out that the gathering with the Lord would come as a surprise. Here, however, the writer of 2 Thessalonians takes pains to show that this coming *is not yet here.* The point of all this, therefore, is to reinforce hope in affliction while not conceding that the day of the Lord is already here.

This text could prove somewhat problematic for preaching. Its vision of vengeance, even if qualified above as "repayment," seems somewhat less than the gospel Paul articulates elsewhere. On the other hand, the text takes seriously the problem of suffering as it relates to the life of faith. Where God's people suffer affliction for their faith, there is a need to talk about how such realities relate to the revelation of God in Jesus Christ. We may not agree with the writer's theological answer, but we cannot evade the question either. The greatest opportunity this text affords may well be in 1:11-12. For a suffering church, it is important to remember that God is still at work and that this work points forward to something later: a coming age in which the name of the Lord will be glorified even in us—and that, by grace.

THE GOSPEL
LUKE 19:1-10 (RCL, BCP, RC)

The familiar story of Zacchaeus offers great homiletical opportunities. Yet hidden in the familiarity of everyone's favorite Sunday school Bible song is a story that embodies Luke's interest in announcing a gospel that, while including Gentiles, still seeks to ground itself in Jewish roots. In the process, Luke continues picking up themes that have recurred in the long trek to Jerusalem that began in 9:51: seeking and finding, sinners and the righteous, rich and poor.

The Jewishness of the Zacchaeus story comes through in his name. He may be an arch–tax collector, the head of the empire's regional office of revenue collection in Jericho, but the character's Jewish identity still comes through in his name, which means "righteous one." And then, almost as a "by the way," at the end of a fairly long sentence in the Greek, it is disclosed that this conflicted, Jewish Zacchaeus is rich. As such, he is in Jewish eyes a sinner's sinner: a collaborator with the hated Romans, one link higher in the administrative chain of command, and wealthy to boot. His name and his occupation already help to drive some of the narrative conflict. His wealthy status calls to mind Jesus' difficult statement to the rich man in Luke 18:25. So when Luke announces that Jesus is coming through town and that Zacchaeus is there, we know something is about to happen.

But then Luke discloses another tidbit of information. Zacchaeus was "trying to see who Jesus was" (19:3). The main verb in Greek means "seeking" and is the same verb used as a rhetorical *inclusio* at the end of our lection in 19:10, where we discover that Humanity's Child (the Son of Man) came to *seek* and save the lost. It may be that Zacchaeus the "seeker" is about to become graciously "sought."

How do we know? Well, Zacchaeus climbs up the tree so that he might see Jesus. But when he's up there and Jesus passes through, well, Jesus looks up at Zacchaeus. As if our text were not already full enough of bizarre reversals, Jesus makes an announcement. He asks Zacchaeus to hurry down, for Jesus is coming to his house.

In that world, staying at someone's house was no small matter. To do so put Jesus at risk of receiving the same kind of marginalization that had befallen the oppressive tax collector he was visiting. This is why the crowd grumbles at the news.

However, when the one you were "seeking" seeks you out first—well, the world looks a bit different. In the face of such graciousness from Jesus, wealthy Zacchaeus does what the other rich man in chapter 18 thought impossible. He doesn't change his attitude about wealth (that's our theological cop-out); instead, he gives up half to the poor and sets aside most of the remainder to pay back anyone he cheated. In short, Zacchaeus repents. But please note one important fact about these verses. Jesus does not apply Grandma's rule: if you are nice and polite, then I'll give you cookies. No, Jesus operates on his own gracious calculus. Repentance is not a prerequisite for grace. Instead, repentance is done under the power of Jesus' gracious seeking out and coming to *Zacchaeus*. Jesus summarizes this reality rather nicely with an audacious saying: "Today salvation has happened to this house" (v. 9). Indeed.

> JESUS OPERATES ON HIS OWN GRACIOUS CALCULUS. REPENTANCE IS NOT A PREREQUISITE FOR GRACE BUT IS DONE UNDER THE POWER OF JESUS' GRACIOUS SEEKING OUT AND COMING TO ZACCHAEUS.

There is an old hymn that helps with Zacchaeus's hard-won insight: "I sought the Lord, and afterward I knew / he moved my soul to seek him, seeking me. / It was not I that found, O Savior true; / no, I was found of thee." Zacchaeus sought, but it was Jesus' seeking that found him and transformed him.

TWENTY-FOURTH SUNDAY AFTER PENTECOST

Thirty-second Sunday in Ordinary Time / Proper 27
November 11, 2007

Revised Common	Episcopal (BCP)	Roman Catholic
Job 19:23-27a or Hag. 1:15b—2:9	Job 19:23-27a	2 Macc. 7:1-2, 9-14
Psalm 17:1-9 or Psalm 98 or Psalm 145:1-5, 17-21	Psalm 17 or 17:1-8	Ps. 17:1, 5-6, 8, 15
2 Thess. 2:1-5, 13-17	2 Thess. 2:13—3:5	2 Thess. 2:16—3:5
Luke 20:27-38	Luke 20:27 (28-33) 34-38	Luke 20:27-38 or 20:27, 34-38

FIRST READING
JOB 19:23-27a (RCL, BCP)

To preach this text on Job is to march homiletically straight into the depths of mystery. It deals passionately with matters of suffering and divine justice. This particular lection adds to that theological difficulty one that is decidedly textual. These lines are some of the most difficult in all of the Hebrew Bible to translate.

One problem that contemporary interpreters have is the familiarity of the old hymn "I Know That My Redeemer Lives." The hymn is a fine one, and an incredible confession of faith. This is probably not what Job means here, however. To preach this text, we need to do the difficult task of staying with Job and carefully unpacking what his words might mean.

Job begins by wishing that his words could be written down (vv. 23-24). As one who has suffered such an injustice, Job wants his case against God to be remembered. The text reflects a kind of intensification of this desire: perhaps a book, or better with iron pen and lead, or how about engraved in rock forever! If he is to die at God's own hand, he wants a record of that injustice for perpetuity.

Then comes the key and trickiest verse. "For I know that my Redeemer lives, and that at the last he will stand upon the earth" (v. 26). The NRSV capitalizes the word "Redeemer," leading one to believe that either God will redeem him, or some other heavenly figure will (beware Christian supersessionism here!). The word in Hebrew, however, is *go'el*. A *go'el* is a family member who (1) avenges your blood if you are unjustly killed, (2) redeems you from slavery, or (3) remits your family land holding if it has passed elsewhere for reasons of debt. Until now, Job has been relentless in his criticism of God for dealing with him so treacherously. What Job envisions is not that the same God will avenge him who harmed him. Job wants a situation in which someone after his death (again, consistent with vv. 23-24) will be there to vindicate him *against* God, which for Job means in God's sight.[1]

Preaching such a text is a great challenge. To take the text seriously means to get in the muck with Job. He cannot understand why God has done such an awful thing to him. He is in the place where no pious platitude, no familiar hymn, no justification of God will wash anymore. Yet in wishing for his vindication before God, there is a strange hope. Job may view

> JOB WANTS A SITUATION IN WHICH SOMEONE AFTER HIS DEATH WILL BE THERE TO VINDICATE HIM *against* GOD, WHICH FOR JOB MEANS IN GOD'S SIGHT.

God as his opponent here, and yet he knows that only God—better, only in God's presence, can he *be* vindicated. In the conclusion of the book, Job almost gets his wish, although God seems to set the terms of their confrontation "out of the whirlwind" (chaps. 38–40). Yet in the end, this may be the place where preaching on this difficult, problematic text can go.

2 MACCABEES 7:1-2, 9-14 (RC)

This lection describes the violent martyrdom of seven brothers and their mother. The setting of the story is the reign of the Seleucid king Antiochus IV Epiphanes. As a Hellenistic king, he sought to secure the loyalty of his Jewish subjects by forcing them to observe Hellenistic ways. When those ways conflicted with Torah, Jews found themselves in a very difficult situation. By refusing the king, they were suspected of rebellion and subjected to torture and even death.

This particular text was probably written during a later historical period, in all likelihood the first century B.C.E. As such, the memory of the seven brothers and their mother helped to encourage Jews to resist the pretentious claims of the powers-that-be. How so? The text also focuses on key theological understandings. First, although the Seleucid king was not to be obeyed, somehow the Jews' own sin had brought on this punishment (the key to this is found in a quote from Deuteronomy 32:36 that appears in verse 6, which is not a part of the stipulated lection). Second, to hold to the Torah was possible, because though the king could separate body from soul, God would in the resurrection of the body vindicate them in the face of their suffering and injustice. Here in this text we begin to see the development of several theological views, such as the bodily resurrection, that are only implicit in other books such as Daniel. As Christians came to value and preserve these texts, the stories of the seven brothers and their mother also became paradigmatic for later martyrologies.

HAGGAI 1:15b—2:9 (RCL ALT.)

Few prophets' work can be so precisely dated as Haggai's: a three-month period during the reign of the Persian king Darius. At this point, the exiles had returned for some time and had not yet rebuilt the Temple. Haggai's prophetic work is to encourage the people to honor God with a new house.

In today's lection Haggai has already managed to motivate the people to work on the new Temple. Some of the older community members, however, who perhaps remembered what Solomon's Temple looked like before the Babylonian exile, complained that the new Temple would not compare. Haggai, as a prophet, acknowledges their concern (2:3) but then goes on to articulate an assurance that God is with them (vv. 4–5), thus encouraging them to persevere in the rebuilding effort. In addition, the prophet announces a divine promise in verses 6–7. In a little while God will appear and, in typical theophanic fashion, shake heaven and earth, and thereby "shake loose" its riches for the Temple. The warrant for this divine action is possession: the gold and silver are, after all, God's (v. 8). As a result, the prophetic word concludes, the new Temple will one day even exceed the old (v. 9), and the people will enjoy a prosperity that has hitherto eluded them (compare Haggai 1:7–11, where the problem of inflation and a lack of fertility are described).

THE PROPHET'S PROCLAMATION GROUNDS THE NEED FOR SUPPORTING AND REBUILDING THE TEMPLE NOT ON GUILT OR THE LATEST MANAGEMENT TECHNIQUE, BUT ON DIVINE PROMISE, DIVINE OWNERSHIP OF ALL CREATION, AND HOPE IN A NEW FUTURE.

Haggai can be instructive for considering a homiletical theology of stewardship. It is important to notice that the prophet's proclamation grounds the need for supporting and rebuilding the Temple not on guilt or the latest management technique, but on divine promise (God is with you), divine ownership of all creation ("The silver and gold are mine"), and hope in a new future ("in a little while"). Perhaps Haggai can help us think through what it means to be God's people together in a way that is different from the bottom-line, me-first mentality of late post-industrial North American capitalism.

RESPONSIVE READING

PSALM 17:1-9 (RCL)
PSALM 17 OR 17:1-8 (BCP)
PSALM 17:1, 5-6, 8, 15 (RC)

The form of this responsive reading is an individual prayer for deliverance from enemies. First there is the cry for vindication (vv. 1-2). Then the psalmist asserts his innocence (vv. 3-5). This may not be a general protestation of sinlessness, but rather a refutation of some false charge that is the source of the threat. Finally, the most promising sections are found at the end of the psalmist's prayer (vv. 6-15). Here the language lays hold of profound imagery of trust: "Guard me as the apple of the eye; hide me in the shadow of your wings" (v. 8). Although there is still venom for the psalmist's opponents and their children (v. 14b), the psalm ends with a profound sense of awakening trust (v. 15).

This psalm opens up for us an interesting connection with other lections for the day. With Job, for example, it asks questions of vindication. But does its awakening language in verse 15 portend something of a view of resurrection? In all likelihood it does not. Still, it offers resonances for us to explore with the liturgical day.

PSALM 145:1-5, 17-21 (RCL ALT.)

See the responsive reading for the Twenty-third Sunday after Pentecost, above.

PSALM 98 (RCL ALT.)

See the responsive reading for the Twentieth Sunday after Pentecost, above.

SECOND READING

2 THESSALONIANS 2:1-5, 13-17 (RCL)
2 THESSALONIANS 2:13—3:5 (BCP)
2 THESSALONIANS 2:16—3:5 (RC)

With the beginning of chapter 2, the writer of 2 Thessalonians begins wading into teachings that help make sense of the Thessalonians' lives under affliction. Chapter 2 is dedicated to clarifying Paul's earlier end-time teachings in that light.

The clarification had to do with some misunderstanding about the Day of the Lord. If chapter 1 was focused on the meaning of what the revelation of the Lord would entail for the Thessalonian community and their persecutors, chapter 2 tries to correct false notions of *when* that day would happen. Whether it arose out of a misinterpretation of an earlier letter (1 Thessalonians?), a forgery of a Pauline letter, or some ecstatic prophecy in the community, the writer wanted to be sure that the community understood the sequence of events that preceded the Day of the Lord. Yes, it would come upon the community in a surprising fashion (1 Thessalonians 4–5), but it would not take place without (1) a rebellion and (2) the revelation of the "lawless one" (v. 3).

THE TEST IS NOT FILLING IN THE RIGHT BLANKS IN
APOCALYPTIC TIMELINES; THE TRUE TEST IS IN THE
LIVING OF THE LIFE OF FAITH IN THE HERE AND NOW.

Apocalyptic literature is full of such scenarios. The times before theophanic events and cataclysms were to be marked by apostasy, or rebellion against authority. For the writer, this would culminate in the "revelation" of the lawless one, a figure reminiscent of the Antichrist in other literature.

Yet the writer is not merely interested in getting apocalyptic timelines straight. The point here, as verses 13ff. demonstrate, is that the sequence of events points to *the salvation of the Thessalonian community*. In an age of special effects in movies and conspiracy thinking in the culture, it is easy to get hung up on timelines for their own sake. This is emphatically not the case for the writer of 2 Thessalonians. "We must always give thanks to God for you . . . because God chose you as the first fruits for salvation" (v. 13). With the knowledge of this delayed timeline, the Thessalonian community is to be empowered to continue steadfast in the faith, whether it is by what they've heard in proclamation or letter. This is the bottom line for a community that waits expectantly. The test is not filling in the right blanks in apocalyptic timelines; the true test is living the life of faith in the here and now. For this reason, the writer closes this section with a prayer to comfort and strengthen the Thessalonians (vv. 16-17). This idea continues in 3:1-5. Although the writer draws attention to the ongoing work of sharing the gospel with others, he or she is quick to connect that to the Thessalonians' own experience and need for the steadfastness of Christ. In their relationship, they share a confidence in the Lord and in each other.

THE GOSPEL

LUKE 20:27-38 (RCL, RC)
LUKE 20:27 (28-33) 34-38 (BCP)
LUKE 20:27, 34-38 (RC ALT.)

With this lection we finally have Jesus in Jerusalem and actually teaching publicly in the Temple. From Luke 9:51 on, we've known that it was necessary for

Jesus to go there and that he would "set his face" toward Jerusalem over the intervening ten chapters of Luke's Gospel. The fact that the passion predictions of Luke also help us to understand the importance of his journey, namely his suffering/rejection and resurrection, points up the importance of today's text. Here Jesus is questioned by the Sadducees about the resurrection. Here Jesus teaches publicly in the Temple about something that was a crucial part of the reason for his whole journey there.

The Sadducees in Jerusalem were a largely priestly party whose reading of the Torah contrasted significantly with that of the Pharisees. Sadducees were the "strict constructionists" of Jesus' day. If it wasn't in the Pentateuch (Genesis to Deuteronomy), they didn't believe it. From Luke's perspective, they are the ideal opponents for a discussion on the resurrection.

Because the Sadducees also represented an elite priestly view, perhaps one even more amenable to the interests of their Roman occupiers, they may have surfaced in Luke's Gospel portrayal as a group that would have wanted to take the upstart Jesus down a peg. Most commentators seem to think that their posing of this question was unlikely to be out of mere curiosity. Luke's Jesus may have represented a threat to the established order from which they benefited.

These issues are partly revealed by the *way* Luke narrates the conflict. Luke the narrator discloses that the Sadducees dispute that there is a resurrection (v. 27) yet nonetheless pose a question that presupposes it as a premise (v. 33). Discerning readers should also note that their question about levirate marriage is drawn from two parts of the Pentateuch (Deut. 25:5 and Gen. 38:8), which the Sadducees point out is what Moses wrote for them (v. 28). They

JESUS POINTS OUT THAT ISSUES OF MARRIAGE DON'T APPLY IN THE RESURRECTION. COMPARING THIS AGE TO THE NEXT IS LIKE COMPARING APPLES TO ORANGES.

are indeed "strict constructionists" on this issue but want to see if Jesus will recognize the absurdity of a resurrection position, what with one resurrected wife for seven resurrected brothers.

Yet here Jesus shows himself capable of careful argumentation. He proceeds along two tracks. First, he talks of the general principle of distinguishing between "the ages." Second, he heads straight into the Sadducees' scriptural stronghold, the Pentateuch itself.

With the first track, he points out that issues of marriage don't apply in the resurrection. Comparing this age to the next is like comparing apples to oranges. Those deemed worthy of resurrection don't need to worry about laws that are applied as a result of death. In fact, these "sons of the resurrection" are equal to the angels and thus belong to God, not to any human person at all. The Sadducees, in other words, have made a category mistake.

With the second track, Jesus pushes the issue further. By reminding the Sadducees of the burning bush story, Jesus does two very clever things. First, he disputes their point about the resurrection with a text from the heart of the Pentateuch itself. Jesus uses the *Torah* to make his case for resurrection. Second, he does so by appealing to the words of God's own self-disclosure at Moses' burning bush as the "God of Abraham, the God of Isaac, and the God of Jacob" (v. 37). Clearly, God is the God of the living, not the dead. Even though the patriarchs died, they live to God, because God's promise to them to be their God is still good.

Why is this important? Luke's Jesus first comes into view in chapters 1–2 of the Gospel as embodying all those Old Testament promises and surrounded by figures like Simeon and Anna, Zechariah and Elizabeth, hoary old Hebrew Bible "types"—all of this described in a Greek literary style that sounds downright Septuagintal. This same Gospel ends with an Emmaus walk on which two of Jesus' own disciples need a brush-up course on the Law and the Prophets, who, Jesus claims, know all about this suffering/resurrection stuff. Luke's tragic gospel of suffering/rejection and resurrection needs this dispute to show that Jesus teaches, lives, and even dies this resurrection thing. So in a culminating moment of his ten-chapter-long journey to Jerusalem, he gets in a Scripture argument. Those of us who read it need to understand: this idea about resurrection is not just about Sunday-school butterflies and pleasant-smelling Easter lilies. Jesus' death and resurrection provoke profound opposition and argument. Jesus is thus willing to teach this truth in the heart of the Temple, about the heart of the Torah, with the heart of his day's elite. The author of Luke-Acts might be quick to point out that the opposition to this teaching is not Jewish alone. Luke's narration of resurrection teaching gets no better reception in Athens (Acts 17:16-34) than it does here in verses 39-40 in Jerusalem. We Gentile-Christians, therefore, have no right to look down our noses at Jesus' opponents. Jesus' dispute about resurrection is with our lives, too, just as its resurrection hope transforms them. So Jesus is willing to head into the heart of our cherished traditions and the ways we use them to protect our privileges, to show how resurrection both arises in those traditions and explodes the privileged categories with which we've surrounded them at the same time.

> LUKE'S TRAGIC GOSPEL OF SUFFERING/REJECTION AND RESURRECTION NEEDS THIS DISPUTE TO SHOW THAT JESUS TEACHES, LIVES, AND EVEN DIES THIS RESURRECTION THING.

One of the most eloquent speeches in American history and certainly one of the most recited is Lincoln's Gettysburg Address. There was a day when schoolchildren would have to memorize the speech to perform in class. As for graduate students, they continue to take apart the rhetoric of Lincoln's brief discourse in countless theses, dissertations, and articles. Clearly, we have learned to rehearse and study its words. Yet the genius of this speech is not just its surface eloquence. In the midst of one of the most death-strewn battlefields of an all-too-bloody American history, Lincoln spoke in just a few words something that took his historical moment to the heart of America's founding documents. "Four score and seven years ago" refers, of course, to the eighty-seven-year-old Declaration of Independence of 1776. It is in that document, Lincoln reminds his hearers, that the confession arises that all "are created equal." Why is this reminder of a national basic truth on a Civil War battlefield so shocking? Until this point, the war between North and South had been read through the Constitution alone: namely, what does the 1791 document and its amendments say about states' rights? Lincoln was reminding his hearers that the Constitution needed to be understood in light of the universal promise of the Declaration of Independence—that the battlefield they gathered in was a tragic space where the conflicted truth of the *whole foundational story of the nation* was being played out in all of its glory and tragedy. Deep within those documents, lurking behind the limitations of a decades-long argument about the constitutional issue of states' rights between slave-holding and free states of the Union, was a transforming truth of the Declaration whose reality could not be denied, even as its painful consequences were still working themselves out.

We who call ourselves Christian know the struggle well. The resurrection is not just a knickknack to be dusted off every spring. It is in fact a deep truth that goes back to the heart of our tradition and whose difficult, transforming word is still working itself out among us. Jesus teaches resurrection to send us to the heart of our traditions, but in a way that breaks open their categories, sometimes even painfully, because in the end he knows that suffering, rejection, *and resurrection* are what our life together is all about.

> THE RESURRECTION IS IN FACT A DEEP TRUTH THAT GOES BACK TO THE HEART OF OUR TRADITION AND WHOSE DIFFICULT, TRANSFORMING WORD IS STILL WORKING ITSELF OUT AMONG US.

Note

1. For a poignant look at this difficult text and some of the issues raised here, see Norman Habel's commentary in the Old Testament Library series, *The Book of Job* (Philadelphia: Westminster Press, 1985), 302–9.

TWENTY-FIFTH SUNDAY AFTER PENTECOST

THIRTY-THIRD SUNDAY IN ORDINARY TIME /
PROPER 28
NOVEMBER 18, 2007

REVISED COMMON	EPISCOPAL (BCP)	ROMAN CATHOLIC
Mal. 4:1-2a or Isa. 65:17-25	Mal. 3:13—4:2a, 5-6	Mal. 3:19-20a
Psalm 98 or Isaiah 12	Psalm 98 or 98:5-10	Ps. 98:5-6, 7-8, 9
2 Thess. 3:6-13	2 Thess. 3:6-13	2 Thess. 3:7-12
Luke 21:5-19	Luke 21:5-19	Luke 21:5-19

FIRST READING

MALACHI 4:1-2a (RCL)
MALACHI 3:13—4:2a, 5-6 (BCP)
MALACHI 3:19-20a (RC)

The prophetic book Malachi is the last book of the Hebrew Bible canon. In many ways, for Christians, it serves as an interesting transition to the New Testament. For example, it mentions the return of Elijah (4:5-6), which becomes the object of some reflection in early Christian literature. For this reason, the book may seem more familiar to Christians than it actually is. Nonetheless, the book is shrouded in more than a little mystery. In all likelihood, for example, the name of the book is probably not the name of the prophet. Malachi, in Hebrew, simply means "my messenger" (see 3:1). So we need to approach this text with some care and not assume we know everything about it or read it in a way that assumes that Jesus has superseded its claim to faith.

MALACHI SEEMS TO PRESUPPOSE A PERIOD WHEN PROPHETIC CRITIQUE WAS FOCUSED ON A CORRUPT PRIESTHOOD AND THE NEED FOR INSTRUCTING A PEOPLE WHO ARE NOT ALTOGETHER WILLING TO STICK WITH TORAH.

Fortunately, scholars do feel some comfort with the historical dating of this book. It comes from the Persian period, probably in the first half of the fifth century C.E. After the return from exile, the life of the people was focused especially on Temple and priesthood. The other major institutions of the people's life, king-ship and prophecy, were either finished off by the earlier Babylonian exile or in the process of dying out. Malachi seems to presuppose a period, therefore, when prophetic critique was focused on a corrupt priesthood and the need for instruct-ing a people who were not altogether willing to stick with Torah, especially as it relates to matters of divorce and Jewish or foreign wives, tithing, and so forth. The fact that Malachi is so concerned with such matters leads many scholars to believe that he was a "cultic" prophet.

The lection for this day is no doubt chosen because of its eschatological focus, which it has in common with both the epistle and Gospel readings for the day. Yet some features of Malachi make it unique and are potentially helpful for the preacher to focus on. Malachi features the use of disputes with the people. In some parts of the book, the peoples' complaints are included in the disputes with the prophet, who is speaking for God. Homiletically, this can help by fore-grounding questions that help make some of the eschatological materials more intelligible today.

In the BCP lectionary, some of these features show up in 3:13-15, where the voices of those who struggle to keep Torah are discussed. Why do Torah when the arrogant and the evil prosper? Nonetheless, there are those among the peo-ple who "revere" the Lord and "think on his name" (v. 16). While clearly not all these divided people will keep Torah in the midst of such corruption, surely this remnant will. These final questions and divisions lay the groundwork for the eschatological material in chapter 4. A day is coming when those arrogant evildoers will be burnt like stubble, and they shall be

> THE PROPHET HOPES THAT SOME OF HIS HEARERS WILL KEEP FAITH BASED ON A PROMISE OF JUDGMENT FOR EVILDOERS AND HEALING FOR THE RIGHTEOUS.

extirpated—"root and branch" (4:1). But for those who do remember and revere the divine name, the sun of righteousness shall arise with healing in its wings (v. 2). The prophet, in other words, hopes that some of his hearers will keep faith based on a promise of judgment for evildoers and healing for the righteous. Here it is important to remember that the image is a two-sided one. Elizabeth Achtemeier points out that God's action of judgment and salvation are treated as two aspects of the same image. When the sun rises on the day of the Lord, its burning will judge the evil (stubble), but its wings (rays) will heal the righteous.[1] Here the text invites us into a difficult yet deep mystery of faith.

For those whose lectionaries continue with the last two verses of the book, there is also the connection with Elijah with the coming day of the Lord (vv. 5-6). The result of this coming, however, is a turning of the hearts of parents and children—a reconciliation that will forestall a divine curse. The point here is that even the last book of the Hebrew Bible is not God's final word. God's judgment is announced not to predetermine who gets burned and who doesn't. There is still time to turn. Though the words of the text sound difficult to our ears, this is where its grace lurks.

ISAIAH 65:17-25 (RCL ALT.)

This salvation oracle in Third Isaiah is important not only as a continuation of the tradition of Isaiah of Babylon's preaching (65:17b reprises, for example, one of Second Isaiah's themes in 43:18), but as a harbinger of later apocalyptic developments. This is not to say that our lection should be reduced to either.

Third Isaiah's context is decidedly postexilic and therefore different from Isaiah of Babylon's. His salvation oracle is given to people likely disappointed after a return to the land and needing some sense of hope for the task of rebuilding. The traditions of Second Isaiah may be important for Third Isaiah, but his context is too different for merely repeating what was said. In fact, it is his use of that tradition in a new time and place that demonstrates how Second Isaiah's prophetic genius was indeed a living one and not a dead one.

This salvation oracle, likewise, is also not to be confused with later apocalyptic visions that use the same kind of language (for instance, Revelation 21). Although the hopes articulated in 65:20-25 are fantastic, they are still decidedly this-worldly. The hope is for long life, undiminished by the seeming curse of a premature death, not the elimination of death altogether (v. 20). The hope is for a fair reward for labor, not its abolition (v. 21). Even the most fantastic hopes about wolf, lamb, lion, and serpent are reprisals of traditions dear to Isaiah (Isaiah 11, Genesis 3) more than anything else. Tellingly, even the serpent's curse is not totally undone, for "dust shall be the serpent's food" (v. 25). The splendid vision, therefore, has a serpentine footnote that refuses to obliterate history and nature. Third Isaiah envisions a new creation not so much as destruction and *creatio ex nihilo*, but as transformation.

> THIRD ISAIAH ENVISIONS A NEW CREATION NOT SO MUCH AS DESTRUCTION AND *creatio ex nihilo*, BUT AS TRANSFORMATION.

And here is the real reason for Third Isaiah's genius, exemplified in this beautifully poetic text of hope. The cause of this transformation and renewal of creation from Jerusalem out will be God's caring presence: "Before they call I will answer, while they are yet speaking I will hear" (v. 24). In the end, this poem of salvation, which speaks such unrelenting promise to the disappointed, hinges on the promise of divine presence, a solicitous Presence who will anticipate the needs of God's people.

Responsive Reading
PSALM 98 (RCL, BCP)
PSALM 98:5-10 (BCP ALT.)
PSALM 98:5-6, 7-8, 9 (RC)

See my comments on the responsive reading for the Twenty-first Sunday after Pentecost, above. Please note how the eschatological tone of the Malachi reading dovetails with that of the end of Psalm 98. Both wait for the coming of the Lord in judgment.

ISAIAH 12 (RCL ALT.)

The reason for the pairing of this responsive reading with the RCL alternative first reading from Isaiah 65 becomes apparent early on. In the first of the two songs that make up the chapter (12:1-3, 4-6) we encounter an important phrase: "For though you were angry with me, your anger turned away and you comforted me" (v. 1). This view becomes a key for hearing the whole book of Isaiah. If, in chapters 1–39, God seems unremittingly "angry," in chapters 40–66 we meet the God of comfort. Thus, from the hinge of Isaiah 12 we can look forward to the soaring prophecy of Third Isaiah. The prophet anticipates it in the future tense with two liturgical notes at the beginning of both songs, "You will say in that day . . ." (vv. 1, 4). More important, Isaiah does so by inviting us to sing along joyfully: "Sing praises to the LORD, for he has done gloriously . . ." (v. 5a).

Second Reading
2 THESSALONIANS 3:6-13 (RCL, BCP)
2 THESSALONIANS 3:7-12 (RC)

With this last section of 2 Thessalonians, the author, writing under Paul's pseudonym, takes up the concrete side of the teaching laid out in chapter 2. Earlier the focus was on making sure that the Thessalonians knew that the end times had not arrived. Now the writer draws out some implications of this for the common life of the community.

Apparently, the excited belief in the imminence of the end times resulted in certain members of the community ceasing to work. If the Lord is coming soon, why bother making a living? Of course, the problem went even deeper than that. Not only were the ones who chose to stop working a drain on the community's resources; they also were meddling in other people's lives—"busybodies" (v. 11), the writer calls them.

In order to keep the community focused on "doing what is right" (v. 13), the writer advises that the Thessalonian community "keep away" from the idle. The implication is that their actions had caused a break in community life. The hope, of course, was that in light of the community's action, and the writer's exhortation (v. 12), the offenders would resume their normal work and provide for themselves. To accomplish this, the writer makes it a point to remind the community of Paul's behavior when he was among them. As an apostle, he had a right to receive the community's aid. He did not avail himself of that aid, however, and worked in order to provide for himself. In this sense, the pseudonymous writer calls for the imitation of that apostolic example.

One important note for preachers: It would be easy to misuse the famous quote from this lection: "Anyone unwilling to work should not eat" (v. 10b). The focus here is on "unwilling." Contemporary ideologies that caricature the poor and unemployed as lazy sometimes use such language to stigmatize them and barely hide a kind of Christian coldheartedness. The focus in this text is very specific. In light of eschatological excitement, some of the community had decided to stop laboring and rely on the community for resources. If we need any extra assurance in this regard, we need only consult the final verse of this lection. The writer ends his warnings with this: "Brothers and sisters, do not be weary in doing what is right" (v. 13).

> NOT ONLY WERE THE ONES WHO CHOSE TO STOP WORK-
> ING A DRAIN ON THE COMMUNITY'S RESOURCES, THEY
> ALSO WERE MEDDLING IN OTHER PEOPLE'S LIVES.

As an expression of Christian vocation, however, the text still has some homiletical value. We live in a time when many people are influenced or at least put at unease by the end-time speculations of those who engage in mass-market religious fear mongering. Over against this, the writer exemplifies a point of view attributed to the reformer Martin Luther: "If the world were to end tomorrow, I would plant a tree today." We who are called to stay faithful in times of cataclysmic change need always and everywhere to remember that our vocation continues, too. In God's grace, in the very face of chaos, we need not "weary in doing what is right."

THE GOSPEL
LUKE 21:5-19 (RCL, BCP, RC)

With Luke 21 at the end of the church year, we enter eschatological territory. This is certainly true when we consider the other texts for the day. Both Malachi and 2 Thessalonians hold our feet to the eschatological fire. Luke, however, is a bit different. Luke is talking about eschatology here, and perhaps with even a few apocalyptic overtones.[2] But Luke has his own interests. Please remember that Luke is the first part of a two-part work, Luke-*Acts*. So whereas other Gospels broach eschatological topics with little explicit vision of church life, Luke fills the gap. To the twenty-four chapters of his Gospel, he adds twenty-eight chapters of Acts. Luke's Jesus can thus envision eschatological issues, but he is committed first to the church as the locus of ongoing life.

This reality about Luke helps make sense of his eschatological discourse in Luke 21:5-19. The language and some of the structure are reminiscent of Mark's apocalyptic discourse in Mark 13. Since Luke seems to have redacted Mark to suit some of his own purposes, the differences are always telling.

In Luke's text, Jesus does not offer his teaching outside the Temple, but remains in the Temple teaching (Luke even reminds the readers at the end of this discourse, 21:37-38, that Jesus *continued* to do so afterward; compare Mark 13:1). When the topic of the future of the Temple is broached and the signs connected with it, Luke's Jesus is very interested in postponing its eschatological significance (vv. 7-8) and

> LUKE IS NOT WILLING TO TALK ABOUT A FULL-BLOWN GENTILE MISSION JUST YET. IN FACT, THIS EVENT WILL BE SAVED FOR THE STORY OF PAUL IN THE UNFOLDING NARRATIVE IN ACTS.

undermining a connection with any single "sign." First, other things must happen: wars, earthquakes, famines, plagues, etc. (vv. 9-11).

Yet before *even these things*, they will arrest you, persecute you, hand you over, and bring you before kings (v. 12), and this will be a time for your testimony (v. 13). This material sounds very similar to Mark's, but the key departure is given right here. Mark goes on to say in 13:10, "And the good news must first be proclaimed to all nations." Luke, however, is not willing to talk about a full-blown Gentile mission just yet. In fact, this event will be saved for the story of Paul in the unfolding narrative in Acts.

These differences make something clear about Luke's agenda with Jesus' eschatological discourse. Luke's Jesus mentions things like arrests and persecutions, being handed over and brought before kings, and the fact that some will be put to death (v. 16), not just because Mark's Jesus says something similar, but because all these events are actually narrated in Acts: persecutions (Acts 4:16-18; 7:52; 8:1b-3; 12:1-5), being handed over to kings and rulers (Acts 12:1-11; 23:24—24:27; 25:13—26:32), and (some) being put to death (Acts 7:54-60; 12:1-2). Just as it was necessary for Jesus to go to Jerusalem and suffer, so also will it be necessary for Jesus' followers in Acts to go witness and, yes, even suffer while they wait for Luke's postponed eschatological end. Luke's tragic Gospel anticipates "opposition" at its outset with Simeon's prophecy about baby Jesus (2:34-35), has Jesus experience rejection at his first hometown sermon (4:23-30), and describes Jesus repeatedly foretelling the necessity of the Son of Man's *suffering* in Jerusalem (9:22, 44-45;

17:25). Now Luke's Jesus postpones a premature equation of the Temple's fall with the end of the world by saying it is *necessary* for other things to happen first (v. 9)—these things, the last ones, will not happen immediately. Instead, Jesus' hearers get something different: a time of witnessing and difficult opposition.

Yet Jesus does not leave his disciples alone with a hugely tragic task before them. He promises them, even in the face of death, that "not a hair of your head will perish" (v. 18). In other words, in the midst of persecution, testimony, and death, they cannot be harmed in any ultimate way. The saying reminds readers of Jesus' words earlier in Luke about not fearing and worrying (12:7). In that context Jesus teaches that the disciples should not worry about anyone who can "kill the body, and after that do nothing more" (12:4). That this image of the hair on their heads should carry the disciples forward is revealed in the second half of Luke's two-part narrative in Acts 27. Here Paul is on the voyage to Malta, ultimately making his way to Rome. Paul is sure in his conviction that he will stand before the emperor there, and encourages the boat's sailors to eat despite their fears with these words in 27:34: "Take some food, for it will help you survive; for none of you will lose a hair from your heads." Even as he prepares for his appeal, his own occasion for being brought before "kings and rulers," the narrator has Paul remind readers of Jesus' teaching and promise.

So it is, for us, too. As bearers of the gospel word, we are given in this transitional moment in North American church life both a difficult task of witnessing and waiting *and a vision of promise to sustain us through it.* Garrison Keillor tells us of a strange gift like this that he was given while fishing with his uncle Al.[3] Even now he can see himself. It's early in the morning, no light yet, and he shivers in the cold. A mist is coming off the waters of the lake that combines with the smell of weeds and his uncle Al's coffee. His uncle makes it a point to whisper to him what to do when the big fish bites. Young Garrison remembers himself lowering his worm on the hook into the dark water, bracing his feet in the boat—all in anticipation of the fish that was about to strike. Keillor concludes, "Uncle Al thought he was taking his nephew fishing, but he made a permanent work of art in my head, a dark morning in the mist, the coffee, the boat rocking, whispering, shivering, waiting for the big one. Still waiting. Still shivering." And here we are, a shivering, waiting church—but continuing forward with this great vision in our heads: "Not a hair of your head," we remember, "not a hair of your head will perish."

> AS BEARERS OF THE GOSPEL WORD, WE ARE GIVEN IN THIS TRANSITIONAL MOMENT IN NORTH AMERICAN CHURCH LIFE BOTH A DIFFICULT TASK OF WITNESSING AND WAITING ALONG WITH A VISION OF PROMISE TO SUSTAIN US THROUGH IT.

Notes

1. Elizabeth Achtemeier, *Nahum—Malachi* Interpretation, ed. James L. Mays (Atlanta: John Knox, 1986), 196.

2. For how "eschatology" and apocalyptic language might relate, see the discussion of apocalyptic forms in my book, *Preaching in the New Creation: The Promise of New Testament Apocalyptic Texts* (Louisville: Westminster John Knox Press, 1999), 6, 30–52.

3. Garrison Keillor, *Leaving Home* (New York: Viking, 1987), 20.

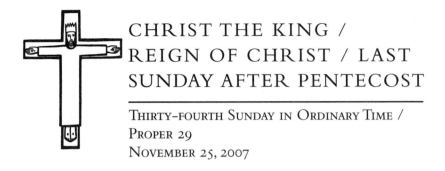

CHRIST THE KING / REIGN OF CHRIST / LAST SUNDAY AFTER PENTECOST

THIRTY-FOURTH SUNDAY IN ORDINARY TIME / PROPER 29

NOVEMBER 25, 2007

REVISED COMMON	EPISCOPAL (BCP)	ROMAN CATHOLIC
Jer. 23:1-6	Jer. 23:1-6	2 Sam. 5:1-3
Psalm 46 or Luke 1:68-79	Psalm 46	Ps. 122:1-2, 3-4, 4-5
Col. 1:11-20	Col. 1:11-20	Col. 1:12-20
Luke 23:33-43	Luke 23:35-43 or Luke 19:29-38	Luke 23:35-43

FIRST READING

JEREMIAH 23:1-6 (RCL, BCP)

This text can be a useful one for Christ the King Sunday not because it is a "prediction" of Jesus, but because it invites us to reflect deeply about kingship and its meaning in a time of suffering and exile. To do so, however, means to take the text and its context with great seriousness. Scholars are very divided as to whether these six verses represent one unit or two. Yet even if they are juxtaposed, their relationship here is nonetheless instructive and homiletically helpful.

We begin with some context. For some time, Jeremiah has been preaching about the coming exile. Now that it has happened, the legitimate Davidic heir to the throne, Jehoiachin, has departed for Babylon. The Babylonians then installed a puppet king, Jehoiachin's uncle, and gave him a traditional throne name, Zedekiah. Although scholars are not in agreement when that latter part of our text was developed (namely, verses 5-6), whether early or late in Zedekiah's reign, nonetheless Jeremiah uses the situation to make his theological points.

Jeremiah begins in verses 1-4 with a woe oracle, although one with surprising salvific components. The "shepherds" who are judged are the leaders, the kings of God's people. Here the exile is explained as a result of their mismanagement of the flock. In exile, the flock is "scattered," and this, says Jeremiah on behalf of the Lord, is the shepherds' fault. Since they failed to attend to their people, now God will "attend" to them. Yet just when you think the woe oracle is done, the prophet adds an uncharacteristic promise in verse 3: "Then I myself will gather the remnant of my flock."

Because of God's gathering, they shall be fruitful and multiply, thus echoing the language of Genesis. Thereafter, God will raise up better shepherds for them and they shall need to fear no more (v. 4). This woe oracle encompasses both judgment and salvation, including a reformed kingship.

Immediately after this come the two verses that sound most familiar to Christians. Out of the tradition of Isaiah 11 (a shoot from the stump), Jeremiah envisions one day a righteous Branch for David. As such, he will be a legitimate king who will do the right thing and thus ensure safety for Judah and Israel (vv. 5-6a). Then comes the prophetic punch line: His name will be called "The Lord is our righteousness," which is in Hebrew an *inverted* form of King Zedekiah's name.

Biblical scholar William Holladay argues that this may be a critique of Zedekiah's kingship.[1] Confronted with puppet king Zedekiah's throne name, the prophet perhaps envisions one day that God will raise up a legitimate Davidic king who will *invert* this puppet king into what is really needed in a king: "The Lord is our righteousness." Although Christians may be quick to ascribe such prophetic hopes to Jesus and leave it at that, a clear embedding of this text's hope in the life and times of the prophet Jeremiah does a far better job of enriching its meaning for us on this day.

> IN EXILE, THE FLOCK IS "SCATTERED," AND THIS, SAYS JEREMIAH ON BEHALF OF THE LORD, IS THE SHEPHERDS' FAULT. SINCE THEY FAILED TO ATTEND TO THEIR PEOPLE, NOW GOD WILL "ATTEND" TO THEM.

2 SAMUEL 5:1-3 (RC)

This text describes David's enthronement over Israel. In 2 Samuel 2:1-7, David is recognized as king of Judah. In this text, Israel, made up of the Northern tribes, also pledges allegiance to him. They acknowledge kinship with him by saying in 5:1 that they are David's "bone and flesh." Saul may have been king, but all along David was providing leadership (v. 2). Moreover, they acknowledge what God has said to David, that he shall be their "shepherd." As a result, they make a covenant with David and anoint him.

On a day like Christ the King, it is interesting to reflect on how these conceptions of kingship—kinship, solidarity, and shepherding—help us understand what it means to call Christ our King. In this way, this Hebrew Bible text can enlarge our understanding of Christ, rather than simply reducing such Old Testament texts to predictions of Jesus.

RESPONSIVE READING

PSALM 46 (RCL, BCP)

While more material on Psalm 46 can be found in the description for this responsive reading on Reformation Day, the psalm offers special interpretive opportunities on Christ the King. Because Christ the King captures an ironic sense of kingship, the elements of change and tumult in the psalm come out all the more strongly. To talk about kingship in this day is to embrace its manifestation not merely in power, but in struggle, difficulty, and change. It is to speak about kingship in the shadow of the cross itself.

PSALM 122:1-2, 3-4, 4-5 (RC)

This well-known responsive reading is one of the psalms of ascent. It may well have been sung in connection with pilgrimages to Jerusalem. While some scholars date the psalm to the postexilic period, it is somewhat difficult to pin down an exact time frame. For our purposes, the connection with the house of David and with the centrality of Jerusalem is significant. In this respect it resonates powerfully with the first reading from 2 Samuel. Within the context of the liturgical day, it emphasizes what kingship means: not merely having power over others, but providing for unity (v. 4) and administering justice (v. 5).

The psalm consists of three parts. The first is the retrospective look of the pilgrims. The first two verses reflect back on what brought them to the city. The next section, verses 3-5, reflects on what Jerusalem means to the pilgrims. From there, the psalm gives a call to prayer. Because the city means so much, the pilgrims are to pray for its peace and prosperity (vv. 6-9). Yet the ultimate reason for such prayerful solicitude is given in the final verse: "For the sake of the house of the LORD our God, I will seek your good" (v. 9). Like bookends standing in the opening and closing verses, the psalmists' words remind that the house of the Lord itself calls forth both pilgrimage and prayer.

> LIKE BOOKENDS STANDING IN THE OPENING AND CLOSING VERSES, THE PSALMISTS' WORDS REMIND THAT THE HOUSE OF THE LORD ITSELF CALLS FORTH BOTH PILGRIMAGE AND PRAYER.

LUKE 1:68-79 (RCL ALT.)

Luke's *Benedictus* makes a wonderful choice for a responsive reading on this day. The text breaks down naturally into two major sections, 1:68-75 and 1:76-79. The first part sounds downright psalmic. It weaves skillfully many quotes from the psalms and other parts of the Hebrew Bible, thus linking the salvation that is being wrought by God through the birth of John and the conception of Jesus into traditional Jewish hopes and dreams. The language here in particular, discerning readers will note, is in the past tense. This is not because it is looking backward. With such language the past tense is used to express a reality that is happening, yet because it is inaugurated by God it is as good as done. The final four verses then turn to focus specifically on John's role in this salvific scheme, echoing the language of Malachi's hope for a coming "Elijah" as well as describing Jesus' significance as the "dawn from on high" (v. 78). The language for Jesus here may also be Davidic, since the Greek word for "dawn," *anatolē*, is also translated in the Septuagint as "branch," a messianic figure used above in Jeremiah 23:5.

Second Reading
COLOSSIANS 1:11-20 (rcl, bcp)
COLOSSIANS 1:12-20 (rc)

With this lection we have the opportunity to consider matters of the reign of Christ from the perspective of the Pauline tradition. I write "Pauline tradition" because the issues of the authorship of Colossians are so complex. Suffice it to say that a place for it among the authentic Pauline letters would be quite precarious. Nonetheless, the line between an actual "undisputed" letter written by Paul (say, the Corinthian correspondence, which may actually be a composite of letters) and Colossians may be less clear than we think. It may be enough to consider how the writer of Colossians seeks to reflect on issues and problems in Colossae, a city in western Asia Minor (contemporary Turkey), in light of a Pauline tradition that wishes to apply, in terms of both form and content, what Paul wrote for a different moment and context.

Like the authentic Pauline letters, this one begins with the requisite addressees in a salutation, a summary of reasons for giving thanks (vv. 3-8), and the beginning of a prayer thereafter. Our lection begins in the prayer itself (v. 11) but quickly distinguishes itself by preparing the readers to deal with matters close to the hearts of the Colossian congregation. It does so in two ways. First, the writer uses language designed to remind the readers of their post-baptismal state (vv. 12-14). Second, it recites what was to them probably a well-known hymn (vv. 15-20). Knowing this, we are able to appreciate better what might be at stake in this seeming esoteric language of today's lection.

The tail end of the writer's prayer in verses 11-12a is focused on strengthening the hearers and encouraging them in patience, endurance, and thankful joy. The basis for this is what "the Father" has done, namely, enabling the Colossians to have a share in the inheritance of the saints in light—language that joins the Colossians to the ancient promises given to the patriarchs and to angels, the "saints in light" (a key issue in the convoluted world of Colossian cosmologies, where figures like angels make life much more difficult and complex). How can this be? The writer reminds the Colossians of baptismal talk. The Father has transferred us already from the dominion of darkness to the Son's kingdom. Yet the writer does more than simply remind of baptism here; he qualifies that transfer to the Son's kingdom by talking about *how* he redeems: through forgiving sins (v. 14).

Having reminded the Colossians of their baptismal status, the writer also reminds them of a hymn, possibly one that they've sung themselves. In doing so, the writer both grounds them in that worship experience as a way of assuaging their fears and modifies that hymn to bring out aspects of Christ's own work. To call Christ "first-born of all creation" and to point out that all of creation was made through him and for him sounds like nice hymnic flattery, until one remembers

> THE WRITER DOES MORE THAN SIMPLY REMIND OF BAPTISM HERE; HE QUALIFIES THAT TRANSFER TO THE SON'S KINGDOM BY TALKING ABOUT HOW HE REDEEMS: THROUGH FORGIVING SINS.

a couple of things. First, invisible things such as thrones, dominions, and powers were just the issues with which the Colossians were struggling. Second, the Christ through and for whom all creation was made is already the head of the body, the church, so that "he might come to have first place in everything" (v. 18). In other words, the church is the place where Christ's lordship, his "kingship," is being made manifest—thus only making clear what was true from the very beginning. Yet here is the Pauline kicker. How does this happen? Through the reconciliation provided by the blood of the cross (v. 20).

Again, the text gives us another view of kingship, this time in a mode conversant with the Pauline tradition. For those who find themselves worried about powers over which they have no control, this christological view of kingship offers an emerging hope sufficient for strengthening and joy—one that is tied to the church now, as the locus of that emerging lordship, and to a Lord who made it possible through the cross.

THE GOSPEL

LUKE 23:33-43 (RCL)
LUKE 23:35-43 (BCP, RC)

Christ the King Sunday focuses on a strange paradox: Christ as *crucified* Lord. Luke's version of this story from chapter 1 on has been a Jewish one. This Jesus, who was celebrated in the first two chapters as the fulfillment of all Jewish hopes and confessed at the same time as a "sign that will be opposed" on old

Simeon's lips (2:34) at the outset, here is crucified with the same tragic ambiguity as when his arrival was first hailed. Crucified, he is surrounded by signs of royalty (figures on the right and left, as in pictures of royal propaganda [23:33]; the inscription over the cross [23:38]), though they are given in irony. In dying, he fulfills Jewish Scriptures (Luke 23:33 = Isa. 53:12; Luke 23:34a = Num. 15:27-31; Luke 23:34b = Ps. 22:18; Luke 24:36 = Ps. 69:21), yet only one person in Luke's story recognizes the cruciform royal truth before him. But we have gotten ahead of ourselves. Let us turn to look at Luke's unique way of confessing our Lord's paradoxical reign on this day.

It is important to note that Luke largely follows Mark's narrative in the first half of our text (23:33-38; compare Mark 15:22-26, 29-32a). Luke has changed the sequence, but his dependence on Mark is fairly clear. An exception is, of course, Luke 23:34a, "Father, forgive them . . . ," which, though unique to Luke, is somewhat disputed textually.

Despite these commonalities, it is important to consider how Luke, who in chapter 1 announced that he was writing an "orderly account," also *departs* from Mark's crucifixion narrative. Whereas Mark refers only briefly to two bandits (Mark 15:27) and how they mocked Jesus (Mark 15:32b), Luke turns what Mark mentions in passing into a self-contained episode (Luke 23:39-43), with a dialogue

CHRIST THE KING SUNDAY FOCUSES ON A STRANGE PARADOX: CHRIST AS *CRUCIFIED* LORD.

that more closely suits Luke's theological purposes. With its placement here, the two "criminals" (the Greek calls them "evildoers") do not merely fulfill Scripture predictions but help to disclose profoundly what Luke's understanding of the crucifixion is and how that relates to Jesus' kingship, both of which are key for preaching on this day.

The first thing to notice in Luke's expanded narrative of the co-crucified is the two criminals' split perspectives. One of them taunts Jesus, just as Mark's bandits did, but more precisely aping the mockery of the leaders and the Roman soldiers that Luke described in verses 35b and 36b. Yet in this tragic moment of crucifixion—when crowds merely "watch" (v. 35a) while leaders, soldiers, and one criminal deride him; when Jesus is surrounded by all the royal signs described above, but they are given only in the form of mockery; when Scripture is being fulfilled left and right, but only as confirmation of Jesus' humiliation—precisely in this abject cruciform moment, one character, the second

A CRIMINAL SEES THE CRUCIFIED CHRIST ON THE CROSS NEXT TO HIM AND ASKS HIM TO EXERCISE HIS ROYAL PREROGATIVE FOR HIS SAKE.

criminal, says this: "Jesus, remember me when you come into your kingdom." A criminal, who acknowledges that he deserves his punishment and that Jesus is innocent, sees the crucified Christ on the cross next to him and asks him to *exercise his royal prerogative for his sake.* And how does Jesus respond? By giving him more than he asked for. The request that the second criminal makes presupposes an eschatology oriented to the future tense. Jesus' response is in the salvific present: "Truly I tell you, *today* you will be with me in Paradise" (v. 43, emphasis mine). Preachers need not trouble themselves over whether Jesus has forgotten about the resurrection of the body and embraced the Greeks' immortality of the soul. The point here is that from the divine perspective, and *within Jesus' own royal prerogative,* the gates to the royal heavenly park of Paradise have swung open to this "evildoer" who precisely in this moment saw Jesus' kingship through the eyes of faith in spite of all the evidence to the contrary.

The moment is a uniquely Lukan one. The second criminal addresses the crucified Christ as "Jesus," the name disclosed at the beginning of Luke's narrative to expectant Mary for the one who will be given the throne of David and "reign over the house of Jacob forever" (Luke 1:31-33). The splitting of the criminals' responses to the crucified Jesus likewise reprises the conflict that Simeon named in chapter 2. The idea that a criminal receives salvation "today" only serves to remind readers of Jesus' action throughout the narrative (for instance, his "today" to Zacchaeus in 19:9). Yet what is the most important key here is that Jesus' last words in the episode finally show what Jesus' kingship is all about. What makes a king? What *really* makes a king? You can strip away all the pomp and circumstance, all the show, all the public demonstrations of power, all the wealth, perhaps even the last shred of human dignity. On the cross, what makes the king has nothing to do with ermine, gold, and courtly retinues. On the cross, the only way to recognize this crucified king is in his power to pardon. How does the old hymn go? "Are ye able to remember / when a thief lifts up his eyes / that his pardoned soul is worthy / of a place in Paradise?" Follow Jesus to the cross and watch every external sign of his kingship stripped away—save one: his power to pardon . . . the *ungodly.* Against all odds and despite all the evidence, Luke's second thief saw the king on his crude throne. Today you can, too.

> ON THE CROSS, THE ONLY WAY TO RECOGNIZE THIS CRUCIFIED KING IS IN HIS POWER TO PARDON.

LUKE 19:29-38 (BCP ALT.)

Luke makes it a point to interpret the entrance into Jerusalem in light of his claims about Jesus' kingship. The untying of the colt is not so much about good logistical planning, but is intended to disclose something theological: "The Lord needs it." While the entrance on the colt brings with it other scriptural implications (Zech. 9:9), it helps here especially to highlight a kingship characterized by peace. Luke even changes the wording of the disciples somewhat: "Blessed is the *king,*" they say (Luke 19:38; compare "the one" in Mark 11:9b). The gloriously peaceful implications of the announcement in 19:38b are also reminiscent of Luke's earlier angelic revelation at Jesus' birth in 2:14. To be sure, Luke also highlights the conflict that comes with the Jerusalem entry, as Jesus and the Pharisees conclude the episode with telling disagreement.

Note

1. William L. Holladay, *Jeremiah 1*, Hermeneia, ed. Paul D. Hanson (Philadelphia: Fortress, 1986), 619.

THANKSGIVING DAY

Revised Common	Episcopal (BCP)	Roman Catholic
Deut. 26:1-11	Deut. 8:1-3, 6-10 (17-20)	Deut. 8:7-18 or 1 Kgs. 8:55-61
Psalm 100	Psalm 65 or 65:9-14	Ps. 113:1-8 or Ps. 138:1-5
Phil. 4:4-9	James 1:17-18, 21-27	Col. 3:12-17 or 1 Tim. 6:6-11, 17-19
John 6:25-35	Matt. 6:25-33	Luke 17:11-19 or Mark 5:18-20 or Luke 12:15-21

First Reading

DEUTERONOMY 26:1-11 (RCL)

This Thanksgiving Day lection helps preachers ground gratitude in Israel's shared liturgical life and overarching story. Although the story is told prospectively, that is, in a future tense that indicates Israel has yet to enter the land, its agenda presupposes a time when the people will live there, when there will be a temple as a centralized place of worship (a recurring focus of the Deuteronomistic tradition in other parts of the canon) where such thanksgiving can take place, and a priesthood relating to it (vv. 2b-3). While the first fruits themselves are important as an embodiment of the promise of land as well as the personalization of the covenant that implies (vv. 1-2a, 4, 10b), the bulk of the text focuses on an important recital of a shared salvation history (vv. 5-10a). Thanksgiving means to *know* the story, to remember, and to rehearse it both *for me* and *for us*. This is all the more true because Israel's story

> THANKSGIVING MEANS TO *KNOW* THE STORY, TO REMEMBER, AND REHEARSE IT BOTH FOR ME AND FOR US.

was one of bondage and freedom. Please note that the five-verse rehearsal of this story omits the Sinai tradition. Clearly this is not because Sinai is unimportant in Deuteronomy—far from it. But here on this day the emphasis is on remembering bondage, freedom, and the promise of the giving of the land. That promise bears fruit not as some abstract thought but in a real worshiper from the actual land, bearing a basket of first fruits, with the assistance of a priest, and at a temple of "God's own choosing." In other words, the remembrance intends community. Please note that the Thanksgiving celebration is not a matter of inward, pious gratitude.

The final verse underlines the proper communal context of thanksgiving: "Then you, together with the Levites and the aliens who reside among you, shall celebrate with all the bounty that the LORD your God has given to you and to your house" (v. 11). The liturgy acknowledges the personal appropriation of the promise but sets it within a wider horizon of shared gratitude.

THE FIRST FRUITS COME FROM SOMEWHERE, THEY HAVE A HISTORY, AND IF THAT ORIGIN AND HISTORY ARE TO POINT FORWARD TO SOMETHING *SHARED*, PERHAPS THEY CAN STILL EMBODY SOMETHING OF THE COMMUNAL NATURE OF TRUE GRATITUDE.

We North American "consumers" are tempted sometimes to celebrate a Thanksgiving without memory—as if the bounty of the land appeared magically and without history, nestled antiseptically on Styrofoam trays covered in shrink wrap on a refrigerated grocery-store shelf and from there hustled home for private consumption. In truth, the first fruits come from somewhere, they have a history, and if that origin and history are to point forward to something *shared*, perhaps they can still embody something of the communal nature of true gratitude. At St. Mark's Lutheran Church in Kitchener, Ontario, they tend to celebrate Thanksgiving with a special meal for the wider community. While such meals happen in countless churches across North America, one thing is unique about St. Mark's Thanksgiving meal. When it comes time to eat, there is no tidy separation of church members and guests, some of whom include the underemployed and the homeless. At St. Mark's, all sidle up to the table and rub shoulders while sharing bounty: working-class folk, pastors, street people, suburban types. Just about anyone who can fit around such a table can still remember that Thanksgivings can't be bought as a private possession, only received and shared as a promised gift.

DEUTERONOMY 8:1-3, 6-10 (17-20) (BCP)
DEUTERONOMY 8:7-18 (RC)

This text from Deuteronomy keeps in view the problem of wealth and the way it can distort memory and thus render gratitude null and void. The writer does not fail to recall the trials of wilderness wanderings, although even they are interpreted through the lens of fatherly discipline. Nonetheless, the blessings of the land are portrayed in such Technicolor splendor that a kind of distracted forgetful-ness of multiplying wealth seems not altogether implausible. Yet the problem of this forgetfulness runs deeper. The Deuteronomist points out that forgetful self-made thinking (v. 17) is a prelude to idolatry, which itself can place Israel under the very same judgment as other nations before them. Consequently, even though the text announces blessing upon blessing, it concludes with warning.

1 KINGS 8:55-61 (RC ALT.)

This lection represents King Solomon's blessing of the people at the dedication of the Temple. Since this section of the long narrative is key to Deuter-onomistic theology, namely, that there be a central sanctuary for worshiping God of God's own choosing, it is the occasion to reflect on how God has indeed kept God's promises and provides the people with "rest" as promised in Deuteronomy 12:10-11. In the process, Solomon also calls the people to continue to keep God's commands so that God might be with them and all the world know that "the LORD is God; there is no other" (v. 60), again hearkening back to an important theme of Deuteronomy. Thanksgiving preachers might consider the relationship of thanksgiving to the promise of "rest" and divine presence in light of the call to ongoing covenant faithfulness.

RESPONSIVE READING

PSALM 100 (RCL)

This well-known hymn of praise serves as the doxology to a collection of kingship hymns in this section of the Psalms (93, 95–99). The psalm reflects a powerful call to universal praise. All earth is invited to join in the praise and to come into God's presence (vv. 1-2). The result of this is knowledge about who we are and what God has done for us (v. 3). Yet the universality of such claims rests on a particular claim. Those so affected by this praise are called in verse 4 to "enter his gates with thanksgiving, and his courts with praise." This is no god in general, but the God who is to be worshiped in the Temple. Nonetheless, this particular-ity is precisely the rationale for all the thanksgiving. It is, in the end, Israel's God who is to be praised in verse 5, because this same "LORD is good; his steadfast love endures forever." On a day like Thanksgiving, on which the claim to divine praise is never a parochially Christian one, it is still good to know not only the God to whom we give thanks, but why it should be *this* God with such a particular his-tory of steadfast love.

PSALM 65 OR 65:9-14 (BCP)

A similar vein of thought runs through Psalm 65. Although the description of this psalm on the Twenty-second Sunday after Pentecost (Thirty-first Sunday in Ordinary Time/Proper 26, above) will provide more information, its *reason* for thanksgiving is key. Psalm 65 places the fullness of divine blessing in nature (vv. 9-13) within a wider context (vv. 1-8). Those of us who lead worshipers in thanksgiving on this day would be wise to ground our thanksgiving in the particularities of the divine/human relationship as well.

PSALM 113:1-8 (RC)

Those fortunate enough to use this responsive reading on Thanksgiving will see the celebration within an important ethical horizon. The description of the psalm on the Twentieth Sunday after Pentecost (Twenty-eighth Sunday in Ordinary Time/Proper 23, above) will supply more about the psalm. Here it is enough to point out that thanksgiving that fails to remember God's special concern for the poor and needy (vv. 7-9) fails to give thanks fully. This is indeed the Lord all can praise on Thanksgiving Day.

PSALM 138:1-5 (RC ALT.)

This responsive reading pairs up nicely with the RC alternative first reading from 1 Kings 8. Both texts point out how God's word is unfailing. However, the unique elements of Psalm 138 are its form, focus, and context. The form is an individual thanksgiving from trouble. The psalm even bears witness to an answer to personal prayer (v. 3). Yet its focus shows that this personal thanksgiving is far from private. In the psalmist's mind, the proof of God's praiseworthiness is not just how "high up" God is, but how God "regards the lowly" (v. 6). God is worthy to receive thanks because God is so unlike others who operate by different valuations of power and might. From here, it becomes possible to consider something of the context of this psalm. Strangely, verse 1b begins the thanksgiving by providing an unusual location: "Before the gods I sing your praise." Could it be that the thanksgiving offered here is done with the awareness that there are other gods, or so-called gods, who are unlike the psalmist's? If so, the psalm may give us a clue for its interpretation. Our thanksgiving may just be a profoundly theological *and* political act.

SECOND READING
PHILIPPIANS 4:4-9 (RCL)

At this point in Paul's letter to the Philippians, he has concluded the body of the letter and turns to the task of saying good-bye. The Greek word usually translated "rejoice" (v. 4) also means "farewell." In this way, Paul matches the tone of this joyful letter with the necessary task of taking leave.

Apart from some of the key phrases, "in the Lord" (v. 4), "the Lord is near" (v. 5), and so forth, the concluding list of exhortations here seems to be a fairly general one. When it comes to the exhortation involving thanksgiving, however, it is important to remember the context of the Philippian letter. The focus of this epistle is being faithful in the face of opposition. Therefore, Paul is not offering general exhortations about being gentle, not worrying, or being thankful here. In a context marked by such opposition, these admonitions take a more compelling shape.

> WE DON'T NORMALLY THINK ABOUT GOD'S PEACE AS "GUARDING" US; PAUL, WHO HAS KNOWN HIS SHARE OF OPPOSITION, WHO IS SPEAKING TO A CONGREGATION WHO MAY BE FACING THE SAME, DOES.

Perhaps this is why verse 7 ends this subsection with a strange benediction: "The peace of God . . . will *guard* your hearts and minds in Christ Jesus" (emphasis mine). We don't normally think about God's peace as "guarding" us; Paul, who has known his share of opposition, who is speaking to a congregation who may be facing the same, does.

The final verses of this lection then conclude with general positive characteristics for the community to embody. The virtues listed here are not peculiarly Christian. However, they are conditioned in two key ways. First, Paul uses his own apostolic example as a kind of Christian commendation of those virtues (v. 8). Second, Paul reminds them that in the process the God of peace will be with them (v. 9).

JAMES 1:17-18, 21-27 (BCP)

On Thanksgiving Day, a text like this one reminds us of two important things. First, God is the ultimate gift giver. Whatever we do, whoever we are, God is the one at work through us by virtue of the power of God's word in us and through God's unchanging nature (vv. 17-18). In this sense, James is right to point out during this, our annual celebration of the harvest, we are *God's* harvest, *God's* first fruits. Yet James is never content to let us hear and receive that truth by itself. Second, therefore, we are to be doers of that word. For this reason James compares those who hear only to people who view their image in a mirror and forget what they look like, in other words, *who they are*. Positively for James, looking into the perfect law, the law of liberty, is exemplified chiefly in the way Christians do the word. This includes taking up the cause of the poor and the oppressed, especially widows and orphans, as well as maintaining purity over against the world.

COLOSSIANS 3:12-17 (RC)

For more background information about Colossians, see the second reading for Christ the King Sunday, below. Here the writer, likely presenting his thought in Paul's name, has begun to turn from his more theological (better, christological) material about the lordship of Christ, baptism, and the church to matters of application. In 3:1, the writer follows Paul's pattern by shifting from indicative to imperative. Whereas in the immediately prior pericope, 3:1-11, the writer tells the Colossians what *not* to do, in verses 12-17 the imperative takes a positive shape. Drawing on a baptismal motif, the writer urges the Colossians to clothe themselves in Christian virtues, above all, love. Preachers should be careful to avoid portraying them as *private*, *individual* virtues. The language of verses 12ff. is in the plural and the concern is with how the Colossians interrelate. All depends, of course, on how the Lord has forgiven and how Christ's peace and Christ's own word dwells among them (the "you" in 3:16a is a Greek plural). In the process, thanksgiving is not only encouraged but also described as a means by which the community participates in the relationship of the Lord Jesus to God the Father (v. 17) in its liturgical life (v. 16b). With this text, preachers on this day can identify thanksgiving as a shared reality among the community of faith, not just a personal attitudinal choice. Because it is also bound up with a shared baptismal identity with which we Christians clothe ourselves, it can lead us more deeply and profoundly into relationship in Christ with God and with those who worship God in Christ.

> PREACHERS ON THIS DAY CAN IDENTIFY THANKSGIVING AS A SHARED REALITY AMONG THE COMMUNITY OF FAITH, NOT JUST A PERSONAL ATTITUDINAL CHOICE.

1 TIMOTHY 6:6-11, 17-19 (RC ALT.)

For introductory material on the letters to Timothy, see the material under the second reading for the Twentieth Sunday after Pentecost (Twenty-eighth Sunday in Ordinary Time/Proper 23, above). In this text, the writer encourages pastors to reflect ethically on the problem of money and wealth. The immediate occasion for words on such matters is the alleged greediness of the writer's opponents (v. 5). Here the writer then shifts to think about the futility of a focus on money, especially given its fleeting nature and our frail humanity (vv. 6-11). With the closing part of our lection, however, the same ethic is presented positively. Here direction is given to "those who in the present age are rich" (v. 17) and how they might set their hopes on God. In doing so, they may discover what true "life" is all about (v. 19).

THE GOSPEL
JOHN 6:25–35 (RCL)

This Thanksgiving Day Gospel lection points proclamation squarely in the direction of Christology. If other texts invite us to reflect in a more theocentric way on God's acts of provision in creation or on God's ongoing acts of nurturance toward humanity in the world, this text from John invites us to consider thanksgiving in a more christocentric way.

Scholars point out that a common mistake in interpreting this discourse from John 6 is believing that Jesus' references to the "Bread of Life" are always and everywhere eucharistic. One can make a good case for that toward the end of the chapter, but in John 6:25–35, one is better off taking a cue from what John has been doing in this Gospel hitherto. We recall that in John 1, Jesus is spoken of as the preexistent *logos*, a figure from wisdom theology. Because this divine wisdom come down is so consistently unrecognized, the dialogues that ensue with him about his identity move strangely, yet graciously, through various misunderstandings: think Nicodemus and birth in chapter 3 or the Samaritan woman and water in chapter 4. In those two cases, as well as here in chapter 6, the confusion is embedded in Jewish understandings of Jesus and "signs." In chapter 6, our lection is preceded by a miracle of feeding with a crossing of the sea. This connection between wilderness feeding and sea crossing functions deeply as an exodus type. The confusion here between Jesus and those who have witnessed these events is whether they represent signs that might confirm Jesus as a new Moses, or, as Jesus tries to do with his discourse, demonstrate how Jesus *himself* is a sign for God. As one might expect, several important Jewish scriptural traditions underlie these conflicted perspectives: Exodus 16:4, Psalm 78:24, but perhaps also Deuteronomy 8:3, which points to the idea that drives much of the dialogical misunderstanding here ("One does not live by bread alone, but by every word that comes from the mouth of the LORD").

So long as Jesus' interlocutors confuse miracle bread for the sign (Jesus gives bread as Moses gave manna), instead of seeing Jesus, God's Word come down from heaven, as the sign ("I am the bread of life" v. 35), they fail to work for real bread that gives life. And how does one work for such bread? Well, not really by working at all, in a sense, but by believing in the one whom God sent (v. 29).

> SO LONG AS JESUS' INTERLOCUTORS CONFUSE MIRACLE BREAD FOR THE SIGN, INSTEAD OF SEEING JESUS, GOD'S WORD COME DOWN FROM HEAVEN, AS THE SIGN, THEY FAIL TO WORK FOR REAL BREAD THAT GIVES LIFE.

Perhaps this text, as a Thanksgiving Day lection, invites us to look past the mounds of food on the average North American table to something more enduring. There is, after all, a perversity about a consumption that leads almost inexorably to a bloated, turkey-induced soporific state of sickness. Yet if our Thanksgiving Day lives seem to bear witness to a confusion about true bread, there remains a constant wisdom through it all if John's Gospel is to be believed. In feast or famine, God provides the Word on which we can feed for true life. Perhaps that Word needs to be spoken again to break through our fascination with brimming gravy tureens and overfed-poultry platters. These, after all, come and go. The Word, by contrast, remains. In doing so, God cuts through the opulent clutter with a strange Word of grace and truth, and performs the one thing that our frenetic, market-based, supersized economy can't commodify: undying, trusting faith.

IN FEAST OR FAMINE, GOD PROVIDES THE WORD ON WHICH WE CAN FEED FOR TRUE LIFE.

THANKSGIVING DAY

NOVEMBER 22/27

MATTHEW 6:25-33 (BCP)

It is important to remember that Jesus' teaching on anxiety follows a saying about wealth that describes the difficulty of "serving two masters." Matthew's teaching portrays the worries of life from a similar perspective. Tellingly, the Greek word for "worry" means to be of a "divided mind" and is reprised several times in the lection (vv. 25, 27, 28, 31). Matthew views such anxiety through his appellation for Jesus' hearers: "you of little faith" (v. 30). Over against such divided consciousness, Matthew's Jesus sets out examples from nature in order to focus his hearers' minds on God's providential goodness. The concerns that cause such worry are linked to things that Gentiles strive after (vv. 31-32), although God knows that they need such things. Disciples, by contrast, need to focus on only one thing (and here we return to the idea of "serving two masters"): the kingdom of God and God's righteousness. To those who are thusly single-minded, God will provide all that disciples need . . . and more.

LUKE 17:11-19 (RC)

See the commentary on the Gospel for the Twentieth Sunday after Pentecost (Twenty-eighth Sunday in Ordinary Time/Proper 23), above.

MARK 5:18-20 (RC ALT.)

This Markan text, which occurs at the tail end of the story of the healing of the Gerasene demoniac (5:1-20), underlines the gratitude and obedience of the man who was healed in contrast to the reaction of others who witnessed the healing (v. 17). The Gerasene man wishes to go with Jesus (v. 18), but Jesus charges him to tell his friends and family about the Lord's mercy on him (v. 19). Interestingly, the final verse implies that the Gerasene did more than was asked. Mark 5:20 reports that he began to "proclaim" (that's gospel language) throughout the *ten cities* of the Decapolis and that *everyone* "marveled." One last note concerns the focus of his proclamation. Jesus charged him to tell about the Lord's mercy; the man, however, told how much *Jesus* had done for him. Perhaps these extravagances are telling for those of us who give thanks on this day.

LUKE 12:15-21 (RC ALT.)

This familiar parable might make for an interesting choice for a Thanksgiving Day sermon. On the surface, the parable seems like a standard negative example story about greed. If New Testament scholar Bernard Brandon Scott is correct, however, the parable may actually be about how to "mismanage a miracle."[1] Scott points out that the kind of big harvest the parable presupposes borders on the miraculous. The extravagance of the harvest is also underlined by the rich man's wealth-management strategy: tear *down* barns and then build bigger ones? Scott notes that there is a long tradition in Israel of storing up now for fallow years (think dreamer Joseph in Egypt or Sabbath-year laws), though the soliloquy of the man makes clear (1) he intends to store up the miraculous harvest for himself and (2) he fully intends to secure his own life with a kind of epicurean ease. That God all of a sudden speaks toward the end of the parable then breaks open the "memo to self" perspective of the rich man who arrogated that right to himself hitherto. When the rich man's death is announced, all that can be heard is God's simple, parabolic question about the vainly stored-up miracle goods: "Whose will they be?" (v. 20b). Scott reminds that the wise person fears God and stores up miraculous harvests to *share*. This fool thought he could take it with him and *keep* it instead. The answer to the divine question, of course, is that the stored-up miracle goods will go to others. That's how God's kingdom works—despite all our rich plans.

Note

1. Bernard Brandon Scott, *Hear Then the Parable: A Commentary on the Parables of Jesus* (Minneapolis: Fortress Press, 1989), 127–40. What follows is my sketchy summary of Scott's insightful chapter.

APRIL 2007

Sunday	Monday	Tuesday	Wednesday	Thursday	Friday	Saturday
1 Passion Sunday / Palm Sunday	2	3	4	5 Holy Thursday	6 Good Friday	7 Easter Vigil
8 Easter Day	9	10	11	12	13	14
15 2 Easter	16	17	18	19	20	21
22 3 Easter	23	24	25	26	27	28
29 4 Easter	30					

MAY 2007

Sunday	Monday	Tuesday	Wednesday	Thursday	Friday	Saturday
		1	2	3	4	5
6 5 Easter	7	8	9	10	11	12
13 6 Easter Mother's Day	14	15	16	17	18	19
20 7 Easter	21	22	23	24	25	26 Vigil of Pentecost
27 Day of Pentecost	28 Memorial Day	29	30	31		

JUNE 2007

Sunday	Monday	Tuesday	Wednesday	Thursday	Friday	Saturday
					1	2
3 1 Pentecost	4	5	6	7	8	9
10 2 Pentecost	11	12	13	14	15	16
17 3 Pentecost Father's Day	18	19	20	21	22	23
24 4 Pentecost	25	26	27	28	29	30

JULY 2007

Sunday	Monday	Tuesday	Wednesday	Thursday	Friday	Saturday
1 5 Pentecost	2	3	4 Independence Day	5	6	7
8 6 Pentecost	9	10	11	12	13	14
15 7 Pentecost	16	17	18	19	20	21
22 8 Pentecost	23	24	25	26	27	28
29 9 Pentecost	30	31				

AUGUST 2007

Sunday	Monday	Tuesday	Wednesday	Thursday	Friday	Saturday
			1	2	3	4
5 10 Pentecost	6	7	8	9	10	11
12 11 Pentecost	13	14	15	16	17	18
19 12 Pentecost	20	21	22	23	24	25
26 13 Pentecost	27	28	29	30	31	

306

SEPTEMBER 2007

Sunday	Monday	Tuesday	Wednesday	Thursday	Friday	Saturday
						1
2	3 Labor Day	4	5	6	7	8
9 14 Pentecost	10	11	12	13	14	15
16 15 Pentecost	17	18	19	20	21	22
23 16 Pentecost	24	25	26	27	28	29
30 17 Pentecost 18 Pentecost						

OCTOBER 2007

Sunday	Monday	Tuesday	Wednesday	Thursday	Friday	Saturday
	1	2	3	4	5	6
7 19 Pentecost	8 Thanksgiving Day (Canada)	9	10	11	12	13
14 20 Pentecost	15	16	17	18	19	20
21 21 Pentecost	22	23	24	25	26	27
28 22 Pentecost	29	30	31 Reformation Day			

NOVEMBER 2007

Sunday	Monday	Tuesday	Wednesday	Thursday	Friday	Saturday
				1 All Saints Day	2	3
4 Reformation Sunday / All Saints Sunday / 23 Pentecost	5	6	7	8	9	10
11 24 Pentecost Veterans Day	12	13	14	15	16	17
18 25 Pentecost	19	20	21	22 Thanksgiving Day (USA)	23	24
25 Last Pentecost / Christ the King	26	27	28	29	30